pastimes

Leisure

pastimes

The Context of Contemporary
leisure

Ruth V. Russell
Indiana University

Leisure

pastimes

Brown & Benchmark
PUBLISHERS

Madison   Dubuque, IA   Guilford, CT   Chicago   Toronto   London
Caracas   Mexico City   Buenos Aires   Madrid   Bogota   Sydney

Book Team

Publisher *Bevan O'Callaghan*
Project Editor *Scott Spoolman*
Production Editor *Terry Routley*
Proofreading Coordinator *Carrie Barker*
Designer *Jeff Storm*
Art Editor *Rachel Imsland*
Photo Editor *Laura Fuller*
Production Manager *Beth Kundert*
Production/Costing Manager *Sherry Padden*
Marketing Manager *Pamela S. Cooper*
Copywriter *M. J. Kelly*

Basal Text *10/12 Garamond*
Display Type *Garamond*
Typesetting System *Macintosh QuarkXPress*™
Paper Stock *50# Mirror Matte*

Brown &Benchmark
PUBLISHERS

President and Chief Executive Officer *Thomas E. Doran*
Vice President of Production and Business Development *Vickie Putman*
Vice President of Sales and Marketing *Bob McLaughlin*
Director of Marketing *John Finn*

A Times Mirror Company

Cover image by © Stephen Simpson/FPG International Corp.

Copyedited by Michelle Campbell; proofread by Kate McKay

dedication

to | **FMK and J & B**

contents

contents

preface

preface

Pastimes is an introductory text. It gathers together the state of the art in leisure science and practice, reflecting as well a wide range of literature from the disciplines of sociology, psychology, economics, political science, and anthropology. More than a text that teaches the foundational meanings and roles of leisure, however, *Pastimes* is also a point of view. This text presents leisure as a human phenomenon that is both individual and collective, vital to survival and frivolous, historical and contemporary, good and bad.

There are three main parts. Part one blends philosophy, religious studies, and the humanities in considering leisure as a condition of being human. Not only do chapters 1 through 4 establish the basic definitions and parameters for studying leisure, they ask readers to consider these concepts from their own personal framework. Part two is a focus on leisure's role in creating and reflecting society. Chapters 5 through 8 build on the personal relevancy of leisure discussed in part one and teach about leisure's contemporary cultural significance. These chapters rely on anthropology, sociology, and psychology concepts. Leisure's personal and cultural vitality are brought to a pragmatic conclusion in part three: leisure's use as a social instrument. Material from recreation and park studies is featured in chapters 9 through 12.

Pastimes is written in a fresh, lively voice. Concepts are illustrated in each chapter with field-based case studies, contemporary research studies, and biographical features. Definitions of terms are boldfaced in the text and defined in the margins, and questions for classroom discussion are offered. The hope is that students will find reading this book an active pursuit. Supplementary teaching materials for the instructor are also available.

Acknowledgments

I owe gratitude to many. This book's character comes from a lifetime of experiencing, thinking, writing, reading, observing, and teaching about leisure. Therefore, I am indebted to my family, friends, pets, colleagues, and students for helping me learn. For assistance in preparing the book, I wish to particularly thank Dr. Frances Stage for reading and critiquing several manuscript drafts, Dr. Sharon Washington for providing unpublished historical materials, Marti May for investigative library assistance, and Kevin Montague for photographic developing help. I also thank the following publisher's reviewers for their useful suggestions: Janice Hedges, California State University; Robin Kuntzler, Lehman College; Douglas McEwen, Southern Illinois University; and Keith Ernce, Ohio University.

Preface

pastimes

We begin our explorations of leisure by considering its significance for us. In a direct yet complex way, leisure helps shape who we are as human beings. It is expressed through our lives and is revealed in our histories, life goals, growth and development, and behaviors. Chapter 1 explores leisure's meanings for us through the humanities and ancient history. These meanings are then contrasted with contemporary definitions. Chapter 2 discusses the qualities of leisure: happiness, freedom, pleasure, intrinsic reward, humor, and others. Chapter 3 offers some explanations and guesses about our behaviors, especially leisure behaviors. Finally, chapter 4 traces the ways leisure helps us grow, mature, adjust, thrive, and age throughout our lives.

Leisure as a condition of being human—personal context

Leisure helps to shape who we are as human beings.

leisure

Even though we may think of leisure casually as having fun, scientists have taken the matter quite seriously.

meanings of leisure

chapter

one

What is leisure?

Leisure is a complex concept with different meanings depending on the context and the person.

Are there clues to the meaning of contemporary leisure in ancient history?

From the beginning of human history, leisure has been a part of everyday life. Legacies from ancient cultures endure today. For example, ancient Greece has given us a spiritual interpretation of leisure, ancient Rome is recognized as the origin of mass recreation, and the Middle Ages has added that touch of guilt we sometimes feel when we choose our favorite pastime over work.

Can leisure be defined through humanities?

Music, art, and literature often mirror the life experiences of their creators. In a song, we can find traces of a social group's use of leisure; a short story can express an individual's personal rapport with leisure; or a painting may depict an entire era's interpretation of leisure.

How is leisure defined today?

Contemporary philosophers and researchers have used a variety of meanings for leisure in their writings. These can be summarized as three types: leisure as free time, leisure as recreational activity, and leisure as a special attitude.

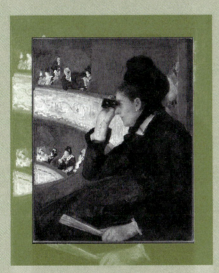

The Hayden Collection.
Courtesy, Museum of Fine Arts, Boston

KEY TERMS

Skiing through a pine forest.

Watching a movie on television. Baking a cake. Leafing through a magazine. Taking a vacation to the beach. Jogging around the block. Knitting a sweater. Winning a game of Monopoly. Spending the afternoon fishing. Coaching a Little League team. Listening to the radio. Talking on the telephone with a friend. Playing in a soccer match. Watching the birds from the kitchen window. Planting geraniums. These and a wide world of other experiences are our pastimes. They are pleasing recreations—ways of spending free time—moments of play. Pastimes are our expressions of leisure, and leisure not only characterizes who we are as people, but our culture as well.

This chapter sets the stage for our consideration of leisure in contemporary society. It is a moment's pause to reflect on the essential humanness of leisure—the foundational meanings of our pastimes. Since leisure is a complex concept that has different connotations depending on the people, place, and time, defining its essence requires journeys to different peoples, places, and times.

First, we define leisure through its reflections in the humanities: literature, art, and music. As humans we have always expressed ourselves through our songs, poems, and paintings, and leisure is often the focus of these expressions. Next, we realize leisure's meanings by examining its origins. Leisure, in various forms and settings, has been part of human life since the beginning. In exploring ancient cultures, we have an opportunity in this chapter to appreciate the enduring quality of leisure. Finally, we explore leisure's contemporary applications. While much of human understanding of leisure (and recreation and play) remains a mystery, you will discover what current philosophers and scientists consider it to be.

The Humanities of Leisure

In creating songs, stories, paintings, poems, and other art forms writers, artists, and composers have turned again and again to certain ideas or themes. These themes grow naturally out of their experiences and frequently express our own half-realized thoughts about ourselves. The song, story, painting, and poem reflect a sense of a particular place, time, and often an individual. Because leisure is so basic to being human, it has frequently been the subject of these reflections; thus, by thinking about the theme of leisure in art, music, and literature, we can understand its meaning.

Leisure is a part of the humanities. When used in education, the term *humanities* refers to the study of philosophy, languages, literature, and the arts. The **humanities** are expressions that interpret the meaning of life, rather than just describe the physical world. We consider the humanities here as a way to interpret the meaning of leisure in life.

Humanities: subjects that seek to interpret the meaning of life.

Leisure and Literature

People read for a variety of reasons, but one basic reason for reading is pleasure. We read because we enjoy it. Reading a novel, short story, or poem is like riding an airplane that speeds us away from ourselves into the worlds of other people and other places—but not too far away.

Fiction writers, dramatists, and poets often write about their feelings, what they know, the times, and the lives they lead. Like looking into a mirror, we can see a reflection of reality in literature. For example, in the United States during the early 1900s, literature often expressed the optimism and conservative ideals of the Victorian Age. Authors of the 1920s wrote about disillusioned and rootless characters. The Great Depression of the 1930s led to literature that protested unjust social conditions. Literature today often features the pains of human relationships. Literature, then, can reflect leisure's meaning. The following are selections from a short story, journal, poem, and novel,—literature that reveals something of people and their leisure.

In John Updike's story "Still of Some Use," notice how the loss of family unity is described through a loss of family pastimes.

When Foster helped his ex-wife clean out the attic of the house where they had once lived and which she was now selling, they came across dozens of forgotten, broken games. Parcheesi, Monopoly, Lotto; games aping the strategies of the stock market, of crime detection, of real-estate speculation, of international diplomacy and war; games with spinners, dice, lettered tiles, cardboard spacemen, and plastic battleships; games bought in five-and-tens and department stores feverish and musical with Christmas expectations; games enjoyed on the afternoon of a birthday and for a few afternoons thereafter and then allowed, shy of one or two pieces, to drift into closets and toward the attic. Yet, discovered in their bright flat boxes between trunks of outgrown clothes and defunct appliances, the games presented a forceful semblance of value: the springs of their miniature launchers still reacted, the logic of their instructions would still generate suspense, given a chance. "What shall we do with all these games?" Foster shouted, in a kind of agony, to his scattered family as they moved up and down the attic stairs.

"Trash 'em," his younger son, a strapping nineteen, urged.

"Would the Goodwill want them?" asked his ex-wife, still wife enough to think that all of his questions deserved answers. "You used to be able to give things like that to orphanages. But they don't call them orphanages anymore, do they?"

His older son, now twenty-two, with a cinnamon-colored beard, offered, "They wouldn't work anyhow; they all have something missing. That's how they got to the attic."

"Well, why didn't we throw them away at the time?" Foster asked, and had to answer himself. Cowardice, the answer was. Inertia. Clinging to the past.

His sons, with a shadow of old obedience, came and looked over his shoulder at the sad wealth of abandoned playthings, silently groping with him for the particular happy day connected to this and that pattern of coded squares and colored arrows. Their lives had touched these tokens and counters once; excitement had flowed along the paths of these stylized landscapes. But the day was gone, and scarcely a memory remained.

"Toss 'em," the younger decreed, in his manly voice. For these days of cleaning out, the boy had borrowed a pickup truck from a friend and parked it on the lawn beneath the attic window, so the smaller items of discard could be tossed directly into it. The bigger items were lugged down the stairs and through the front hall and out; already the truck was loaded with old mattresses, broken clock-radios, obsolete skis, and boots. It was a game of sorts to hit the truck bed with objects dropped from the height of the house. Foster flipped game after game at the target two stories below. When the boxes hit, they exploded, throwing a spray of dice, tokens, counters, and cards into the air and across the lawn. A box called Mousetrap, its lid showing laughing children gathered around a Rube Goldberg device, drifted sideways, struck one side wall of the truck, and spilled its plastic components into a flower bed. As a set of something called Drag Race! floated gently as a snowflake before coming to rest, much diminished, on a stained mattress, Foster saw in the depth of downward space the cause of his melancholy: he had not played enough with these games. Now no one wanted to play.

So begins Updike's story that originally appeared in *The New Yorker* magazine in 1980. Updike, whose fiction usually includes deep uneasiness mixed with humor over changes of relationships within a family, has used in this story "fun and games" as an explanation of family awkwardness. This loss of family intimacy isn't limited to divorce situations. For example, can you remember the end of a particular family custom that your parents expected to continue, such as playing cards on the patio in the summer, going to sports events together, or spending vacations at the same place?

In Maya Angelou's poem "Harlem Hopscotch," the rhythm of a chant that accompanies a children's street game expresses a serious social problem.

Harlem Hopscotch

One foot down, then hop! It's hot.
    Good things for the ones that's got.
Another jump, now to the left.
    Everybody for hisself.
In the air, now both feet down.
    Since you black, don't stick around.
Food is gone, the rent is due,
    Curse and cry and then jump two.
All the people out of work,
    Hold for three, then twist and jerk.
Cross the line, they count you out.
    That's what hopping's all about.
Both feet flat, the game is done.
    They think I lost. I think I won.

In the poem Angelou uses the children's game of hopscotch to vent frustration and a sense of betrayal. While the poem is about the injustices of race and social class, it makes light of it by putting it into a rhythm of a classic children's pastime. What do you think is meant by the game's outcome in the last line?

A journal entry by May Sarton defines leisure in terms of peace and quiet.

September 15th

> Begin here. It is raining. I look out on the maple, where a few leaves have turned yellow, and listen to Punch, the parrot, talking to himself and to the rain ticking gently against the windows. I am here alone for the first time in weeks, to take up my "real" life again at last. That is what is strange—that friends, even passionate love, are not my real life unless there is time alone in which to explore and to discover what is happening or has happened. Without the interruptions, nourishing and maddening, this life would become arid. Yet I taste it fully only when I am alone here and "the house and I resume old conversations."

> Reprinted from JOURNAL OF A SOLITUDE by May Sarton, with the permission of W. W. Norton & Company, Inc. Copyright © 1973 by May Sarton.

This is the first entry in *Journal of a Solitude,* published in 1973. Sarton is a poet, novelist, children's book author, and writer of nonfiction, and in this journal she celebrates the warmth of being at home alone. For her, leisure is a kind of rest for the spirit as she contemplates the change in seasons, the blooms in her garden.

The excitement of preparing for an evening out, even for the vampire Khayman in Anne Rice's novel *The Queen of the Damned,* published in 1988, reflects the special feelings of anticipating pleasure.

> In London, past midnight in a darkened store, he found his vampire clothes. Coat and pants, and shining patent leather shoes; a shirt as stiff as new papyrus with a white silk tie. And oh, the black velvet cloak, magnificent, with its lining of white satin; it hung down to the very floor.

> He did graceful turns before the mirrors. How the Vampire Lestat would have envied him, and to think, he, Khayman, was no human pretending; he was real. He brushed out his thick black hair for the first time. He found perfumes and unguents in glass cases and anointed himself properly for a grand evening. He found rings and cuff links of gold.

> From Anne Rice, *Queen of the Damned.* Copyright © 1988 by Anne Rice. Reprinted by permission of Alfred A. Knopf, Inc.

Khayman's attitude toward getting dressed is itself part of the joys and freedoms experienced in leisure. Leisure is just as much anticipation as it is the actual event or experience. Can leisure also be the reminiscence following the experience?

Leisure and Art

Wherever and whenever people have lived, they have always had an interest in order. We enjoy certain patterns of contrast and balance for their own sake. We show this delight in form and design when we dress up or wear jewelry, mow the lawn, doodle during class, and select the color and chrome markings for our automobiles. We simply like making things look better. This is also the function of a painting or a sculpture. We receive an aesthetic experience from seeing it.

The use of design and color have a commemorative function, too. The most important events in our religious, social, and political life are reflected in art. From earliest times, people have used some formal visual symbol to mark an event or preserve an idea. For example, prehistoric peoples used drawings on cave walls to celebrate a hunt. The ancient Greeks represented their high regard for physical strength in their statues of gods and goddesses. Today, when we take pictures of relatives at family reunions, we record the occasion in visual form to make it memorable. We are visually marking the event in order to heighten our sense of its importance.

In other words, art mirrors what a culture considers beautiful and important. Artists, as sensitive members of their society, imagine, dream, think, feel, and communicate in the context of their world. Their art becomes a reflection of their time. Since our curiosity here is about leisure, let's continue our humanities exploration by finding what is considered beautiful and important about leisure through art.

Since we've already mentioned the ancient Greeks, let's continue to examine their approach to leisure. To the ancient Greeks, a human being's health and happiness were supremely important. Specifically, the Greeks admired the beauty and agility of the human body (fig. 1.1). Since it was through the perfection of their bodies that human beings most resembled the gods, sports were a spiritual as well as physical activity.

The numerous ancient Greek sculptures of humans remaining today communicate that life was good and was meant to be enjoyed. The nude male body in action at gymnasiums was a daily experience, and sculptors had ample opportunity to observe the body's proportions and musculature.

In the fifteenth through seventeenth centuries in China, gardening was developed into a fine art and an expression of leisure as nature. Many types of gardens were popular. For example, the courtyard garden was designed to be viewed through a framed window opening (fig. 1.2). Although it was possible to have a general view of this type of garden from a balcony, one usually walked around the garden in a long covered corridor, looking through lattice windows that framed the view. The garden was planned as a series of colorful pictures, often of a carefully placed rock or tree, differently viewed as one moved around it (Tregear 1985).

Perhaps one of the more prominent reflections of leisure in art comes from the impressionist period. **Impressionism** is a style of art that presents an immediate "impression" of an object or event. Impressionist painters try to show what the eye sees at a glance. The compositions typically seem informal and spontaneous. While painters and other artists have created impressionistic

Impressionism: a painting style that achieved a vividness simulating reflected light.

works in several periods of history, the term impressionism is most commonly applied to the work of a group (mostly French) of painters exhibiting in Paris from about 1870 to 1910. What is the impression of leisure in this art?

The painting *Terrace at Sainte-Adresse* by Claude Monet depicts vacationers (fig. 1.3). Painted in 1866, it is the view from a window of his aunt's villa where Monet stayed that summer. Out in the water are a number of ships, varying from the pleasure boats moored on the left, to the steamers on the right. The ships include a mixture of old and new ships that represent the transition of sail to steam. There is another and related transition represented in the painting. In the middle distance is a fishing boat (just above the parasol) that suggests the local and traditional life at Sainte-Adresse, France, before its transformation by tourists. This reflects what was happening at that time in most of coastal France. Fishing villages were being molded into modern resorts, marked by broad avenues, sidewalks, formal gardens, and huge buildings. Shortly after the scene depicted in Monet's painting, municipal

Figure 1.4 Mary Stevenson Cassatt. *Woman in Black at the Opera.* 1879.

The Hayden Collection. Courtesy, Museum of Fine Arts, Boston

authorities and owners of villas began filling in or leveling land, pushing landings, porches, and roads out toward the water, and creating artificial spaces for the visiting Parisians, leaving nothing for the fishermen and shopkeepers who had once lived there (Herbert 1988).

Mary Stevenson Cassatt's *Woman in Black at the Opera,* painted in 1879, presents a woman in "matinee" clothing, using her upward-tilted opera glasses to scan the audience (fig. 1.4). With a bit of humor, Cassatt also has a man in the distance leaning out of his box to point his glasses in our direction, emphasizing the pervasive idea of the time of spying on one's society

(Herbert 1988). We also learn from the painting that leisure defined the upper class of this era.

One of the more important features of leisure for upper-class Parisian society of the late 1800s, as captured by impressionist artists, was the racetrack. Its prominence in art was out of all proportion to the short racing seasons—a week in April, four days in late May, and an equally brief period in September (Herbert 1988). The races were the center of the elaborate social world of the upper class, involving balls and parties, and grand strolls by people dressed in the latest fashions up the wide boulevards of Paris. For example, Edouard Manet incorporated the races at the Longchamp racecourse into his conception of modern Paris. In his 1864 painting *The Races at Longchamp,* several horses race toward us, watched on the left by a crowd along the fence inside the privileged oval (fig. 1.5). Behind them are several carriages, the nearest one driven by two uniformed coachmen, and bearing two women with raised parasols. These women, the prominent woman standing in the foreground, and the gentleman escort on horseback to the left seem not to be watching the race. Like other Parisian entertainments of the time, the races were distractions as much as attractions (Herbert 1988). The social rituals at Longchamp did not require constant attention to the race.

Enjoying restaurants and cafes was also an important pastime for Parisians at the time. There are many paintings from the impressionist artists depicting women and men enjoying each other's company over food and drink. Pierre-Auguste Renoir's painting *The Luncheon of the Boating Party,* begun in the summer of 1880, shows the terrace of the Restaurant Fournaise (fig. 1.6). It identifies a riverside restaurant whose customers were boaters and their friends. In fact, boating was another leisure activity associated with the upper class. Boating then, as today, was relatively costly and a conspicuous form of leisure.

The well-known *A Sunday on La Grande Jatte* by Georges Seurat depicts an urban scene of a relaxed group of middle-class Parisians on a Sunday outing (fig. 1.7). Here leisure is portrayed as quiet relaxation. Although the clothes

Figure 1.5 Edouard Manet. *The Races at Longchamp.* 1864.

Courtesy of The Fogg Art Museum. Harvard University Art Museums. Bequest of Grenville L. Winthrop.

Figure 1.6 Pierre-
Auguste Renoir. *The Luncheon
of the Boating Party.* 1881.

The Phillips Collection,
Washington, D.C.

are updated, this same scene is replayed in many urban parks on Sunday afternoons today. In this painting, we notice a shift away from the impressionist
portrayal of everyday pleasures as casual and lighthearted. Instead of informal
arrangements, everything here seems as posed as an old-fashioned family por-
trait. Instead of indistinct forms, such details as a bustle, parasol, or stovepipe
hat are geometrical. This style is a part of the postimpressionist period in western art and Seurat's system was called *pointillism.* The painting's effect is created by thousands of dots of uniform size applied to the canvas in a calculated
way (Fleming 1986).

Even this brief glance at leisure through the impressionist art of the late
1800s reveals that leisure was paramount in Paris. Indeed, idle hours and entertainment greatly expanded during this time, particularly for the upper class.
By the end of the century, the life of Paris was dominated by theaters, opera,
cafes, restaurants, dances, racetracks, gardens, and parks. Tourists began to
flock to Paris to enjoy the elegant urban culture. All this is portrayed in the
thousands of paintings by the impressionist artists Edouard Manet, Pierre-
Auguste Renoir, Claude Monet, Edgar Degas, Mary Stevenson Cassatt (an
American), and others.

While impressionism is most commonly applied to art, the idea of por-
traying impressions of things also applies to music and literature. In literature,
impressionism means expressing the immediate sensations of events. Impressionist music is usually based on atmospheric effects. Claude Debussy and
Maurice Ravel of France, for example, wrote music with sounds that suggest
such images as moonlight, waterfalls, and fireworks.

Bruegel and Me and Julio

At a recent session of the Leisure Research Symposium, Dr. Michael Blazey of California State University, Long Beach presented his work comparing the depiction of play in sixteeth- and twentieth-century popular art forms. He studied Peter Bruegel's sixteenth-century painting *Children's Games,* which has long been presented to scholars of play as a pictorial encyclopedia of children's play of that era. The painting is a depiction of the variety of play expressions in sixteenth-century European culture.

In the modern era, another art form that depicts popular culture is the music video. In 1988, Paul Simon recorded the song "Me and Julio (Down by the School Yard)" with video images of teens and young adults playing on an urban playground. Dr. Blazey, in his study, drew strong parallels and contrasts between the arts of Bruegel and Simon. "Over 80 games have been identified

in the painting," he wrote. "Many of these games remain common to the present time. The video presents popular playground activities." At least four of these games are found in *Children's Games* (Blazey 1990, 8).

The presentation of these two works side by side reveals strong parallels despite a time difference of over four hundred years. Colors and action blend in both works to create innate realism. A panoramic view of the school yard in the video creates the same sense of activity found in the painting. Perhaps the most striking contrast, according to Dr. Blazey, is how adults are depicted in both works. In the painting, adults are absent, however, the children are playing in the heart of a city square, a place normally reserved for transacting business. In the video, the playground is presented as a place only for children, and adults are not allowed to enter.

Figure 1.7 Georges Seurat. A *Sunday on La Grande Jatte.* 1884.

Georges Seurat, French, 1859–1891, A Sunday on La Grande Jatte—1884, oil on canvas, 1884–86, 207.6 x 308 cm, Helen Birch Bartlett Memorial Collection, 1926.224. Photograph © 1994, The Art Institute of Chicago. All Rights Reserved.

Leisure and Music

Music is perhaps the most basic and universal activity of humankind. It has existed in some form from the earliest days because humans are born with a great musical instrument. For thousands of years, music was the simple and natural sound of the human voice. Through the centuries, music has taken many forms and reflected many ways of life. Today in Western cultures people express themselves through jazz, rock, opera, gospel, classical, rhythm and blues, country, and other musical styles.

In the United States, for example, there are an estimated 1,500 symphony orchestras, with annual attendance at concerts believed to exceed 25 million people. There are over 900 American organizations that produce operas, presenting more than 7,000 performances each year. There are over 40 million amateur musicians, and professional musicians in 1989 sold over $3.3 billion worth of cassette recordings and $2.6 billion worth of CD recordings (Recording Industry Association of America, Inc. 1989).

Music reflects much about a people and their society. In keeping with our exploration of the humanities of leisure, how might music portray leisure? We begin with the folk music from the mountains of West Virginia. The early and hardy settlers of the mountains of then western Virginia brought with them a musical legacy from England and Scotland (Boette 1971). All social gatherings started with songs—some happy, some sad, some religious, some worldly. These songs were handed down from one generation to another, and until recently, without aid of a written record. Some of the songs laid forth moral lessons as does this one called "The Young Man Who Wouldn't Hoe Corn":

I'll sing you a song
And it won't detain you long
Concerning the young man who wouldn't hoe his corn.
The reason why I cannot tell, for this young man was always well.

He planted his corn in the month of May
And in July it was knee high
And in September there came a frost
And all this young man's corn was lost.

He went to his nearest neighbor's door
Where often times he'd been before,
And when his courtship it came on
She asked him if he'd hoed his corn.

He hung his head and began for a sigh
Saying, "Kind Miss, I'll tell you why—
I've tried, I've tried and I've tried in vain
But I don't believe I'll raise one grain."

"Then why do you come to me for to wed,
When you can't raise your own cornbread,
Single I am and single I'll remain
For a lazy man I won't maintain."

He hung his head and he went away
Saying, "Kind Miss, you'll rue the day,
You'll rue the day as sure as you're born
For giving me a sack cause I wouldn't hoe my corn."

From "The Young Man Who Wouldn't Hoe Corn," collected by Marie Boette,
Wirt County, West Virginia.

What about leisure do you think this song portrays? One interpretation is that in the song leisure is considered as laziness or not being productive. It is doing nothing. Accordingly, the young woman in the song shuns such idleness. As we will discover later in this chapter, not doing one's work has frequently been considered wrong. Leisure as nonproductivity has quite a history of disrespect and even sinfulness.

When Witold Rybczynski, author of *Waiting for the Weekend* (1991), described his experience listening to Vivaldi's classical work *The Four Seasons,* it is in terms of the pleasing mystery of the music. He is engaged by the descriptive character of the melody. He also told of the sonnets Vivaldi wrote to accompany the music. The sonnets depict the changing climate of the four seasons through such scenes as peasants celebrating the harvest, a hunter setting out at first light, and the comfort of a winter fireside. Rybczynski comments that the celebration in the music of things pastoral is poignant, since the composer was sickly and often housebound, yet it also reflects the eighteenth century's fashionable preoccupation with the idealization of nature.

Listening to the lyrics of contemporary music, we find other meanings of leisure. In the rap song "People Everyday," recorded by the group Arrested Development, leisure is expressed as hanging out in the park with a radio tape player—resting—and putting one's soul at ease. Michael Jackson, in the song "Remember the Time," expresses the park differently. Here the park is remembered as a place for falling in love. In the same song, the beach too is remembered this way. Leisure is also used as a context for remembering the past in K.T. Oslin's "Old Pictures." In this country music song there are recollections of a little girl playing dress up, a little boy playing a cowboy, and the Saturday matinee movie. Leisure is sometimes used as metaphor in music. As exampled in k.d. lang's "Wash Me Clean," romantically desiring someone is like swimming—swimming through my veins.

There are, of course, many more sculptures, paintings, poems, stories, and songs that we could use to extend this excursion into leisure's portrayal in the humanities. What other examples can you find? As you listen to your CDs, visit an art museum, or read a novel, look for references to leisure's meaning. Next we trace leisure's definitions in history.

Classical Histories of Pastimes

It is not really known where civilization, that is a settled community life and the social institutions necessary to support it, originated. However, the story of how it evolved once it began is known. The retreat of the last glaciers (about eleven thousand years ago) initiated successive periods of cultural evolution from primitive hunting and gathering societies to the development of agriculture and animal husbandry, to ultimately, the urbanization and industrialization of modern societies.

Radiocarbon dates suggest the domestication of goats in the Near East as early as 8000 B.C. and sheep in Turkey about 7500 B.C. (Fellmann, Getis, and Getis 1990). Evidence also exists that African peoples were raising crops of wheat, barley, dates, lentils, and chickpeas on the floodplains of the Nile River as early as 18,500 years ago (Fellmann, Getis, and Getis 1990).

It seems likely that agriculture and animal husbandry were not an "invention" motivated solely by the need for food but were the result of other needs as well. For example, plant dyes were universally collected for personal adornment or article decoration. Also, mood-altering plants were gathered, protected, and cultivated by all primitive cultures. Indeed, there is persuasive evidence that early cultivation of grains was not for grinding and baking as bread but for brewing as beer, a beverage that became important in some cultures for religious, nutritional, and pleasure reasons, and that may have been a first and continuing reason for settling into stable civilizations.

As people gathered together into communities, new and more formalized rules of conduct naturally emerged. We see the beginnings of governments. Writing and mathematics became common. Social stratification emerged. Religions became more collective and organized, and work occupations became increasingly specialized. These social and technical developments were initially confined to specific geographic locations and eventually diffused from these points of origin to other peoples. Geographers term these original centers of innovation **culture hearths,** and they are viewed as "cradles" of a particular system of civilization (fig. 1.8).

Culture hearths: original centers of civilization. Significant innovation and invention made them cornerstones for the development of more advanced civilizations.

The earliest culture hearths were found in Egypt, Mesopotamia, the Indus Valley of the Indian subcontinent, northern China, southeastern Asia, and in several locations in Africa and the Americas (Fellmann, Getis, and Getis 1990). They arose in widely separated areas of the world, at different times, and under differing circumstances. Our contemporary meanings of leisure were shaped by the ancient histories of these early culture hearths. Let's explore some of them.

The Kingdom of Kush

Africa has been called the "birthplace of the human race." The oldest evidence of humanlike creatures found anywhere in the world is bones and other fossils discovered at many sites in eastern and southern Africa. Scientists think that

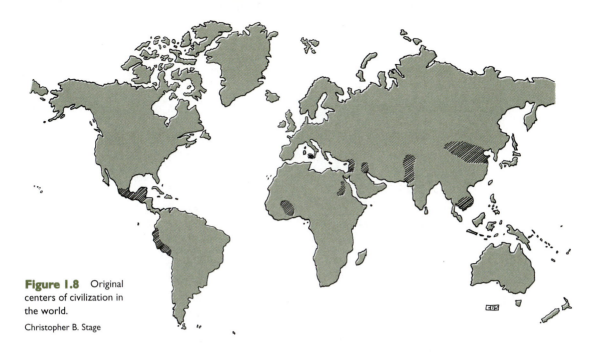

Figure 1.8 Original centers of civilization in the world.

Christopher B. Stage

various ethnic groups of people lived throughout Africa when agriculture was developing there. For example, Black Africans lived in the Sahara when it was a grassland. Hunters tracked game, fishing communities lived on the catch from lakes and rivers, and farmers grew grain and raised livestock. About 4000 B.C., Africa's climate gradually became much drier. Farmers moved southward. By about 1500 B.C., the Sahara had become what is today the world's largest desert and a barrier to the easy movement of people between northern Africa and the rest of the continent.

Meanwhile, the fertile soils of the Nile Valley supported some of the greatest civilizations in world history. Known then as Upper Egypt and Lower Egypt, they were magnificent centers of government and trade until Roman armies conquered the entire north coast by 30 B.C. Just south of Egypt, a kingdom called Kush arose about 2000 B.C. To begin our story of leisure in ancient cultures we direct our curiosity here.

Kush (located in what is today the country of Sudan) was an important center for the exchange of art and ideas (*Pan-African Market Place* 1993). This Black African kingdom was the center of learning. The Kushites shared their knowledge of especially politics, religion, and the use of metals with civilizations to the south. There were several invasions of Kush by the Egyptians to the north, but when they were free from Egyptian influence, they developed new styles in art and architecture, used their own language, and invented a system of writing. Scientists guess that these new art styles included metalwork and wooden sculpture. Such avid use of art and craft appears to be the Kush legacy for leisure.

While there is still mystery about how the Kush kingdom ended, some historians suggest that there was a gradual decline following an invasion in 23 B.C. by the Romans who then occupied Egypt to the north. As a visitor to Sudan today, you may still see the ancient Kush sites.

Ancient Greece: Glorious Leisure

When I'm cross-country running alone something wonderful comes over me. After a mile or so I begin to concentrate just on my breathing and the strong feeling of my body moving. All my worries disappear and I seem to float into a sensation of being for real.

(Anonymous college student 1993)

Describing a leisure experience in such a spiritual manner most likely originated from the ancient culture of Greece. The early Greeks were perhaps the "first people in the world to play, and they played on a great scale" (Hamilton 1942). Ancient Greek children played with toys widely recognized by today's children: jacks (called knuckle bones then because the jacks were the knuckle bones of an animal), kites, and marbles. Amphitheaters were built where music, dance, and drama festivals took place yearly. Even *proxemos,* whose prime function was to assist fellow citizens traveling abroad, were the forerunners of today's tour guides.

Another legacy of ancient Greece is organized sport. Scholars believe that sport contests might have originally been offered at the funerals of fallen heroes to give their spirits pleasure. Excavation at the ancient Olympic site in western Greece shows that it was used for such an observance for many years before the first formalized Olympic games took place there in 776 B.C. Later, these games were held in honor of Zeus. Part religious event and part sports event, all the buildings on the site were either for worship or for athletics (fig. 1.9).

The Olympic Games were held every four years, and the only contest in the first thirteen Olympiads was a footrace of about 180 meters. Through the years, longer running races were added to the event, as well as other types of competition. Later contests included horse races, weight lifting, boxing, and the pentathlon, which consisted of javelin and discus throwing, a sprint foot race, long jump, and wrestling. A savage and sometimes deadly sport called pancratium, which combined boxing and wrestling, was introduced in 648 B.C.

When the Romans later conquered Greece, the games soon lost their religious meaning, and the contestants became interested only in winning money. In A.D. 394, the Emperor Theodosius ordered the games ended because of their decline in quality, and no Olympic Games were held for more than 1,500 years.

The essential point is that in ancient Greece, for the first time in the history of civilizations, pastimes were taken very seriously.

If we had no other knowledge of what the Greeks were like, if nothing were left of Greek art and literature, the fact that they were in love with play and played magnificently would be proof enough of how they lived and how they looked at life (Hamilton 1942).

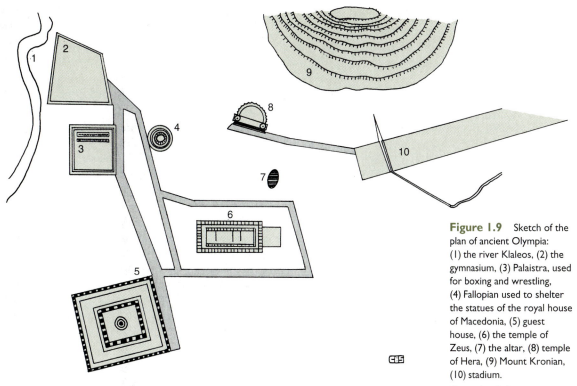

Figure 1.9 Sketch of the plan of ancient Olympia: (1) the river Klaleos, (2) the gymnasium, (3) Palaistra, used for boxing and wrestling, (4) Fallopian used to shelter the statues of the royal house of Macedonia, (5) guest house, (6) the temple of Zeus, (7) the altar, (8) temple of Hera, (9) Mount Kronian, (10) stadium.

Christopher B. Stage

Within two centuries Greek art, music, poetry, literature, philosophy, and sport reached lofty heights.

The ancient Greek term for leisure was ***schole,*** meaning to use free time wisely for oneself (Ibrahim 1991). It meant being occupied in something desirable for its own sake: music, poetry, oratory, debate, and inquiry into the nature of things. Toward this goal Plato established the Academy, a place for reading, writing, discussion, and thinking forms of pastimes. Leisure for the ancient Greeks meant pursuing intellectual leisure as much as it meant physical exertion in game and sport. It may surprise you that this Greek word for leisure, *schole,* was the origin of the English word *school.*

The Greek word *schole* also became *skole:* a drinking song. The aristocrats from Athens loved to celebrate. On occasion at the end of the day, they held a rousing banquet. At the banquet, the guests at first concentrated on enjoying the food. Next came the *symposium,* which was a drinking session. By the throw of the dice, the amount of water mixed with the wine was controlled (Engs 1993). During the *symposium,* acrobats and magicians would be called in to entertain. Riddles might be posed for the guests or games organized.

Our inheritance from ancient Greek philosophers is significant as well in terms of contemporary meanings of leisure (Goodale and Godbey 1988). Above all, the search for a philosophy of the good life and ways to attain it are particularly of their origin. The philosopher Plato was interested, for example,

Schole: an ancient Greek term for leisure, meaning to use free time wisely for oneself.

in the benefits of music and gymnastics. He believed that there were spiritual and physical rewards to be gained from the pursuit of such activities. To Socrates, knowledge was required in choosing the best pleasures. The "good life" was the life of right choice and conduct.

Throughout his writings, Aristotle conveyed ideas and, more importantly, ideals concerning the role of leisure in humankind's quest for a good life. In understanding the classical thinking about leisure, there is no better teacher than Aristotle. For Aristotle, leisure was activities performed for their own sake. Leisure was the freedom from having to be occupied (and having an occupation) and was the necessary condition for happiness. He believed the goodness of anything was found in the realization of its uniqueness, and for human beings, he determined that the most unique quality was the power to think. Thus, Aristotle believed a life of contemplation was the proper use of leisure. He wrote ". . . that what is best and most pleasant for any given creature is that which is proper to it. Therefore for man, too, the best and most pleasant life is the life of intellect, since this life will also be the happiest" (Aristotle, *Ethics*).

Aristotle also believed that a lifetime should not only be devoted to thinking noble and divine thoughts, but to doing civic and productive good deeds as well (Hemingway 1988). For Aristotle, this was leisure too—taking responsibility for enhancing the goodness of individuals and community.

The ancient Greeks believed in balance in life, the importance of developing both the mind and the body, and a kind of holistic and spiritual leisure. The Greek concept of leisure was one of participation, learning, and zestful living. The life of leisure for the Greek was a very complex ideal; leisure was an essential element in the culture. It was a matter of knowledge and health leading to virtuous choices and conduct which, in turn, led to true pleasure. Leisure, then, was not just a weekend or a vacation. It was a lifetime.

There is one element of the story of ancient Greece that we reject in today's conceptualization of leisure, however. The aristocratic leanings of the philosophers of this period meant that the leisure ideal just described was restricted to only the elite male "citizens." We must remember that the culture of this period (and others) was built on the backs of slaves. The work of providing food, shelter, and clothing was done by slaves. Only citizens (about 20 percent of the population) were free to pursue the leisure ideals of Greek culture. Today, we are much more egalitarian, and we reject leisure if it refers to the privileges of an elite class supported by the labors of others.

Ancient Rome: Leisure as Spectacle

No one knows how or when Rome was founded. Nonetheless, Rome eventually prospered, and the use of both military and political methods paved the way for its march to supreme power in the region. Rome engaged in wars with its neighbors—Greece, Syria, Egypt, and Macedonia—and as "confidence followed victory" (Ibrahim 1991), a policy of expansion resulted. Thanks to multiple conquests, Rome grew larger and richer. Although they borrowed a good deal of Greek philosophy and copied Greek art and architecture, the ancient Romans had a more practical notion about leisure.

biography   Aristotle

Plato taught Aristotle how to think philosophically, but Aristotle learned the lesson so well that he is the better teacher for all of us (Adler 1978, ix–x).

Aristotle (384-322 B.C.) was a Greek philosopher, educator, and scientist. Undoubtedly, he was one of the most influential thinkers in Western culture. This reputation extends, as well, to the influences of his writings about leisure.

He was born in 384 B.C. in the northern Greek town of Stagira, the son of the personal physician to the king of nearby Macedonia. Some historians believe that Aristotle may have lived his early years recklessly but soon made his way to Plato and the Academy in Athens and studied under this master teacher for twenty years (Simpson 1989). In spite of Aristotle's recognized intellectual genius, the opportunity to replace Plato upon his death as head of the Academy was impossible, because it was felt that the honor must go to a native of Athens.

Aristotle left Athens and became the tutor to Alexander, grandson of the Macedonian king. This new assignment paid off when Alexander later conquered all of Greece and ascended to the throne. Under the support of Alexander the Great, Aristotle returned to Athens and founded the Lyceum. The new school immediately surpassed the Academy in prestige and was particularly noted for its teaching of the natural sciences. This was a fruitful time for Aristotle, and much of his written work was authored then.

In spite of this, the Athenian citizenry remained at odds with Aristotle because of his friendship with Alexander, who had conquered them. When Alexander unexpectedly died, the Macedonian rule in Athens quickly fell, and Aristotle was forced to leave Athens to avoid the same fate as Socrates. He left saying he would not give the city-state "a second chance to sin against philosophy" (Simpson 1989). Only a few months after fleeing Athens, Aristotle became ill and died.

Box Figure 1.1   Aristotle.
Christopher B. Stage

The Romans faced the tedious problem of overseeing an immense empire. This meant that the need for social order took precedence over the individual's need for personal freedom. Life in the early Roman Empire in the third century B.C. was simple, yet discipline and careful regulation were required. People worked hard and lived frugally. Early Roman society provided limited opportunities for leisure activity.

Later, as Roman conquests produced greater wealth and military captives of sufficient numbers to be exploited, free time increased. Thus, the practical need to control a growing middle class with increasing time free from work was responded to with the provision of large-scale entertainments. As opposed to the Greek idea of an intellectual and spiritual leisure, many Romans participated in gaudily expressed pastimes. For example, there were heated public baths, the *campus martius* (parade grounds for various ball games), and grand athletic exhibitions. The preferred form of theater was the *mimus,* a form of low farce. Often, the middle classes were spectators to absurd and revolting pleasures: gladiators fought each other, often to the death; and condemned criminals and Christians were sometimes thrown to wild animals. Leisure was used as a form of social control based on the policy of "bread and circuses."

Beginning about 31 B.C. the ***ludi,*** or public games, became annual events in the Roman calendar (Ibrahim 1991). For example, the *Ludi Megalesia,* a yearly festival commemorating the Roman victory over Hannibal, lasted between April 4 and April 10. The *Ludi Romani,* an appeal to Apollo and to avert pestilence in the summer heat, took place from the fourth to the twelfth day of September, and the *Ludi Plebei,* games of the commoners, lasted from November 4 to November 17. By the end of the Roman Empire the calendar included 175 official holidays, with 101 for theatrical entertainments, 64 devoted to chariot races, and 10 given over to gladiatorial combats (Roberts 1962).

The games became a means whereby rulers and officials could win popular favor, as they had great drawing power among the masses. They took place in specialized buildings. The oldest of these, the Circus Maximus, was built for horse races that included trick-riding, mock cavalry battles, and chariot racing. Amphitheaters hosted gladiatorial combats, with the largest—the Colosseum—holding thousands of spectators. Another spectacle held in the Colosseum only once was the *naumachiae* (Ibrahim 1991), a ship battle requiring the flooding of the Colosseum floor. The greatest of all *naumachiae* was staged by Claudius outside Rome in Lake Fucine. A total of nineteen thousand men boarded a fleet of fifty ships and battled each other beginning at 10:00 A.M. By 3:00 P.M., three thousand of them were dead (Butler 1972).

Excesses in the name of leisure by the close of this ancient period had degraded the Roman people and their culture. While rich cultural developments occurred during this time in architecture, sculpture, painting, poetry, and oratory, the leisure tastes of the masses lead to a depravity that some historians consider an important factor in the demise of the Roman Empire. The preponderance of passive and barbaric entertainment, which sapped the will of the spectators, perhaps was too much for the classical traditions of civic responsibility. Rome could not withstand the constant pressure of aggressive invaders and finally fell in A.D. 476.

Ancient China: One Fifth of Humanity

Zhonghua Renmin Gongheguo is the official name of today's People's Republic of China. It means the Middle Kingdom. According to ancient Chinese belief, the area we call China is situated, cosmologically, in the center of the universe. Thus, the concept of centricity has been prevalent in Chinese philosophy and ethics. For example, the quest for harmony, life balance, calmness, order, and peace is central to the teachings of Confucius. In Western cultures,

Case $Study$ **Super Bowl Frenzy**

Here we are in the year 2005, and once again it is Super Bowl time! As the frenzied excitement of the big event builds, I can't help but remember its history. Do you remember when it was just a football game? One Sunday afternoon in Los Angeles in 1967, when the Green Bay Packers tromped the Kansas City Chiefs (35–10), sportswriters described it as a "super" event for professional football. There were 61,946 fans in the stadium. Even five years later, television had barely discovered the commercial value of the game; sponsors paid only $100,000 for 30 seconds of Super Bowl TV time.

Since these humble beginnings, organizers of the Super Bowl really have developed something "super." Let's take this year, 2005, as an example, The expected attendance in stadium seats is 120,000 people. An additional 20,000 people are predicted for the ten glass bottom blimps that will float above the stadium and 30,000 more people will choose to watch the game from special atmosphere controlled "tents" that feature large screen televisions equipped with experience sensors that send not only the sights and sounds of the action on the field to the viewers, but the smells as well. Hundreds of gambling windows are, of course, available in both the stadium and tents, and game-day-only wagers are expected to be over $6 billion.

Indianapolis, the host city, expects to bring in $15 billion in visitor revenues, which will help offset the cost of its five thousand-acre Super Bowl Megacomplex. This new facility not only includes the stadium and television viewing tents, but three resort hotels with restaurants and recreational facilities plus thirty independent restaurants each featuring a different cuisine. On the site there is also an underground road system and two underground parking lots that will accommodate 50,000 cars each, two shopping malls (one featuring only sport equipment and memorabilia), a 100 prisoner jail, an accident clinic with twenty-four hour medical staffing, and a world-class athletic training center.

This year's festivities will take place over three weeks in July to capitalize on Americans' typical vacation time. It will include a bungee jumping tournament and a velodrome bicycle endurance race. As has become a Super Bowl tradition, a wire will again be installed across the top of the stadium for the tight rope performances. This year over $25 million is expected to be won from the marathon bingo games. By the way, this year's bingo match-ups will be televised and may be viewed on closed circuit TVs from anywhere in the complex.

Of course, marching bands will entertain in daily "battles of the bands," and fifty bands will be part of the two hour half-time show. We can't forget the hundreds of eating contests that are planned over the three weeks: pies, pizzas, hot dogs, watermelons, and sushi. In the air over the stadium, glider planes will do stunt flying; skydivers will attempt to break world records; and the U.S. Air Force will give flying and target firing demonstrations.

Speaking of the military, a full-scale mock battle between two battalions of the U.S. Marines will be waged in the stadium the day before the game. The latest in warfare land machines will engage in realistic conflict for thousands of spectators. The kick-off for this year's edition of the hit TV show *American Gladiators* will also be taped in front of stadium audiences. For those not able to get enough action, virtual reality helmets will be sold afterward, so they can experience the game right down on the field.

On game day itself, all expectations will be exceeded! Although the half-time extravaganza is being kept secret, I can tell you that as part of the pregame action, each starting player from both teams will enter the field, in full uniform, leading leashed leopards. After one parade around the field, waving to the crowd, players and leopards will face-off in simultaneous wrestling matches (mostly staged, of course) for the warm-up period. After the game, a demolition derby of eighteen-wheeler trucks will take place, and to the delight of the crowd, completely tear up the turf on the field. But, who cares, there's plenty of time before next year's Super Bowl to grow the grass back.

Questions to Consider and Discuss

1. How do you react to this case study? What do your classmates think about it? Is it pure fantasy? Do you think it is plausible? Why or why not?

2. In your opinion, are there kernels of truth in this case study in terms of typical leisure pursuits in the United States now? What clues do you have from this year's Super Bowl?

3. The ancient Roman period is often remembered for its use of leisure as a spectacle. Large-scale entertainments, sometimes cruel and violent, were used to control a large middle class that had lots of free time. What parallels can you draw between the ancient Roman expression of leisure and today's?

(This case study was inspired by an article by Joseph E. Curtis, Super Bowl XXXV: The Ultimate Recreation Event, *Parks and Recreation Magazine*, January 1992, pp. 52–57. Used with permission.)

scholars also write about the quest for harmony, life balance, calmness, and order as a definition for leisure.

When the Chinese refer to their history, they are speaking of times which are already legendary. The Middle Kingdom's written history dates back approximately four thousand years. However, in spite of the symbolism of China's official name and the importance of harmony and calmness, the history of China has been turbulent. Brief periods of peace and prosperity have alternated with times of chaos, famine, poverty, war, and revolution. In spite of this, China has been the most highly populated country on earth since history has recorded this information. Thus, it is meaningful for us to consider contemporary leisure's roots within this culture hearth.

The story of leisure in ancient and medieval China is framed by the histories of the imperial dynasties (table 1.1). To this day, the existence of the first dynasty recorded in Chinese historical writings—the Xia dynasty (approximately the twenty-first to sixteenth century B.C.)—is disputed. Much later, with the arrival of the Han dynasty (206 B.C.–A.D. 220), China was united politically, and a lifestyle resembling that of the ancient Greeks evolved (Ibrahim 1991). During the Han dynasty, Confucianism became the official doctrine, which among other things resulted in an educated upper class devoting itself to fine

Tourists at the Great Wall of China near Beijing, China.

© Ruth V. Russell

Table 1.1

An Abbreviated Chronology of Chinese Dynasties

Dynasty	Time Period	Notation
Xia	c. 21st–16th century B.C.	Its existence is debated
Shang	c. 1600–1111 B.C.	An aristocratically minded society
Zhou	c. 1111–221 B.C.	An unsettled and warring period
Han	206 B.C.–A.D. 220	A period of great geographical expansion
Tang	A.D. 618–A.D. 907	A culturally rich and vital time
Song	960–1279	Impressive developments in commerce and agriculture
Ming	1368–1644	Surpassed Europe both economically and technically
Qing	1644–1911	The end of China's imperial rule

arts. The goal was also to prepare a broadly cultivated person in both the literary and martial arts—an ideal of a harmonious body and mind.

Later, the Tang dynasty (618–907) was an important chapter in the story of leisure's beginnings in China. Culturally, this was a period of enormous vitality, especially in the seventh and eighth centuries. China became a cosmopolitan society—rich in music, literature, and the visual arts (Tregear 1985). Even today, poems dating from the Tang dynasty are regarded as unsurpassed. Interestingly, based on the idea of a square world, the Tang capital (which is the city of Xi'an today) was laid out like a chess board.

Two types of people evolved during the dynasty periods in China: the governing class and the peasants. The governing and merchant classes of people, the male gentry, lived in a large household with many servants, wives, concubines, children, and grandchildren. Their residences consisted of a series of buildings set at right angles and separated by a series of courtyards. Each building was designed to produce some special advantage. For example, one may have been best suited for admiring the moonlight, another for making music, another for banquets. Specialized servants were kept: chess players, acrobats, painters of chrysanthemums, writers, musicians, and tellers of riddles. A text cited by Ibrahim (1991) lists fifty-five varieties of performers, including those with extraordinary talents: tellers of obscure stories, imitators of street cries, imitators of village talk, slight-of-hand experts, and kite flyers.

The masses in ancient China, on the other hand, were the peasants who tilled the land. Although they were legally free, they could be sold or transferred to other households. During the Song dynasty (960–1279), however, the peasants became more prosperous, and had more free time for play and entertainment (Fitzgerald 1933). By the later years of this dynasty, the entire population of the towns celebrated particular festivals. For example, according to Gernet (1962), the day might begin with people offering sacrifices at a sacred place, watching ceremonies performed at the altar, and finally making merry in the streets—sometimes for days. "Pleasure grounds" were vast covered markets where crowds gathered to watch a theatrical presentation, see a marionette show, take lessons in singing, or even be entertained by dancing turtles! The gentry, as well as the peasants, could learn to play the xylophone or tell a joke.

Leisure and Muhammad's Early Empire

Muhammad, which means praised one, was the founder of the Islamic religion and one of the most influential people of all time. Not only was he able to correct many injustices in a wild and lawless ancient Arabia, but his preaching revealed another meaning of leisure still retained by people today.

Muhammad was born in the city of Mecca in A.D. 570. When he was thirty-five years old, a flood damaged the Kaaba—the most sacred shrine in Mecca. Because of his moral excellence, Muhammad was chosen to set the sacred stone in one corner of the Kaaba back into place. Muhammad frequently spent his free time meditating alone in a cave on Mount Hira, and one night a vision appeared to him. Muslims believe that the vision was the angel Gabriel, who called Muhammad to be a prophet for God. From this beginning, Muhammad spent his life leading his people in a great religious movement. Within a hundred years after his death in A.D. 632, followers of Muhammad (Muslims) had carried his teachings into other parts of the Middle East, North Africa, Europe, and Asia. Today, there are about 500 million followers of Islam throughout the world.

While early Muslims had already learned Muhammad's philosophy of leisure through one of his sayings, "Recreate your hearts hour after hour for the tired hearts go blind" (from the Hadith), the leisure activities of the emerging leisure class resembled a more aristocratic notion. Following the death of Muhammad and during the expansion of the Islamic faith into Egypt and North Africa, contact with foreign ideas often conflicted with interpretations of the teachings of Muhammad.

For example, Muhammad had frowned on certain forms of leisure activities, particularly music and poetry. However, poetry as a pastime for the listener was to later return. Other instances of pleasure for the wealthy in the early Islamic empire can be found. According to Stewart (1967), even new forms of pastimes were developed. In the Qur'an (the Islamic holy book), paradise for the faithful is envisioned as a verdant garden where chosen men recline on beautiful carpets next to rippling water and delight in the fragrance of flowers. Thus, these lush gardens were recreated by wealthy Muslims and Arabs alike who spent hours there among the pavilions, pools, and fountains. During the day they relaxed, conversed with friends, and played chess. At night, entertainment was provided by salaried musicians. Hired performers danced until dawn. When the Persians were converted to the religion of Islam, a number of their pastimes, such as backgammon, were also introduced to the Muslim elite.

Women, as early as this ancient period, were already segregated from men (Ibrahim 1991). Even though Muhammad had sought to limit the practice of polygyny (marriage to more than one wife), the upper-class wealthy man typically practiced it and kept his wives and children in a special place within the palace. This was called the harem, and here the lifestyle of wealthy Muslim women was enlivened by a variety of diversions, among them, receiving visitors, game playing, reading, and telling stories. Music became a favorite despite its prohibition in early Islam. Even though the harem had its own bath, women's weekly visit to the public bath was an "outside" diversion. Here she could soak in varying temperatured pools of water, have her finger tips tinted with henna, move to a lounge for lunch, and later join in singing.

Similar to ancient Greece, such was not the case for the masses of people in ancient and medieval Islam. Slaves, although prohibited by Islamic law, nonetheless, did most of the work. For these people, the religious and public festivals provided the chief source of leisure (Ibrahim 1991). As example, the Festival of the Prophet, celebrating Muhammad's birthday is described by Lane (1836) as twelve days and nights of amusements. Rope dancers, singers, and reciters of romantic stories entertained under large tents. On the side streets around the tents, a few swings were erected and numerous stalls were set up for selling treats, such as sweetmeats.

Ancient New World Societies

Now let's think about the early societies of the New World. In North America beginning around A.D. 500 and predominantly in the southeast of what is now the United States, successful agriculture permitted the growth of large population centers, which in some instances approached true urban proportions even by today's standards. These were the cities of the Creek, Choctaw, and Chickasaw people. Archeologists believe they had elaborate art forms and a rich ceremonial life (McNickle 1988). Another North American example is the ancient civilization of the Cahokia people who lived near what is today St. Louis around A.D. 1000. At its peak of development, the main Cahokia site was home to over thirty thousand inhabitants and extended over an area of more than five square miles (Fowler 1978). This site is believed to be the ceremonial and political center for a larger metropolis that served a series of villages within a thirty to fifty mile radius. By studying the drawings on pottery remains, archeologists have guessed that these people also enjoyed a rich ceremonial life. People with deformities were often elevated in the society as religious leaders or shamans believed to have supernatural powers (Chapman and Chapman 1983).

The history of the Mayas and the Aztecs offers an even more extensive glimpse of the ancient meanings of leisure in the Americas. For example, the Mayas developed a magnificent civilization in what is now part of Mexico and several countries in Central America. At their peak around A.D. 300, the Mayas were particularly distinctive for being the first people in the Western Hemisphere to develop an advanced form of writing. Also among their cultural legacies are remarkable examples of architecture, painting, pottery, and sculpture.

Religious festivals provided a favorite pastime for the Mayas. The Mayan year was divided into eighteen months of twenty days each, leaving an extra five day "lucky" period. Each month had its special festivals (Ibrahim 1991). Music was provided by various kinds of drums, while dancers and dramatists performed. The passion of the Mayas was the game of *pok-a-rok*. This was played with a ball on a long, rectangular court, with spectators seated on both sides. Similar to basketball, the goal was to pass the ball through a stone ring—often as high as thirty feet—using only the elbows, knees, and hips (fig. 1.10).

Much later, around the 1400s, the Aztec people ruled a mighty empire in Mexico. The Aztecs had one of the most advanced civilizations in the world. They built cities as large as any in Europe at that time and had highly developed religious and social systems. The center of Aztec civilization was the Valley of Mexico. The largest city was Tenochititlan which occupied an island in Lake Texcoco and today is Mexico City.

Like the ancient Mayas, religion was extremely important in Aztec life. People devoted much of their time to religious practices. The Aztecs worshiped hundreds of divinities (gods and goddesses), each of whom ruled one or more human activities or aspects of nature. War was an important means of obtaining prisoners to sacrifice to these gods. During the many religious ceremonies of the Aztecs, human sacrifice often played a role. Priests slashed open the chest of a living victim and tore out the heart. The Aztecs believed that the gods needed human hearts and blood to remain strong. Worshipers sometimes ate portions of a victim's body, perhaps thinking that the dead person's strength and bravery passed to anyone who ate the flesh.

Most religious activities took place inside walled ceremonial centers. These centers included a temple, gardens, living quarters for the priests, sacred water pools for ceremonial cleansing, and racks to hold the skulls of sacrificed victims. In addition, many ceremonial centers had a playing court for another game that resembled basketball called *tlachtli*. The players tried to hit a ball through a ring with only their hips and knees (Von Hagen 1967).

Aztec society had four main social classes: nobles, commoners, serfs, and slaves. Nobles owned private land or received government land for use during their term in public office. Commoners made up the majority of the population, earning a living usually by farming family plots or doing craftwork. Their typical household included a husband and

Figure 1.10 The Mayas' favorite game was *pok-a-rok*.
Christopher B. Stage

wife, their unmarried children, and a number of the husband's relatives. Boys were educated by their father until about the age of ten and girls learned household skills at home until they married at about age sixteen. Serfs worked the land held by nobles and remained on the land when a new noble acquired it. Slaves were considered property, but their children were born free. Many slaves had been captured in war or were criminals or people who could not pay their debts.

These social class distinctions made a difference in how leisure was experienced. For example, leisure for the commoners mostly focused on arts and crafts and the religious ceremonial centers. Anthropologists have speculated about and been awed by the elaborate lifestyles of those in the noble class. For example, according to Farb (1968), the luxury of the palaces included a great number of dancers kept for amusement and royal zoos.

Medieval Europe

The Middle Ages was the period between ancient and modern times in western Europe, extending from the end of the Roman Empire (about A.D. 400) to the 1500s. The Middle Ages is also known as the medieval period, from the Latin words *medium* (middle) and *aevum* (age).

With the fall of the Roman Empire, a weakened culture was unable to turn back the invasions from the north. These invasions divided the huge Roman Empire into kingdoms, called *manors*. Each manor kept its own laws and customs. These large estates were controlled by a few wealthy landowners or lords (landlords). Most other people became poor peasants who worked the manor land for the lord.

Under the manor system towns lost their importance, and many were abandoned and eventually disappeared. Education and cultural activities were almost forgotten; few people could read or write. The arts of literature, architecture, painting, and sculpture, part of the ancient Greek and Roman legacy, were abandoned.

The Catholic Church became the main civilizing force at this time. According to church teachings, the main goal of life was abstinence from worldly pleasures. As monasteries expanded, more people lived under the Church system of hard labor, good works, and self-deprivation. Leisure, and associated pleasures, were considered against this religious ideal.

During the tenth and eleventh centuries, a system of **feudalism** was established. Again Europe was divided into many kingdoms and hundreds of wealthy men with such titles as prince, baron, duke, or count, became rulers of their own fiefs. Under feudalism, these noblemen who controlled the land also had political, economic, judicial, and military power. Even the church, which had its own princes and fiefs, was part of the feudal system. Life continued to be difficult. War, disease, famine, and a low birth rate kept the population small. People lived only an average of thirty years. There was little travel.

There were three types of people in medieval Europe: the wealthy noblemen who governed the fiefs and did all the fighting; the clergy who served the church; and the peasants who worked on the land to support themselves, the

Feudalism: the system of political organization in Europe from the ninth to about the fifteenth centuries; the service of tenants to a lord.

clergy, and the wealthy class. Let's look at the lives of each of the groups as a way of continuing the discovery of leisure's early meanings.

The noblemen's life centered around fighting. They led their knights, wearing heavy armor and riding war horses, into many land wars. As might be guessed, they were particularly interested in two outdoor pastimes: hunting and tournaments (Labarge 1965). Hunting with hounds and falconry were most popular, and tournaments were mock fighting events between two groups of knights. However, when unruly squires created wild melees, a new variation of the tournament developed—the Round Table (Labarge 1965). This was a social occasion, accompanied by jousting with blunted weapons, wrestling, dart-shooting, and even skipping contests. The church tolerated these activities reasoning that they had "useful" outcomes of providing food from the hunt and training young knights at the tournament.

The castles of the noblemen were not only mighty stone fortresses, but also settings for pleasures. In the great hall of the castle, the lord and his knights ate, drank, and were entertained at the firesides. Minstrels, who were musicians, acrobats, jugglers, and storytellers all in one, entertained the group. They also played dice, backgammon, checkers, and chess. In fact, to be good at chess was a mark of knightly quality (Ibrahim 1991). Unlike our current form of chess, however, which depends on creative problem solving, the simpler form played in the Middle Ages used dice; thus, the chess piece moves were determined by chance. Again, the church originally did not approve but later relinquished if the chess game was not played before noon on Sunday.

The clergy consisted of wealthy noblemen who devoted their lives to the church. These bishops ruled over their own large fiefs and often enjoyed pastimes much like other noblemen. Social drinking, gambling, secular music, and theatrical performances were officially regarded as sinful, but clergy frequently took part in such activities in connection with religious events (Chubb and Chubb 1981). Monks, who lived in a monastery, spent a certain number of hours each day studying, praying, and taking part in religious services more in line with the official teachings of the church.

Finally, peasants had few rights and were almost completely at the mercy of their lords. Entire peasant families farmed both the lord's fields and their own and also performed whatever other tasks the lord demanded, such as cutting wood. The peasant also had to pay many kinds of rents and taxes to the lord, so money was scarce. The only free time for the peasants of the Middle Ages was on Sundays and certain church-declared saint's days. Although the church sought to censure it, dancing, singing, and general partying typically filled these days. The songs of the day were usually sacrilegious and vulgar (Ibrahim 1991). Fairs, held for peasants in conjunction with church holidays, featured the antics of trained monkeys and performers, such as fire-eaters and sword swallowers.

Medieval civilization reached its zenith in the eleventh to the late thirteenth centuries. During this time, many capable lords provided strong governments, relative peace, and a generally higher quality of life than under the feudal system. As a result, the people were able to turn their attention to new ideas and activities. For example, students gathered at magnificent stone cathedrals where scholars lectured. Eventually, these students and scholars formed new organizations called *universities.*

The Renaissance

- Line your doublet with taffitie, taffitie is lice-proof.
- Never journey without something to eat in your pocket, if only to throw to dogs when attacked by them.
- At sea, remove your spurs; sailors make a point of stealing them from those who are being seasick. Keep your distance from them in any case; they are covered with vermin.
- In an inn-bedroom which contains big pictures, look behind the latter to see they do not conceal a secret door or a window.

(Travel described by a tourist in the 1600s; cited from Hudman 1980)

By about 1300, medieval Europe began to give way to modern Europe—a period in European history called the **Renaissance.** In the three hundred years of the Renaissance era, great changes in ways of experiencing leisure occurred when compared to leisure in the Middle Ages. We conclude this section by briefly recognizing these changes.

Renaissance: the transitional period between medieval and modern times in Europe, marked by a humanistic revival of the arts and literature.

The Renaissance spread throughout Europe during the fifteenth and sixteenth centuries. It swept away customs that had dominated for almost a thousand years, and the new ideas and attitudes about leisure that emerged influence our lives today. While the period is noted for its advancement of strong national governments, dramatic increases in commerce and trade, and a weakening of the power of the Catholic Church, probably the greatest achievements came in scholarship and the arts. This was the age of such artists as painters Michelangelo, Raphael, and Leonardo da Vinci; sculptor Donatello; playwright William Shakespeare; and author Cervantes.

This was also an age of adventure and curiosity. People became fascinated with the world and the people around them. They set out on dangerous voyages to explore unknown lands. Books about travel began to flood England, and it became a widespread custom for young gentlemen to complement their education with travel (Hudman 1980). Perhaps we can count this period the birth of modern tourism.

Renaissance is a French word meaning rebirth. During this time, there was a renewed interest in those things human—languages, literature, the arts. This emphasis formed a new philosophy known as **humanism,** which glorified the human being.

Humanism: a way of looking at the world that emphasizes the importance of human beings. Humanities is education based on the philosophy of humanism.

Literature, drama, music, painting, and ballet flourished under the sponsorship of nobles and royalty. Theaters and opera houses were constructed, and troupes of actors, singers, musicians, and dancers were in high demand. The wealthy became patrons of the arts and arranged formal dances, exhibitions, banquets, hunts, and masquerades. The middle class tried to copy the upper

Table 1.2

Contemporary Definitions of Leisure

Leisure is
- **Free time**—time free from obligations
  "To me, leisure is the weekend."
- **Recreational activity**—nonwork kinds of activity
  "To me, playing golf and watching TV are leisure."
- **Attitude**—a self-actualized life perspective
  "To me, getting the most out of the day is leisure."

class by participating in less extravagant festivities and the pursuits of gardening and hunting. Even children's activities stressed intellectual and creative pastimes, such as studies in art, music, and science (Bucher, Shivers, and Bucher 1984).

Today's Meanings and Connotations

Because words are basic tools of communication, it is important that we consider the contemporary meanings of the word used most frequently in this book: leisure. In an effort to understand the meaning of the word *leisure,* researchers and philosophers have produced a large body of literature. In considering contemporary pastimes in this book, the meaning of leisure can be gathered from the three definitions listed in table 1.2. First, leisure is described as free time. Next, leisure is defined as nonwork activity. Finally, leisure is considered a state of mind, an attitude. Before examining each definition individually, let's consider two cautions. Since leisure means different things to different people, setting the contemporary foundation for its meaning will necessarily be complex. People do not always mean the same things even though they use the same words. For example, saying a particular college course is "difficult" will probably be differently defined by an undergraduate student, a graduate student, and a professor.

A second difficulty is that word meanings change over time and between contexts. Saying you "love" ice cream has a different connotation than saying you "love" your parents or mate (Bammel and Bammel 1992). So it is with leisure. We've already discovered how different ancient cultures experienced leisure in different ways. Also, does the leisure we enjoy by ourselves have the same meaning as the leisure we enjoy with our friends?

Leisure as Free Time

Today, leisure is commonly considered time free from obligations—time at one's own disposal. According to this definition leisure is considered leftover time apart from that time a person is obligated to work. This means that leisure is quantifiable, and it is possible to talk about leisure in terms of amounts of it possessed. We often look forward to weekends and holidays because we will have more leisure, that is, more time to do what we freely choose. When we retire from employment, we look forward to more leisure; day upon day of time to fill as we please.

This quantifiable definition of leisure as free time has led to comparative research. For example, time-budget studies make it possible to contrast the leisure of different population groups and different cultures.

In a few Mediterranean and Latin American countries the custom of siesta is observed, giving workers time off in the middle of the afternoon. In Asunción, Paraguay, for example, the typical workday begins at 8:00 A.M. and lasts until about 1:00 P.M. Then, stores and offices close while workers go home for a large lunch and a long nap. They are back to work from about 5:00 P.M. to 8:00 P.M. After work, there is free time for social events, typically beginning around 10:00 P.M. and often lasting until after 1:00 A.M. Thus, instead of a single long period of sleep at night, many Paraguayans take two long naps each day.

Greece has traditionally observed similar workday customs. In 1977, however, the Greek government tried to change the official workday to 9:00 A.M. to 5:00 P.M. to conform to western European customs as preparation for membership in the European Economic Community (EEC). Workers reacted with wildcat strikes, and customers stayed away in protest. The government was defeated, at least temporarily, and allowed businesses to return to the split-shift schedule (Chubb and Chubb 1981).

People's perceptions of free time influence the ways they use it. If free time is regarded as a privilege, it is likely that the individual will try to use it wisely and fill it with experiences that are personally and/or socially beneficial. Some see free time as a chance to escape temporarily from the physical and emotional stresses associated with their work or routine duties, and they spend their leisure trying to get away from it all. Others perceive free time as an empty space that, if left unfilled, becomes something negative. To these people, leisure becomes intimidating, and they feel anxious to fill the vacuum.

Wearing and Wearing (1988) have suggested that leisure as free time is not a very useful conceptualization for women because many women do not believe they deserve or have the time to engage in leisure. Further, Deem (1986) found that the leisure time available for women is often fragmented and interrupted by the roles of mother and wife. This matches Henderson and Rannells's (1988) distinction of women's free time as only small "minute vacation" time blocks.

Leisure as Recreational Activity

A second definition of leisure is participation based. In this connotation, leisure is considered nonwork activity, commonly called recreation activity. This is the predominant definition of leisure held by those professionals working in the park and recreation fields. Accordingly, leisure is games, sports, social interactions, arts, crafts, rest, travel, dance, drama, hobbies, day dreaming, etc. Although some vagueness prevails, most people can easily explain what they do for leisure and it is usually in the form of an activity.

The activities people engage in for leisure are diverse. Recreational interests of people range from model airplane building to playing cards, yet in an important multinational survey conducted in the mid-1960s by Alexander Szalai, the participation patterns of 27,860 adults in twelve countries revealed some common patterns. While somewhat dated (1972), these findings are generic enough to be respected. For example, the majority of this large sample participated in media-type activities. About 80 percent of the respondents watched television, and over 50 percent listened to the radio. Reading newspapers, magazines, and books was the second set of activities in order of participation importance. This was followed by social interaction activities, such as visiting friends, attending a party, and having conversations.

Leisure activity participation differs according to population groups. To illustrate, Boyd and Tedrick (1992) interviewed eleven elder, black women. Most of the women were widowed and lived alone in an urban setting in the United States; their finances were meager. The study found their leisure patterns focused on television watching, going to the senior center, attending church, reading the Bible, and listening to the radio. When asked to describe their most memorable leisure experience, four of the women mentioned a trip and three a religious experience.

In spite of its common usage, many writers have pointed to a problem in defining leisure as an activity. Is making a ceramic pot a recreational activity for everyone all the time? Is tennis leisure when it is played on Saturday at the local park and something else when played in a required physical education class or by a touring pro? When is mowing the lawn or washing the dishes a leisure activity? How might we solve this paradox?

While leisure as an activity means nonwork, it does not mean a purposeless activity. According to Dumazedier (1974) leisure activity has purposes. Leisure activity is focused on relaxation, diversion, refreshment, and re-creation. Thus, only those activities that satisfy these purposes can be considered leisure. Is it really this simple? The requirement of relaxation, for example, can be met by a wide array of activities: sleeping in on Saturday morning, competing in a triathlon, baking a cake, bird watching, or window shopping at the mall.

Kelly has offered another solution to the confusion by concluding that "no activity is always leisure because of its form. Almost anything may be an obligation under some conditions" (Kelly 1982, 21). Therefore, an activity is leisure when it is freely chosen and benefits the participant. It is how the person doing the activity feels about it, not the activity itself, that makes it leisure.

Leisure as an Attitude

Defining leisure as free time or as recreational activity appears to yield more objective and visible results. On the other hand, defining leisure as an attitude or state of mind appears to be more subjective. This definition maintains that "leisure is not in the time or the action, but in the actor" (Kelly 1982, 22). The leisure attitude is a way of life, a philosophy about living, a psychological condition.

Almost poetically, Pieper (1963) explained it thus: "Leisure, like contemplation, is a higher order than the active life. . . . It involves the capacity to soar in active celebration, to overstep the boundaries of the workaday world." To illustrate, a team of researchers (Hull, Steward, and Yi 1992) studied the states of minds of ninety hikers during a short but strenuous dayhike. One interesting finding was related to leisure's definition as a psychological condition. The hikers in the study described their feelings during the hike as those of complete satisfaction. This is not surprising given the scenic beauty of the area, yet these feelings of satisfaction were found to be virtually independent of the activity, setting, and characteristics of the experience. For the hikers, feelings of self-satisfaction, positive outlook, and happiness varied little with the type of scenery being viewed, the degree of exertion (downhill versus uphill), or with the accomplishment of reaching the destination. These feelings were more a state of mind.

Although the psychological condition of leisure suggests it is simply a matter of "feeling good," the connotation goes beyond this. Leisure is an entire way of being—an opportunity for building purpose into life—capable of providing opportunities for self-expression, self-achievement, and self-actualization. Leisure is engaging in flights of imagination, developing talents, looking at things in new ways, and being ourselves.

Summary: Multiple Meanings

Leisure is a multifaceted concept. In order to understand its contemporary expression, this chapter played with various definitions. The meanings of leisure were considered from three perspectives: the humanities, ancient culture histories, and current connotations.

To initially demonstrate leisure's various meanings, literature, art, and music offered glimpses of leisure as an interpersonal unifying force, emotional outlet, source of peace and quiet, contact with nature, idleness, excitement, sociability, and others. In comparing ancient cultures, we also discovered leisure's multiple meanings, as well as the roots of contemporary definitions. For example, the nature of leisure as spectacle in ancient Rome parallels today's expression of leisure in many modern societies.

Finally, leisure was described based on current definitions. Here the various definitions were grouped according to theme: leisure as free time, leisure as recreational activity, and leisure as attitude or state of mind.

References

Adler, M. J. 1978. *Aristotle for everybody.* New York: Bantam Books.

Angelou, M. 1986. *Maya Angelou: Poems.* New York: Bantam Books.

Anonymous college student. 1993. Comment made during class discussion in recreation and park administration course at Indiana University.

Aristotle. 1963. *Ethics. Book X.* Chapter 7. London: Dent.

Bammel, G., and L. L. B. Bammel. 1992. *Leisure and human behavior.* Dubuque, IA: Wm. C. Brown Publishers.

Blazey, M. A. October 1990. Bruegel and me and Julio: A comparison of 16th and 20th century popular art forms depicting play. Paper presented at the Leisure Research Symposium, National Recreation and Park Association Congress, Phoenix, AZ.

Boette, M. 1971. *Sing hipsy doodle and other folk songs of West Virginia.* Parsons, WV: McClain Printing Company.

Boyd, R., and T. Tedrick. October 1992. Leisure's role in the lives of older, black women. Paper presented at the Leisure Research Symposium, National Recreation and Park Association Congress, Cincinnati, OH.

Bucher, C. A., J. S. Shivers, and R. Bucher. 1984. *Recreation for today's society.* Englewood Cliffs, NJ: Prentice-Hall.

Butler, J. 1972. *The theatre and drama of Greece and Rome.* San Francisco, CA: Chandler.

Chapman, C. H., and E. F. Chapman. 1983. *Indians and archaeology of Missouri.* Columbia, MO: University of Missouri Press.

Chubb, M., and H. R. Chubb. 1981. *One third of our time? An introduction to recreation behavior and resources.* New York: John Wiley & Son, Inc.

Curtis, J. E. 1992. Super Bowl XXXV: The ultimate recreational event. *Parks and Recreation* 1:52–57.

Deem, R. 1986. *All work and no play? The sociology of women and leisure.* Milton Keynes, England: Open University Press.

Dumazedier, J. 1974. *Sociology of leisure.* New York: Elsevier North-Holland.

Engs, R. 1993. Interview by author. 10 March.

Farb, P. 1968. *Man's rise to civilization.* New York: Avon.

Fellmann, J., A. Getis, and J. Getis. 1990. *Human geography: Landscapes of human activities.* Dubuque, IA: Wm. C. Brown Publishers.

Fitzgerald, C. P. 1933. *China: A short cultural history.* New York: Praeger.

Fleming, W. 1986. *Arts and ideas.* New York: Holt, Rinehart and Winston.

Fowler, M. L. 1978. Cahokia and the American bottom: Settlement archeology. In *Mississippian settlement patterns,* edited by B. D. Smith. New York: Academic Press.

Gernet, J. 1962. *Daily life in China.* Stanford, CA: Stanford University Press.

Goodale, T. L., and G. C. Godbey. 1988. *The evolution of leisure: Historical and philosophical perspectives.* State College, PA: Venture Publishing.

Hamilton, E. 1942. *The Greek way.* New York: W. W. Norton.

Hemingway, J. L. 1988. Lesiure and civility: Reflections on a Greek ideal. *Leisure Sciences* 10:179–91.

Henderson, K. A., and J. S. Rannells. 1988. Farm women and the meaning of work and leisure: An oral history perspective. *Leisure Sciences* 10:41–50.

Herbert, R. L. 1988. *Impressionism: Art, leisure, and Parisian society.* New Haven and London: Yale University Press.

Hudman, L. E. 1980. *Tourism: A shrinking world.* Columbus, OH: Grid Inc.

Hull, R. B., IV, W. P. Steward, and Y. K. Yi. 1992. Experience patterns: Capturing the dynamic nature of a recreation experience. *Journal of Leisure Research* 24, no. 3:240–52.

Ibrahim, H. 1991. *Leisure and society: A comparative approach.* Dubuque, IA: Wm. C. Brown Publishers.

Kelly, J. R. 1982. *Leisure.* Englewood Cliffs, NJ: Prentice-Hall.

Labarge, M. W. 1965. *A baronial household of the thirteenth century.* New York: Barnes & Noble.

Lane, E. W. 1836. *An account of the manners and customs of the modern Egyptians.* New York: Dover.

McNickle, D. 1988. Americans called Indians. In *North American Indians in Historical Perspective,* edited by E. B. Leacock and N. O. Lurie. Prospect Heights, IL: Waveland Press.

Pan-African MarketPlace. 1993. Come home to Sudan, a nation full of potential and promise! *Pan-African MarketPlace* (September):1–2.

Pieper, J. 1963. *Leisure: The basis of culture.* New York: New American Library.

Recording Industry Association. 1989. *The 1991 information please almanac.* Boston: Houghton Mifflin.

Rice, A. 1988. *The queen of the damned.* New York: Ballantine Books.

Roberts, V. M. 1962. *On stage: A history of theatre.* New York: Harper & Row.

Rybczynski, W. 1991. *Waiting for the weekend.* New York: Viking Penguin.

Sarton, M. 1973. *Journal of a solitude.* New York: W. W. Norton.

Simon, P. 1989. *Me and Julio.* Burbank, CA: Warner. Videocassette.

Simpson, S. 1989. Aristotle (384–322 BC). In *Pioneers in Leisure and Recreation,* edited by H. Ibrahim. Reston, VA. The American Association of Health, Physical Education, Recreation, and Dance.

Stewart, D. 1967. *Early Islam.* New York: Time.

Szalai, A. 1972. *The use of time: Daily activities of urban and suburban populations in twelve countries.* The Hague: Mouton.

Tregear, M. 1985. *Chinese art.* New York: Thames and Hudson.

Updike, J. 1989. Still of some use. In *Life studies: A thematic reader,* edited by David Cavitch. New York: St. Martin's Press.

Von Hagen, V. W. 1967. *The ancient sun kingdoms of the Americas.* London: Panther Books.

Wearing, B., and S. Wearing. 1988. "All in a day's leisure": Gender and the concept of leisure. *Leisure Studies* 7: 111–23.

having a good time

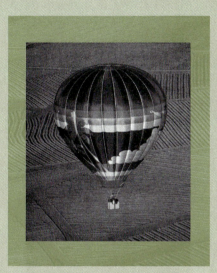

Digital Stock

PREVIEW

What do we mean when we say leisure is "having a good time"?

Even though we may think of leisure casually as having fun, philosophers and scientists have taken the matter quite seriously. "Having a good time" in leisure involves the qualities of happiness, pleasure, freedom, intrinsic reward, play, game, laughter and humor, solitude, spirituality, risk, and even boredom.

Is leisure all these qualities?

No, at any single moment leisure can be characterized by one or more of these qualities. For example, a summer spent at a seashore cottage may be described as leisure because you feel free and alone. A quick climb to the top of a rock face may be experienced as risk, spirituality, and even a game.

two

Are you having a good time?

While this may appear a trivial question—one that often becomes a tease or a joke—much of most people's life is spent in the pursuit of a good time. Having fun is often what is thought of when considering leisure. Leisure is almost always looked upon with favor, and almost everyone wants it. It is not something unpleasant, punitive, or threatening but is both a reward and a way of being that provides personal benefit.

Leisure is not a withdrawal from life, rather it is an engagement in living. Your pastimes—how you experience leisure—has an effect on the kind of person you are, as well as an effect on the character of your society. In fact, our leisure makes us complete. How we spend our leisure is a reflection of not only our interests, but our character and personality as well.

What is involved in this good time? What are the qualities of leisure? In this chapter, we seek to portray the nature of leisure by characterizing its experience. In doing this, we go beyond leisure's definition. We focus on the variety of ways leisure is felt.

Happiness

Happiness, morale, psychological well-being, and life adjustment are all indicators of the overall quality of our inner experience. Definitionally slippery, happiness is often considered the extent to which we have positive attitudes and feelings about various aspects of our life.

In his classic book devoted to the subject of happiness, Bertrand Russell (1968) laid some foundation for understanding this quality. He claimed that happiness is the possession of zest. Using the illustration of a person who approaches a meal with a good appetite, appreciates the food, and eats heartily until full, Russell defined zest as enjoying life because it is interesting and we are hungry for it. Russell also maintained that achieving happiness is very difficult. "My purpose is to suggest a cure for the ordinary day-to-day unhappiness from which most people in civilized countries suffer" (p. 5). Among the advice Russell has given for being happy is this one: "The secret of happiness is this: let your interests be as wide as possible, and let your reactions to the things and persons that interest you be as far as possible friendly rather than hostile" (p. 111).

A complete presentation on happiness could fill this entire book, so extensive have been speculations about happiness and how to achieve it. Therefore, we will discuss only briefly the role of happiness in leisure. We make our connection between happiness and leisure from two perspectives: classical philosophies and current beliefs about achieving happiness.

A question that occupied much of the philosophy of Aristotle was how the good life should be lived. His answer from the beginning was that the best life is *eudaimonia,* which most translations today interpret as happiness or personal well-being (Sylvester 1991). How did Aristotle mean it? Was his view that *eudaimonia* was a state of mind characterized by feelings of contentment

Bertrand Russell (1872–1970) was a Welsh mathematician and philosopher. He wrote over forty books on subjects as diverse as philosophy, mathematics, education, sociology, politics, and sexuality. Among them are *Mysticism and Logic* (1918), *Marriage and Morals* (1929), and *Has Man a Future?* (1962), for which he received the 1950 Nobel Prize for literature.

Most interesting about Russell, perhaps, was his outspokenness which involved him in many controversies. During World War I, he was dismissed from Cambridge University and imprisoned because of his pacifist views. In 1940, protests against his liberal views on religion and morals caused the College of the City of New York to cancel his appointment as a professor. Attempts to oust him from Harvard University the same year failed. In 1962 he was again imprisoned, briefly, for his efforts to ban nuclear weapons.

In the preface of his book *The Conquest of Happiness* (1968), Russell wrote, "No profound philosophy or deep erudition will be found in the following pages. . . . I [only] venture to hope that some among those multitudes of men and women who suffer unhappiness without enjoying it, may find their situation diagnosed and a method of escape suggested" (p. iv). In his "recipe" for happiness, he begins by presenting the causes of unhappiness. They are such things as competition, boredom, fatigue, and envy. One of the ingredients for the happy person highlighted in the book is zest, or enthusiasm for a variety of pursuits in life. Like a cat that will not relax in an unfamiliar room until it has sniffed at every corner, humans must remain zealous in their explorations. As the traveler who seeks to "make the acquaintance of people who typify the locality, observe whatever is of interest either historically or socially, eat the food of the country, learn its manners and its language, and come home with a new stock of pleasant thoughts for winter evenings" (p. 116), zest is a way to happiness.

and satisfaction? That is, happiness is all in the mind? According to the scholar Sylvester, psychological happiness is not what Aristotle meant by *eudaimonia*.

To Aristotle, classical *eudaimonia* was not determined by subjective feelings of well-being, rather by the more objective character of the activities of life. This meant that happiness is an action, moreover a good action, and leisure is a part of that action. It is having the ability to choose and engage in worthy pursuits. Thus, happiness depends on leisure, and for Aristotle, only moral and "good" activities are inherently leisure. Unhappiness, then, is when one cannot do good things.

This was the classical sense of leisure and happiness. What about today's contemporary society? What makes us happy? During the past twenty years, hundreds of studies have sought to answer the question with no agreement. Some have predicted that age is a factor in happiness. Older people tend to be less happy in some studies and happier in others. Some studies suggest that women are happier than men and that having good health makes one happy. Having friends, enough money, and a career that matches your talents and interests have also been connected to happiness in research studies. Being creative and having a nurturing personality have also been linked with happiness, but what about the role of leisure?

In revisiting the relationship between leisure and happiness according to age, we find numerous **gerontological** studies indicating that involvement in leisure activity facilitates successful aging. For example, one of the earliest

Gerontology: the study of aging and the aged.

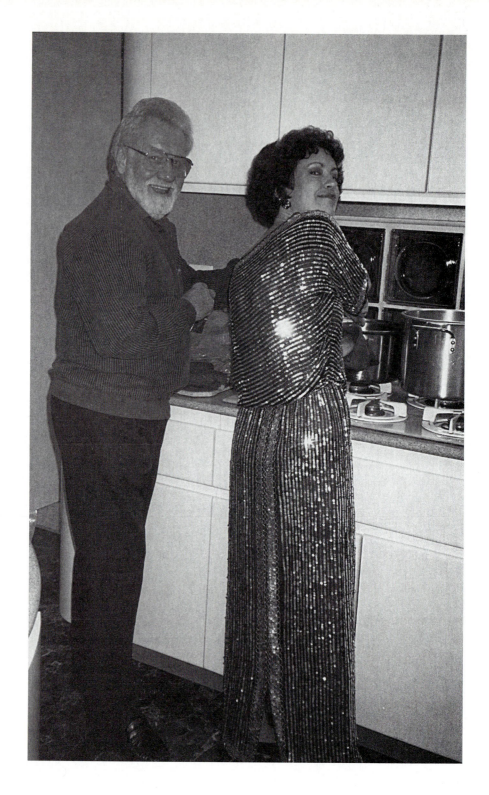

Research indicates that participation in leisure activities relates to the happiness of adults.

© Ruth V. Russell

studies on this topic (DeCarlo 1974) found that a large amount of daily recreational activity was more highly correlated with successful aging than was small amounts of infrequent activity. This study also found that intellectual types of pastimes had the highest relationship. In contrast, another early study (Peppers 1976) found that people engaged in active, social, and external forms of leisure activity were happier than people who engaged in passive, individual, and homebound activities. An investigation of retirees by Heppe and Ray (1983) demonstrated that frequent participation in cultural activities, social and service organizations, and crafts and hobbies yielded a greater likelihood for life happiness.

Research has also suggested that childhood pastimes are related to happiness in middle age. These studies (such as Brooks and Elliott 1971) have concluded that successful adjustment to growing older depends less on how active a person is than on whether her or his activities developed out of life-long interests.

The weight of the evidence from these findings does indicate that participation in leisure activities in general relates to the happiness of older persons. The key to this relationship seems to be the significance or meaning of the activity. To what extent is there a commitment to the role of leisure in daily life? Several studies in gerontology have focused on this question as well.

In order for participation in leisure to make people happy, an important qualifier is the person's satisfaction with this participation. More recent studies have affirmed (Keller 1983; Ragheb and Griffith 1982; Russell 1987) that in order for activities to be satisfying and thus contribute to life happiness, they must be able to maximize an individual's abilities, produce challenge, be interesting, and elicit pleasure. Thus, the value of leisure for happiness is not only determined by how often one engages in it, but also by its meaning within life.

Pleasure

Leisure is pleasing. In almost all characterizations of leisure, reference is made to pleasure. What is pleasure? In popular discourse the word is used in many ways. Pleasure comes from listening to favorite music, being with a friend, petting our dog, or winning a lottery! There is sexual pleasure, the pleasure of eating to one's "heart's content," and perhaps the elation from taking drugs.

These uses of the word seem to be saying that pleasure is basically the satisfaction of a desire. Of course, it is not that simple. In their book *The Evolution of Leisure* (1988), contemporary leisure philosophers Goodale and Godbey described many understandings about pleasure. Drawing on beliefs about pleasure that originated in ancient Greece, these authors help interpret current attitudes about pleasure. These ancient attitudes are cynicism, skepticism, stoicism, epicureanism, and hedonism.

Cynicism refers to the belief, established in the fourth century B.C. by Antisthenes, a disciple of Socrates, that virtue rather than pleasure is the chief goal of life. This perspective argues that the wise person is one who looks

Cynicism: distrust of human nature.

with contempt on all the ordinary pleasures of life and lives without regard for riches or honors. Among the enthusiastic followers of Antisthenes and cynicism was Diogenes, who carried the principles to extreme. It is said that he ate only the coarsest bread and slept in a bathing tub. Authorities have argued about the original source of the word *cynic,* but in ordinary modern speech, a person who sneers at the idea that goodness exists in human nature is often called a cynic.

Skepticism: suspended judgment.

Skepticism was another philosophical movement that originated in ancient Greece. As in the contemporary use of the word, skeptics doubted everything. This school of thought tried to weaken people's confidence in observation and reason as trustworthy guides to understanding the world. They believed that one can be certain of the nature of her or his observations, but cannot be sure that these observations reflect the real world. Thus, according to the skeptics, what a person thinks is water might be a mirage. Although we can thank this view for challenging and clarifying such concepts as probability, astrology, and magic, skepticism also taught people to withhold judgments on everything if they wanted mental peace. In other words, the wise person should simply try to live a neutral life. This attitude toward pleasure says that one should accept whatever is conventional.

Stoicism: impassiveness.

Stoicism holds the middle perspective about pleasure. It is a philosophical attitude that compromises between the rejections of pleasure represented by cynicism and skepticism and the promotions of pleasure in epicureanism and hedonism. In its modern usage, the word means indifference to both pleasure and pain. Originating also in ancient Greece and then spreading to Rome through about 300 A.D., stoic philosophers believed that all people have within themselves reason. This individual reason further relates each person to all other people and to the universe. This belief, therefore, provided a theoretical basis for the contemporary notion of **cosmopolitanism**—the idea that people are citizens of the world.

Cosmopolitanism: not bound by local or national habits or prejudices.

Stoicism maintains that people achieve their greatest good—happiness— by following reason, freeing themselves from passions, and concentrating only on things they can control. Thus, the Stoics did not seek pleasure in life. They accepted good fortune without joy and bore misfortune without complaint— very much the modern philosophy "you win a few; you lose a few."

Epicureanism: belief that more permanent pleasures are best.

Epicureanism sought to free humans from fear. Named after the ancient Greek philosopher, Epicurus, this belief taught that the human mind, which was disturbed by fears of the gods and goddesses, and fear of death, could be freed by seeking moderate pleasures. The Epicureans concluded that there were two kinds of pleasures. The more superior were intellectual pleasures, such as contemplation and appreciation. The more inferior pleasures were those that responded to the senses, such as sexual drives and hunger. Pleasure, to the Epicurean understanding, could best be gained by living in accordance with prudence, virtue, moderation, justice, and friendship.

Finally, we consider **hedonism.** Located on the other end of the scale from cynicism, this philosophy held that pleasure was the highest goal of life. In fact the term *hedonism* comes from the Greek word *hedone,* meaning pleasure. While the Epicureans based their philosophy on the idea that pleasure was an important human goal, they believed that people should seek pleasures of the mind rather than pleasures of the body. The wise person, they thought, avoided pleasures that might later cause pain. In contrast, those who believed in hedonism included the body, fame, power, and wealth as other sources of pleasure. To some critics hedonism is little more than a rationalization for self-indulgence.

The ancient perspectives about pleasure—cynicism, skepticism, stoicism, Epicureanism, and hedonism—have influenced contemporary notions of leisure as pleasurable. An individual's own unique casting of leisure in his or her life can be described according to these different perspectives about pleasure. For example, some forms of leisure, such as swimming and dancing, are considered pleasurable by some people because of the pleasurable sensations to the body (hedonism). For other people, such physical pastimes are considered immoral because of their sensual nature (Epicureanism).

Another way to link pleasure with leisure is to consider various kinds of pleasure that may result from our pastimes. While numerous sensations of pleasure result from leisure, they can be grouped into three categories: (1) sensory, (2) expressive, and (3) intellectual (Smith 1991).

Sensory pleasures are often found in such everyday activities as eating, some forms of children's play, music, sex, and sports. These activities are pleasurable because they directly stimulate the body. For example, in an investigation by Dimberg (1987) people's response to musical tones was measured physiologically. The facial EMG technique was used to detect different body reactions to tones of low intensity (75 dB) and high intensity (95 dB). High-intensity tones evoked an increase in corrugator muscle activity. (The corrugator muscle is used when frowning and other negative emotional expressions.) Likewise, the subjects indicated they thought the lower-intensity tones were more pleasing. What do these findings suggest about the pleasure value of very loud music?

Expressive pleasures from leisure, on the other hand, are based on the use of creativity. As a result of the activity something is produced which gives pleasure (fig. 2.1). Painting, sculpting, composing music, and film-making are examples. This type of leisure pleasure can be confused with sensory pleasure. For example, listening to rock music may trigger sensory pleasure, while composing a piece of classical music will be an expressive pleasure. The distinction is not so much in the type of music (rock vs. classical) but in the differences between expressions of listening and composing.

Finally, intellectual pleasure from leisure seems to belong to the activities of thinking. While some everyday examples might include fantasizing and day-dreaming, the more rare pleasure of studying is also an intellectual type of

Hedonism: the idea that pleasure is the chief goal in life.

Figure 2.1 The sculpture *The Napper* by Duane Hanson gives expressive pleasure to travelers in the Orlando, Florida, airport.

© Ruth V. Russell

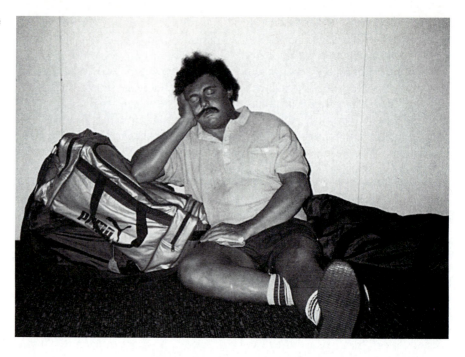

pleasure. Only a few people derive most of their pleasure from intellectual sources. For philosophers, mathematicians, and even mystics pleasure primarily comes from their minds and not their actions.

Now let's look at pleasure from a very different perspective: biological. Although most writers about leisure recognize pleasure as an essential component, those who conduct research on leisure experiences have not studied pleasure in leisure directly. Hamilton (1989) attempted to fill this void by investigating whether leisure induces increases in dopamine (a pleasure producing neurotransmitter) in blood plasma levels. While the subjects in his study (thirty female undergraduate college students) perceived the leisure experienced in the laboratory as pleasurable, no differences in their plasma levels were found.

Most of the study of pleasure as a biological phenomenon comes from research outside leisure literature. Several classic studies by the psychologist James Olds (Olds 1960; Olds and Milner 1954) first demonstrated that pleasure had a biological basis. Olds discovered that stimulating the limbic system of the brain produced pleasure in laboratory rats. A portion of the limbic system is now called the pleasure area of the brain. Direct stimulation of the limbic system is so powerful that it even overwhelms the desire for water and food. Years of experimentation on these areas of the brain have determined that this is one of the strongest drives in animals (Smith 1991).

The limbic system also exists in the human brain. In experiments by Robert Heath (cited in Smith 1991), mental patients were provided a set of implanted electrodes and a button. He noted that the patients used the buttons frequently. According to them, it felt good and made them feel happy.

The improvement of their moods ranged from general pleasure to a profound euphoria that lasted up to several days.

The next step in the inquiries was to determine if animals would voluntarily engage in some behavior that would yield no reward other than the pleasure of doing it, as in the leisure behavior of humans. Using the sensory stimulation of a pure white light that was shone into their eyes, monkeys in Campbell's (1973) experiments voluntarily switched on the light. When the color of the light was changed every fifteen minutes, the monkeys kept flashing the light for over four hours, indicating that animals do engage in behavior solely for pleasure.

In fact, most activities in which an animal engages in the natural world are done for pleasurable stimulation only. An animal does not eat to get nourishment; it eats to get pleasure. Does this sound unlikely? If an animal's mouth is numbed so it cannot taste or feel food during eating, the animal may starve to death (Smith 1991). Research by Ziegler (1975) further indicated that overeating may be due to a malfunctioning of the nerve that registers oral tactile sensations, such as kissing, smoking, and eating. In his experiments with animals, the destruction of this nerve (called trigeminal) not only stopped the sending of the pleasurable feelings of eating, but also stopped any interest in eating.

Freedom

It's 5:00 P.M. and a typical Tuesday evening for the American suburban family is about to begin. As usual, lots of leisure is on tap for this evening. The parent leaves work and picks up the younger child from band practice at the school. At home, the parent fixes a microwave dinner, and the child eats it in eight minutes. Next, the parent herds the child back into the car and makes the drop-off at the Scout meeting on the way to the community theater play rehearsal, which begins at 6:00 P.M. Meanwhile, another parent and a teenager arrive home at 6:20 P.M. There is a small conflict over use of the car for the evening, but it is solved. At 6:50 P.M., this parent drops the teenager off at track club practice, does some quick grocery shopping for the small dinner party they're having tomorrow, and picks up the child from the Scout meeting. They return home, and the parent drops off the child at the door. The child is instructed to do homework but watches TV instead. Racing off, the parent hurries across town to participate in a 7:30 P.M. tennis match for the city tournament.

Meanwhile, the first parent, having finished the rehearsal, stops by the tennis courts to watch a bit of the match and then drives over to the track and picks up the teenager at 8:30 P.M. They drive through a restaurant for a hamburger, soda, and fries for the teenager's dinner on the way home. The tennis playing parent gets home at about 10:00 P.M. The family is together now. Did everyone get dinner?

Let's dissect the leisure in this scenario. The family members participated in music, sports, and drama—oh, and yes, the Scout meeting, too. Thanks to efficient time management and sharing the two family cars, they squeezed a lot of leisure into the evening. Was the family's freedom, even within their leisure, limited?

Leisure is commonly considered to involve freedom. As children, we first discover freedom, its delights and dangers, in playing. As formal education gradually replaces play, we begin to experience constraints upon our freedom. This is the beginning of a long process of adjustment that will last our entire life. We have to learn that we cannot always do what we want when we want. Thus, it may appear hopeless to consider freedom as a condition of contemporary leisure. Nonetheless, current descriptions suggest that leisure cannot survive when freedom is curtailed. Let's explore the connections: leisure as freedom "from" and leisure as freedom "to."

First, leisure is temporary "freedom from" the necessities of life. Leisure is time free from work and obligations. It is a kind of compensation for work. When people work at their jobs overtime without pay, they are usually rewarded instead with "comp" or compensatory time, that is, some time off later.

Leisure as freedom "from" something is a bit problematic. Since this suggests that leisure is an escape from work, those who do not work could be considered unworthy of leisure. The "freedom from" notion of leisure suggests that freedom must be earned. After all, how can one have free time when one does not have obligated time? Another difficulty with this concept of leisure is that the time becomes an end in itself (Goodale and Godbey 1988). Accordingly, what is done with that time is less important.

Let's consider an illustration of these problems. A few years ago I interviewed three women who were "serving time" in prison. I wanted to explore how leisure was experienced with all constraints on time removed. I reasoned that these women, whose only obligations were three meal times and one hour of yard exercise each day, had large amounts of free time. In talking with the women about how they spent their time, I learned some surprising things.

First, how they used their free time wasn't very meaningful for them. They considered their daily activities (reading, writing letters, watching television, and crafts) more as "killing" time—doing things to make the time pass. Second, they didn't see the long expanses of unobligated time each day as free time. Because they always had this time, day after day, and because this free time certainly wasn't perceived as a reward for doing something, their sense of freedom, as it applied to time, was nonexistent. As a result they felt they had absolutely no leisure.

Continually, these three women commented: "But I cannot choose to do what I really want to do!" This justifies why in most approaches to leisure and freedom, the focus has been on freedom of choice, or freedom to experience a particular personal expression. Consequently, leisure also implies the ability to choose something we want to do, preferably among two or more desirable alternatives. This second sentiment—freedom to choose—is a central element in leisure. As the three women in prison told me, "If we do not want to do anything, there is no point in being free."

This freedom "to" notion of leisure means there is no such thing as purposeless leisure. To have leisure we must make choices, take actions. We must make a decision about what to do and what not to do. Leisure means grasping the possibilities of choice of pastimes, and being able to choose involves perceiving options and resources as real opportunity. This all implies that leisure is also the outcome of an ability to do what one wants. What does "ability" to choose leisure mean? Let's look more closely at this concept.

According to the writings of Bregha (1991), leisure is a matter of ability. To Bregha there are three kinds of ability needed for engaging in leisure: possessing personal qualities, having the means, and receiving permission. First, freedom to experience leisure involves possessing personal qualities, such as knowledge and physical ability. This not only includes having information on what is available or permissible, but also having knowledge of oneself, knowledge of what is good, and knowledge of the consequences of actions. Were such knowledge absent, every choice would be made blindly. Leisure, according to Bregha, is linked to knowledge and wisdom—possessing the ability to choose with intelligence and responsibility.

Before you accept this ability to choose leisure proposed by Bregha as completely useful, let's think about a possible argument to it. The claim here is that in order to be free to experience leisure meaningfully we must first have knowledge about what we choose to do. Does this mean that babies, or others without adequate knowledge, have no leisure? Is it like saying that no laughter exists unless you first know what is funny and what is not funny?

Second, for Bregha (1991) the ability to experience leisure involves having the means. Throughout history, wealth has always been perceived as a factor in having leisure. Wealth (especially the possession of property) and leisure have even given rise to an old notion of "the leisure class." To a great extent, unfortunately, this link still exists today. Many forms of leisure activity require participation fees, equipment, clothing, transportation to special locations, and expensive training. Have you priced jogging shoes lately or admission to a museum?

Third, to Bregha (1991) the ability to do what one wants requires permission. Since few forms of leisure, except perhaps daydreaming and contemplation, can be experienced without at least the passive consent of our neighbors or civic authorities, the ability to leisure requires sanction from others. For example, there are city ordinances against playing music too loudly, restaurants are open only at specific times and days, we may jog only on public property unless we have authorization to enter land that is privately owned, and we cannot plant a garden unless we own the plot or are given permission to use the land.

The inability to enjoy leisure because of sanctions or fear of punishment is often the result of societal or institutional rules. For example, gays and lesbians may go to gay bars and clubs because they are free there to be themselves. Some societies, such as the United States, have not given permission for them to experience certain social forms of leisure such as dancing.

Is this discussion of freedom beginning to make it seem like leisure is difficult, fragile, and almost impossible for people today? If leisure is freedom, did the suburban family in their typical Tuesday evening in the opening of this section really have leisure? According to Bregha, they did not:

> Much less free than superficially believed, much more manipulated than publicly admitted, much less educated than generally thought, modern man (sic) appears to be lacking precisely those components of leisure that make it such an exacting state of being; self-knowledge and inner peace.

(Bregha 1991, 51)

Leisure is our most precious and fragile expression of freedom. Leisure requires freedom to choose and choice, in turn, requires awareness of preferences, a sense of direction, and ultimately, the authority to strive for a goal. In other words, leisure is as much freedom to do something as freedom from something.

Intrinsic Reward

So, what is the ultimate payoff? What are the potential benefits of leisure to you and society? Research has given ample evidence of the rewards of leisure. For example, rewards to individuals from leisure include physical well-being, emotional health, sense of identity, sense of community, learning, relaxation and renewal, self-esteem, personality development, social interaction, and adventure. For our communities and the broader society, leisure has economic and cultural development value. In addition to all these, there is a singular benefit that makes leisure unique among all other human experiences. This is leisure's **intrinsic reward.**

Intrinsic reward: the benefit of doing something is the satisfaction gained from doing it.

Frequently, leisure is valued in and of itself. Intrinsic meaning is found simply in experiencing. Leisure gives us a sense of living for its own sake. Cross-country skiers often exclaim about sensations of peacefulness and physical exertion while gliding along. Artisans may explain their interest in working with clay on the potter's wheel because of the elastic, smooth substance responding to their hands. Dancing could be described as moving to a rhythm within. Hikers often stress the experience of being a part of the beauty of the natural environment. These are all intrinsic rewards. There is no external payoff, such as losing weight, getting a job promotion, or finding new friends. The experience itself is enough. "I do it just because I like it." (See Csikszentmihalyi 1975.)

The impetus for research on intrinsic motivation began with the somewhat surprising finding that primates taught to solve complex problems showed less interest in the task when offered extrinsic incentives (such as food) than when no rewards were offered (Harlow 1953). Later experimental investigations with humans matched this. The offering of a reward for engaging in an activity that was initially intrinsically interesting seemed to alter a person's future enjoyment of the experience.

For example, Lepper, Greene, and Nisbett (1973) conducted a study with preschool children who initially showed a high interest in drawing activities in the classroom. For the study, the children were divided into three groups. Those in the first group were told that if they would draw pictures they would receive a "good player award." Children in the second group also engaged in drawing and

Many studies have attempted to understand the influence of the family by observing its impact on a child's behavior. This study by Kevin Rathunde (1988), on the other hand, attempted to understand the subjective experience of the family for the child. To gather this information, Rathunde used a research procedure called the Experience Sampling Method (Csikszentmihalyi, Larson, and Prescott 1977).

Approximately 193 freshman and sophomore high school students were given electronic pagers and a booklet of questionnaires. The youth carried their pagers for one week and were sent seven to nine random signals daily between the hours of 7:00 A.M. and 10:00 P.M. during the weekdays and 7:00 A.M. and midnight on the weekend. Each time they were beeped they were instructed to fill out one of the questionnaires. The questionnaire assessed how they felt at the moment they were beeped on several dimensions, including how positive or negative they were feeling, how much self-esteem they felt, and how much intrinsic reward they felt.

Prior to the week of responding to the random electronic pager signals, the students had been assessed through several tests and scales about qualities of their family life. Subsequently, they were assigned to one of two family types. Type one was a family that provided choices in order to give the student control, clear feedback on successes and failures, appropriate rewards, trust, and a balance of challenges. This family was labeled an autotelic family. Autotelic means having a purpose in itself; thus, this type of family gave the youth opportunities for intrinsic reward, as we'll see from the results. A context that typically provides too little or too much of these qualities was referred to as a nonautotelic type family.

When the teens received the beeper signals while at home, as expected, those who perceived their family context as autotelic showed a strong pattern of more positive home experience. For example, these teens reported experiencing higher levels of concentration, more sociability, more cooperative spirit, greater self-concept, and an elevated sense of intrinsic reward.

Also, when the teens received the beeper signals while at school, results indicated that teens who perceived their family context as autotelic showed similar results. They felt happier, more cheerful, had higher self-concepts, felt more alert and in control of their situation, and believed they were intrinsically motivated. The results when the teens were beeped while studying or doing homework were similarly positive.

To Rathunde, more important than knowing that the autotelic type of family is functioning smoothly and successfully, was knowing why this is the case. Rathunde looked to the concept of intrinsic reward for his clue. In the study results, intrinsic reward showed the strongest differences between the two types of families. "The adolescents in the autotelic environment were feeling more in control of their actions, they wished to be doing what they were doing, and they were more involved with it" (p. 360). Part of the success of the autotelic family, reasons Rathunde, is that in these families the teens are not experiencing an oppression of their natural need for intrinsic reward—to be self-determined. He goes on to conclude that one of the best ways for a family to provide an appropriate amount of opportunity for intrinsic reward for children is by facilitating family play.

received the same award for doing so at the conclusion of the session but were not told about the reward at the start. Those in the third group engaged in the drawing activities but were neither told they would receive an award, nor did they receive an award.

Two weeks later, the children were unobtrusively observed in their classroom, and the duration of time they spent drawing pictures was monitored. Results confirmed that those children in the expected award group later showed less interest in drawing than those children in the unexpected and no award groups. In addition, the quality of the pictures the children drew in the expected award group was judged to be poorer than those drawn by the children in the other two groups.

These research studies bring up a fascinating concern for those involved in the provision of leisure services. In such systems as city park and recreation departments, resorts, and YMCAs, the promise of an external award in certain leisure activities has become traditional. For example, sporting events, tournaments, marathons, etc. usually offer trophies, ribbons, and other prizes for top performances. The expectation that this will occur has been ingrained since the competitive games in ancient Greece, yet research on the matter indicates that offering an extrinsic award alters internal interest. Players may "work" for the reward rather than participate for the reasons inherent in the activity. If this occurs leisure is lost, because intrinsic reward is a vital quality of leisure.

Play

Play, as part of the spirit of leisure, is human nature itself. Play is an existential phenomenon; it elevates us to the seriousness of frivolity. Play is a spontaneous act. It involves the carefree suspension of consequences, a temporary creation of its own world. Play is not for the sake of a final goal; it is motivated by the enjoyment of living.

While play is now associated with the activities and spirit of children, this notion has not always existed. The concept of play as the domain of children or at least as childlike behavior did not emerge in Western cultures until the early seventeenth century (Kando 1980). This is because the conceptual category of "child" itself did not appear until then. Before this, at the time of the Middle Ages in Europe, there were two types of people—adults and little adults. As paintings by Durer and Breughel show, the facial traits, clothing, and behaviors of children in medieval periods are ruthlessly adultlike. Children were not excluded from adult spheres, such as taverns, workshops, or bedrooms. While people played then as they always have, it was not perceived as being childlike.

The history of play's definition since that time has frequently connected play to children. Friedrich Nietzsche, a German philosopher in the late nineteenth century, once commented, "Really to play, one must play like a child" (Bammel and Bammel 1992). Then in the twentieth century, de Grazia wrote, "Play is what children do, frolic and sport . . . Adults play too, though their games are less muscular and more intricate" (de Grazia 1964).

From a cultural perspective, however, play is pervasive in all human activity—for children and adults both. Even in modern societies play is universal. To illustrate, the writings of Johann Huizinga (1949) can be consulted. As a historian, Huizinga made a generalization about play for all written human history. His point was that all forms of civilization begin as play, that culture arises as play. To make his point, he drew examples from the more "serious" domains within modern society. For example, what else is law, he asked, but a playful way of settling disputes? Court scenes become "plays" and lawyers jockey for position so the facts can "play themselves out."

It is still easy to see the pervasiveness of play in the adult world today. The popularity of television game shows and adult toys, such as karaoke machines are obvious examples, but there are many others. Golf and squash are often used as a medium for transacting business deals. Baseball, now common in many countries, mimics combat.

All the "play" on words that exists in the English language adds to the documentation that play is pervasive with adults. Some enjoy "playing the stock market," while others "play the horses." When someone asks us a touchy question we "play dumb" in order to avoid the discomfort of the answer. In the domain of interpersonal relationships, we "play up to someone," "play along," "play both ends against the middle," and "make a play for someone."

The question that has been most enduring for scientists and philosophers is that basic curiosity: why do people play? Why is it important for human behavior to include playfulness? Since the eighteenth century, according to Ellis (1973), at least fifteen different theories have emerged to explain play. These theories have been derived from the knowledge bases of biology, psychology, and sociology. In reviewing the more common of these theories, we'll use Ellis's classification system: first the older theories, then more recent theories, and finally, the most contemporary theoretical perspectives (table 2.1).

One of the oldest and most often quoted theories to explain play is the surplus energy theory. This explanation claims that when the organism has more energy than can be stored, it is released in play. Play is the safety valve for burning up more physical energy than is needed. Even as observed by Darwin, one's tensions, both mental and physical, could be expended through a play outlet (Barnett 1978).

Another early theory viewed play as preparation. According to the preparation theory, play is trying out behaviors that will be useful in a future phase of life. Coming from a biological perspective, this theory considers play as a practice of instinctual urges needed for survival of the species. Explaining mostly children's play, this theory maintains that the stimulus for play is preparation for adult life. Children play house, doctor, and school because they are practicing for these roles.

The relaxation theory explains play as an activity that allows the individual to recuperate from fatigue and stress. When tired from work, people play. Opposite from the surplus energy notion, the relaxation theory claims that energy expended for survival activities is replenished during play.

A Brief Comparison of Play Theories

Table 2.1

Category	Theory	Definition	Critique
Older theories	Surplus energy	Burning up excess energy	Helps justify the role of physical play for problem youth; doesn't explain nonphysical play
	Preparation	Practice for adult life	Doesn't explain adult play
	Relaxation	Recuperation	Doesn't explain children's play or adult play that is similar to work
More recent theories	Catharsis	Letting off emotional steam	Has intuitive appeal in its field application, yet often aggressive behavior increases aggressive behavior
	Behavioristic	A response to a pleasurable stimulus	Overlooks the role of individual differences, yet boosted play as a topic worthy of serious study
	Psychoanalytic	Mastering disturbing events or thoughts	Initiated the practice of careful observation of play and of play as a therapy
Contemporary theories	Arousal seeking	Seeking optimal stimulation	Has more research support
	Competence-effectance	To have an effect on things	Requires more research testing

These and other theories, dating back to the early part of the twentieth century, were based mainly on notions of instinct and levels of energy. They have often been labeled "arm chair" theories because they have limited support in research. They are mostly the result of philosophers and writers reflecting on that which they have casually observed. Furthermore, they are considered less useful explanations of play because they do not define all play. The preparation theory, for example, is only useful when describing children's play, while the relaxation theory is only useful when describing adult play. More recent theories represent attempts to be more inclusive.

One recent theory is the catharsis theory. It is similar to the surplus energy theory except it focuses on pent up emotional energy rather than surplus physical energy. This theory describes play as a safety valve for the expression of emotions. Play is viewed as a means of purging oneself of negative feelings, of reducing hostilities. Throwing a hard baseball toward a batter is a socially acceptable way of expressing anger, frustration, or aggression.

A behavioristic explanation labels play as simply a form of learning. Based on the propositions of early twentieth-century psychologists, such as Hull and Skinner, play is connected to the stimulus response mechanisms of human behavior. Play is considered pleasurable in that it is reinforced by praise, recognition, and status and thus is learned and repeated.

The psychoanalytic explanation, first developed by Sigmund Freud, viewed many forms of play as symptoms of psychological illness. It claims that play repeats an unpleasant experience to reduce its seriousness or to simulate control over its consequences. In other words, play is a method of mastering disturbing events or thoughts and reducing nervous tension. For example, such high-risk play as skydiving or bungee jumping might indicate a death wish, or children play dentist as a way of coming to grips with an upcoming office visit.

More substantiated by research data, recent theories of play have been useful in furthering the investigation of play. The behaviorists, for example, while overlooking the role of individual intellectual and personality differences, boosted play as a topic worthy of serious study. Also, while the psychoanalytic perspective is often criticized today because of its emphasis that play is motivated by unpleasant experiences, it served well in initiating play as a form of therapy. These theories are still explored in studies today and remain credible in some quarters as at least partial explanations of why people play.

The most contemporary explanations of why people play have been more holistic and are often composites of earlier theories. For example, the arousal seeking theory views play as a complexity generating activity. It incorporates the catharsis and behavioristic theories. Perhaps grounded in the catharsis theory, and directly opposite the behavioristic notion, the competence-effectance theory explores the joy of being a causal force. Let's review these two theories in greater depth.

The main goal of play, according to arousal seeking theory, is intellectual and physical stimulus. People need a certain level of physical and mental activity. For example, workers without enough to do invent games, such as sports betting pools. Bored college students in class sometimes make a game out of counting a particular mannerism of the professor. The arousal seeking theory is based on the judgment that individuals strive to maintain an optimal state of stimulus. While different for everyone, there is a level of arousal that is our most efficient. Play is a way individuals can create the complexity required to maintain this level of arousal. On the other hand, the competence-effectance theory refers to the need to produce effects, to be a cause of things taking place or being produced. Play is seen as a tool in this drive to gain positive feelings from the effects one produces.

Each theory of play has an element of truth, yet none are sufficient to fully explain why we play. Research progress, though considerable, has not

Figure 2.2 The game
ends in two more moves.
Can you list those moves?

Christopher B. Stage

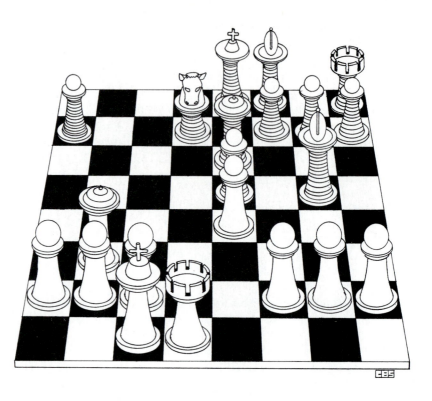

determined one best explanation, yet this should not cause us to lose sight of the core of play as a characteristic of leisure. Play does not occur because it is useful. Play has no commercial or material value. Even though play provides many physical, social, and emotional benefits to the player, and to the entire animal and human species for that matter, in the most immediate and personal sense, play is outside ordinary life. It is a place of enchantment and wonder.

Game

The diagram in figure 2.2 shows the concluding position of one of the most celebrated short brilliancies in the history of chess. New Orleans prodigy Paul Morphy won the game in September 1858, playing in a box at the Paris Opera against the Count Isouard and the Duke of Brunswick. Morphy is White. Black has just made the fifteenth move. The game ends in two more moves. Can you figure out the next two moves?*

Over 10 million people regularly play chess; yet people play all kinds of other games, too. In addition to chess, checkers, bridge, Scrabble and the like, we also play war games, money games, status games, and dating games. In fact, games and gaming have been studied extensively by people who have

*Answer: 16. Qb8 ch. KtxQ 17. Rd8 check and mate

little to do with the study of leisure (Bammel and Bammel 1992). Mathematicians and computer programmers use games to help solve particular analyses. Psychologists and psychiatrists use games, such as psychodrama, as a therapeutic tool. What is the connection between games and leisure?

One clue may be the origin of the word. The English word *game* is related to the old German word *gaman,* which means glee. Thus, the original meaning of the word *game* is not far from that of play—spontaneous, nonserious, and gleeful expression. Increasingly, however, social scientists have assigned *game* a different meaning from play. *Game* today refers to a more highly structured, organized, and regulated form of activity (Kando 1980).

A game is a contest. It may be a contest with yourself, such as in the card game solitaire, or occur between two or more people or teams. Without the prospect of winning or losing, games lose some of their appeal. Even in tic-tac-toe each participant wishes to win. Through cunning, manipulation, logic, luck, or even cooperation, the desired outcome is winning (fig. 2.3).

Figure 2.3 Unlike traditional games, many new games are won through cooperation rather than competition.

Christopher B. Stage

Figure 2.4 A life-sized chess game.
© Ruth V. Russell

biography   Monopoly

In the heart of the Great Depression when the average person was either broke or about to be, Charles B. Darrow offered an illusion of wealth. He dreamed of escaping the summer heat of Philadelphia and going down to the New Jersey shore seventy-five miles away. He was, of course, in no position to do this. He had lost his job as a heating engineer and was walking dogs for rich people (Goldensohn 1987). Nonetheless, he dreamed about the wide boulevards of Atlantic City and cool breezes on the boardwalk.

One day, Darrow sat down at his kitchen table and put his fantasy of cooler and richer times on paper. He invented a board game using the street names that intersect with Atlantic City's boardwalk. Each player would get $1,500 to restart life by the shore and another $200 every time they circled the neighborhood. Darrow called the game Monopoly.

In those days it was hard to restart your life in reality, so people began dropping in at Darrow's house to play Monopoly. As demand for the game increased, Darrow put his engineering skills to work, producing 100 sets in his basement, which he sold for $4 each. Making all those deeds, hotels, houses, and counterfeit $100 bills by hand while profiting only $1.75 on each game, he quickly tired of small-scale manufacturing. He brought the game to Parker Brothers in New York.

At Parker Brothers, he met with opposition. Though the company executives played Monopoly all afternoon, they said it took too long, and rejected it, enumerating "52 fundamental errors" (Goldensohn 1987). Meanwhile, Monopoly was spreading by word of mouth. So a local printer began to help Darrow make the games. By 1934, 17,000 orders had come from department stores across the country. Parker Brothers reconsidered, and in 1935 Darrow retired to the country to raise orchids at age 46 with the first of many royalty checks. He became a millionaire within 10 years (Goldensohn 1987).

Monopoly, the idea of amassing money and property, has sold over 100 million copies in thirty-two countries. It has been translated into nineteen languages. Today, it is still a best-seller.

This means that a game must have rules. This is what distinguishes games as simple or complex; the more complex the rules, the more complex the game. In watching children play a game, you may notice how the rules are often casually developed (and changed) as the game goes along. Other games require not only a rule book, but a referee to interpret and apply the rules.

There are other characteristics of games. For example, games can be classified according to whether they require a particular place: a special table, field, room, or court. Other games are played anywhere the players meet. Another characteristic of games is the use of particular equipment. While some games, such as tag, require no equipment, others require cards, dice, markers, a racquet, a board, a ball, or some other tool. Some professionalized games require a great deal of specialized equipment, as well as special rooms to store it (fig. 2.4).

A third characteristic of games is a specific time span. Time, in other words, often dictates who wins. Games, such as charades or basketball, are focused on beating the clock. Other games, such as Monopoly, are relatively indifferent to time.

Another, and perhaps the most important characteristic of games is that they are in some way artificial. They take place as a synthetic counterpart to real life. The contest of the chess match is the artificial enactment of a medieval war. Monopoly is the counterfeit experience of capitalism.

The type of play required in a game is the final characteristic. Callois (1961) distinguished four types of game: agon, alea, mimicry, and ilinx. Agon, which means competitive, includes most sports and games, such as football and checkers. Alea games require luck, and winning is a matter of fate. Mimicry games involve role playing, such as children's make-believe play. Ilinx games involve vertigo and other sensory stimulation, such as hang gliding and drug use. When many people think of games, they usually think of only agon type games, such as football, baseball, and board games. Callois's categorization indicates that games have a much wider range of meaning. The distinctions have also been useful in describing contemporary and sometimes harmful uses of games—drinking games, for example.

Laughter and Humor

Laughter and humor are essential to human beings. You might informally confirm this by surveying the quantity of films in the comedy section of the local video rental store or by checking the yellow pages in the telephone book under comedy clubs, or counting the joke books on the shelf at a bookstore. Without the joy and elation of laughter and humor, life is one serious, tension-filled downward spiral. People who cannot occasionally laugh at their failures and mock their successes are doomed to a wretched life. Jokes, cartoons, parodies, tall tales, puns, imitations, silliness, clever insults, and intentional misunderstandings free us!

We laugh in very diverse situations. This is why it is very difficult to explain why we laugh. The oldest, and probably still most widespread theory of laughter is that laughter is an expression of a person's feelings of superiority over other people. Labeled the superiority theory (Morreall 1983), the explanation is that the laughing person thinks of herself or himself as wealthier, better looking, more virtuous, or wiser than he or she really is. Laughter, then, is self-congratulatory. This theory dates back to Plato, for whom laughter involved a certain malice toward other people (Plato, *Republic*). Aristotle agreed in considering laughter as a form of derision (Aristotle, *Rhetoric*). Since in laughing we are concerned with what is base, Aristotle insisted that too much laughter is incompatible with living a good life.

The relief theory, on the other hand, claims that laughter is physiological—a venting of nervous energy. For example, children often get the giggles in church, adults snicker at jokes about sex, and comedians get laughs from poking fun at the bungling of public figures. We laugh as a release of denied feelings or social restrictions. The letting go of nervousness is accomplished through laughter, according to Spencer (1911) the theory's founder, when inappropriate feelings build up.

Another explanation of laughter is the incongruity theory (Morreall 1983). While laughter for the superiority theory is the feeling of triumph, for the incongruity theory it is an intellectual reaction to something that is unexpected. The idea is quite simple. We live in an orderly world where we have come to link certain patterns and characteristics to events. We laugh when we

$\mathcal{C}$ase $\mathcal{S}$tudy   College Drinking Games—Just Fun and Games?

Quarters—the game is played in a group with rotating turns. A quarter and a glass of beer are the required items of game equipment. The object is to bounce the quarter off the table and into the glass. The players who succeed may give the glass to anyone else at the table, who must then drink all the beer in it. Each player is given two tries to get the quarter in the glass. Should he or she miss on the first try, there is the option of passing the quarter to the next player or taking a second turn. Players who make it the second time may present the glass to anyone else. If they miss, however, they themselves must drink it. The idea when playing this game is to be the last one left, that is, to drink everyone else under the table.

Drinking games, such as Quarters, are considered common among college students. This is particularly true for male peer groups and more structured college organizations, such as fraternities and ROTC units. Women have been observed to play along with men, but all-women games are not very common. Group sizes for playing a drinking game can be as few as three to five persons or sometimes as many as sixteen to eighteen persons will participate. About ten players are ideal.

Have you ever played a drinking game? Did you win the game? What does it mean to win in a drinking game? Are these real games? What do they harm? The strategic manipulation of other players to consume alcohol could be considered as competition and, legitimately, a game. Is it really a game?

The main reason for engaging in these games is to get one another drunk and/or to embarrass one or more of the players. This means that one person will be a target (typically, a female player if there is one in the game or a light drinker), and the rest of the players will consistently manipulate the game to ensure that the target person is forced to drink the most. The games' strategies seem to work. According to the research of Engs (1993), the majority of college students who drink heavily and play drinking games experience hangovers (95.5 percent), nausea or vomiting (77 percent), and drive a car afterwards (69 percent).

An anthropological study conducted at Texas A&M University (Green and Grider 1990) sought to understand drinking as a game. Based on observations of 117 drinking games played in college bars over a four year period, the study concluded that these games were based on the concept of reversal of competence.

Whereas in more traditional games the most capable player is the winner, in drinking games the least competent player (i.e., the one who has to drink the most) is considered the winner. It is a position much like being "it" in children's games (Gump and Sutton-Smith 1965). This is called a reversal of competence, and Green and Grider consider it to be at the heart of the aggressive game behavior of American college students.

The result of playing drinking games is drunkenness and loss of control. Because of the game elements of chance and competition, players of drinking games cannot avoid these negative end results. Competence (avoiding getting drunk) is not valued by fellow players. Incompetence, or the reversal of competence, is the goal. According to Green and Grider's research, the most entertaining drinking games, in the minds of the players, are those that victimize the participants and result in a demonstration of extraordinary drinking capacity or silliness. Unlike games proper, argue Green and Grider, good performance is not rewarded.

Also, unlike genuine games, the action in drinking games does not stop when a player achieves a particular goal (such as a set number of points). Instead, the game ends when enough players become so drunk that the action falls into a shambles. For these and other reasons Green and Grider's research conclusion was that drinking games cannot be considered games.

Questions to Consider and Discuss

1. What makes a game a game? Based on the discussion in this section of the chapter, what do you consider the essential ingredients of a game? Also, in reviewing the types of games developed by Callois, how would you categorize drinking games?

2. Do you agree with the conclusion of Green and Grider that drinking games are not real games? What support do you and your classmates have from your own experiences to either agree or disagree with this conclusion?

3. There is a great deal of concern on college campuses in the U.S. about excessive and irresponsible drinking by students. Students are often injured and sometimes die as a result. How does this case study on drinking games demonstrate another kind of "injury" to the players?

experience something that doesn't fit these expectations. For example, we laugh at the punchline of a joke because it does not fit what is "normal" in the situation.

The superiority, incongruity, and relief theories all have their roots in historical writings. All seem to explain different circumstances or motivations for laughter. Putting them together into a more contemporary and comprehensive rationale, Morreall (1983) claims that laughter simply results from a pleasant psychological shift. It is a natural, physical expression of pleasure. The source of the pleasure is enjoying an embarrassment, some sudden and unexpected event, and the release of pent-up energy. All these feel good and can cause us to laugh.

Laughter is different than humor in that humor is one source of laughter. As suggested by the incongruity theory previously discussed, what separates humor from simpler kinds of laughter stimuli is that it is based on a conceptual change, a jolt to our picture of the way things are supposed to be. Humor is based on simple surprise and incongruity. What an individual finds humorous (or incongruous) depends on what his or her experience has been. This experience varies from person to person, culture to culture, and time to time. For example, adults from different cultures often fail to appreciate each other's humor because they don't have the same picture of the world. This is why a joke is often not funny when it is translated into another language. Not only do we have difficulty appreciating the humor of different cultures, but we sometimes find humorous the ordinary customs of a different culture. What people find funny also varies between different times in history within a single culture. For example, when the use of the fork was introduced in England a few hundred years ago, people found this new eating instrument extremely funny (Morreall 1983). What is humorous also varies according to one's educational level, profession, and gender. To illustrate, compare the cartoons and jokes in two different publications, such as the *New Yorker* and the *National Enquirer* or the *New York Times* and a college newspaper. How would you characterize the typical readership of each of these according to the form of humor?

Humor is an aesthetic experience (Morreall 1983). Just as we appreciate a beautiful painting, the performance of a dancer, and a fine work of literature, humor similarly appeals to our sense of appreciation. A painting is appreciated because of the use of color or brush strokes. A joke is appreciated because it is incongruent with reality. Above all, both the painting and joke are enjoyed for their own sake; they have no other purpose. A frozen lake is enjoyable to look at and so are ducks landing on it. The beauty and humor of both are reasons for looking at them.

Laughter and humor are therapeutic. In a hospital near Atlanta, Georgia, there is a "laughing room" in which patients are encouraged to watch funny movies and read humorous books. The purpose is to help them get well. The hospital reports that the laughing room decreases people's need for pain medication and serves as an antidepressant. Maybe ideas like this began with Norman Cousins when he published the book *Anatomy of an Illness* (1979). From personal experience and through interviews with others, he demonstrated that humor can be a therapeutic aid in overcoming illness. Laughter, and the positive attitudes required by it, can stimulate endorphins in the brain, which are natural painkillers. Voltaire once commented, "The art of medicine consists of amusing the patient while nature cures the disease."

Because humorous moments are considered aesthetic experiences that contribute to well-being, humor can be considered a quality of leisure. It is no accident of language that we "play" a musical instrument and "play" a practical joke. In the book *Play: It's Not Just for Kids!* (Broadus and Broadus 1987), the following suggestions are offered for finding more humor, and thus leisure, in life:

1. Find and cultivate a friend or two with whom you can laugh regularly.

2. Use lunch time to relax, play, and laugh. One of the worst practices is the working lunch where people stuff food in their mouths while their minds work full speed. They never notice the pleasure of the food or the company.

3. Schedule time and places to exercise the laughter muscles. The theater, movies, stand-up comedians, humorous writers, and even occasionally television programs afford opportunities for laughing.

4. Take frequent laughing vacations—a minute, thirty minutes, an evening, or even a few days at a laughing seminar.

Ritual

In Denmark, a disciplinary procedure for prisoners awaiting trial is solitary confinement. Confinees spend twenty-three hours a day in a small cell. They are allowed two half-hour periods of exercise alone, but their isolation is otherwise interrupted only by visits to the toilet and the delivery of meals. In spite of being allowed books, radio, television, and letters, many inmates complain of restlessness and insomnia. They find it particularly difficult to measure the passage of time, so they invent rituals to give structure to the day. When these rituals are interrupted, even by visits from a lawyer, the prisoners become upset.

Ritual is defined as a set of acts (originally involving religion or magic) with their sequence established by tradition and stemming from everyday life (Ibrahim 1991). Perhaps most importantly, ritual evokes some kind of collective behavior.

Beverly Hungry Wolf, in recording the ancient ways of the women of her tribe, the Blood People of the Blackfoot nation in Canada, offers an example of the ritualization of everyday behavior. In the following quote she describes meal time in her grandmother's home.

Ritual: any formal and customarily repeated act.

The first person that she always served was her husband; that is the proper way in our customs. She would put his meat and potatoes and bread in a bowl. . . . She would put his knife and fork right in the bowl: we don't lay them out on the side. . . . Only after he was completely served did she set up the places and food for the others. . . . The most honored guests sat closest to him, just on the other side of him and his bundles. The people who had medicine pipes and beaver bundles always sat closest. . . . Of course, the men always sat on the north side of the tipi and the women on the south. . . . But the women never sit cross-legged. They sit with their legs either folded back to one side or else straight out.

Brief quotation from *The Ways of My Grandmother* by Beverly Hungry Wolf. Copyright © 1980 Beverly Hungry Wolf. Reprinted by permission of William Morrow & Company, Inc.

Another example of the ritualization of everyday experiences is the public bath. Miracle (1986) described his visit to the hot springs mineral baths of Arkansas as a ritual. He explained his bath experience according to three ritualized stages. First, time is spent in the locker room before the bath. There, separation from normal life is accomplished by segregating the sexes, removing clothing, and putting on a plain white sheet. The second stage is entry into the bathing room. There, a stylized form of interaction occurs as young, athletic attendants direct all movements from the whirlpool tub to the steam baths to the massage. Finally, incorporation back to normal life begins in the cooling room and is completed when the bather returns to the locker room and dresses.

There is much to suggest that humans are born with the need for regular and mutual affirmation (Ibrahim 1991); thus, ritual is pervasive in leisure settings. Even more directly, leisure itself as an everyday experience has been ritualized. For example, on an individual level, we all tend to express our leisure in ritualistic ways. How do you enter a swimming pool for the first time? Do you usually dive in off the side, dive in from the board, use the ladder, jump, or walk down the shallow end steps? Most of us follow a consistent pattern.

On a broader, collective scale the leisure expressions of entire cultures are to large extent ritualized, too. For example, holiday rituals are shared by families and communities. On Thanksgiving in the United States most families have exactly the same dinner menu: roast turkey, stuffing, mashed potatoes and gravy, cranberry sauce, and pumpkin pie. In many communities in the U.S. the Fourth of July is always recognized with a parade and fireworks.

Have you been to summer camp? How much of the day's activities included ritual? Were you awakened every morning by reveille? Was grace sung in the dining lodge before meals? Was the last night's campfire always lit by "fire from heaven"? Did the counselors serenade the campers to sleep the first night?

Ritual in leisure is not simply habits. Ritual and leisure have both meaning and function beyond the pragmatic. In fact, leisure and ritual have been described as sharing certain characteristics. For example, both involve intrinsic reward—having meaning in itself—with no ulterior or extrinsic end sought (Grimes 1982).

Much of the ritual of leisure is of the type labeled by Erving Goffman (1959) as interaction ritual, or decorum. Decorum is nonessential, as is decoration, but is practiced because it enhances social interaction. An example of this is the Japanese tea party. An invitation to have tea is often laden with rules for a lengthy interaction between host and guest. The host must make specific movements in the preparation and serving of the tea and the guests must respond with specific actions. While not as frequently expressed in contemporary Japan, the ritual of this social interaction of sharing a cup of tea is still taught to young people.

Solitude

In the opening paragraph of the previous section on ritual, an example of solitude used as a punishment or a tool for social control was presented. Aloneness as an emotional health problem has also been the subject of research. Studies suggest that loneliness has powerful destructive social consequences. For example, the suicide rate among young people has doubled in many countries within the past ten years. One of the major contributing factors to this increase is an intense sense of loneliness (Derelega and Winstead 1986).

The Armed Services are increasingly concerned with the loneliness of men and women on active duty. For example, a study of loneliness and the leisure behavior of unaccompanied enlisted personnel at the U.S. Naval Base in Guantanamo Bay, Cuba (Shelar 1991), found that the longer individuals had been on their tour of duty and the higher their rank, the less lonely they were prone to be. Also, nonlonely personnel participated in mass media activities, such as watching television, reading, listening to the radio, and going to the movies, as well as social activities more often than the lonely. The lonely were generally less motivated to participate in any leisure activities.

Loneliness and alienation are not merely by-products of modern society but a natural part of being human. Time spent alone, often free time, is an integral part of living. This means that solitude can offer not only problems and constraints but unique positive opportunities as well. In this section, we explore this other face of solitude—its quality in leisure.

For starters, recall the popularity of the card game solitaire! While we typically think about leisure as a social and companionable experience, being alone at leisure can also produce enjoyment and fulfillment. Let's discuss another common leisure experience—reading. Reading, like so much of leisure, is not necessarily easy. Reading makes demands on our skills; it requires our concentration and our attention. Observe this in some familiar reading behaviors around you: workers reading on the commuter train, a child sitting up in a tree reading, reading while eating lunch or while ironing. Have you noticed how reading isolates the readers from the ordinary business around them? The fun of reading, then, like so many solitary activities is in its escapist nature. Everyday routines are forgotten for a moment; we can get away from our problems.

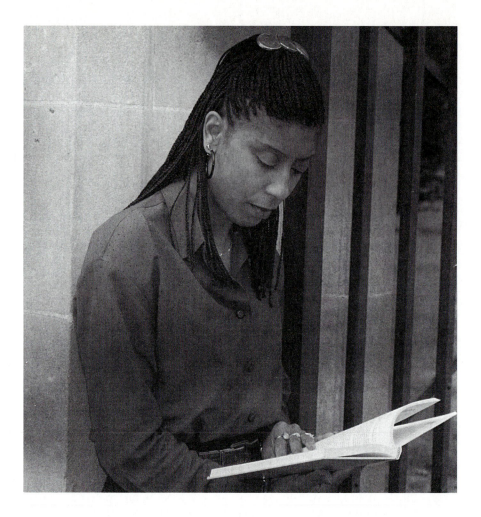

Reading demonstrates how leisure needs its own specific time and space. Leisure provides for the human being a special and separate form of being. Leisure has the potential to give you the time of your life in those rare moments when you feel you have all the time in the world. Leisure returns us to our own world, or "a sphere of privacy" (Davies 1989, 111).

How does leisure grant us a world of our own, a sphere of privacy? Leisure, in a sense, is a form of **narcissism.** Through moments of solitude in leisure, we are allowed to return to ourselves. Admiral Byrd's account of spending the winter of 1934 alone in an advanced weather base in the Antarctic perhaps best illustrates this:

Narcissism: love of self.

> Aside from the meteorological and auroral work, I had no important purposes.
> There was nothing of that sort. Nothing whatever, except one man's desire to
> know that kind of experience to the full, to be himself for a while and to taste
> peace and quiet and solitude long enough to find out how good they really are.

(Byrd 1938, 7)

Contemporary cultures make the peace of solitude difficult to attain. The telephone is an ever-present threat to privacy. In cities, it is impossible to get away from the intrusions of noise and people. Most occupations require working with and around other people. This may be why some people describe driving a car as leisure. It is considered relaxing and refreshing—simply because they are alone and temporarily unavailable to others. (Unless, of course, one has a car telephone!)

Moreover, solitude, argues Anthony Storr in the book *Solitude: A Return to the Self* (1988), provides opportunities of creativity. He tells the life stories of such creative people as Beethoven, Goya, Kipling, and Beatrix Potter—all of whom were alone at crucial periods in their lives. Storr claims that when we are free to be ourselves, individuals accountable only to ourselves, "free of obligations, duties, fears, and hopes" (p. 201), we have the ability for creativity of any kind.

Spirituality

Going to church on Sunday is the thing I look most forward to in the entire week.

(From the diary of "Louise," in Russell 1984)

Spiritual experiences are among the most fundamental human expressions. While leisure, due to its connotation as pleasure, may appear an inappropriate context for the more reverent aspects of spirituality, religion is the most important form of leisure for some people. To understand the meaning of spirituality in leisure, we must clarify that we are not necessarily referring to religion as compulsory attendance at mosque, church, or temple nor are we referring to the official doctrines of religious organizations. As history has demonstrated, organized religion has at times considered leisure evil or at least as laziness. Instead, we consider the spirituality of leisure through the phenomena of celebration and concentration.

The sabbath tradition, which has its origin in Judaism several centuries before Christ, was a day in the week for expressing gratitude and thanksgiving. Work ceased on that day for celebration. For Christians, the sabbath is on Sunday; in the Muslim world, Friday is the sabbath day. For many religions, the only requirement for the day is attending a worship service. The rest of the day is spent as the individual pleases.

To religious philosophers such as Josef Pieper (1963), it is this link with celebration that characterizes leisure as an affirmation of the joy of being human. As Pieper wrote, "The soul of leisure, it can be said, lies in 'celebration' . . . But if celebration is the core of leisure, then leisure can only be made possible and justifiable on the same basis as the celebration of a festival. That basis is divine worship" (p. 56). Also in worship arise such festivities as music, dance, and drama. Often these expressions become part of the pattern of worship for the structured celebrations of churches, temples, and mosques.

All cultures are resplendent with the spirituality of celebrations. Even in more secular, contemporary Western cultures, holiday celebrations are still practiced as at least a partial response to a sacred authority. For example,

In the Saint Peter festivals of a small town in the southern Colombian Andes, the *Hombre al Reves* (Upside Down Man) is a typical costume used to jest about the general disorder of life (Gradante 1986).

Christopher B. Stage

Christmas in France still claims the greatest number of celebrants, followed in January by the Epiphany. Easter is also celebrated, and Saint John's Day remains the traditional feast of midsummer. All Saint's Day and Virgin Mary Day are occasions for family members to get together, and these occasions remain alive as religion-based celebrations. Other formerly religious holiday celebrations have given way in contemporary France to more secular purposes. For example, the Pentecost has expanded into three days that are used today for traveling and camping (Ibrahim 1991).

Now we come to the second connection between leisure and spirituality: concentration. To Pieper (1963), leisure is a spiritual attitude similar to worship. He declared that leisure is an inward calm of silence and peaceful concentration. Leisure is a receptive occasion for steeping oneself in a thoughtful consideration of things greater than oneself.

The essence of spiritual thought is the belief that life has purpose. The struggle to know and the power of the unknown give birth to spiritual values and beliefs. A person's work hours spent earning the means of survival provide a purpose for life, in one sense, but humans search for purpose beyond mere survival. It is a search for meaning beyond the physical aspects of survival. We struggle to understand existence beyond the time necessary to provide basic needs. Leisure provides an opportunity for individual expression that is well suited to such personal inquiry. The nature of leisure itself promotes philosophical reflections on life.

One of the most commonly cited examples of this notion of spirituality and leisure as concentration is the wilderness experience. Early writers frequently used the descriptive language of spirituality, mysticism, or emotional transcendence to describe their experiences in the wilderness. They viewed the wilderness as a source of psychic energy. Today, perhaps more than ever, people consider the outdoors as a place for the human spirit. To many people, natural areas are important settings for answering the deepest questions of human existence and for contemplating the unifying power behind life and things. Through history, we have gone to the woods, oceans, plains, deserts, and rivers to discover the spiritual riches within ourselves. The outdoors is a place where we cannot escape the fundamental truth of what we are.

Risk

Ocean cruising is an example of an exotic and esoteric way of living. Cruisers are people who sail the oceans of the world for years at a time for pleasure rather than profit. They forsake the security and safety of land-based life for the formidable challenges of the high seas. Many give up careers and other "productive" activities. In making this choice, they deviate from the usual goals that

Western society judges people should seek. Their lifestyle requires much effort, involves considerable danger, and provides no extrinsic rewards, such as fame or money. Why, then, do they do it?

In research conducted by Macbeth (1988), cruisers reported that the risk is viewed more as a challenge to one's own skill and competence, and within the realm of personal control.

> Our lives lay in our hands alone—no one knew where we were. . . . I also had the notion that I was in control of the sea that I could see around me—a foolish idea, I suppose. . . . Yet as long as we paid proper respect to the might of the ocean I felt sure that our tiny ship would be safe (p. 8).

This kind of risk is in stark contrast to the random risks individuals face from crime and cars in modern everyday life.

Similarly, when people who choose to scale vertical rock faces or shoot white-water rapids in slender kayaks explain why they do it, they seldom begin by talking about risk. Activities, such as rock climbing, white-water kayaking, and other high risk events, are explained more often as providing other sorts of rewards. More important is the knowledge that one is able to cope with the universal fears of height or speed. Risky forms of leisure are felt to give a sense of freedom, control over self and the environment, and escape from the ordinary routines of life. The benefit of developing close friendships with fellow risk takers are also frequent testimonies. For example, in the research of Haggard and Williams (1991), kayakers not only claimed thrill seeking and adventure to be important attributes of the experience but also the social, playful, athletic, independent, outdoorsy, and conservation aspects of running white-water rapids.

Thus, we see that risk is a quality of leisure, too. In fact, some risk is inherent in nearly all physical forms of leisure. Even such activities as crafts, not normally considered risky, can become dangerous to participants under certain conditions. The monetary risks of spending large amounts of free time in gambling casinos or at the racetrack are notorious, because while there is also a chance of winning, there is also the risk of losing. The risk of injuring self-esteem when having a poem you've written read aloud to an audience is also a ready example of risk in leisure.

A recent concern by professionals who provide organized leisure experiences for people is that the risk factor in some pastimes should be minimized. Worry about the potential for injuries and even death to persons who participate is very real, and agencies should avoid negligence in promoting unnecessary risks to participants. This often means providing instruction to beginners, safety equipment and information, and proper maintenance of facilities. However, the natural element of risk from leisure cannot and should not be eliminated. It is one of the motives for engaging in such activities.

Boredom

In *Twilight Zone: The Movie,* people are shown in a nursing home wasting away. They appear supremely bored—no smiles, no action, no hope. Then Scatman Crothers shows up to teach them how to start enjoying life even

A state park bobsled run is an example of a leisure activity with the element of risk (Pokagon State Park, Indiana).

© Ruth V. Russell

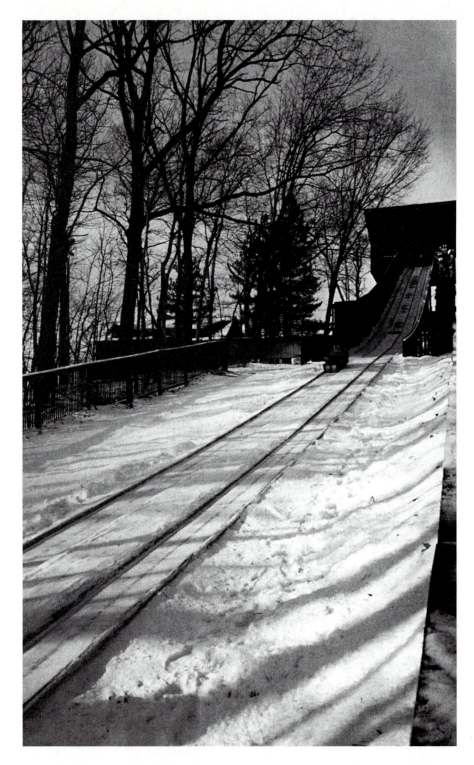

though their circumstances and futures are dismal. At one point he says, "When you stop playing, you start dying. You need another summer, another game to look forward to" (Broadus and Broadus 1987).

At last we come to boredom. Boredom has been, perhaps, one of the great motivational powers throughout human history. Crimes have been committed and accidents resulted from efforts to escape boredom. Heavy alcohol use, poor mental and physical health, and even abuse of the natural environment have been attributed to boredom.

Boredom is a human emotion that occurs when there is not enough meaningful life experience. According to Bertrand Russell (1968) "boredom is essentially a thwarted desire for events, not necessarily pleasant ones, but just occurrences such as will enable the victim of ennui to know one day from another. The opposite of boredom, in a word, is not pleasure, but excitement" (p. 36). While a certain ability to tolerate boredom is essential to a well adjusted contemporary life, boredom is generally considered a problem to solve.

The connection between boredom and leisure is already familiar to us. Leisure is often seen as an antidote to boredom. When a child complains of boredom during a school vacation, a parent's typical response is to suggest something recreational. Increased recreation and park services have been promoted as part of the solution to the boredom of chronic unemployment. As Neulinger (1974) indicated "the moment boredom enters, leisure leaves and once leisure enters, boredom is inconceivable" (p. 141). Despite this commonsense notion, the availability of empirical data to support the connection between boredom and leisure has become available only recently.

An inquiry by Ragheb in 1990 tested the relationship between leisure activity and boredom, and the results supported the commonsense conclusion that leisure counteracts boredom. Among the findings were the following points:

- As participation in leisure activities goes up, a sense of boredom goes down.

- As satisfaction with leisure experiences increases, a sense of boredom decreases.

- Those leisure activities most likely to reduce boredom are social activities, sport participation, outdoor recreation, and reading.

- Cultural activities, sport spectating, hobbies, and mass media experiences (television and movies) are less likely to reduce feelings of boredom.

Meanwhile, Iso-Ahola and Weissinger conducted research that seems to contradict this common sense. They developed the notion of leisure boredom. How would you answer the following questions?

1. For me, leisure time just drags on and on.

2. In my leisure time, I usually don't like what I'm doing, but I don't know what else to do.

3. I waste too much of my leisure time sleeping.

4. Leisure time activities do not excite me.

(Iso-Ahola and Weissinger 1990, 10)

These and other questions in the questionnaire helped Iso-Ahola and Weissinger discover that boredom can occur during leisure. If you agreed with these questions, your perception is likely to be that leisure is boring.

Leisure boredom results when people feel they cannot escape a meaningless leisure routine, they are constrained from satisfying leisure activity by too many obligations, or free time is forced on those who do not have sufficient leisure skills (Iso-Ahola and Weissinger 1990). Thus, research suggests that boredom is possible during leisure time and during leisure experiences. In fact, some studies (Keen 1977; Tokarski 1981) report that boredom in leisure is a significant problem.

Some of the conclusions drawn about leisure boredom from the research follow:

- People who do not have the awareness that leisure can be psychologically rewarding are most likely to perceive leisure as boredom.

- People who do not have the skills that facilitate leisure involvement are most likely to perceive leisure as boredom.

- Leisure time has the greatest potential of all human arenas to produce feelings of boredom.

In spite of their differences, there is one concept on which the research concurs and that is the importance of having personally meaningful leisure. Leisure for the sake of filling time does not seem to eliminate boredom. Rather, having personally satisfying leisure (Ragheb 1990) and having more than a meaningless leisure routine (Iso-Ahola and Weissinger 1990) helps reduce or control boredom.

Summary: Leisure Qualities

As we have discovered in this chapter, the "having a good time" nature of leisure can be experienced in many ways. When we experience leisure we may be happy, intrinsically rewarded, and alone. We also may experience a sense of pleasure, freedom, playfulness, and spirituality during leisure. Leisure may involve risk, ritual, game, and humor. It can also be described as boredom.

What we did not explore in this chapter is that leisure has also been described as a human right, as self-realization, and therapeutic. It is a political, economic, and educational tool. Reminiscence has also been described as a leisure experience, and the list of qualities goes on. What is most important is that one's pastimes affect the kind of person one is. Our pastimes make us complete because they include these qualities.

References

Aristotle. 1984. *Rhetoric. Book II.* Chapter 12. New York: Modern Library.

Bammel, G., and L. L. B. Bammel. 1992. *Leisure and human behavior.* Dubuque, IA: Wm. C. Brown Publishers.

Barnett, L. A. 1978. Theorizing about play: Critique and direction. *Leisure Sciences,* 1, no. 2: 113–29.

Bregha, F. J. 1991. Leisure and freedom re-examined. In *Recreation and leisure: Issues in an era of change,* edited by T. L. Goodale and P. A. Witt. State College, PA: Venture.

Broadus, C., and L. Broadus. 1987. *Play: It's not just for kids.* Waco, TX: Word Books.

Brooks, J. B., and D. M. Elliot. 1971. Prediction of psychological adjustment at age thirty from leisure time activities and satisfactions in childhood. *Human Development* 14: 51–61.

Byrd, R. E. 1938. *Alone.* New York: G. P. Putnam's Sons.

Callois, R. 1961. *Man, play, and games.* Glencoe, IL: Free Press of Glencoe.

Campbell, H. 1973. *The pleasure areas.* New York: Delacorte Press.

Cousins, N. 1979. *Anatomy of an illness.* New York: W. W. Norton & Co.

Csikszentmihalyi, M. 1975. *Beyond boredom and anxiety.* San Francisco: Jossey-Bass.

Csikszentmihalyi, M., R. Larson, and S. Prescott. 1977. The ecology of adolescent activity and experience. *Journal of Youth and Adolescence* 6: 281–94.

Davies, M. 1989. Another way of being: Leisure and the possibility of privacy. In *The philosophy of leisure,* edited by T. Winnifrith and C. Barrett. New York: St. Martins Press.

DeCarlo, T. J. 1974. Recreation participation patterns and successful aging. *Journal of Gerontology* 24, no. 2: 438–47.

de Grazia, S. 1964. *Of time, work and leisure.* Garden City, NJ: Doubleday and Company.

Derelega, V. J., and B. A. Winstead, eds. 1986. *Friendship and social interaction.* New York: Springer-Verlag.

Dimberg, U. 1987. Facial reactions and autonomic activity to auditory stimuli with high and low intensity. *Psychophysiology* 24:586.

Ellis, M. J. 1973. *Why people play.* Englewood Cliffs, NJ: Prentice-Hall.

Engs, R. 1993. Drinking games endanger college students' health. *Indiana Daily Student,* 28 August, 2.

Goffman, E. 1959. *The presentation of self in everyday life.* New York: Doubleday.

Goldensohn, M. 1987. Genial pursuits. *TWA Ambassador Magazine* (December):52, 73–75.

Goodale, T. L., and G. C. Godbey. 1988. *The evolution of leisure: Historical and philosophical perspectives.* State College, PA: Venture.

Gradante, W. J. 1986. The message in the mask: Costuming in the festival context. In *The many faces of play,* edited by K. Blanchard. Champaign, IL: Human Kinetics Publishers.

Green, T. A., and S. A. Grider. 1990. Reversal of competence in college drinking games. *Play and Culture* 3:117–32.

Grimes, R. 1982. *Beginnings in ritual studies.* Lanham, MD: University Press of America.

Gump, P. V., and B. Sutton-Smith. 1965. The "it" role in children's games. In *The study of folklore,* edited by A. Dundes. Englewood Cliffs, NJ: Prentice-Hall.

Haggard, L. M., and D. R. Williams, 1991. Self-identity benefits of leisure activities. In *Benefits of leisure,* edited by B. L. Driver, P. J. Brown, and G. L. Peterson. State College, PA: Venture.

Hamilton, E. 1989. *Plasma HVA levels and contrived leisure experiences of female college students.* Unpublished dissertation, Indiana University.

Harlow, H. F. 1953. Learning and satiation of a response in intrinsically motivated complex puzzle performance by monkeys. *Journal of Comparative Physiological Psychology* 43:289–94.

Heppe, G., and R. O. Ray. October 1983. Recreational activity breadth and intensity and the relationship to life happiness of older adults. Paper presented at the Leisure Research Symposium, Kansas City, MO.

Huizinga, J. 1949. *Homo ludens: A study of the play element in culture.* London: Routledge & Kegan Paul.

Hungry Wolf, B. 1980. *The ways of my grandmothers.* New York: William Morrow and Company.

Ibrahim, H. 1991. *Leisure and society: A comparative approach.* Dubuque, IA: Wm. C. Brown Publishers.

Iso-Ahola, S. E., and E. Weissinger. 1990. Perceptions of boredom in leisure: Conceptualization, reliability and validity of the leisure boredom scale. *Journal of Leisure Research* 22, no. 1:1–17.

Kando, T. M. 1980. *Leisure and popular culture in transition.* St. Louis: C. V. Mosby Co.

Keen, S. 1977. Chasing the blahs away: Boredom and how to beat it. *Psychology Today* 4:77–84.

Keller, M. J. October 1983. The relationships between leisure and life satisfaction among older women. Paper presented at the Leisure Research Symposium, Kansas City, MO.

Lepper, M. R., D. Greene, and R. E. Nisbett. 1973. Undermining children's intrinsic interest with extrinsic reward: A test of the "overjustification" hypothesis. *Journal of Personality and Social Psychology* 28, no. 1:129–37.

Macbeth, J. 1988. Ocean cruising. In *Optimal experience: Psychological studies of flow in consciousness,* edited by M. Csikszentmihalyi, and I. S. Csikszentmihalyi. Cambridge: Cambridge University Press.

Miracle, A. W. 1986. Voluntary ritual as recreational therapy: A study of the baths at Hot Springs, Arkansas. In *The many faces of play,* edited by K. Blanchard. Champaign, IL: Human Kinetics.

Morreall, J. 1983. *Taking laughter seriously.* Albany, NY: State University of New York.

Neulinger, J. 1974. *The psychology of leisure.* Springfield: Thomas.

Olds, J. 1960. Differentiation of reward systems in the brain by self-stimulation techniques. In *Electrical studies on the unanesthetized brain.* New York: Hoeber-Harper.

Olds, J., and P. Milner. 1954. Positive reinforcement produced by electrical stimulation of septal area and other regions of rat brain. *Journal of Comparative Physiology and Psychology* 47:419.

Peppers, L. G. 1976. Patterns of leisure and adjustment to retirement. *The Gerontologist* 16, no. 5:441–46.

Pieper, J. 1963. *Leisure: The basis of culture.* New York: The New American Library.

Plato. 1992. *Republic. Book V.* Chapter 4. New York: Knopf. 452.

Ragheb, M. G. October 1990. The contribution of leisure participation, leisure satisfaction, and a set of social psychological variables to boredom. Paper presented at the Leisure Research Symposium, Phoenix, AZ.

Ragheb, M. G., and C. A. Griffith. 1982. The contribution of leisure participation and leisure satisfaction to life satisfaction of older persons. *Journal of Leisure Research* 14, no. 4: 295–306.

Rathunde, K. 1988. Optimal experience and the family context. In *Optimal experience: Psychological studies of flow in consciousness,* edited by M. Csikszentmihalyi and I. S. Csikszentmihalyi. Cambridge: Cambridge University Press.

Russell, B. 1968. *The conquest of happiness.* New York: Bantam.

Russell, R. V. 1984. *Correlates of life satisfaction in retirement.* Unpublished dissertation, Indiana University.

Russell, R. V. 1987. The relative contribution of recreation satisfaction and activity participation to the life satisfaction of retirees. *Journal of Leisure Research* 19:273–83.

Shelar, V. D. 1991. Loneliness and leisure among young adult military personnel in Guantanamo Bay, Cuba. In *Recreation: Current selected research, Vol. 2,* edited by F. N. Humphrey and J. H. Humphrey. New York: AMS Press.

Smith, S. L. J. 1991. On the biological basis of pleasure: Some implications for leisure policy. In *Recreation and Leisure: Issues in an era of change,* edited by T. L. Goodale and P. A. Witt. State College, PA: Venture.

Spencer, H. 1911. On the physiology of laughter. *Essays on Education, Etc.* London: J. M. Dent.

Storr, A. 1988. *Solitude: A return to the self.* New York: Ballantine Books.

Sylvester, C. 1991. Recovering a good idea for the sake of goodness: An interpretive critique of subjective leisure. In *Recreation and Leisure: Issues in an era of change,* edited by T. L. Goodale and P. A. Witt. State College, PA: Venture.

Tokarski, W. November 1981. Some social psychological notes on leisure, the meaning of leisure, and life styles. Paper presented at the WLRA Leisure Research Conference, Twannbert, Switzerland.

Ziegler, H. P. 1975. The sensual feel of food. *Psychology Today* 8:62–67.

explanations and speculations

What influences our pastime choices?

There are multiple explanations because leisure behavior is complex and dynamic.

Can leisure be explained theoretically?

There are several theories that attempt to explain the meaning, conditions, and function of leisure.

Are these theories supported by research?

Research has demonstrated that the theories explain aspects of leisure behavior; however, more theoretical work is needed for a comprehensive explanation.

What role do life situation factors have in influencing our pastime choices?

Numerous characteristics about our lives, such as our occupation, income, education level, family and friends, religion, residence, and others shape our leisure interests and needs.

three

Digital Stock

KEY TERMS

Personal community   75
Theory   80
Hypothesis   81
Multidisciplinary   81
Paradigm   88
Autotelic   96

pastimes is complex and changing. We are far from understanding exactly the causal relationships. Why did you choose to take a vacation last summer? How did you choose where to go and what to do after you got there? Were you tired from a stressful year; want to go someplace inexpensive because your finances were a bit low; or did you more or less "need" to go because your family insisted? As you begin to answer this (or the alternative question of why you chose not to have a vacation!), you quickly begin to realize that your reasons are numerous and often interrelated.

In spite of this complexity, the question of "why" has intrigued leisure philosophers and professionals over the decades. This chapter is an overview of some of the explanations for leisure behavior. First, a brief summary of the factors that frequently affect a person's pastime choices is presented. These factors are typically about a person's life situation, such as personal income, occupation, available resources, and the influence of family and friends. Next, a person's state of mind helps explain leisure behavior, and this is presented in this chapter in discussions of theoretical propositions.

Situational Factors That Affect Leisure Behavior

The number of factors that play a role in the determination of what, why, and how we pursue our pastimes is great. Age, the topic of chapter 4, is important. Gender, race, and ability levels are also important influences considered in chapter 11. Many other factors exist, such as income, occupation, educational level, family and friends, geography of residence, religious beliefs, government regulations, availability of transportation, and the presence of crime or war. In this section, we will briefly discuss some of these factors.

Even though leisure is often contrasted with work, numerous research inquiries have suggested that leisure behavior is, in part, determined by our process of preparing for work and our actual type of employment. For example, some investigators indicated that people in professional occupations experience a greater variety of pastimes and participate more frequently in certain activities (White 1975). Even though generalizations are often misleading, research has suggested that professional workers are also more likely to engage in strenuous exercise, and those in lower-prestige occupations are likely to spend more time watching television. On the other hand, such activities as gardening, listening to the radio, and picnicking tend to be equally attractive to those in all occupations (Godbey and Parker 1976). The reason these data may be misleading is the simultaneous effect of other factors. That is, less affluent persons, who are typically those in lower-prestige occupations, have a reduced ability to engage in certain pastimes. Also, one's level of education, which contributes to occupational choices, is a factor in leisure behavior. Let's explore these two factors further.

Income and education are examples of powerful influences on how we express our leisure. Higher levels of education tend to accompany higher levels of personal income, which can be spent on pastimes. To illustrate, researchers of tourism report that tourists with higher incomes stay longer and spend more money per day than do those with lower incomes (Mill 1986). In essence, leisure opportunities in technological cultures are more accessible to those with higher incomes. This is why poverty is such a double tragedy. While participation in leisure activities improves the quality of daily life, they tend to be less available to economically disadvantaged people who perhaps need them most.

There is another interesting connection between money and leisure. In some situations, leisure actually provides direct financial benefits to participants. Obvious examples are occupations where participants are paid for engaging in a leisure activity. Trekking and fishing guides, fitness instructors, professional athletes, artists, musicians, and others receive pay for what began as leisure pursuits. Also, some leisure activities improve health or fitness, which increases the wage-earning potential of people.

Education's contribution to leisure pursuit choices is also direct. Education, in and of itself, can contribute to people's ability to participate in leisure. In addition to education's contribution to the reading, writing, and math skills frequently required in leisure pursuits, attitudes toward leisure can be altered by education as well. Those who learn while young that leisure is a valuable and meaningful part of everyday health and happiness are more likely to experience positive leisure as adults. Courses and extracurricular programs in school can introduce children and young adults to art, music, dance, drama, the outdoors, sports, literature, and games, which become useful skills later. Thus, beyond enabling higher levels of leisure spending, education is an important determinant of the type of leisure behavior.

Another explanation of leisure behavior is the influence of family and friends. When the family is a well-developed part of a person's social structure, the leisure attitudes and preferences of parents, grandparents, brothers, sisters, aunts, uncles, and cousins are typically strong predictors of an individual's pastimes. This is because people are most impressionable and learn most readily from those with whom they come into closest contact during their childhood and youth years. Think about the influence of your own family in your current interests of camping, theater, or sports. Early exposure to certain types of activities often sets the pattern for later leisure behavior.

Much of adult leisure is not explained by the interests of the family. As human beings, we are members of other types of social groups as well. Thus our peer groups, neighbors, workmates, friends, as well as our families, are important determinants of our pastime interests. The concept that describes this is called **personal community.** Personal community is the relationships with and socialization by work partners, friends, parents, and mates (Field and O'Leary 1973). Since we usually belong to more than one personal community, the impact on leisure is multiple. We engage in different pastimes with different personal communities. For example, we play board games with our families, go to parties with our friends, and eat lunch with our work colleagues.

Personal community: relationships with others with whom we interact daily.

Another determining factor in leisure behavior is place of residence. Geographic location affects the nature and accessibility of opportunities for

Interests in activities, such as bird watching, are often set at early ages by our families.
© Ruth V. Russell

pastimes and thus pastime choices. Some pastimes are not universally available because of climate and topography. Today, most people's choice of residence is influenced by the availability of employment. Beyond this, residences are chosen according to style of housing, neighborhood qualities, and cost. Additionally, more people now consider the availability of recreation opportunities when selecting their residence. Golfers like to live near a golf course; water sport enthusiasts seek to live near lakes, rivers, or oceans; families with young children try to locate near playgrounds or parks.

If a downtown urban location is chosen, a wide range of commercial and cultural activities are typically available, yet activities requiring large space, such as gardening and hunting or children's play areas, may be less common. When a suburban location is chosen, local government sponsored parks, youth sports programs, and indoor recreation facilities may be more readily available, yet opportunities to view live theater or enjoy diverse restaurant cuisine may be more limited. Apartments and condominiums are often selected because of their very ability to offer greater opportunities for leisure. Not only does the resident have more time because maintenance of the property is provided by the management, but most condominium complexes also offer an array of recreation facilities, such as swimming pools, tennis courts, jogging trails, and picnic shelters.

Leisure is also becoming a more important consideration in choosing the overall geographic location. Significant numbers of people are moving to warmer climates, the coasts, and mountains based on a desire to live lifestyles focused on their leisure interests. For example, in the United States, 75 percent of the federal government managed recreation land for outdoor pursuits is located in the west; Arizona is considered an important retirement state. Some people choose to live in New York City to be near the Lincoln Center for the Performing Arts. Aspen, Colorado, draws residents because of its world-class skiing and trendy nightlife. In other words, leisure is a prime consideration for many people in the choice of where to live.

Religion is also a factor that commonly influences leisure behavior. Most religious organizations are concerned with human behavior and, therefore, often teach doctrines about leisure behavior in particular. For example, certain days and/or hours of the day are considered sacred and reserved for religious celebration. This sacred time may involve silent meditation, singing, and dancing. The effect of religious beliefs on nonsacred time is also wide ranging, depending on the doctrine of the religion. For example, some religious beliefs affect leisure expression by designating certain activities as "good" and others as "evil." This has resulted in bans on specific films, books, music, art, and television programming. Other religious organizations, on the other hand, use recreational activities as a means for spreading their particular religious creed and provide recreational events for members, such as social groups, camps and resorts, and sport facilities. For example, the United Methodist Church, a Protestant religious denomination, provides a social club (MYF—Methodist Youth Fellowship) for young members. Another Methodist denomination, the African Methodist Episcopal Church, frequently offers sociability for members at lunch held immediately following the Sunday worship service.

Governments, as well, regulate much of our leisure behavior. Fish and game laws stipulate where and when people may fish and hunt; laws require boaters to wear life jackets and motorcyclists to wear helmets; city curfew laws limit the pastimes of teenagers; there are requirements for wearing swim suits at beaches; ordinances rule against skateboarding and rollerblading; and strict health codes regulate restaurants, bars, resorts, and campgrounds. While we typically think of government regulations as restrictive, some actually stimulate leisure expression. Governments sponsor recreation services, such as museums, parks, sports facilities, cultural centers, libraries, and tourist facilities, as well as contribute financial support to privately managed theater groups, arts councils, and other organizations.

Another factor that affects leisure behavior is transportation. The availability of various methods of transportation in providing access to particular leisure places varies considerably. In some locations, walking is still important. Elsewhere, public transportation, private cars, boats, or aircraft dominate. A family residing in rural Alaska uses a bush plane almost exclusively to reach recreation sites, whereas someone living in downtown Paris relies more on walking and public transit systems to get to museums, parks, and cafes.

An interesting comparison of the impact of transportation development on the recreational "distance" of people is presented in figure 3.1. It has only been about 150 years since rapid changes in transportation began to contribute to leisure behavior. Before then, most people were confined to opportunities they could reach on foot. In the mid-1800s, steam-powered boats and locomotives widened the average person's ability to travel to such places as resorts and sports events. Today, the train can even be used to transport you and your car to a vacation destination. The automobile, which was a relatively expensive novelty at first, had comparatively little impact on most people's leisure-related

Figure 3.1 Transportation inventions have increased the accessibility of certain pastimes (Chubb and Chubb 1970).

Christopher B. Stage

Changes in travel distance for a one-day recreational trip.

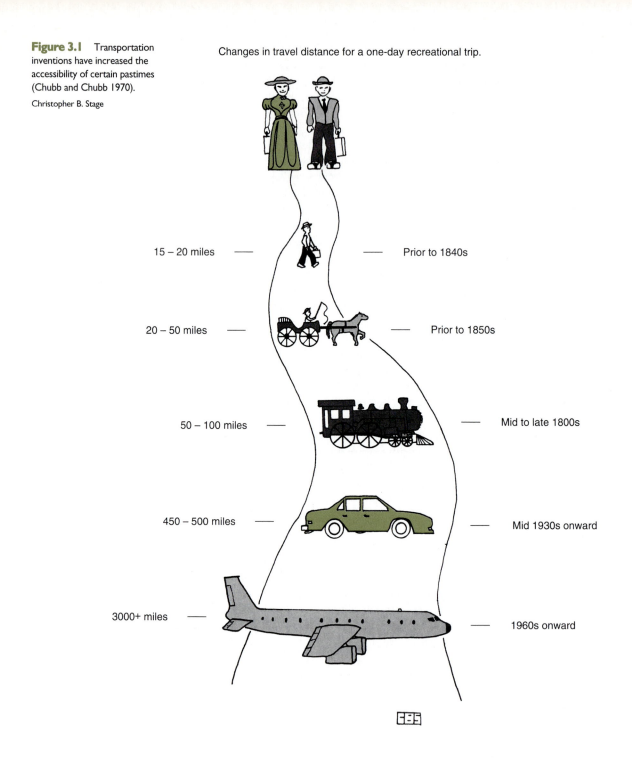

15 – 20 miles —   — Prior to 1840s

20 – 50 miles —   — Prior to 1850s

50 – 100 miles —   — Mid to late 1800s

450 – 500 miles —   — Mid 1930s onward

3000+ miles —   — 1960s onward

travel when it was invented. However, the mass production that followed World War I brought car ownership within the reach of people of moderate incomes as well. Similarly, the airplane has become a major factor in the flow of pleasure travel; it has greatly increased the accessibility of certain kinds of pastimes and locations.

There is another aspect of transportation that affects leisure behavior. Frequently, getting to a particular destination is considered a favorite pastime in itself—a realization by many cities where recreational forms of transportation, such as trollies, funiculars, streetcars, and dinner trains have been revitalized. Walking, biking, and canoeing from inn to inn have become popular vacations as well. Even riding a mule down into the canyon at Grand Canyon National Park in Arizona is a part of the fun of getting there!

Crime and other depreciative behaviors are major determinants of our pastimes. They reduce our opportunities in multiple and often subtle ways, but primarily they place limitations on people's freedom to enjoy themselves as they please. Some neighborhoods in many of the world's cities have areas where residents consider themselves prisoners in their apartments. Here, older adults are particularly affected. Fear of robbery, assault, rape, or murder affects the leisure potential for people of all ages in many locations. For example, in a study of midwestern urban and suburban park users' perceptions of safety and security, Westover (1985) discovered that one-fourth of the users felt unsafe when alone in the park during the day.

Finally, particularly meaningful in this decade, is the determining factor of war. We are reminded, as wars rage in several parts of the world, that war and civil disorder greatly affect people's living conditions and their opportunities for leisure. This effect is felt mostly by people from the directly involved regions or countries, of course, but the effects are not confined there. The well-being of many other countries also suffers. For example, in the past when conflicts involved oil-producing countries a decrease in the supply of oil resulted. This meant gasoline shortages around the world, which in turn resulted in canceled auto and airline vacation trips. Of course, this is inconsequential to the life-threatening impact of war on those in war zones.

At a more local level, gang wars between neighborhood groups can also disrupt the daily lives of people. These wars affect the safety of not only schools, streets, and subways, but also recreation centers, playgrounds, parks, and commercial amusements. Regardless of who wins the ethnic, political, religious, or gang war, it takes years for all factions involved to overcome the losses to natural resources, housing, and economies. Frequently, valuable cultural treasures, such as art and architecture, are lost forever.

These and other life-situational factors, while they do not single-handedly explain leisure behavior, taken together help shape its expression. For example, while watching television is a universally popular activity, the types of programs watched, amount of time devoted to them, time of day and days of the week the television is on are behaviors influenced by these situational factors. Nonetheless, care should be taken that an understanding of the relationships between leisure and income, education, geography, occupation, family and friends, and religious beliefs do not lead to stereotypes.

Figure 3.2 A model for
how theories are constructed.

From James F. Murphy, *Concepts
of Leisure,* Second Edition, by
Allyn & Bacon. Adapted by
permission.

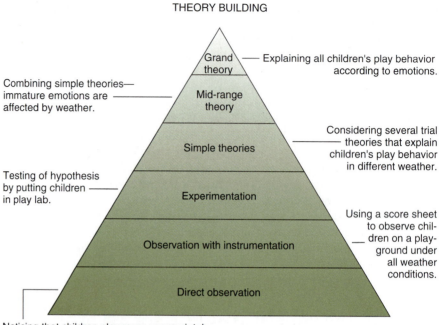

THEORY BUILDING

Grand theory — Explaining all children's play behavior according to emotions.

Combining simple theories—immature emotions are affected by weather. — Mid-range theory

Simple theories — Considering several trial theories that explain children's play behavior in different weather.

Testing of hypothesis by putting children in play lab. — Experimentation

Observation with instrumentation — Using a score sheet to observe children on a playground under all weather conditions.

Direct observation

Noticing that children play more appropriately on sunny days on the playground.

Theoretical Explanations for Leisure Behavior

Now we turn to more internal, attitudinal factors that influence our pastimes. These factors are explored in this section according to theories. Let us begin by considering what a **theory** is.

Scientific theory is a set of interrelated, testable propositions. Every science attempts to explain itself by developing theories. The goal of a theory is to summarize existing knowledge, provide an explanation for observed events, and predict the occurrence of as yet unobserved events on the basis of the principles in the theory. How does this happen?

Initially, a theory may simply be an effort to describe an observed event, such as the behaviors of children on the playground on sunny days versus cloudy days. Ultimately, however, an attempt is made through theory to explain an entire social domain, such as leisure's role in the quality of all life. This notion of building a theory through a series of steps is graphically represented in figure 3.2.

According to the diagram, the process begins at the bottom level of direct observation and continues through an ongoing search for more refined and precise explanations. At the first level, observation leads to the development of conceptual groupings. For example, suppose we go to our nearest school playground and observe children ages six through eight every day during recess.

Theory: a plausible body of principles used to explain some behavior or event.

Based on our numerous opportunities to watch their behavior, we notice that on sunny days their play behavior is more systematic and controlled. They are considerate of each other, play more traditional games, and use the play apparatus more appropriately. On overcast and windy days, on the other hand, we notice their play is more erratic, active, and uncontrolled. More fights occur and the noise level is higher.

The second level of theory building might involve specific observation procedures that measure the presence of certain behaviors. To illustrate, let's suppose that now in observing the children on the playground we use a score sheet, which helps us record the number and type of abusive play behaviors, air temperature, wind speed, and humidity for each observation period. We also interview the playground adult supervisors and a sample of the children about how they feel at particular times during recess.

The next stage involves the testing of **hypotheses.** Suppose that based on the data we collected in the previous stage, we develop a hypothesis that says that the cooler, more humid and windy the weather, the more unconventional the childrens' play behaviors on the playground. We test this hypothesis by placing samples of children into a controlled weather play laboratory and measuring the degree of self-control in their actions according to different combinations of weather conditions. (Such "play" labs do exist!)

Hypothesis: a tentative assumption made in order to test its logic.

Now the first level of actual theory composition is possible. These are tentative propositions that explain specific sets of relationships. Suppose we develop three of these trial theories for the children's playground behavior. One claims moist, cool, and windy weather frightens children so that they act out their fears in their play. Another says that moist, cool, and windy weather requires more human energy to function within it, so that while the children's play appears uncontrolled, it is actually an over application of physical energy. A third trial explanation is that children need to feel in control of their environment, and the erratic play during bad weather reflects these attempts.

At the next level, middle-range theory, a combination of related explanations at a more abstract level is sought. Perhaps children react in fearful and uncontrolled ways to weather because their emotional development is not yet mature.

Finally, the highest level of theory development permits the deduction of many small theories and resolves contradictions among the small theories. Such a grand theory attempts to explain all of any given type of phenomenon. For example, a useful grand theory for our illustration is that leisure is a reflection of personal emotional states; that is, we play as we feel.

Some theories that try to explain leisure behavior are developed only at the conceptual level; that is, they represent ideas which have not been widely tested and validated. Other leisure behavior theories are in transition between simple theory and middle-range theory. Even for those theories that have been extensively tested, the **multidisciplinary** nature of leisure and the variations in leisure behavior require such a broad explanatory approach that the task has been difficult. The rest of this chapter summarizes the dominant leisure theories and their research support. Notice that none of the theories completely explain all leisure behavior for all people.

Multidisciplinary: from many fields of study.

Compensation and Spillover

One explanation for people's leisure behavior is actually a combination of two approaches: spillover theory and compensatory theory. Even though these two theories provide opposite explanations for leisure behavior, the basis for both is satisfaction in work.

According to compensation theory, leisure for some people is a compensation for the deadening rhythm of the work-a-day existence. As described by Wilensky (1960), a person, particularly a blue-collar worker, engaged in repetitive, low-skilled, and machine-paced work, will seek the precise opposite activity for leisure. An auto mechanic might choose poetry writing, and a professor might enjoy rebuilding an antique car. Whenever an individual is given the opportunity to avoid a regular routine, especially if it is ungratifying, he or she will seek a directly opposite activity. This explains why people who perform physical work choose to spend their free time resting, or why those who work indoors prefer outdoor pursuits.

Opposite to the compensatory explanation, Wilensky described a spillover effect for some individuals' pastimes. According to the spillover theory, work will "spill over" into leisure. That is, leisure will be a continuation of what is experienced, especially if it is enjoyable, in one's work. An auto mechanic might go home after work and build a boat and a professor might spend the evening hours reading. Leisure becomes an extension of the skills and attitudes used at work. This explains why people who are sedentary at work are often not interested in physical pastimes, or why those who work indoors might be uncomfortable in the forest.

Notice how for both of these theories leisure is explained according to its response to work. Leisure can be different from work (compensation theory) or a repeat of work (spillover theory). Which theory applies depends on the amount of satisfaction found in the work. Also notice how these theories contribute to stereotypes about social status and leisure behavior. These theories claim to explain why the construction worker goes bowling once a week, likes fast motorcycles and boats, and watches professional wrestling on television, and why the corporate executive plays golf at the country club, travels to exotic places, and attends symphony concerts. Often such stereotypes are wrong and unfair. For example, you perhaps know a construction worker who enjoys listening to classical music on the radio while working or a corporate executive who unwinds on the weekend by driving drag racing cars. The injustice of such a status basis for leisure was the very concern of Karl Marx and Fredrich Engels. Engels, a German revolutionary of the late 1800s who in collaboration with Marx established Communism, wrote:

> On Saturday evenings, especially when wages are paid
> and work stops somewhat earlier than usual, when the
> whole working-class pours from its own poor quarters
> into the main thoroughfares, intemperance may be seen
> in all its brutality. . . .

(Engels 1892, 118)

Engels complained that workers, forced by the conditions of their labors, exploded out of the factory gates and the deadening rhythms of the job to the thrill of the barroom brawl. According to the compensatory theory, as later interpreted, we use our free time to balance the agony we endure while earning a living. Engels's examples were workers who drink as a form of psychological compensation for the drudgery of daily work. Other examples may be coal miners who prefer pastimes spent outdoors (Bammel 1977), and urban people who pursue leisure activities in the countryside (Burch 1969).

Engels also inspired the spillover theory of leisure behavior, yet his thesis was about the spillover of the negative aspects of work. Engels, as updated by Wilensky (1960), maintained the:

> Worker goes quietly home, collapses on the couch, eats
> and drinks alone, belongs to nothing, reads nothing, knows
> nothing, votes for no one, hangs around the home and the
> street, watches the "late-late" show, lets the TV programmes
> shade into one another, too tired to lift himself off the
> couch for the act of selection, too bored to switch the
> dials (p. 544).

Contemporary examples are not necessarily so negative. For instance, in support of the spillover theory, we might cite a tour director who chooses travel as a favorite pastime or a police officer who enjoys spending off-duty hours cruising the streets of the city.

The idea, nonetheless, is that leisure is a response to work. Thus, both the compensation and spillover theories attempt to explain leisure behavior in relation to the activities and status of employment. In so doing, it is assumed that work is the central meaning of human life.

The Contributions of Dumazedier

An important scholar of leisure in contemporary times has been Joffre Dumazedier. Dumazedier, a French sociologist, attempted to explain leisure behavior according to its purpose. His research and writings (1967, 1974) pointed to three main functions of leisure: relaxation, entertainment, and personal development. Each function represents one aspect of why adults select particular social or cultural activities, travel, and sports. Dumazedier called this a tripartite theory of leisure because of these three functions.

Relaxation "provides the individual recovery from fatigue," entertainment "spells deliverance from boredom," and personal development "serves to liberate the individual from the daily automatism of thought and action" (1967). Dumazedier's explanation of "why" was essentially that leisure is an activity to which an individual and society turn at will for these three purposes. For example, Dumazedier suggested that holiday celebrations are practiced in contemporary society because they enhance social cohesion. He, likewise, explained the popularity of cafes in France as being due to their functions of socializing and entertainment.

Dumazedier's predominant contribution is what his theory suggested about the future of leisure. Because he considered leisure purposeful in satisfying human needs for relaxation, entertainment, and self-development, he claimed that the opportunities for leisure in the twentieth century were unprecedented. Thus, the essence of the tripartite theory is that leisure is more important for human life than work. He predicted that a time would come when personal growth, not working for a living, will be life's primary motivator and that leisure will become the primary goal in life.

Dumazedier's theory is simple, which may explain its lasting appeal. The uncomplicated notion that people engage in leisure because it offers opportunities for important human growth and expression is perhaps too idealistic, however. Thinking about your friends and family, what do they do when they have more free time? Do they simply watch more television? Can people have too much leisure? On the other hand, maybe Dumazedier was correct. He suggested that concern for personal growth should be primary, and work should support that growth. This sounds reasonable when we remember that people frequently resign from work and typically retire from it, too. Leisure is constantly with us from birth to death, so perhaps everything else is subordinate to it.

Leisure Types

John Kelly (1972) developed a theory that explained leisure according to four types. He diagrammed the theory as a square with four cells, as shown in figure 3.3. In general, the diagram illustrates that people experience different kinds of leisure depending on the amount of free choice they have and the activity's meaning to them.

In the first cell of the diagram, unconditional leisure occurs when an activity is chosen for its own sake, for satisfactions intrinsic to participation. Kelly labeled this "unconditional" leisure (1972, 166). Something about the activity provides the primary reason for doing it. This could be because the activity is exciting, personally expressive, creative, or emotionally fulfilling. For example, while reading a good book you become completely immersed, unable to tear yourself away from it, even forgetting what time it is.

In the second cell of the diagram, according to Kelly, recuperative and compensatory leisure make up for some deficit or loss. For example, coming home from work and listening to music as a way to unwind or taking a brisk morning walk as a way to clear the head for studying would be described as

Figure 3.3 John Kelly's theory of types of leisure. Percentages refer to proportions of experience for a research sample.

From John R. Kelly, *Leisure.* Copyright © 1982 by Allyn & Bacon. Adapted by permission.

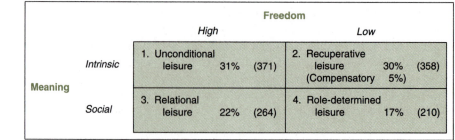

A mid-morning cup of coffee with a friend can be called relational leisure.
© Ruth V. Russell

recuperative. The purpose is rest and relaxation. Also, some leisure is engaged in as a compensation for the constraining conditions of work, parenthood, school, caring for an aged parent, and even the weather. For example, during final exam week a college student goes to the movies as a way to get away from studying for a while.

In relational leisure (cell three), activities are chosen because of a desire to be with others. Leisure occurs because friends or family have chosen it or as a way of being with people we enjoy. Relational leisure is not done because someone else expects it but because it is a valued means for expressing the relationship. Going camping with your family because you enjoy their companionship, taking a child to the zoo because you want to spend some meaningful time with him or her, or having a mid-morning cup of coffee with a colleague because you are friends could all be explained as relational leisure.

Finally, Kelly theorized about role-determined leisure (cell four). Some leisure occurs as a way of satisfying the expectations of others. Parents attend a Little League game to cheer for their child. A boss invites employees to a back-yard cookout to show appreciation for their hard work. Leisure that is done with other people in order to meet a perceived role obligation—as parent, boss, friend, roommate—is motivated by a desire to maintain the relationship.

Notice that the four types of leisure are different according to the degree of freedom of choice for the activity and the activity's meaning. Thus, unconditional leisure involves a great deal of freedom of choice and is done for intrinsic reasons, while role-determined leisure has minimal freedom of choice and is done for social reasons. Thus, the answer to why people choose particular pastimes is not the activity itself but the meaning received from the activity. This theory explains why, for example, going for a jog for one person could be completely obligatory (as a way to avoid feeling guilty about eating too much the day before), and joyously invigorating and liberating for another.

Satisfactions as Explanation

Another theoretical perspective of leisure is, like Kelly's, based on categories of activity meanings. Bev Driver, a researcher for the U.S. Forest Service, believed that leisure was beneficial, especially leisure occurring in natural environments. In the 1960s, he and colleagues began some early examinations of the motivations for choosing water and forest related leisure. They discovered that people engage in outdoor forms of leisure for the following reasons: (Driver 1977):

1. Social: social recognition, family togetherness, being with friends, meeting new people, sharing experiences.

2. Personal development: achievement, reinforcing self-image, competence testing, discovery, learning, physical fitness.

3. Experimental: sensory stimulation, risk-taking, tranquility, nostalgia, testing limits.

4. Nature appreciation: enjoyment of scenery, closeness to nature, seeking open space and privacy.

5. Change: rest and escape from pressures, routines, crowds, and weather.

Later, Driver and his colleagues broadened their task to identify human needs that could be gratified by leisure behavior in general. After a great deal of research, the list of needs was increased to nineteen (Driver, Tinsley, and Manfredo 1991):

1. Enjoy nature: scenery and being in nature.

2. Physical fitness.

3. Reduce tension: escape role overloads and daily routines, slow down mentally.

4. Escape physical stressors: seek tranquility and solitude, escape crowds and noise.

5. Outdoor learning: exploration, nature facts, geography.

6. Share similar values with friends and others.

7. Independence: autonomy, being in control.

8. Family relations: both kinship with and escape from family.

9. Introspection: spiritual, personal values.

10. Be with considerate people: a kind of social security.

Understanding why people behave in leisure as they do has been used by managers of parks to respond to the needs of visitors.

© Ruth V. Russell

11. Achievement/stimulation: skill development, competence testing, endurance, social recognition, self-confidence building.

12. Physical rest.

13. Teach/lead others.

14. Risk-taking.

15. Risk reduction: risk moderation and prevention.

16. Meet new people.

17. Creativity.

18. Nostalgia.

19. Agreeable temperatures.

Driver's efforts to explain leisure behavior have proven valuable to leisure service managers. For example, as was Driver's original motivation thirty years ago, understanding why people behave in leisure as they do has been used by managers of forests and parks to respond to the needs of visitors. Driver's list of satisfactions from pastimes has been used to specify management objectives and mechanisms for providing recreation experience opportunities for people.

Neulinger's Paradigm

Paradigm: a pattern or model for how something works.

John Neulinger, an American psychologist, developed a **paradigm** to explain leisure. He was most concerned with those factors that make a distinction between leisure and nonleisure. Neulinger's theory maintains that perceived freedom is the primary determining characteristic. Perceived freedom means how much choice one feels they have in determining their own actions. Was it their choice (perceived freedom) or did they do it because they felt they had to (perceived constraint)?

Of secondary importance is motivation. According to the theory, motivation for a person's actions is a matter of degree between intrinsic reasons, doing it for its own sake, and extrinsic reasons, doing it for a pay-off or to avoid a punishment.

Neulinger divided these qualities across a "state of mind" continuum to explain different leisure experiences. For example (fig. 3.4), the paradigm makes the distinction between leisure and nonleisure along the dimensions of perceived freedom and intrinsic/extrinsic motivation. It does this by dividing these dimensions into six types of psychological states of mind (Neulinger 1976).

State of Mind One. This represents the purest form of leisure—an activity freely chosen for its own sake. This pure leisure requires freedom from external control and brings intrinsic rewards. Neulinger's pure leisure is the same as Kelly's unconditional leisure. It not only requires "a complete mastery of oneself in terms of total freedom from inner constraints, but it also implies the condition of being able to enjoy the satisfactions derived from intrinsic rewards without having to pay attention to potential extrinsic ones" (Neulinger 1981, 31).

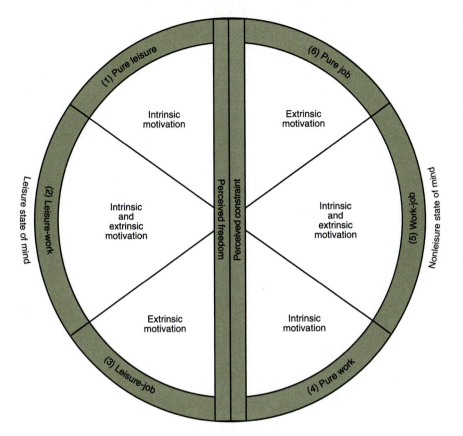

Figure 3.4 Neulinger's paradigm distinguishes leisure from nonleisure by the amount of perceived freedom and type of motivation.

Based on John Neulinger, *To Leisure*, by Allyn & Bacon.

State of Mind Two. This type of leisure represents a wide range of experiences—all of which are freely chosen yet are both extrinsically and intrinsically rewarding. The activity is satisfying not only in itself but also in terms of its payoffs. For example, perhaps for you doing antique furniture refinishing, chores around the house, or gardening may be characteristic of this leisure-work state of mind. An important distinction is that a person can quit whenever she or he pleases.

State of Mind Three. This is leisure-job according to Neulinger. It is a type of leisure one engages in without coercion, but the satisfaction comes from external payoffs. For some people, playing cards for money (when you don't need the money) or lifting weights in order to look better (not on doctor's orders) might fit this state of mind. The activity, while reflecting an experience of perceived freedom, is only extrinsically rewarding, thus resembling a job. Some consider this leisure-job state of mind to be the same as recreation, doing something you freely choose for a reward external to the activity.

These three states of mind represent, according to Neulinger's paradigm, different explanations of leisure experiences. To Neulinger, the essential characteristic of leisure is that the person perceives him- or herself as the originator of the behavior, being able to quit whenever desired, and being under no pressure to continue (Neulinger 1981, 32).

The following editorial by American writer Ellen Goodman appeared in newspapers across the country in August 1993.

There was a Catskill comedian who used to tell a story about his first time away from home and home cooking. After a week in Army boot camp his stomach started to feel funny. He was convinced that something was terribly wrong with his digestive system, maybe his entire body.

Well, after much medical consultation, the problem was diagnosed. For the first time in his life he wasn't suffering from heartburn.

I think about him every summer during the dangerous season of vacations. People, even presidents, get away from the office for a week or two, and if they're not careful, they lose their disequilibrium.

They wake up in the morning and feel funny. They realize that something's missing. Where has the stiffness in the neck gone? What happened to that old familiar stress lurking in the right quadrant of the brain?

They go through the checklist of personal items that are lost. The ironclad hinges that hold the jaw tight have let go and their teeth aren't doing the midnight shift of grinding. The tension band around the eyebrows has released its death grip on their mental outlook.

It becomes clear too that the medicine cabinet of over-the-counter items advertised on evening news shows has stayed untouched for days. The symptoms have disappeared. The symptom-bearers are feeling abnormal. Abnormally well.

Suddenly, the bio is feeding back subversive messages that say that unwork may be good for them. It begins to seep around the edges of their consciousness that maybe the work ethic is not the same as the pleasure principle. It occurs to them that if labor was all it's cracked up to be, we wouldn't celebrate Labor Day with a day off. We'd celebrate with overtime.

At this point in the season, any sensible adult with a decent job, a refinanced house, a non-vested pension plan, and a primal fear of ending up on a sidewalk with a shopping cart begins to panic. They begin to suffer from re-entry phobia.

For this reason, as a public service, I have assembled a handy reference sheet to grasp all during vacation. Lest we forget, lest we fear, this is to help us remember what is normal in the everyday workaday world.

Normal is . . . being woken up in the digital dawn by a radio playing a reveille of murder, mayhem, rock, roll and news of the latest failed foreign policy.

Normal is . . . saying the same six words to your children before the 7:30 A.M. school bus: Hurry up, hurry up, hurry up.

Normal is . . . getting dressed in clothes that you buy for work, driving through traffic in a car that

---

State of Mind Four. This is considered a nonleisure behavior because it is done under perceived constraint for intrinsic reasons. Neulinger called it pure work. Examples could include doing homework when students are interested and even enjoyably involved but, nonetheless, reflects a mandatory responsibility. Given free choice they would not do the homework, but they still find it engrossing.

State of Mind Five. This type is work-job—activities engaged in under constraint but having both intrinsic and extrinsic rewards. The awareness of constraints is present and, therefore, makes the behavior nonleisure, no matter how satisfying. The average employment situation may produce this state of mind. The work experience is satisfying in and of itself. For example, the staff of one large municipal recreation and park department rated their job as highly meaningful and usually personally satisfying, but they did complain

you are still paying for, in order to get to the job that you need so you can pay for the clothes, car and, especially, the house that you leave empty all day in order to afford to live in it.

Normal is . . . following a time plan that requires you eat breakfast before you want it because otherwise you might be hungry for lunch before you can break for it.

Normal is . . . spending all day in a sick building with windows that don't open and a thermostat that is seasonally dysfunctional, in order to make the environment consistently comfy and user-friendly for the mainframe computer.

Normal is . . . solving complex emotional problems of sibling rivalry and adolescent moral dilemmas of right and wrong, in three-minute telephone segments in midafternoon under the disapproving eye of a supervisor who lives alone with a parakeet for which he has health insurance.

Normal is . . . socializing by E-mail with friends who work no more than 30 feet away.

Normal is . . . being required to wear a beeper so that your boss can call you out of an important meeting at the critical point in order to find out how it's going.

Normal is . . . sitting at a desk all day, under artificial light, eating machine food, hemmed in by four walls, with a plastic plant, a telephone, a Rolodex, a

sense of déjà vu and a manager who says you better start "thinking outside the envelope."

And of course, normal is . . . being grateful for your job because in two more years, if they don't downsize or move the office to Singapore, if the company isn't bought out, the technology hasn't become obsolete, and the entire work force hasn't been put on part-time, you'll be entitled to three weeks off.

Now, there, don't you feel it? That old burning sensation creeping up the digestive tract. This vacation too shall pass. Pretty soon everything will be back to normal.

Questions to Consider and Discuss

1. What do you think is Goodman's rather tongue-in-cheek message in this editorial? What is she saying about work? What is she saying about leisure?
2. Do you personally know anyone who leads the "normal" lifestyle of which Goodman writes? Describe them to your classmates.
3. How might Neulinger's paradigm of leisure help interpret Goodman's perspectives on work and leisure? In which state of mind would you place the "normal" state versus the "vacation" state from the editorial?

about low salaries. They also indicated on a survey they would quit or retire immediately if given the financial opportunity (Russell 1993).

State of Mind Six. Behavior in the pure job category represents a complete opposition to leisure. It is an activity engaged in by necessity and under constraint. There is no reward in and of itself but only through a payoff resulting from it. Having to work at a job in its most negative connotation—in order to earn a living only—is categorized as pure job. It has no other redeeming qualities.

These last three states of mind represent nonleisure experiences. They all share a sense of constraint and a lack of perceived freedom. It is that lack of freedom that, according to Neulinger, classifies them as nonleisure.

What is important to realize about Neulinger's theoretical contribution is that the paradigm represents a psychological orientation with behavior attributed solely to self rather than to external forces. This means that leisure's

biography Mihaly Csikszentmihalyi

Mihaly Csikszentmihalyi's focus on psychology began as a very personal interest. In October 1944, relatives argued with his mother that Venice, Italy, was not enjoyable at this time of year—too many mosquitoes—and the theaters would all be closed. His mother ignored their advice and left Budapest, Hungary, with ten-year-old Mihaly and his sister on the early train. Later that day, the advancing Russian army bombed the bridges, placed the city under siege, and within three months more than half of Mihaly's relatives were dead. He and his family had taken the last train out (Shore 1990).

Mihaly was born in 1934 in Fiume, Italy, where his father served in the Hungarian foreign office. As a child he spoke German with his nanny, Hungarian with his parents, and Italian with his friends. During summers in the 1930s, he returned to Hungary and stayed in the mountains with his mother's family. However, the arrival of World War II interrupted this happy pattern. Mihaly and his family spent the war exiled in Venice where the Hungarian diplomatic corps had gathered.

After the war, Mihaly and his family were placed in an internment camp for several months and then released "with apologies" (Shore 1990). His father then took a post at the Hungarian foreign office in Rome. When the Soviets installed a Communist government in Hungary, he resigned, refusing to return to his homeland. Instead, he used his savings to buy a restaurant, which became one of Rome's most fashionable spots.

By now Mihaly was growing up. After quitting school he worked a variety of jobs. He helped out at his father's restaurant, painted posters for American movies showing in Rome, worked as a travel agent, served as manager of a hotel, and led tour groups around Europe, yet questions about the war continued to plague him. He remembered vividly his relatives at the train station imploring them to stay in Budapest. "I wondered at the time, 'How can people be so mistaken about things?' This was an example of mass delusion or a denial of reality that seemed extremely important for me to figure out. I was stunned by how out of touch people were and their lack of sensitivity to their own emotions or their own well-being" (Shore 1990, 34).

In the winter of 1952, eighteen-year-old Mihaly was in Switzerland; his pockets were empty. He searched Zurich for an activity that would keep him warm and not cost anything. The solution was a free lecture given by a psychologist—Carl Jung. Inspired, he began to read Jung's books, then the works of Freud, and finally, anything he could find on psychology. Ultimately, his new love led to his departure for the United States to study psychology. In 1956, at the age of twenty-two, Mihaly arrived at Chicago's Dearborn Street Station with $1.25 in his pocket. He knew no one and spoke only the little English he had picked up from reading American comics in a Rome newspaper.

Five months later, he passed the high school equivalency exam and enrolled at the University of Illinois at Chicago. Because the psychology curriculum there was behavioristic, having little in common with his reading of Freud and Jung, he transferred two years later to the University of Chicago. He worked as a night auditor at a hotel from 11:00 P.M. to 8:00 A.M., reconciling the hotel's accounts. He attended classes in the morning and slept in the afternoon. He earned his B.A. in 1960.

As a doctoral student, Mihaly began to feel that much of psychology was consumed with the pathological aspects of life. He was interested in the positive dimensions of existence as he continued to reflect on his earlier war concerns—the blindness people have to their self-interests. He began to study creativity. For his Ph.D. dissertation, completed in 1965, he studied a group of art students. "I was puzzled about why they were so taken with what they were doing without any extrinsic rewards and I realized people seek activities for their own sake—and this was generally what people in the past have called happiness" (Shore 1990, 34). This became the focus for a lifetime of research and writing on the theory of flow.

"Most people nowadays are aware of the importance of health and physical fitness. But the almost unlimited potential for enjoyment that the body offers, often remains unexploited. Few learn to move with the grace of an acrobat, see with the fresh eye of an artist, feel the joy of an athlete who breaks his own record, taste with the subtlety of a connoisseur, or love with a skill that lifts sex into a form of art" (Csikszentmihalyi 1990, 94).

explanation is psychological rather than economic, as in the work of Marx and Engels, or sociological, as in the perspective of Kelly.

Flow

One day, doctoral student Mihaly Csikszentmihalyi was wondering about the motivations of art students he observed while attending his own classes at the University of Chicago. Why were they so frantically involved in something that for most would pay no money and provide no status? Once they finished a painting or sculpture they often seemed to lose all interest in it. Later, as a professor at his alma mater, Csikszentmihalyi studied the behavior of rock climbers. Why would someone cling by their fingers to a cliff hundreds of feet off the ground? No money would be earned from this act or recognition from others, and there would always be the likelihood of injury.

Over the past twenty-five years, Csikszentmihalyi and his colleagues have studied thousands of people—rock climbers, artists, chess players, basketball players, dancers—all people who seem to be spending time doing what they really want to do. These inquiries have led to one of the more popular and universal theories about leisure called *flow*.

Flow is a word that Csikszentmihalyi uses to describe a state of being in which you become so involved in some activity or thing that nothing else seems to matter. It is an experience so compelling, so gripping and absorbing, so satisfying, that you do it for the sheer pleasure of it. Csikszentmihalyi discovered that people reached this optimal experience through different activities but in similar ways. For example, a long-distance swimmer described the feeling of crossing the English Channel almost identically to the way a chess player felt during a tournament. The elderly Koreans liked to meditate and teenage Japanese liked to swarm around in motorcycle gangs, but they described how it felt in Csikszentmihalyi's research in almost identical terms (1990).

These common reasons have become the major elements of flow theory. In the research, when people reflected on how it felt when their experience was most positive, they mentioned at least one, and often all, of the following characteristics.

First, the activity is challenging and requires skills. Flow, or an optimal experience, is most likely to occur when there is some exertion for which we have the appropriate skills. This is not limited to just physical exertion and skill but mental and emotional efforts as well. For instance, one of the most frequently mentioned enjoyable activities the world over is reading. Reading is an activity that requires the concentration of attention and has a goal, and to do it one must know the rules of written language (Csikszentmihalyi 1990).

One of the most common ways to find challenging activities that require skill is through competition. This is the source of the great appeal of games and sports that pit a person or team against another or themselves. For the skilled, the challenges of competition can be stimulating and enjoyable. "But when beating the opponent takes precedence in the mind over performing as well as possible, enjoyment tends to disappear. Competition is enjoyable only

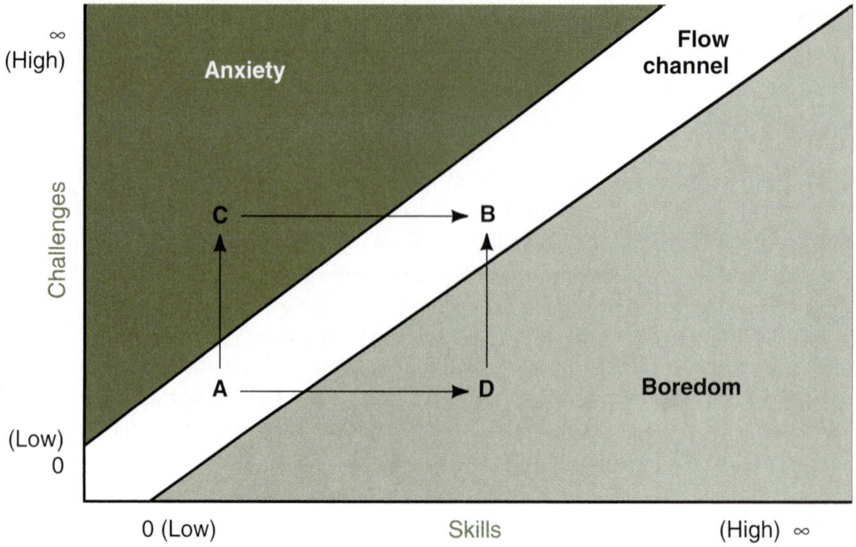

Figure 3.5 Diagram illustrating one of the characteristics in the flow theory.

Diagram on page 74 from *Flow: The Psychology of Optimal Experience* by Mihaly Csikszentmihalyi. Copyright © 1990 by Mihaly Csikszentmihalyi. Reprinted by permission of HarperCollins Publishers, Inc.

when it is a means to perfect one's skills; when it becomes an end in itself, it ceases to be fun" (Csikszentmihalyi 1990, 50).

For all the activities reported by people in Csikszentmihalyi's research, enjoyment occurs at a specific point: whenever the opportunities for action perceived by the individual are equal to his or her capabilities. Playing chess, for instance, is not enjoyable if the two opponents do not have comparable skills. The less skilled player will feel anxious, and the more skilled player will feel bored. This is diagrammed in figure 3.5.

In the diagram the two important dimensions of an experience, challenges and skills, are represented on the two axes. Let's suppose the activity is a basketball game. When a junior high school team plays another junior high school team (A), the players are likely to enjoy themselves because the level of difficulty is just about right for the rudimentary skills of the players. The teams are approximately matched. Likewise, in the final game of an NCAA championship (B) there is the possibility that the players will have a satisfying and absorbing experience, because their skill is evenly matched. While the level of challenge in the game is certainly more difficult than in the junior high game, the skill level of the players is also advanced.

These two situations would result in an optimal, or flow experience, according to the diagram. However, as we all know, there is also opportunity for anxiety and boredom in an activity. In situation C in the diagram, the junior high team is quite likely to experience anxiety if it played a college team, and a college team probably would experience some boredom if it played a junior high team (D). This is a simplistic example, of course, but according to the theory, every flow activity—whether it involves competition, chance, expression, or any other effort—has this in common: it transports the person to a new level of performance.

Second, action and awareness merge. When we are experiencing an activity as flow, our attention is completely absorbed by that activity. There is no excess "psychic energy" left over to consider anything other than the activity. All our attention is focused. This is a universal and distinctive feature of an optimal experience. People become so involved in what they are doing that the activity becomes spontaneous, almost automatic. They stop being aware of themselves as separate from the activity.

For example, a dancer describes how it feels during a good performance, "Your concentration is very complete. Your mind isn't wandering, you are not thinking of something else; you are totally involved in what you are doing. . . . Your energy is flowing very smoothly" (Csikszentmihalyi 1990, 53). This complete concentration is not constant, or long lasting, of course. Any lapse in concentration will erase the flow feeling, yet while it lasts, we feel effortlessly consumed by the exertion required for the action.

The third characteristic is concentration on the task at hand. Related to the previous element of flow, the merging of action and awareness, concentration on the task at hand also explains optimal experiences. According to researchers of the flow theory, one of the most frequently mentioned dimensions of flow is that, while it lasts, one is able to forget unpleasant aspects of life. This is because enjoyable activities require a complete focusing on doing the activity. Think about times when you've gone for a run, attended a party, read a novel, or skied down a powdery slope. Remember how surprised you were when the activity was over and you realized that not once had you worried about your daily problems?

When one experiences flow, only a select range of information can be allowed into awareness. Therefore, all the troubling thoughts that ordinarily keep passing through the mind are temporarily interrupted. As reported by a dancer, "Dance is like therapy. If I am troubled about something, I leave it out of the door as I go in [the dance studio]" (Csikszentmihalyi 1990, 59). A comment attributed to Edwin Moses, the great hurdler, "Your mind has to be absolutely clear. The fact that you have to cope with your opponent, jet lag, different foods, sleeping in hotels, and personal problems has to be erased from consciousness—as if they didn't exist" (Csikszentmihalyi 1990, 59).

The fourth characteristic is the loss of self-consciousness. When we engage in activities that require us to concentrate on the task at hand and that is experienced as a merging of action and awareness, a loss of self-consciousness is a natural by-product. When an activity is thoroughly engrossing there is not enough energy left over to allow us to consider ourselves. In flow there is no opportunity for self-scrutiny.

Further, the loss of the sense of self is sometimes accompanied by a feeling of union with the environment. For harp players, this may mean being extremely aware of a merging of every movement of their fingers into the sound and rhythm of the orchestra. In a sense, this feeling is not really a loss of self but a transcendence of the self into the music, the rock face, the chess board, or the ballet. Csikszentmihalyi (1990) describes this as a feeling that the boundaries of our being have been pushed forward.

The fifth characteristic is clear goals and feedback. It is possible to achieve such complete involvement in a flow experience partly because the goals of the activity are clear, and the feedback is immediate. For example, the tennis player always knows what to do: return the ball over the net. Each time we hit a tennis

The feedback these children receive from the experience of releasing newly hatched turtles in a conservation project is immediate and clear.

© Ruth V. Russell

ball we know whether or not we have done it well. The more challenging the goal achieved, the more enjoyment, which explains why climbing a mountain or cultivating Bonsai trees can be so personally rewarding. Some people have even reported having leisure experiences that they considered life changing because of a sense of mastery over something challenging.

Csikszentmihalyi claims that sometimes the goals for an activity are invented at the moment of the experience. He uses teenagers enjoying impromptu interactions with each other, such as telling jokes, teasing each other, gossiping, or talking dirty, as an example. The goal of such encounters emerges by trial and error, and is rarely explicit. Nonetheless, it becomes clear to the teens what the rules are and what being successful looks like!

The nature of the immediate feedback from the activity's performance varies widely. In tennis, it is getting the ball within the white lines. In rock climbing, it is feeling the wind from the cliff top. In gourmet cooking, it is receiving compliments from the dinner guests. In coaching a youth sport team, it is seeing a child be a good sport. Almost any kind of feedback can be enjoyable. What matters is that it is directly related to the goal sought.

The sixth characteristic is a sense of control. The flow experience is also typically described as involving a sense of control. For some people, this means not worrying about losing control, which is typical in many situations of everyday life. While it is actually possible to lose control during a flow experience—a rock climber may fall and break a leg, or a Poker player may lose a month's salary— the perception of being in control is an important aspect of the experience.

Essentially, activities that produce flow experiences, even the most risky ones, allow the doer to feel in control. Csikszentmihalyi maintains that people enjoy not the sense of simply being in control but the sense of exer-

Autotelic: an activity that has a purpose in itself.

cising control in challenging situations. Ironically, only when the outcome is doubtful and one is able to influence that outcome can people really know whether they are in control.

The seventh characteristic is the transformation of time. One of the most common descriptions of optimal experience is that time no longer seems to pass as it ordinarily does. In most situations, it seems to pass much more quickly. People have reported through Csikszentmihalyi's research that they lose track of time while experiencing flow and are surprised that so much time has passed. As described by a ballet dancer, "I see that it's 1:00 in the morning, and I say: 'Aha, just a few minutes ago it was 8:00.'"

Is this distraction from time simply a by-product of the intense concentration in the activity, or is this element of flow a part of the positive quality of the experience itself? Csikszentmihalyi has concluded that "although it seems likely that losing track of the clock is not one of the major elements of enjoyment, freedom from the tyranny of time does add to the exhilaration we feel during a state of complete involvement" (1990, 67).

Eighth, the activity is an **autotelic** *experience.* According to flow theory a key element of an optimal experience is that it is an end in itself. Even if initially undertaken for other reasons, the activity consumes us by becoming intrinsically rewarding. As also shown in Neulinger's paradigm discussed previously, Csikszentmihalyi believed that a completely enjoyable activity is done not with the expectation of a future benefit, but because the doing itself is the reward.

Ask anyone who has climbed a mountain why they did it, and the answer is usually "because it was there." Going for a jog because you are trying to lose weight is not an autotelic experience, whereas going for a jog because you like to feel the strength in your lungs and muscles is an autotelic activity. A sailor reported, "I am spending a lot of money and time on this boat, but it is worth it—nothing quite compares with the feeling I get when I am out sailing" (Csikszentmihalyi 1990, 67).

Self-As-Entertainment

The final theory we will review is the Self-As-Entertainment construct, and it was developed by Mannell (1984). The Self-As-Entertainment (S-A-E) theory is based on individual personality differences. It attempts to characterize the ways people differ in their ability to fill free time with personally satisfactory activity. In other words, people who are high on the personality trait of S-A-E perceive a match between the free time they have available and their capacity to meaningfully fill it. They do not experience time as "hanging heavily on their hands" or feel that their free time is "wasted." On the other hand, individuals low on this trait perceive that they have "too much free time" and that there is frequently "nothing to do" (Mannell 1984, 232–33).

In explaining the theory, Mannell has used the comments often made by parents about their children. How often have we heard a parent make comparisons between children concerning their ability to play by themselves or to entertain themselves? Have we not also noticed some people always seem engaged and involved in something during their free time, while others frequently seem at a loss for what to do with their time? This is the first factor of the S-A-E theory: people differ in their ability to satisfyingly fill free time.

A second factor is people not only differ in their ability to fill free time, but they also differ according to the ways they seek entertainment or diversion during their free time. Mannell hypothesized that some people use their "self" as the primary basis or means of filling their time. They have the capability to enjoyably entertain themselves. Research has tentatively suggested that some prerequisite skills for this way of filling free time may be the ability to engage in fantasizing and make-believe and using knowledge stored in memory. Those who do not tend to rely on the "self" as the source of entertainment, Mannell has indicated, seek diversion through external situations. They rely on social and physical opportunities. Thus, their friends or television are their way of filling free time.

Researching for Verification

As we already realize, leisure is a difficult aspect of human behavior to comprehend. The theoretical explanations available attempt to describe the meaning, conditions, and functions of this complexity, and each leisure theory has weaknesses and strengths in its ability to do this. Therefore, like any field of endeavor, the propositions that make up these theories are constantly subject to further questioning, empirical testing, and revision. The following is a discussion of some of the research efforts to test leisure theory.

Initially, various early investigations were made to validate the spillover and compensatory theories. For example, research indicated that those who work productively and are excited by their jobs tend to choose stimulating and wholesome pastimes. Those with dull jobs either compensate radically, or their dull work routine spills over into nonstimulating leisure expressions (Parker 1971).

Meissner (1971) found that social interaction on the job is related to social interaction in free time. He suggested a spillover explanation for the lack of social interaction in the leisure of those whose work requires minimal sociability. Another study (Kelly 1976) found that although getting away from work was seldom the main reason for choosing particular leisure activities, it was of secondary importance in choosing about 25 percent of the activities.

Indeed, the compensation and spillover theories are helpful in explaining the leisure behavior of some people some of the time. That is, they are useful in understanding some of the leisure behavior of those who work. What about those who are retired, children, or unemployed? Why do two workers doing the same job choose opposite kinds of leisure? These pastime choices cannot be explained by the spillover and compensation theories.

Research based on Kelly's theory of the four types of leisure has typically focused on proportions of each in people's lives. For example, a study of three American communities (a university town in the Pacific Northwest, a mill town in the Midwest, and a new suburb of Washington, D.C.) revealed a profile of what adults did for leisure and why (Kelly 1978). A slight majority of the leisure (31 percent) reported by the sample was considered unconditional leisure—involving high freedom of choice and intrinsic meaning for the participants. Thirty percent of the leisure was recuperative, 22 percent was relational, and 17 percent was role-determined leisure (fig. 3.3).

Do some kinds of activities tend to be chosen for some kinds of reasons more than others? That is, are some activities more often unconditional and others usually role determined? According to Kelly's (1982) research, while no activities always have the same meaning for everyone, some activities tend to be chosen for intrinsic reasons and others are generally a response to perceived role expectations. For example, Kelly considers arts, crafts, hobbies, creative home projects, and some sports as more often than not unconditional in nature. Also, reading, television viewing, listening to music, daydreaming, and some travel tend to be chosen for their ability to relax or change pace. Activities such as eating out and parties are viewed as relational, while pastimes experienced with family members are typically considered as role determined.

However, as Kelly's research has cautioned, any categorization of activities can mask subtle but important exceptions. As Kelly explained, "cultural activities tend to be more unconditional if they involve the effort of going somewhere on a schedule and more recuperative if they are passive and done at home . . . family activity tends to mix the positive satisfactions and role constraints rather than consist of just one or the other" (1982, 168–69).

Next, a great deal of research has been conducted by many scientists in many countries on Driver's theoretical position that leisure is motivated by the satisfactions it provides. In fact, the nineteen categories of leisure satisfaction were originally derived from exploratory research. Most recently, however, testing a research tool designed to measure Driver's ideas has been the focus. This tool is called the Recreation Experience Preference (REP) questionnaire, which has been used since about 1982 (Driver, Tinsley, and Manfredo 1992).

In one study (Driver and Cooksey 1980), the REP questionnaire was administered to randomly selected users of the parks along the Huron River in Michigan. Results indicated that for those who were camping in the park, escape from daily routine was the most important satisfaction. On the other hand, for those who chose to swim in the river, physical rest was the highest ranking satisfaction. Those who engaged in boating indicated they did so in order to enjoy nature.

In another study (Driver, Tinsley, and Manfredo 1992), for hikers along the Arkansas River in Colorado the most significant explanations for their behavior were enjoyment of the scenery and exploration. For those engaged in fishing, a desire for tranquility, physical rest, and being in nature best explained the leisure behavior. Do these results match your own experiences? Do you go hiking and fishing for similar reasons?

Much research has also focused on Csikszentmihalyi's flow theory. Information from lengthy interviews and questionnaires have been collected over two decades from several thousand respondents by Csikszentmihalyi and his colleagues. At first, they interviewed only people who spent a great amount of time and effort in activities that were difficult yet provided no obvious rewards, such as money or prestige: rock climbers, composers of music, chess players, and amateur athletes (Csikszentmihalyi 1975). Later studies included interviews with people doing ordinary activities. For example, individuals were

Antiflow

Following the work of Csikszentmihalyi, research by Maria Allison and Margaret Duncan (1987) sought to identify the nature of flow for working women. Was it more likely to occur at work, home, or while engaged in pastimes? In addition, they attempted to discover the contexts in which working women experience the greatest sense of boredom, frustration, or what they called *antiflow*. Seen as the opposite of flow, antiflow was considered by the researchers as meaningless, tedious activity that offers little challenge, is not intrinsically motivating, and creates a sense of lack of control. "Insofar as flow represents absolute enjoyment, antiflow represents extreme disdain or dislike for an activity" (Allison and Duncan 1988, 120).

In conducting the research, extensive interviews were conducted with two groups of working women: eight professionals from a university setting that included faculty and research associates, and twelve blue-collar women employed as factory workers and service workers. The average income for the professional women was twice as high as for the blue-collar women. Eleven were married, six were divorced heads of household, and three were not married. Allison and Duncan organized their findings according to experiences of flow and antiflow in the work setting and the nonwork setting.

Professional and blue-collar women had very different experiences on the job.

During the interviews it became clear that the blue-collar women felt frustrated, bored, and unchallenged at work:

> The thing I hate most about work is the boredom. There are times when I get really busy, but there are often times, a lot of times, when there's nothing to do. You stand around and watch the clock—I hate it.

> No stimulation, little new to do. Supervisory staff not willing to deal with people at the bottom—they don't work with us but against us. There's a lot of conflict.

Thus, their work experience became a source of antiflow. The professional women, on the other hand, more often found their work experience very challenging and stimulating:

> To be totally absorbed in what you are doing and to enjoy it so much that you don't want to be doing anything else, I don't see how people survive if they don't experience something like that . . . if I went to work every day and just had to sort of wait 'til Miller Time, just do my work and have no feeling of getting anything out of it, I'd look for something else to do.

> . . . freedom and liberation from boredom—that is the most prevalent

asked to describe how it felt when their lives were at their fullest, when what they did was most enjoyable. These people included urban Americans—surgeons, professors, clerical and assembly line workers, young mothers, retired people, and teenagers. In addition, Csikszentmihalyi and other scientists conducted studies with respondents from Korea, Japan, Thailand, Australia, various European cultures, and a Navajo reservation.

The research that both created the flow theory and that now tests it essentially asks why is play enjoyable, while the things we have to do everyday are often boring? Why is it that one person will "experience joy even in a concentration camp, while another gets the blahs while vacationing at a fancy re-

characteristic of having my career . . . you cannot be bored because in this subject there are continually new discoveries, just reading about it is fascinating to me. My enthusiasm for reading about these things is greater than ever.

Thus, professional women claimed to experience their greatest sense of flow at work, whereas blue-collar women experienced flow predominantly at home and during leisure. Whereas the work setting yielded different reactions from professional and blue-collar women, the nonwork setting (home, family, personal relationships, leisure) elicited many similar experiences for both groups. For example, circumstances likely to be described as flow by both professional and blue-collar women included the following activities and situations:

With my daughter, seeing her happiness, seeing her fascination with a toy, putting a puzzle piece in upside down and watching her work with it.

Friendships, very close friendships, very very important to share things with. To me, life wouldn't work well without that.

Sewing, making afghans and quilts. . . . I do this for about four hours a day.

I play golf, going to a good concert, I like feeling uplifted. . . . Reading an exciting novel. . . . I have a dog I just love. I play with him a lot, they don't demand anything, they give it all, and you've got it all right there.

Traveling . . . we love to travel . . . we can go when we want, where we want, and do what we want.

My biggest treat is to sit and drink a glass of sherry . . . and watch old movies . . . and work on my needlework.

The major source of antiflow within a nonwork setting derived from household chores.

In summary, Allison and Duncan's research found that all women reported intense flow experiences when interacting with other people—especially their children. Similarly, creative, active pastimes provided flow experiences for both professional and blue-collar groups of women. Professional women were more likely to consider work as an opportunity for flow. For all women, the more repetitive household tasks were occasions for antiflow. For blue-collar women, on the other hand, repetitive and unchallenging tasks were more likely experienced at work as well, and work was a prime source of antiflow for them.

sort" (Csikszentmihalyi 1990, 71–72)? Study results have found that what makes such activities as music, rock climbing, dancing, sailing, and chess conducive to flow is that they make optimal experience easier to achieve. The rules involved require the learning of skills, setting of goals, feedback, and control. The activities require concentration and involvement and are as distinct as possible from the reality of everyday existence. For example, in sports, participants dress up in eye-catching uniforms and enter special enclaves that set them apart at least temporarily from ordinary mortals. Play, pageantry, and sports are constructed to help participants (and spectators) achieve an ordered state of mind that is enjoyable. Flow activities provide a state of being that is an end in itself, as the following sample studies illustrate.

Larson (1988) assessed high school students working on a research paper for English classes. Some students were interviewed at about the time they were completing their papers (Larson and Csikszentmihalyi 1982). Others filled out questionnaires on repeated occasions before, during, and after starting the assignment (Larson 1988), which took several weeks. As can be imagined, students experienced a wide range of emotions during the writing experience. Some experienced anxiety and described their feelings as "flustered," "overwhelmed," and "scared" (Larson 1988, 153). Others were bored:

> . . . when I have all these notecards it's all there, but it's a job to put it down on paper. I know what I want to say, but having to put it into words was boring. I'm just kind of a robot repeating what other people say.
>
> (Larson 1988, 158)

Some students, however, reported flowlike involvement in their writing. "All of my brain was there." "I felt really powerful, like I had the information in the palm of my hand and could mold it any way I wanted." Some students even used the word "flow" to describe the rapt involvement with their work (Larson 1988, 164).

From a different perspective, Logan (1985) illustrated flow in a more unusual setting: solitary ordeals. This is fascinating because solitary situations are not typically considered enjoyable. Logan described Christopher Burney's many months in solitary confinement as a prisoner of the Nazis during World War II. He created a flow state by mentally making a catalogue of every fact on every object within his view. He asked often absurd questions of himself about his bed, walls, blanket, and even the toilet. Papillon (Charriere 1970), in solitary confinement in the penal colony in French Guiana, also created absorbing mental activities, such as counting the hours, minutes, and seconds he had left to serve. Solitary confinement is punishment designed to deprive a person of a most precious feature of life: freedom. As researchers have found, however, a key feature of the flow experience is centering attention on a specific thing, which in turn creates a sensation of freedom.

Finally, what sort of testing has Mannell's Self-As-Entertainment theory received? In general, research on personality factors influencing leisure behavior has been simplistic and limited. Nonetheless, some work in support of the Self-As-Entertainment personality trait has been accomplished. For example, Iso-Ahola and Mannell (1984) found support for the idea that too little or too much free time is perceived by people as a constraint on their leisure behavior.

One particularly fascinating study relative to the theory was the earlier research of Singer (1961). It was an investigation of fantasy in nine- to thirteen-year-old children. Children clinically assessed as low and high fantasizers were brought individually into an office and told that astronauts (a highly desirable occupation for this group of children) must be able to wait patiently for extended periods of time. Each child was then asked to wait as long as he or she could while the researcher sat and worked at his desk in the same room. High fantasizers were able to wait three times as long as low fantasizers. The fantasizers were quickly lost in their daydreams and inner thoughts, while the non-fantasizers appeared restless and bored. One interpretation of these findings is that those who had high abilities in fantasizing were able to fill the time by using themselves as sources of entertainment.

Summary: What We Do and Do Not Understand about Leisure

These ways of explaining leisure help us understand our own and others' pastimes. In fact, we realize that our choices and interests are due to multiple factors. For example, such life-situation characteristics as our income, occupation, educational level, network of family and friends, residence, religious beliefs, and others are all part of the explanation.

Also, there are several theories based on our attitudes, skills and perspectives that attempt to explain our leisure choices and interests. For example, the compensation and spillover theories maintain that in leisure we do the same as or opposite of what we do at work, depending on how satisfied we are with our work. For Dumazedier, leisure's explanation is in its purpose: the satisfying of human needs for relaxation, entertainment, and self-development. Kelly's theoretical work also explains leisure in terms of its function. These functions are recuperative, relational, role determined, and unconditional.

Meanwhile Driver's theoretical explanation is according to the satisfactions derived from leisure. He identified nineteen satisfactions in all. Neulinger's contribution to leisure theory was in highlighting the importance of freedom of choice and intrinsic motivation in determining if something is experienced as leisure or not. Mannell added personality differences to the theoretical explanations. He proposed that people differ in their ability to fill free time with satisfying activity.

Finally, perhaps the most widely known leisure theory comes from Csikszentmihalyi. This is the flow theory, and it describes the optimal experience of being so involved in something that nothing else seems to matter. Csikszentmihalyi discovered through his research that although people reach this optimal experience through different activities, the qualities of the activities are similar. These qualities are that the activity is challenging and requires skill, it has clear goals and provides feedback, there is a merging of action and awareness, and it is an autotelic experience. There is also a loss of self-consciousness, concentration on the event at hand, a sense of control, and a transformation of time.

All the theories discussed here have research support, yet in comparison to the theory development model explained earlier in this chapter, some are still at the conceptual level of development, while others are simple to middle range theories. We have not yet achieved a grand theory to explain leisure. In tallying what we know and don't know at this point, however, two conclusions seem evident: (1) none of the theories are able to thoroughly explain leisure behavior because (2) leisure behavior is complex and unique. It is no easy task to understand the meaning, conditions, and functions of leisure expression under all circumstances. Like any field of endeavor, the theories that currently seek to explain leisure are constantly subjected to further questioning, research testing, and revision. Which theory do you think best explains your own pastime interests and expressions?

References

Allison, M. T., and M. C. Duncan. 1987. Women, work, and flow. *Leisure Sciences* 9, no. 3:143–61.

Allison, M. T., and M. C. Duncan. 1988. Women, work, and flow. In *Optimal experience: Psychological studies of flow in consciousness,* edited by M. Csikszentmihalyi and I. S. Csikszentmihalyi. Cambridge: Cambridge University Press.

Bammel, G. 1977. Leisure in Appalachia. *West Virginia Recreation and Parks Review* (May–June):5–7.

Burch, W. 1969. The social circles of leisure. *Journal of Leisure Research* 1, no 2:143.

Charriere, H. 1970. *Papillon.* New York: Morrow.

Chubb, M., and H. R. Chubb. 1981. *One third of our time? An introduction to recreation behavior and resources.* New York: John Wiley & Sons.

Csikszentmihalyi, M. 1975. *Beyond boredom and anxiety.* San Francisco: Jossey-Bass.

Csikszentmihalyi, M. 1990. *Flow: The psychology of optimal experience.* New York: Harper & Row.

Driver, B. L. 1977. Unpublished Reports. Fort Collins, CO.: Rocky Mountain Forest and Range Experiment Station.

Driver, B. L., and R. W. Cooksey. 1980. Preferred psychological outcomes of recreational fishing. In *Catch-and-release fishing as a management tool: A national sport fishing symposium,* edited by R. A. Barnhart and T. E. Roelofs. Arcata, CA: Humboldt State University.

Driver, B. L., H. E. A. Tinsley, and M. J. Manfredo. 1992. The paragraphs about leisure and recreation experience preference scales: Results from two inventories designed to assess the breadth of the perceived psychological benefits of leisure. In *Benefits of leisure,* edited by B. L. Driver, P. J. Brown, and G. L. Peterson. State College, PA: Venture.

Dumazedier, J. 1967. *Toward a society of leisure.* New York: The Free Press.

Dumazedier, J. 1974. *Sociology of leisure.* New York: Elsevier North-Holland, Inc.

Engels, F. 1892. *The condition of the working class in England in 1844.* London: Allen and Unwin.

Field, D., and J. O'Leary. 1973. Social groups as a basis for assessing participation in selected water activities. *Journal of Leisure Research* 5 (Spring):16–25.

Godbey, G., and S. Parker. 1976. *Leisure studies and services: An overview.* Philadelphia: Saunders.

Goodman, E. 1993. Soon, vacation will end and all will be back to "normal." *The Herald Times,* 27 August, editorial.

Iso-Ahola, S., and R. C. Mannell. 1984. Social and psychological constraints on leisure. In *Constraints on leisure,* edited by M. Wade. Springfield, IL: Charles C Thomas.

Kelly, J. R. 1972. Work and leisure: A simplified paradigm. *Journal of Leisure Research* 4:50–62.

Kelly, J. R. 1976. Leisure as compensation for work constraint. *Society and Leisure* 8, no. 3:73–82.

Kelly, J. R. 1978. Leisure styles and choices in three environments. *Pacific Sociological Review* 21:187–207.

Kelly, J. R. 1982. *Leisure.* Englewood Cliffs, NJ: Prentice-Hall.

Larson, R. 1988. Flow and writing. In *Optimal experience: Psychological studies of flow in consciousness,* edited by M. Csikszentmihalyi and I. S. Csikszentmihalyi. Cambridge: Cambridge University Press.

Larson, R., and M. Csikszentmihalyi. 1982. The praxis of autonomous learning. Unpublished manuscript, University of Chicago.

Logan, R. D. 1985. The flow experience in solitary ordeals. *Journal of Humanistic Psychology* 25, no. 4:79–89.

Mannell, R. C. 1984. Personality in leisure theory: The self as entertainment. *Society and Leisure* 7:229–42.

Meissner, M. 1971. The long arm of the job. *Industrial Relations* 10:239–61.

Mill, R. C. 1986. Tourist characteristics and trends. *Literature Review: The President's Commission on Americans Outdoors.* Washington, DC: Government Printing Office.

Murphy, J. F. 1981. *Concepts of leisure.* Englewood Cliffs, NJ: Prentice-Hall.

Neulinger, J. 1976. The need for and the implications of a psychological conception of leisure. *The Ontario Psychologist* 8 (June):15.

Neulinger, J. 1981. *To leisure: An introduction.* Boston: Allyn and Bacon.

Parker, S. 1971. *The future of work and leisure.* New York: Praeger.

Russell, R. V. 1993. Employee perceptions of work-place barriers to change. Technical Report prepared for Indianapolis, IN, Department of Parks and Recreation.

Shore, D. 1990. The pursuit of happiness. *University of Chicago Magazine* (Winter) 28–35.

Singer, J. 1961. Imagination and waiting behavior in young children. *Journal of Personality* 29:396–413.

Westover, T. N. 1985. Perceptions of crime and safety in three midwestern parks. *Professional Geographer* 37, no. 4:410–20.

White, T. H. 1975. The relative importance of education and income as predictors in outdoor recreation participation. *Journal of Leisure Research* 7 no. 3:191–95.

Wilensky, H. 1960. Work, careers and social integration. *International Social Science Journal* 12:4.

leisure and human development

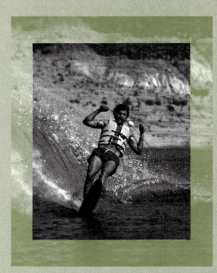

Digital Stock

PREVIEW

How is life span related to leisure?

Life is experienced both as a continuous process and as change. Leisure stimulates and eases the transitions of change yet remains constant throughout life.

How does leisure affect my emotional development?

Leisure teaches us joy, affection, and other positive feelings and helps us cope with anger, fear, anxiety, and other negative feelings.

How does leisure affect my social development?

Leisure helps us achieve and remain vibrant within a social network.

How does leisure affect my physical development?

Leisure is a tool for developing motor control when young and an aid to staying physically healthy when old.

How does leisure affect my intellectual development?

Leisure is a prime medium for learning and keeping sharp such skills as language, intelligence, and creativity.

four

Humans, animals, and plants are born,

mature, and die. This cycle of life is marked by both expected and surprising transitions. Certain experiences in human life are certain because life contains some continuity. We are what we are today based in part on what we were yesterday; we are college students today because we did well in high school and in elementary school before that. Life is experienced as a continuous and connected process, yet we also experience change in life; there are surprises. As a child we may have met a counselor at camp whose role modeling made us want to become a teacher when we thought we wanted to be a lawyer. At a party we may become outgoing and jovial, when our usual manner is reserved and quiet. Life is also, then, unexpected.

This chapter is about the continuities and changes across the life span as they relate to leisure. How do our pastime expressions and interests change as we move through our life cycle? Do they change in significance or meaning as we age? We will take a **life span development** approach in considering these questions. In other words, instead of studying each age group separately, we will view human life as an uninterrupted process. We will use developmental tasks—cognitive, social, physical, and emotional—and how leisure relates to them across life for the organization of the chapter.

Life span development: the changes and continuities of life from birth to death.

Leisure and Physical Development

Katharine

> I'm really crazy about sports. Since I'm the third kid in my family and have only older brothers, I've grown up able to fend for myself. I learned early the importance of running fast and hitting back. In grade school I was proud of my reputation as being strong. I even got a hernia when I was in the first grade by lifting up this big sixth grader. I love to tell people about that.
>
> There was never any question that I wouldn't be good at sports, and not "girl" sports either. I HAVE tried those, of course. First ballet when I was six and seven, then came gymnastics. Mom even made me take tennis lessons the summer after seventh grade. Now that I'm in ninth grade I feel that there is no longer any need to check it all out. I've found what I really like: running.
>
> I could hardly wait for high school. They actually have two running seasons here. In the fall I can go out for cross country, and in the spring they've got track. I'd rather run than anything else in the world. My friends Lee and Nyagon are runners too and the three of us go everywhere together, but we especially like to run together. I always want to be a runner.

The strength of the relationship between leisure and physical development is constant across the life span, but the nature of the relationship changes. Physical benefits from leisure shift from developing motor control in children, to sustaining health during the middle years, to reducing the decline in physical capabilities in older adulthood. Will Katharine be a runner all her life as she hopes? Yes, perhaps, but not necessarily a competitive one. Let's

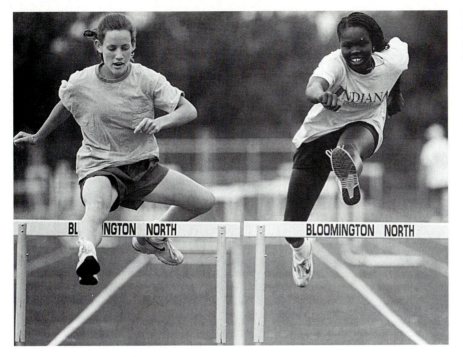

Katharine and Nyagon—
teens are typically involved in
physical forms of leisure.
© Toni L. Sandys

begin our exploration of leisure and physical development across the life cycle by considering children.

A baby whose day of birth is this year can look forward to a life expectancy of about seventy-six years. Seventy-six years, on average, of physical movement in defiance of gravity! Movement actually begins before birth, however. These prenatal movements include kicking, body posture changes, and thumb-sucking. Perhaps in preparation for the new and challenging environment, babies emerge with remarkable and practiced physical skills.

Infancy is a time when the newborn is struggling to master its own body, and play provides an important tool in this struggle. Early learning is the result of movement, and an infant's egocentric and individualistic play is almost all movement based. While an infant's movements seem random, such variety is important to his and her early movement experiences.

By two years of age, the baby has begun to develop basic locomotor skills, such as running, jumping, and hopping and such nonlocomotor skills as turning, pushing, pulling, kicking, and catching. With this increased mobility, play becomes more social and interactive, but basic development still centers around satisfying individual physical needs (Bammel and Bammel 1992).

These early play experiences are crucial for acquiring motor skills basic to later success in life. Children don't separate work from play. To them, play is the all-encompassing business of childhood—their method of sorting out the world and preparing for adulthood. Through physical play, children develop their growing bodies, learn muscle control and coordination, and move from a helpless state to physical accomplishment and competence.

Eleven-year-old Randy Durham locked his eyes on the target and with arms straight and steady, raised the gun and fired. His victim screamed and staggered to the ground, but he wasn't dead. The bullet had only grazed his arm. As he was trying to crawl to safety, Randy was ruthless. He finished him off with a single bullet to the head. While the victim's body bled and convulsed, Randy had already shifted his attention to a new threat entering through the doorway. Randy has been shooting people for the past two weeks in a video arcade. The video game he plays, Mad Dog McCree, is his favorite because it is realistic. Real people replace cartoons (Patterson 1992). Randy fires electronic bullets at a fifty-inch screen. For $1 per play, he gets to shoot people, making them scream, gasp, and die.

Like the pool sharks and pinball wizards before them, "vidkids" have invaded the world and are just as controversial. For better or worse, electronic games have become a popular form of entertainment. Home video players support a $5 billion a year industry (Oppenheim 1987). With games selling for up to $300 apiece, the pressures to own the "in" toy is tremendous.

Meanwhile, a town in Colorado reported a link between commercially sponsored game machines and a rise in petty thievery among school-age children. A survey of some 700 game arcades in New York City indicated that there were drug-related activities going on in more than 50 percent of them (Oppenheim 1987). Some city governments have passed laws to regulate who can play and when.

There are arguments on both sides, of course. Are video games destructive or supportive of physical, intellectual, and emotional development? Proponents say they are a wholesome entertainment that enhances physical and mental skills. Opponents say the users (predominantly preadolescent boys) skip school, squander their allowances, and hang out in unsavory places. Let's hear out this debate.

Pros	Cons
The games are entertaining. At least they're better than staring at the TV.	A lot of things are more entertaining than TV. Since when is TV a good measure?
They're not just passive. They really get kids involved.	Between TV, video games, and school, kids are spending most of their time sitting.

Pros	Cons
They develop good eye/hand coordination. You've got to be fast.	Kids are really expert at pushing a button, but that's because they spend so much time at it.
They can play the games solo; the machine becomes the competition.	Machines are a poor substitute for interacting with a human being. Even when they're playing together, kids are playing beside each other, not with each other.
The games actually help kids develop a greater attention span and train them not to be so easily distracted.	Kids who need flashing lights and beeps to focus on are later going to have a problem with a printed page that just sits there.
The games offer an opportunity to learn problem solving.	The games build a false expectation. Problem solving in life is not so simple as pushing a button.
The games offer a positive release. They are a modern and safe form of fantasy.	The games are basically aggressive. They focus on violent themes of attack and destroy. Kids are pushed into a prefabricated fantasy rather than creating their own.

Questions to Consider and Discuss

1. Which side of the argument do you think wins the debate? What do your classmates think? Why do you and your classmates support the side you chose?
2. Do some library research to locate research articles on video and electronic games. What evidence do these studies offer in support of either the pros or cons of the argument?
3. Take a field trip to your local toy store and/or computer store. As you study the kinds of video games currently available, how would you characterize their play value? Are we beginning to see games that go beyond blasting and zapping moving targets? Are more games designed to encourage cooperative play?

Table 4.1

Comparisons of Fat (Average Skinfolds) and Average Fitness Levels by Age and Gender, 1960 to 1980

Dimension Measured	Boys		Girls	
	Age 6	Age 9	Age 6	Age 9
Sit and reach (flexibility in in.)	13.23	12.61	14.10	14.05
Sum of Skinfolds (fat in mm.)	24.56	32.07	30.55	39.16
Sit ups (strength in #/60 sec.)	18.41	27.89	17.79	25.49
Mile walk/run (endurance in min. and sec.)		10.37		11.35

From J. G. Ross and R. R. Pate, "The National Children and Youth Fitness Study II: A Summary of Findings" in *Journal of Physical Education, Recreation, and Dance*, December 1987, pgs. 55-56.

Between the ages of about six and twelve the amount of muscle tissue doubles in the typical child. Because of their soft and flexible bone structure, children can absorb many blows without fractures, and additional flexibility comes from the development of supple connective tissue around their joints. Thus, physical exercise continues to be a necessary developmental component, particularly for promoting normal bone growth.

Increased motor control does not simply and automatically occur with maturation; the child's body develops in part from the physical demands placed on it. Playing with ropes, mastering climbing and balancing equipment on the playground, and learning to control balls give children additional opportunities to expand neuromuscular coordination and strength. Through these physical play experiences, the beginnings of social development are staged.

During middle childhood, physical development occurs along two major body directions. These are called the cephalocaudal and the proximaldistal axes (Gordon 1962). This means that physical ability development proceeds downward from the head and outward from the body center. For example, children just learning to write often move their whole bodies, including the tongue. Only later can they confine the action to the fingers, the hand, and a little arm motion. Play experiences are needed that progress from gross muscle movements to finer muscle movements to maximize physical development.

Are children in North America engaged in sufficient physical play experiences? Discouragingly, the answer is no. One study (McGinnis 1987) found one-third of the children and youth studied were not physically active enough, resulting in concern for children's physical health. Another related study also found that, overall, children weigh more and have more body fat than they did just twenty-five years ago (table 4.1). Up to 25 percent of teenagers in North America are obese. Some degenerative diseases that were once thought to begin in middle adulthood now have their roots in childhood.

In other words, even though children are more active than other age groups, activity isn't enough for good health. Conditions, such as increased body fat, not only affect their physical capacity but their self-esteem and social development as well. While medical evidence overwhelmingly supports the importance of physical play, some predict that children will spend increasing amounts of time in sedentary activities. For example, a study conducted in Arlington, Virginia, (Flinchum 1988) found that the most frequently used kindergarten equipment included record players, videos, small blocks, and computers.

Now, let's consider the next stage in the life cycle: adolescence. Pinpointing the beginning (and end) of adolescence is very difficult. Individual human bodies mature at different rates. Two thirteen-year-old boys could actually be up to five years apart in maturity due to differences in their developmental timetables. This wide-ranging passage from childhood to adulthood has, since the late nineteenth century in industrialized countries, been regarded as a particularly difficult transition. The major initiator of the transition is physical change. In fact, the word **adolescence** is Latin and means to grow up.

Adolescence: the state or process of reaching maturity.

In growing up, teens experience growth spurts, the appearance of visible secondary sex characteristics, changing body proportions, hormone increases, and alas, acne. No wonder a poll of ninth graders found that over 50 percent "had problems in connection with their own bodies" (Gordon 1962, 330). These changes, and the often accompanying traumas, can affect concepts of self that go beyond the physical. If appropriately selected, active forms of leisure can help teens cope with their social and psychological awkwardness as well. For example, one college student remembered this time in his life this way:

> By the time I reached adolescence, I had become quite successful in Little League baseball and junior high basketball. It was at this time in my life that I was labeled as an "athlete." This became important in the development of my social activities as well. I attended a small high school where social cliques were common. By participating in sports, I was in the "athlete" clique of friends.
>
> (Meyer 1993, 2)

For him, physical leisure activities made social acceptance possible. As another young adult remembered, sports helped her emotional adjustment:

> As a teenager entering high school, I decided to run cross country. This decision was made partly because I was overweight. I cannot stress how important that one decision was. I lost weight and met many upper classmen before school even started. As a result, my first day of high school was not so scary. This was because I had more self-confidence.
>
> (Evans 1993, 2)

Teens are typically involved in physical forms of leisure. Most have developed enough strength, flexibility, height, weight, endurance, and motor control to participate fully in adult activities. Sports participation, particularly

For teens, TV watching is the most preoccupying activity.
© Ruth V. Russell

competitive experiences, are important for teens because they not only provide healthful exercise but offer sources of self-confidence and social status. Teens are, therefore, the most physically active of all the age groups, even though high interests in television watching carry over from childhood. For the teen, the passive experience of TV remains the most preoccupying activity, absorbing about four to five hours of free time per day (Kleiber and Richards 1985).

Formerly, strong **sociocultural** pressures in Western societies like the United States suggested that girls should cease physical activity in adolescence. Thus, historically, teenage boys have had more opportunities for physically active pastimes, and consequently, have been more likely to develop greater strength and endurance than girls. However, in recent decades there has been an explosion in girls' and women's competitive sports. Since 1970, for example, the number of female tennis players has risen from 3 million to 11 million. In 1980, more than a million girls under the age of nineteen were playing soccer, compared to almost none in 1970. Currently, about 33 percent of all high school athletes are female—a 600 percent increase in less than ten years (Conger and Petersen 1984).

> Sociocultural: a combination of social and cultural factors, such as societal attitudes, rewards, and institutions.

When individuals become workers or college students and/or begin their own families in late adolescence and early adulthood, their physical capabilities and energy are usually at a peak. Most seek a wide assortment of active recreations, with participation in strenuous sports typically continuing. Interests in high-risk activities, such as skiing and rock climbing, begin to be fully developed as well.

Usually by the late twenties or early thirties, leisure and physical development begin to shift their relationship. Biological maturity—when bone density is greatest and most physical skills peak—occurs for individuals about this time (Bammel and Bammel 1992). Participation in strenuous and high-risk sports gradually decreases. This happens both because of decreasing vigor and increasing time commitments to careers and families. As a counterforce, however, is the high-level skill development that has taken place through years of practice, which makes some sports even more enjoyable for young adults.

Perhaps what is most important about leisure's role in physical development in adulthood, however, is its utility for sustaining health. Physical pastimes keep adults healthy. From research, we can substantiate this claim in many ways. Some examples follow.

Regular physical activity leads to a reduced resting heart rate and lower blood pressure levels, thus reducing the incidence of hypertension (Seals and Hagberg 1984). Exercise reduces blood glucose levels, increases the effectiveness of endogenous insulin, and delays the development of certain forms of diabetes (Paffenbarger, Hyde, and Dow 1991). Sustained physical activity leads to a decrease in fat body mass and an increase in lean body mass, which increases the metabolism and lowers the risk of obesity. This is directly related to a decrease in coronary heart disease, sudden cardiac death, and stroke (Caspersen 1989).

Physical activities increase muscle strength and improve the structure and function of ligaments, tendons, cartilage, and joints. This, in turn, helps prevent conditions leading to chronic back pain (Tipton, Vailas, and Matthes 1986). Physical activity, particularly weight-bearing and strength-building activities, help sustain bone mass and reduce the incidence of fractures. It also helps prevent osteoporosis (Smith and Raab 1985).

Regular moderate physical activity reduces the symptoms of mild or moderate depression and anxiety, thus improving self-image, social skills, mental health, and perhaps cognitive functions (Taylor, Sallis, and Needle 1985). Finally, longevity is increased by an active lifestyle in adulthood (Paffenbarger, Hyde, and Dow 1991).

To illustrate, a total of 16,936 men who had graduated from Harvard University were studied from 1962 through 1978. The study was an attempt to identify lifestyle characteristics, including various types of physical activity, related to rates and causes of death (Paffenbarger et al. 1986). As can be concluded from some of the findings reported in table 4.2, participation in sports decreased mortality. Actively playing any type or amount of sport is generally experienced more vigorously than walking or climbing stairs and makes a stronger contribution to longevity in adults.

For millions of people, however, physical limitations are a daily reality. Heart conditions, arthritis, hypertension, impairments of the back, spine, joints, arms, legs, hips, visual and hearing impairments, and many other conditions affect close to one-quarter of the American population (Austin 1986). For those who face the challenges of physical disabilities, leisure offers a special opportunity. Leisure experiences improve the quality of life. They are a bridge to fuller participation in the activities of living for persons with disabilities. They bring pleasure into difficult daily life and enhance functioning. For example, one study demonstrated the effectiveness of an outdoor adventure leisure experience in enhancing friendships between persons with and

Table 4.2

Risks of Death by Types of Weekly Physical Activity

	Weekly Physical Activity			Relative Risk of Death (Percent)
	Walk 6+ Miles	Climb 36+ stairs	Active Sports Play	
No Activity	−	−	−	100
One out of three activities	−	−	+	69 ⎤
	−	+	−	72 ⎬ 80
	+	−	−	93 ⎦
Two out of three activities	−	+	+	66 ⎤
	+	−	+	48 ⎬ 62
	+	+	−	82 ⎦
All three activities	+	+	+	53

From R. S. Paffenberger, R. T. Hyde, A. L. Wing, and C. Hsieh, "Physical Activity, All-Cause Mortality, and Longevity of College Alumni" in *New England Journal of Medicine, 314,* 605-613.

without disabilities (Anderson, Schleien, and McAvoy 1992). As a result of five- and three-day canoe trips, strong group cohesiveness developed, with an improvement of attitudes among the participants toward each other despite their differences in physical ability.

Leisure also minimizes physical disabilities. In therapeutic recreation services, sports activities are often promoted as useful in maintaining and enhancing physical functioning. For example, a person who enjoyed downhill skiing before a double leg amputation, can be taught how to continue this interest with special ski equipment. In a study of teens involved in a wheelchair tennis program, results demonstrated that the experience increased their perception of their physical competence (Hendrick 1985). In another study of an exercise program involving physically active recreation (swimming and running), children with asthma were able to increase their work tolerance and decrease their resting heart rates (Rothe, Kohl, and Mansfeld 1990).

In spite of the efforts of therapeutic recreation services such as these, antidiscriminatory government laws, and greater sensitivity by the general population, people with disabilities participate less frequently in all types of leisure activities. For example, movie going is a popular adult pastime. While 78 percent of the general population attended in 1987, only 22 percent of persons with disabilities went to the movies (Hartman and Walker 1989). These results indicate that there are barriers to leisure participation. These barriers can be environmental, such as the sand on the beach for a wheelchair user, or attitudinal, such as a feeling of self-consciousness in social situations by a person with a hearing impairment.

Normal physiological changes that affect leisure continue to occur with advancing age. As all human bodies get older, they gradually become less flexible and endurance is reduced. For example, between the ages of forty and sixty-five more body fat is carried, subcutaneous tissue slowly changes, the face becomes wrinkled and thinner, and the skin and external organs lose their elasticity. After age fifty, the number of muscle fibers steadily decreases.

Even with up to 50 percent deterioration in many organ systems, an individual can still function adequately. The ability of human beings to compensate for age-related changes attests to a significant amount of reserve capacity. In most instances, the normal physical changes of aging need not diminish a person's quality of life. By remaining physically vigorous through leisure and by making activity and environmental modifications, life's pleasures can continue. For example, pacing the amount of physical exertion throughout the day can enhance an adult's adjustments to physical changes. Also, many of the physiological functions that were once assumed to deteriorate irreversibly with normal aging are being reevaluated by researchers. Even people who begin a regular exercise or sport program late in life have experienced significant improvements in their heart and lung capacity.

Nonetheless, the proportion of individuals starting vigorous pastimes appears to decline with age (Iso-Ahola, Jackson, and Dunn 1994), even though older adults identify physical exercise as one of the important needs satisfied by leisure expression (Ostrow 1980). Perhaps this will change as new generations reach advanced age. Because most individuals do not make radical adjustments in their participation as they age and because physically active older adults have a history of participation in vigorous sports, the so-called baby boom generation which popularized the fitness movements may experience aging in physically different ways.

Leisure and Emotional Development

Chris

Chris had looked forward to his graduation for a long time. As an architecture major, he'd spent more years at the university than he'd imagined he wanted to. Now as he looked back, those six years had been maybe the best he would have. There always seemed to be opportunities for a good time. The campus theater, orchestra, art museum, winning basketball and football teams, bar outings and parties every week, and the student recreational sports center made him feel like he belonged to a health club. He could work out, play racquetball, and go for a swim anytime he wanted.

In fact, he hadn't realized how good he'd had it until taking this job with the firm six months ago. Now he's at his desk from eight to five every weekday. Plus, he has a half hour commute each way. His new friends—associates at work—live scattered about the city, so they rarely are able to get together on the weekends. Chris' fun now seems to be restricted to noon squash games at the YMCA, which is next door to the office, and an occasional dinner out in connection with entertaining potential clients. On weekends, he watches sports on television and fiddles with his sound system.

Chris realizes he needs to perk up his life. Should he learn to play golf so he can play with his work associates on the weekend? Maybe join a singles club and meet someone interesting? He has more money now than he did in college; maybe he should buy season tickets to the city opera, but they're so expensive, and there's the downtown parking problem. He used to enjoy working with his model trains when he was in high school. Should he call home and have it shipped down to him? No. He rationalizes that he should have outgrown that hobby.

All people go through the process of learning how to deal with their feelings. Some are very good feelings, such as joy, affection, and sensuality. Others, such as anger, fear, anxiety, jealousy, frustration, and hurt are not pleasant at all. Leisure is often considered an emotional state, a feeling of joy, or a positive state of mind. Now let's explore leisure's role in the development of emotional health, beginning again with children.

One day a little boy was occupied, as usual, apart from the other children at the playground. He was drawing in the dirt with a stick. A kitten came into the playground and walked across the drawing the boy was making. The child stiffened and turned livid. With all his might, he swung his fist at the kitten, barely missing its tail as it escaped.

Young children have all the basic emotions of adults, but their expression of these emotions is immediate, impulsive, and direct. The boy on the playground, as with most children, will grow up learning to manage and enjoy his emotions according to coping strategies, so the immediacy is more controlled and socially appropriate. Play is an important ingredient in this emotional development.

One of the **emotions** that children must learn to deal with is the tension caused by fear and anxiety. In a classic study of children's fear, Jersild and Holmes (1935) found that younger children are most likely to be afraid of specific things, such as strange people and noises. Children of about five to six years of age show an increased fear of imaginary or abstract things, such as fantasized creatures, the dark, and being alone.

Emotions: psychic and physiological reactions.

Freud (1955) argued that play helped humans master fear and anxiety. He claimed that if children were not allowed to deal with traumatic events through play, they could become psychopathic adults. To date, research has found some evidence that confirms this view. For example, Symmonds (1946) was among the first to find a relationship between anxiety reduction and fantasy in young children. Later studies by Barnett (1984) supported the importance of play used by children to neutralize anxiety they feel. Part of the rationale for providing play activities and materials for hospitalized children is the emotional benefit.

For children, what characterizes the relationship between leisure and emotions? One connection is through a concept called **locus of control.** Locus of control is a personal perception about the source of power in life. External locus of control is perceiving that we have no control, we are merely pawns moved by forces beyond our control. Internal locus of control is the perception that we are the origin of our own life events and is related to successful coping in both young and older persons. In terms of leisure's role, we know that the more time children spend in a supervised child-centered play program the more internal in their focus they become (Bolig 1980). An example is the playplace (or *legeplads*)

Locus of control: the perception of the source of control in one's life. The belief by an individual that events in life are the result of personal actions is internal locus of control, and the belief that events in life are the result of fate or powerful others is external locus of control.

research

I'd heard about a kid in Florida whose mother picked him up after school every day, drove straight to the mall, and left him there until it closed—all at his insistence.

I'd heard about a boy in Washington who, when his family moved from one suburb to another, pedaled his bicycle five miles every day to get back to his old mall, where he once belonged.

(Kowinski 1989, 348)

These stories aren't that unusual. The mall is a common gathering place for a large number of North American youth. Teenagers now spend more time in the mall than anywhere else but home and school (Kowinski 1989). In one study (Anthony 1985) teens' use of the shopping mall as a "hangout" was investigated. Through interviews with fifty-one adolescents who use the mall plus ten hours of mall observations, it was found that many teens visit the mall regularly to watch members of the opposite sex, play video games, see friends, shop, and people watch. While it is mostly by their choice, some of the time they spend in the mall is a result of circumstances of modern society—single-parent households, both parents working full-time, and commercialism. Are these children being harmed by spending their free time at the mall? What else does the research say?

Over a six-week period, extensive interviews were regularly conducted, day to day, with adolescent frequenters of a shopping mall (Lewis 1989). This study found that the teens exhibited a good deal of alienation from both family and school. They used the mall as neutral ground on which to create a fragile but mutually supportive community.

The International Council of Shopping Centers commissioned a study, which they published along with a guide to mall managers on how to handle the teenage incursion. The study found that "teenagers in suburban centers are bored and come to shopping centers mainly as a place to go.

concept from Denmark (Bruya 1988). At Bornenes Jord (The Children's Earth) in the city of Arhus, there is a large sand play area under shade trees with small farm animals to be cared for, two small children-built playhouses, and a stream with a paddle wheel, water-stopping wooden plugs, and pulley system that let the children route the water through a series of troughs.

Children's use of fantasy is another interesting aspect of leisure and emotional development. Researchers (Barnett 1984) have observed that children use fantasy play to reenact sources of emotional distress. This often happens by changing the outcome of the stressful event or reversing roles to achieve a more pleasant result. Perhaps you remember playing doctor and giving your stuffed animals shots or imagining you were your school teacher and yelling at the "students" to stay in their seats.

In moving from childhood to young adulthood, adolescents often display a curious combination of the emotionally mature and the childish. This mixture is often awkward, but it serves an important developmental function. Each stage in life presents its developmental challenges that require new skills, and

Teenagers in suburban centers spent more time fighting, drinking, littering, and walking than did their urban counterparts, but presented fewer overall problems" (cited in Kowinski 1989, 349).

The report further observed that teens congregated in groups of two to four, predominantly at locations selected by them rather than by the management. This probably has something to do with the installation of game arcades in malls, which allows management to focus teens into contained areas away from the major adult shopping traffic. The report concluded that mall managers should actually encourage the teenage presence because, after all, mall kids are being preprogrammed there to be consumers, heading for a life of hard-core shopping.

The abundance of products in the mall, plus the pressure to buy them, may contribute to the phenomenon that psychologist David Elkind calls "the hurried child": kids who are exposed to too much of the adult world too quickly, and must respond with a sophistication that does not match their still tender emotional development (Kowinski 1989). Growing up in a high-consumption society adds pressure to children's lives. How is a preteen girl to respond to form-fitting designer jeans and sexy tops marketed specifically for her?

Finally, Karen Lansky of Los Angeles has researched the subject and has expressed her conclusions about the effects of the mall on teens. "Structure is the dominant idea, since true 'mall rats' lack just that in their home lives, and adolescents about to make the big leap into growing up crave more structure than our modern society cares to acknowledge," she says (cited in Kowinski 1989, 351). The mall, in other words, has become a parent, providing a home of warmth (Strawberry Shortcake dolls), support ("We do it all for you"), and even cooking (the food court) through brightly lit glass. The problem with this, as Karen sees it, is the mall as a parent encourages passivity and consumption. Such values as initiative, self-expression, and empathy are not taught at the mall.

most psychologists agree that in adolescence two emotional tasks must be successfully accomplished: achieving greater autonomy and forming an identity.

The fundamental question of "Who am I?" characterizes the early teen period. The young person tries out many kinds of personal identities, experiments with different kinds of relationships, learns to see his or her behavior as the result of individual choice, and explores his or her emotional capacities. This is a main function of leisure in adolescence; it provides a context for experimenting. The more relaxed environment of recreational activities can be viewed as a safe haven in which teens can try out various roles and behaviors.

This is why it is important for youth to explore a variety of leisure interests (Kelly 1982). For some, such school activities as competitive sports and extracurricular clubs are central. For others, the sociability outside school is more important. Finding out who we are is serious business and often takes place for teens on the playing field, in the gymnasium, in the band or art room, at the Scout meeting, or perhaps in the shopping mall and the street corner.

The teen is not alone in these settings. As the young person enters junior high or middle school, the world widens and the range of acquaintances broadens. In general, the teen's peer relationships fall into three broad categories: the crowd, the **clique,** and individual friendships (Conger and Petersen 1984). At their best, these forms of peer relationships can help teens deal with their own complex feelings and those of others, as well as develop their identity—most frequently through shared pastimes. As one fifteen-year-old girl expressed it: "A best friend to me is someone you can have fun with and you can also be serious with about personal things." Unfortunately, peer relationships are not always so favorable. Adolescent friendships can be fickle, offering more painful ways of developing emotional maturity. Worries over social acceptance and rejection are potent at these ages.

College students are also engaged in discovering their identity. At this stage in the life cycle, leisure is a vital context for breaking with the personal identities associated with family and home community. Several emotional transitions occur: emergence of a focused sexuality and greater social and economic independence from parents (Kelly 1982). The college years are a time of trying out new possibilities for a future social and personal identity. This is a time for learning, exploring, and testing adulthood. Universities and colleges aid in this process by providing "real world" simulations. Students can participate in politics through student government and in a profession through practicums and internships. These are thought of as preparations for real work and community responsibilities.

Likewise, social events, intramural sports, spring break trips, activity clubs, and other campus experiences are crucial for the development of future selfhood. Sports participation produces status for students that helps establish physical and social self-esteem. Campus organizations provide ways of experimenting with attitudes of influence, dissent, and cooperation. Being with others at concerts, sport events, and in the TV lounge of the residence hall can lead to building a new reality of the self in relation to others.

Campus recreation also plays a role in reducing the stress some college students experience. For example, Ragheb and McKinney (1992) found that the more students participated in recreation activities, the less they perceived experiencing academic stress. The study concluded that the greater satisfaction students experienced with their pastimes, the lower their perceived academic stress.

For many of us, there is another emotional transition between the high school and college periods and settling into long-term relationships and parenting. More and more, women and men are assuming regular careers while still single (Kelly 1982). For those with higher education levels and clear career aspirations, marriage or long-term commitments to another significant person may be delayed until the first steps of work establishment are accomplished. For others, during this time there may be some urgency in getting settled with a life mate. Either way, this requires, as it did for Chris in the opening of this section, a different emotional reliance on leisure.

For both those who prefer to wait in selecting a life partner and those who seek to establish a family, leisure focuses on meeting interesting people and pursuing relationships. Thus, leisure interests at this life cycle stage tend to

Clique: an exclusive group of persons.

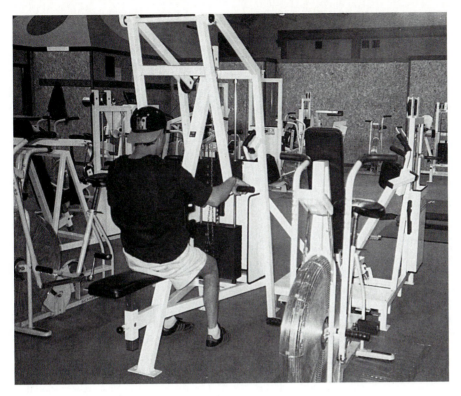

The more college students participate in recreation, the less their perceived academic stress.
© Ruth V. Russell

be social. Especially if they live alone (and over 13 million Americans do), leisure is expected to help keep loneliness at bay.

The years from thirty-five to forty-five have been called the "deadline decade" by Gail Sheehy in her book *Passages*. Others have labeled it the "mid-life crisis." Divorce and career change occur with increasing frequency. Essentially, this crossroad brings the realization of one's limitations. Predictable at this point in life is a sense of depression and stagnation. Some people experience tumultuous struggles within themselves and with others. Married persons with children often find their recreation patterns disrupted and restricted. Some resent the change from the more adventurous and free lifestyle they enjoyed at earlier life stages. Others welcome the stable, noncompetitive, and predictable leisure patterns of family life.

The years between middle and old age have been labeled the "reintegration" period of the life cycle (Rapoport and Rapoport 1975). Emotionally, this is the time in which adults reevaluate themselves and their lives, and the meaning and worth of one's life commitments and investments are weighed. A person may take a second look at his or her personal relationships, community, career, and pastimes. Are they worth it? Are they producing the fulfillment they once promised?

Part of this emotional transition may be motivated by a relaxation of previous commitments and role requirements, such as parenting and career building, yet a part also seems to be a consequence of a sense of running out of time.

One response may be to make a radical change such as divorce, a second career, or a move across the country. Another is to engage in a pruning and cultivation operation, in which elements of life that no longer bear fruit are clipped away with care taken not to damage the integrated whole life. Promising new possibilities are grafted onto the main tree.

(Kelly 1982, 149)

In either case, the free choice nature of leisure makes it a prime medium for life evaluation and alteration. New pastimes can be tried with minimal changes to relationship and work commitments. New hobbies and interests—tennis, traveling, art collecting—can be pursued. With increased time and resources, men and women in this reintegration life stage can bring former leisure interests back into their lives. Leisure is allowed to again become more personally satisfying and a more important life priority. There are many exceptions, of course, but life during this stage can be very emotionally satisfying, involving some or all of the pastime experiences of all the other age groups. These adults may have the time and money to explore many pastimes they missed earlier in life.

Another change in adult leisure before retirement is an increase in the proportion of experiences chosen primarily for their own sake, for intrinsic reasons. Whether the activities change or not, the motivation seems to become more related to self-satisfaction. Why is this so? The Rapoports (1975) suggested that emotions of depression, boredom, isolation, and entrapment may dominate during this period. The loss of the parental responsibility may leave an emotional void. Some may rush to fill the void with activity: a new hobby, job, house, or relationship. The motivation for participating in pastimes becomes more focused on what they can contribute to the person's sense of well-being.

As we approach the retirement years, one underlying emotional preoccupation is anticipation (Rapoport and Rapoport 1975). This anticipation of the future may be positive or negative. Some look forward to retirement, to escaping the routine of the job, and to having time for leisure that is not restricted to weekends and holidays. Others are not as sure about what they will do without the structure of employment. Leisure can be a part of retirement preparation decisions. Should I sell this home and move into a smaller place that will require less maintenance and give me more free time? Maybe I should move into a retirement center where the days are filled with planned leisure events. Should I buy the motor home so I can travel?

Alongside these dangers, there is continuity as well. In this time of transition, people generally continue the pastimes of previous years. If they have fulfilling life patterns outside of work, this may be a time of excitement and anticipation. If not, it may be a time in which thoughts of the future are frightening.

When retirement does arrive, the impact of the unconstrained schedule, less income, and shift in central life role away from work may be quite significant. Adjustments may be difficult and take time. While depression, loneliness, and apathy may characterize some retirees, these tend to be people who have less psychological preparation for retirement, as well as those who were less happy with their lives before retirement. When the quality of the nonwork aspects of life

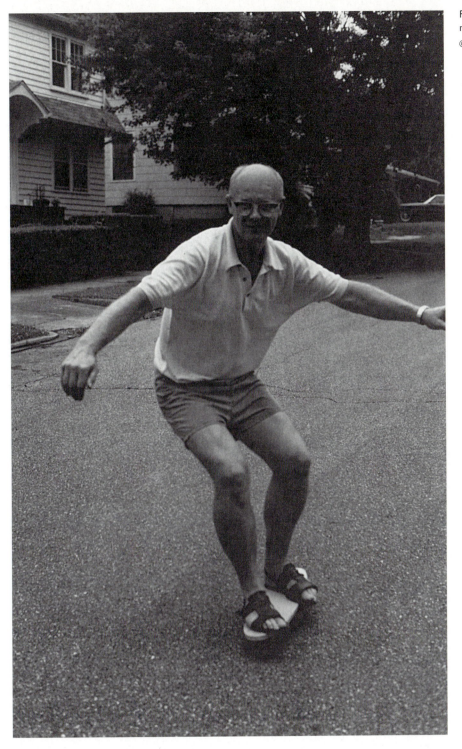

have been high, retirement is more likely to be viewed as an opportunity rather than a loss (Russell 1987). Psychological adjustment can be aided by trips, projects, and the expansion of favorite leisure activities. Feelings of competence, social esteem, and community acceptance can be derived from leisure involvement both before and during retirement. As leisure identities become more important to our selves, they can continue to provide both a sense of worth and opportunities for fulfillment.

Eventually, the death of a spouse or companion becomes a reality for many. The companion of most of life, especially for leisure, is gone. Many widows and widowers demonstrate great powers of adaptation. The loss of a spouse or significant person creates loneliness. It also changes the context of leisure. Instead of being a member of a couple doing things with other couples, the older adult who has lost a mate now needs to establish new relationships for leisure. The loss requires a rebuilding of other roles in leisure expression. For most people, grief does not permit an acceptance of the new freedom until the process of working through the loss has been accomplished, but once begun, leisure can help with the emotional healing.

Leisure and Intellectual Development

Bill

"Jerry, over here!"

Bill waved to his friend and colleague from across the crowded restaurant. Jerry spotted Bill and began to make his way through the smoke and noise. They were at that once a year sales conference they both looked forward to, mostly for the chance to catch up on each other's lives since the conference last year. Bill and Jerry had been friends since high school when they played football together. They still found it amazing, after all these years, that they ended up in the same occupation.

"So, good to see ya, how's it going old buddy?" Bill greeted, with a likewise boisterous thump on Jerry's back.

Jerry sat down at the table and began looking for the menu.

"So what's new with you?" asked Bill.

After they'd bragged about their favorite baseball teams, gossiped about a mutual former girl friend, spoken guardedly about the upcoming election, and complained about their adolescent kids who were learning to drive, they got around to talking about their jobs.

"You know," said Bill, "things have finally changed for me at work. You remember how down I was this time last year about the boredom of it all. I just couldn't imagine surviving until retirement the way I was feeling. It seemed that day after day, it was the same old thing. Nothing ever challenged me—nothing interesting to think about. In fact, I think I quit thinking! I was on automatic."

Jerry nodded and waited, knowing Bill would take his time in telling this.

"I guess I was in real danger of actually being fired. I couldn't seem to make the sales, and as the company's profits went down because of the economy, we needed sales people who were problem solvers. That sure wasn't me! But then about six months ago, things began to change. I don't know how, but thank goodness they did.

Now I'm having a ball at work. I've begun to be a whole lot more creative in serving my districts. I don't know what you'd call it but my thoughts are more playful. I'm able to see new solutions to the company's problems, solutions that I'd never thought of before. I've never considered myself to be a creative thinker; I've always been so practical. But this has really been fun!

Jerry nodded again and looked around for the check.

Beginning our exploration of leisure and intellectual development again with the childhood period of life, it has long been thought that one of the main contributions of a child's play is to cognitive skills. Specifically, play has been linked to the development of two modes of thought: **convergent** and **divergent thinking** (Vandenberg 1980).

As long ago as the late 1800s, it was theorized that one of the important functions of play for children was that it enhanced problem-solving or convergent thinking ability. Play is still regarded as an opportunity to develop the skills needed to solve a variety of problems. This is because a child's playful experience with objects and procedures can be applied to real-life issues. By exploring and manipulating objects in play, children learn the properties of not only those objects but their potential for application to various other problem situations as well (Barnett 1990). For example, Sylva and her colleagues (1976) found that children who were allowed to play with materials that would later be used in a task, actually performed that task better than children who had no opportunity for the same play experiences.

As well, there are two common views about the way play contributes to divergent thinking ability. The first considers the spontaneous nature of play as important to the development of thinking ability. This means that play provides the child with a broad repertoire of skills and responses used with a flexible approach to effectively solve a problem.

A second way play relates to divergent thinking is through the symbolic nature of much of a young child's play. Several theorists (Barnett 1990) suggested that play enhances the child's transition from concrete to abstract thought processes, because of the way children's play frequently uses nonreal things to represent real ones. Make-believe play appears to be the key link. Thus play contributes to creativity by increasing the child's repertoire of novel associations with objects. Perhaps play creates a more flexible attitude toward the world that can be carried into adulthood.

Another domain in which leisure and intellectual development are commonly linked in childhood is language. Sounds, syllables, words, and phrases provide children with a rich source of play material. Infants discover the joy of vocal play when starting to babble. By the time they are uttering their first words and sentences, preschool children have begun to playfully manipulate grammar, rhyme, nonsense words, and multiple meanings. For example, children sometimes play with word patterns as if they were practicing a grammatical drill: Hit it / Sit it / Slit it / Mit it (Schwarts 1981). School age children have an underground oral tradition of rhymes, jokes, and incantations that they have passed on to each other for generations.

Convergent thinking: using information to find one right answer.

Divergent thinking: thinking in different directions.

Make-believe play helps children develop divergent thinking.
© Jane Duffy

The idea that play and language are interrelated is not surprising since both serve several joint functions in the young child's life: (1) both involve a communicative function, and (2) children use both play and language to experiment and learn about themselves and others (Barnett 1990). Whereas play clearly comes before language in the growth of a child, play is, in a sense, a form of language because it incorporates symbolic as well as social interaction.

Piaget (1926), a famous child psychologist, discovered that playing out a story forces a child to become actively involved in an experience. In order to physically recreate the events of a story, the child must create a mental representation of events and then engage in social interaction to coordinate the playing. A number of studies (Lowe and Costello 1976) support this, demonstrating a relationship between symbolic play and language during the early states of language acquisition in children with and without language impairments.

From a great number of investigations, it is clear that mental abilities increase rapidly from birth through adolescence but not at the same rate. That is, the fluid measures of mental ability, such as perceptual speed, conceptualizing the relationship of objects in space, psychomotor speed and coordination, develop more rapidly. These abilities depend most heavily on flexibility, adaptability, and speed of information processing. On the other hand, the crystallized measures of mental ability (word fluency, general information, and verbal comprehension) develop more slowly. These are influenced more by experience and acquired knowledge. Thus, the average young person's score on perceptual speed reaches 80 percent of her or his ultimate peak score by about age twelve, while the 80 percent level for verbal comprehension is not reached until age eighteen and for word fluency later than age twenty (Conger and Petersen 1984).

While general intelligence measures seem to indicate a leveling off during young adulthood, with a slight decline in middle age and a more rapid decline in old age (Baltes, Reese, and Lipsitt 1980), some mental abilities improve well into the middle years. For example, intelligence test scores for vocabulary and information comprehension continue to improve in the mid-thirties. Recent longitudinal research suggests that more intellectual abilities than previously thought are retained into the sixties and beyond, particularly when experience, knowledge, and judgment are required (Botwinick 1977). However, older adults do less well on tasks that depend on speed and memory.

The relationship of leisure to the intellectual development of middle aged and older adults can be demonstrated in several ways. For example, keeping mentally sharp can be aided by intellectually challenging pastimes, such as board and card games, book clubs, attending lectures, and learning new hobbies. **Creativity** is also an excellent demonstration of leisure and intellectual development in older age. Creativity is playful thinking; it is an uninhibited associative freedom of thinking that can result in unique approaches to new situations. According to several studies, creativity can improve across the life span (Lorenzen 1989). To illustrate, the research conducted by Dawson and Baller (1972) used an experimental group of thirty-five people who were sixty-five years old and older who took an oil painting class for several weeks. The researchers compared this group with a control group of university students who took a similar course. At the end of the course, the two most highly rated paintings were painted by members of the older group. The older group significantly exceeded the student control group on measures of satisfaction derived from the art class and showed greater continued interest in art as well.

Creativity: the ability to be imaginative. To make something new rather than to imitate.

An even more interesting study on creativity and leisure in adults was conducted by Rothschadl (1993). This study focused on everyday creativity (rather than that of artists and musicians). A variety of questionnaire and interview results from older women respondents indicated an important link: creativity can itself be considered leisure. For example, from one of the interviews:

> I dance with the music and even if I don't get up
> and dance, I'm dancing in my mind because I just love
> dancing so much and the movement of the music is so
> spontaneous, it just comes out and that's what I always
> think of creativity as being.
>
> "Theresa," age 75 (Rothschadl 1993, 89)

In this study, the kinds of leisure activities considered creative varied widely, but the majority included literary and mental activities (reading, studying, attending classes), social activities (visiting friends, talking on the phone), gardening, and handwork. This link between creativity and leisure may be what Bill in the opening scene of this section found in his job. He discovered how to put playful thinking, or creativity, back into his occupation.

biography

Jean Piaget

Jean Piaget (1896-1980), a Swiss psychologist, won fame for his studies on the thought processes of children. Born in Neuchâtel in 1896, Piaget had already published a scientific article by the age of eleven about the albino sparrow. By age fifteen he had published articles on mollusks (Ginsburg and Opper 1969). One of these papers resulted in an offer to the post of curator of the mollusk collection at the Geneva Natural History Museum. Piaget declined the position in order to complete his high school studies.

As a teenager, Piaget spent one summer vacation with his godfather, Samuel Cornut, a Swiss scholar, who was to have considerable influence on him. Cornut felt that his godson's horizons were too restricted in the natural sciences and decided to introduce the youngster to philosophy. Piaget's readings were broadened, and this eventually led to a special interest in epistemology (Ginsburg and Opper 1969). Epistemology is the branch of philosophy concerned with the study of knowledge, and that summer's holiday had a life-altering effect on Piaget.

In 1921, Piaget began to do research in child psychology which soon became focused on the intellectual development of children. This was his area of study for the rest of his life (including constant study of his own three children). By the time of his death in 1980, he and his associates had published more than thirty books on the subject.

Piaget's goal was to define children's gradual attainment of increasingly effective intellectual abilities. His

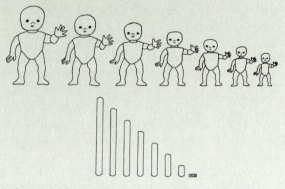

In Piaget's dolls and sticks experiment, children were asked which stick went with which doll. Their success determined where they were in the preoperational stage of cognitive development.

Christopher B. Stage

work led him to conclude that children pass through four stages of mental development. First, during the sensorimotor stage from birth to two years, they obtain a basic knowledge of objects through their senses. How does this happen according to Piaget? By four or five months, infants generally reach out, grasp, and hold objects. These simple skills, together with their developing perceptual skills, equip them for more varied play with objects. This

Leisure and Social Development

Marguerite

Dear Nan,

Sorry I haven't written sooner, but as these things go, my usual quiet days got busy all at once. The kids came home for a visit and brought the grandchildren too. They live so far away now, and I rarely get to see them. Still, the stress of having so many of them here, cooking and all, has exhausted me. And all those dirty towels! I've had to call my friend Peggy in to help me clean up the house.

Speaking of Peggy, we're planning a wonderful trip for this winter. We're going to go to Costa Rica and join an ecology study tour. This will mean we spend a lot of time in rain forests. Our friends here think we're nuts to do such a thing. They call it crazy; we call it living! I promised myself when I retired that I would make time for all those

kind of play, in turn, lays the groundwork for developing complex thinking and language.

Piaget explained it this way. Following the simple explorations of objects, by nine months, most infants explore objects more actively. They wave them around, turn them over, and test them by hitting them against something nearby. By about twelve months, they stop first and examine objects closely before putting them in their mouths. By fifteen to eighteen months, they try to use objects as they were intended. For example, they make a doll sit up, feed it with a spoon, or put it in the driver's seat of a toy truck. The play becomes still more realistic by twenty-four months. Toddlers take dolls out for walks and line up toy trucks and cars in the right direction. These accomplishments in what Piaget termed object play are important to children's cognitive development. Their play with objects demonstrates a memory for repeated events, an ability to match actions with objects, and the development of an understanding of the social world through pretending.

Next, children enter the preoperational stage. Children from about age two to seven years of age develop such skills as language and imagination. The purpose of these skills is to help the child build some facsimile of the outside world within him- or herself. The child develops the ability to see our action at one point in time, store that information in memory without performing the act, and at a later time imitate the act.

Later, from about seven to eleven years of age, children begin to think logically. Essentially, this concrete operational stage is when children begin to use symbols. In experiments with young children, Elder and Pederson (1978) found that the youngest children (two and a half years old) needed props similar to the real object for their pretending games. However, the three and a half year olds could pretend that a hairbrush was a pitcher and even pretend to use a pitcher with no props at all.

Finally, in Piaget's fourth stage of formal operations, which lasts from about eleven to fifteen years of age, children begin to reason realistically about the future and to deal with abstractions and possibilities. In other words, older children are more likely to be able to approach a problem by trying to imagine all the possible relationships. Their thought is richer, broader, and more flexible.

Piaget's work on the sensorimotor and concrete operations stages of cognitive development have had substantial verification through the research of others. There is considerable more question, however, about the universal and age-specific nature of the fourth stage—formal operations. For example, investigators have found some aspects of formal thinking in highly intelligent younger children, and some adolescents and even adults never acquire true formal operational thought because of either limited ability or cultural differences (Conger and Petersen 1984).

things I couldn't do when I worked. And as you know at the top of my list is traveling. Aren't I lucky to have a long time friend like Peggy who's free to go with me?!

And I see Maude Jones from time to time too. She's a little dumpy now, has lost a bit of her shape, but it doesn't seem to stop her from finding romance. You won't believe this Nan, but she's dating. Some widower named Jack. That's all I can remember about him, except that he takes her out to dinner alot.

I've recently made some new friends at the center. Although I never thought I'd be the type to be a regular at that senior center down on 3rd avenue, I did start going for the creative writing classes. Now I'm also taking the poetry class. I'm going to be reading one of my new poems to the group on Friday.

As you can tell, I'm enjoying myself somewhat these days. Sometimes I think I ought to feel guilty about it, but if one is not to please oneself in old age, when is one to please oneself?!

Well, I'll close for now and promise to write more often. I hope all is well with you.

Love,

Your sister Marguerite

Human infants are born into an environment rich with social expectations, norms, and traditions. A social heritage with standards of behavior awaits them. An infant, however, has no awareness of this. Infants have no sense of themselves as individuals or of their relationship with their environment. They cannot recognize themselves in a mirror, have not developed a sense of trust, and have no knowledge of the expectations for them by those who care for them.

A dramatic series of changes takes place during the first two years of human life. Children become aware of their environment and the ways they can act upon it. They become aware of family relationships, themselves as a girl or a boy, responses to others, and what is good behavior and bad behavior. Play, of course, is a prime teacher in a child's social development.

The importance of the peer group in teaching social skills has been documented. This sort of research is difficult to conduct using human babies, but several interesting studies using animals highlight this point. Harlow (1969) learned that even brief daily play sessions between infant monkeys raised with surrogate mothers fully compensated for their lack of real mothering. Another study by a team of biologists and psychologists (Rosenzweig and Bennett 1976) found that rats that spent four to ten weeks in an enriched play environment with frequent changes in playthings differed markedly from the rats in impoverished environments without playthings. They were considerably better adjusted at maturity.

Early studies of **peer** relations in human children have charted the development of six different levels of social interaction (Craig 1983):

1. Unoccupied play. Unfocused play,

2. Solitary play. Child plays alone,

Peer: one who is of equal standing with another, usually based on age, status, and grade.

This group of older adults enjoys white-water rafting in Costa Rica.

© Ruth V. Russell

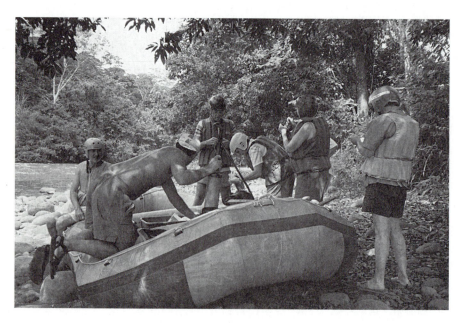

3. Onlooker play. Child's interaction is limited to just observing other children,

4. Parallel play. Children play alongside each other but do not interact with each other,

5. Associative or interactive play. Some interaction in play,

6. Cooperative play.

These levels predominate at certain age levels.

Two-year-olds engage heavily in onlooker and parallel play. At a day care center you can observe that younger children especially watch older children's play and tend to play by themselves, even when around other children. The four- and five-year-olds show increasing amounts of associative play and cooperative play. They are able to play little games that loosely require others, and their play changes in reaction to others. Finally, six- and seven-year-olds can interact for relatively longer periods of time while fully sharing materials and helping one another. According to some scholars (Barnett 1990), if youngsters are not given opportunities to experience interactive and cooperative play, adult social maladjustment or a sense of exclusion from their social group may result. The play group is an important context for learning such social skills as empathy, role-taking, self-control, and sharing.

As children grow older, their play begins to involve ritual. They make decisions about taking turns, set boundaries, and stipulate rules about what is and what is not permitted. Have you ever watched children in your neighborhood play hide and seek, tag, or red rover? It is fascinating to listen to them negotiate the ritual of the game. Such play helps them learn about winning and losing, about fitting their behavior into certain patterns of rules, and about how their actions affect others.

Learning social roles is another developmental task that relies on the benefits of play. Dramatic play is one of the major types of play that involves taking roles. For example, playing house helps children practice family roles, and pretending to be an astronaut teaches children about adult work roles. Such play involves not only imitation of patterns of behavior but also novel ways of interaction. Dramatic play—imitating, pretending, and role playing— gives children the opportunity to project themselves into other personalities and see themselves in a broader range of adult roles.

One adult social domain taught by early play experiences that is interesting to explore further is **sex role.** This is our most fundamental self-concept. Child psychologists suggest that much of the basis for an individual's sex role identity is acquired by age three and is primarily a result of the different ways parents treat male and female babies (Craig 1983). For older children parents, teachers, peers, and even television and book characters reinforce sexual stereotypes.

Sex role: societal ideas of what is appropriate masculine or feminine behavior.

Ideas about what is appropriate masculine and feminine behavior pervade nearly every culture, and children are put under strong social pressure to conform to these sex role expectations. Let's see how this pressure is expressed in leisure. Mothers and fathers play with male and female infants quite differently. Fathers' play tends to be physical and arousing rather than intellectual as in the case of mothers' play. Parents allow boys more freedom to display aggressive behavior and to engage in more vigorous activities with toys (Barnett and Kane 1985). Boys receive more gross motor stimulation from parents, while girls receive more verbal stimulation. A mother is more likely to pick up a daughter than a son, an action that restricts range and exploration possibilities (Bammel and Bammel 1992). Both mothers and fathers tend to disapprove when sons play with dolls.

The difference between older boy and girl game preferences has been considerably reduced during the past forty years: girls of today are more like boys in their game choices than was the case in the early 1920s (Sutton-Smith and Rosenberg 1971). Girls in about the fourth, fifth, and sixth grades now tend to prefer more "masculine" games. Boys, in turn, have decreased their preferences for those games that have been somewhat adopted by girls, ultimately reducing their total play options.

Play for girls in middle and late childhood occurs more often in small groups, in private places, and mimics adult social relationships. It is also more spontaneous, freer of rules, and more cooperative than boys' play. In contrast, boys at this stage experience more controlled competitive games. These differences in play reinforce sex role identities and help ensure that children will grow up behaving in ways appropriate to their sex.

In our culture, adolescence has traditionally been viewed as a difficult period in the lives of children and their parents. Changes in social development are prime contributors to this challenge. If an adolescent is to become truly adult and not just physically mature, he or she must fit into a social world: achieve independence from parents, establish workable and enjoyable relationships with peers, and decide on and prepare for a meaningful vocation.

Autonomy: emotional, social, and physical independence from others. The ability to self-govern.

The development of **autonomy** is central to any exploration of the social tasks of adolescence, not only because autonomy itself is important but because it is related to the accomplishment of the other tasks necessary for functioning in a social world. The teen must become adjusted to the demands and the privileges of independence. What is expected in every culture is that the adolescent should achieve an appropriate balance of independence from parents, teachers, and other adults. An important context for developing autonomy is in peer group friendships and social leisure experiences.

Most teens are attached to a social group which has considerable power to shape pastime interests and behaviors. During middle childhood and preadolescence, the child's peer relationships tend to center around neighborhood play groups and same-sex groups. Largely informal at first, these children's groups become more highly structured with increasing age. Aspects of formal organization, such as special membership requirements and elaborate rituals appear. Throughout these middle childhood years boys tend to be more involved with groups than girls. Girls tend to have more intimate, individual relationships than boys, a precursor, perhaps, of later lifelong friendship patterns of men and women.

For American teens, the traditional vehicle for fostering relationships has been the social institution of dating. Under favorable conditions, dating presumably serves a number of useful functions: developing social and interpersonal skills in relations with peers, providing an opportunity to meet peers, and enabling occasions for sexual discovery (Conger and Petersen 1984). To some extent, these goals may be realized. In contrast, European youth, who do not date at such young ages nor as seriously, do not exhibit the same degree of poise and nonchalance as American teens (Conger and Petersen 1984).

Dating conditions are not always favorable, however, as teens are often aware. Dating may also promote a lack of genuineness, dishonesty, and at times competitiveness. "While we usually think of the dating system as helpful preparation for later, deeper relationships, the personal qualities that the system actually rewards (with popularity) are not always the ones that will make for a good marriage, or good parenting, or meaningful relationships in adulthood" (Craig 1983, 356).

Nonetheless, such "romantic" leisure is an important context for testing sexuality and for establishing ways of lovingly relating to others. In fact sexuality is a preoccupation in the development of selfhood for many adolescents, and sexual activity itself can be a major pastime. Parties, movies, dances, concerts, driving, and just being with someone else provide the settings for adolescent sexuality.

Teens often develop same sex physical attachments. Crushes, sexual play, and even exhibitionistic "contests" with persons of the same sex are common for younger adolescents. Both boys and girls form very deep relationships with best friends in the younger teen years. For some, that special

Most teens are attached to a social group which has considerable power to shape their pastime interests and behavior.

© Ruth V. Russell

friendship takes the form of extended communication and helps develop peer trust. These teens then move from the same sex romantic relationship to the beginnings of opposite sex relationships. Others develop their sexuality through homosexual relationships, and this becomes their normative social pattern. Researchers are not yet able to explain the causes of sexual orientation, and there are still questions about leisure's role in homosexuality and heterosexuality. The importance of games and play for children and of sport and social recreation for teens, suggests that the factors relevant to the development of sexual orientation should be researched and understood more fully.

While romance and sexuality are emerging dimensions of teenage social relationships, they are by no means the only ones. Friendships are also important and often take on an increasingly crucial role in development. As individuals become independent of their families, they depend more on friendships to provide emotional support and to serve as testing grounds for new values (Douvan and Adelson 1966). With close friends, teens are able to accept their identity because of the feelings of acceptance and being liked by others. Between the ages of twelve and sixteen particularly girls demand greater loyalty, conformity, and intimacy from their friends. Adolescents also tend to become more aware of peer groups and are concerned about whether or not their group is "in." For at-risk youth, the negative factors of substance abuse, gangs, and pregnancy have an impact on their ability to define their personal identity as well.

At the point of leaving school, young adults are propelled into more adult roles related to the social institutions of family, the economy, and the community. For many, these can be exciting times of exploring new possibilities for life, filling out new aspects of social identities, and looking for possible futures. More and more, young adults are taking full-time work roles while still single. For them, leisure is predominantly social and commercial, taking place in bars, clubs, restaurants, resorts, and apartment complexes. Leisure serves largely as a means for meeting others. On the other hand, over 90 percent of the population gets married at some point (Kelly 1982), and the impact of this transition on leisure depends on whether residence, employment, and family size change as well. Nonetheless, the likelihood that leisure activities will be done together increases, and some formerly separately experienced activities may decrease as leisure becomes an important context for building a relationship.

When there are two incomes, leisure activities may still include more expensive forms, such as eating out, shopping, and weekend trips. The time and the money spent for leisure tend to be restricted by the births of children for families in all income levels. The first change in leisure that new parents realize is the loss of freedom. Parents of young children cannot engage in spur-of-the-moment pastimes outside the home, and at-home pastimes become more interrupted and crowded. Leisure activities and the amount of leisure time are more restricted until children can live more independently.

At this life stage, leisure activities also usually take place in or near home and with the family. While there is the old adage that the "family that plays together stays together," research suggests that this may not necessarily be so. As an example, a study by Freysinger (1994) found that leisure experienced between children and their parents was satisfying only for the fathers. This may be because leisure with children is one of the few ways that fathers interact with their children; hence, it may be more valued by them. For the mothers, on the other hand, experiencing leisure with the children may be perceived as just another duty of daily care giving.

As the children grow older and become more involved in their own lives and relationships, parents' energies are often adjusted to refocus on their own career development. Thus, the dual focus on the children and their activities (making particular demands on transportation) and the job and efforts for career advancement, yields even greater restrictions on the parents' leisure. Research by Kelly (1982) on North American parents at this life stage concluded that unconditional leisure, or leisure for its own sake, is less significant in overall priorities than at other life periods.

As children leave the family and assume more fully their own lives, both the children and their parents grow more independent, although this varies according to ethnic group differences. Three different leisure patterns seem to be the main options for the "empty nest" couple. Some use their new freedom to turn back to the marriage for leisure partnership and satisfaction. Others turn outward and seek new and separate social groups and activities. Finally, some pour themselves into a greater work engagement by launching new careers or increasing civic responsibilities, thus continuing the restrictions on their leisure expression.

The postparental period prior to retirement is lengthy and potentially disruptive to social relationships. If the marriage or significant relationship remains intact, the importance of companionship in the leisure of the couple is critical. In fact, a failure in this is a major factor in divorce at this life stage (Kelly 1982). Leisure may also become more important as some of the pursuits laid aside during parenting are taken up again. This is also a renaissance time for middle aged adults who have not reared children, as their careers tend to stabilize and become financially rewarding. Now life brings an opportunity to think about oneself and develop more personally satisfying life patterns.

As people grow into old age, the nature of their social roles and relationships changes again. The way older people interact in their social worlds of family, friends, and neighbors is affected by physiological, situational, and even economic changes. For example, with children long gone from the home, without the daily contacts with co-workers, or because of the death of a partner or spouse, older retired people lose a critically important context for social involvement. As Marguerite wrote in her letter to her sister in the opening of this section, leisure often becomes a major social area in which former relationships are renewed and new friends made.

This is very important, because older adults who are part of well-defined friendship groups tend to have more positive self-concepts and higher morale than those not part of such groups (Blau 1981). Friends, in other words, are

The "empty nest" couple sometimes seeks new social groups and activities.
© Ruth V. Russell

more important than family in enhancing life satisfaction in old age. There are three explanations for this: (1) people have more in common with their peers, (2) friendship is more rewarding because it is not obligatory, and (3) friendship involves older adults in the larger society more than family relationships do (Adams 1986).

As is typical throughout the life span, the type of social interaction with friends varies by gender in old age. Women in general have more intimate, diverse, and intensive friendships than men, who tend to have more casual acquaintances (Matthews 1986). For many men, their wives are their only confidants, a circumstance that may make widowhood devastating for them. In contrast, women tend to satisfy their needs for intimacy throughout their lives by establishing close friendships with other women and, therefore, are less dependent emotionally on the marital relationship.

Both men and women tend to select friends from among people they consider their social peers—those who are similar in age, sex, marital status, sexual orientation, and socioeconomic class. The type of living environment also affects the nature of social relationships. Age segregated environments, such as retirement communities where organized leisure activities and facilities are frequently provided, offer a ready opportunity for friendships.

Finally, what about the leisure pursuits themselves? Disagreement regarding the value of leisure activities for older adults is reflected in the gerontological literature. The argument is not over whether leisure is an important life force in old age but over the nature and extent of leisure's role. For example, can leisure in retirement replace the work role? Several research studies maintain that leisure provides a personally meaningful alternative to the job, especially when the retired person has good health and an adequate income, and when the leisure activities build upon preretirement skills and interests. Going further, some researchers have suggested that leisure is central in maintaining a positive life experience (Russell 1987).

Although there are wide variations, leisure activity patterns among older persons have been identified. For example, most leisure time is not spent in public recreation programs developed specially for the elderly. The proportion of persons engaged in community organizations, sports, exercise, and outdoor recreation declines consistently by age, with the activities of those of age seventy-five and older becoming more sedentary and home-based. There are some gender differences, however. Older men are more likely to participate in outdoor activities, such as fishing, sports, and community organizations, while women tend to pursue handiwork and crafts, socialize, attend cultural events, and read (Hooyman and Kiyak 1993).

Overall, compared to younger people, older people are more likely to engage in solitary and sedentary pastimes, such as watching television, visiting with family and friends, and reading. However, it is important to recognize that compared to only a decade ago, older people today are choosing activities far more like those of people twenty years younger than themselves. After all, as the closing line of Marguerite's letter—an adaptation of a line in a novel by

Vita Sackville-West (*All Passion Spent*) and originally spoken by the eighty-eight-year-old character Lady Slane—reminds:

If one is not to please oneself in old age, when
is one to please oneself? There is so little time left!

(Sackville-West 1984, 67)

Summary: The Themes of Leisure Through the Life Span

The cycle of life contains both certainty and uncertainty. Leisure's role in human development from birth to death is also both expected and surprising. This chapter was about leisure's continuities and changes throughout life in four areas of development: physical, emotional, intellectual, and social.

The role of leisure in physical development continues across the life span, but the nature of its role changes. For infants and children, play is the main source for developing motor skills. In the middle years, leisure helps sustain physical health, and in older adulthood, leisure reduces the decline of physical capabilities. Leisure in intellectual development plays a similar role. For children, leisure is the tool for learning. It helps teach problem solving, thinking, language, and other cognitive skills. For adults, leisure's importance is in maintaining previously acquired mental abilities, as well as more fully developing others. For example, leisure and creativity are linked.

Next, while leisure itself is often considered an emotional state, it also has a role in the development of emotions and emotional health. For children, play is important in learning coping strategies for managing emotions. Later, leisure becomes the setting for the adolescent transition into emotional maturity. In adulthood and old age, leisure is a prime medium for life evaluations and alterations. Finally, leisure is important for social development. Through leisure, children are able to acquire appropriate skills for social interaction, cultural ritual, personal autonomy, and sex roles. When people grow into older adulthood, leisure is often the sole connection to the social world.

Leisure is one of the most important aids for growing, maturing, and achieving old age. Leisure is part of our entire life. While the nature of its role may change from helping us learn how to enter and function in life to helping us find graciousness in leaving it, it is constantly with us.

References

Adams, R. G. 1986. A look at friendship and aging. *Generations* 10:40–43.

Anderson, L., S. J. Schleien, and L. McAvoy. October 1992. Integration through adventure: Preliminary results of a three year longitudinal study. Paper presented at the Leisure Research Symposium, National Recreation and Park Association, Cincinnati, OH.

Anthony, K. H. 1985. The shopping mall: A teenager hangout. *Adolescence* 20:307.

Austin, D. R. 1986. Recreation and persons with physical disabilities. *A Literature Review: The President's Commission on Americans Outdoors.* Washington, DC: Government Printing Office.

Baltes, P. B., H. W. Reese, and L. P. Lipsitt. 1980. Life-span developmental psychology. *Annual Review of Psychology* 31:65–110.

Bammel, G., and L. L. B. Bammel. 1992. *Leisure and human behavior.* Dubuque, IA: Wm. C. Brown Publishers.

Barnett, L. A. 1984. Young children's resolution of distress through play. *Journal of Child Psychology and Psychiatry* 25, no. 3:477–83.

Barnett, L. A. 1990. Developmental benefits of play for children. *Journal of Leisure Research* 22, no. 2:138–53.

Barnett, L. A., and M. J. Kane. 1985. Environmental constraints on children's play. In *Constraints on leisure,* edited by M. G. Wade. Springfield, IL: Charles C Thomas.

Blau, Z. S. 1981. *Aging in a changing society.* New York: Franklin Watts.

Bolig, R. 1980. The relationship of personality factors to responses to hospitalization in young children admitted for medical procedures. Columbus: The Ohio State University.

Botwinick, J. 1977. Intellectual abilities. In *Handbook of the psychology of aging,* edited by J. Birren and K. W. Schaie. New York: Van Nostrand.

Bruya, L. D. 1988. *Play spaces for children: A new beginning.* Reston, VA: American Alliance for Health, Physical Education, Recreation, and Dance.

Caspersen, C. I. 1989. Physical activity epidemiology: Concepts, methods, and applications to exercise science. In *Exercise sports sciences reviews, vol. 16,* edited by K. B. Pandolf.

Conger, J. J., and A. C. Petersen. 1984. *Adolescence and youth: Psychological development in a changing world.* New York: Harper & Row.

Craig, G. J. 1983. *Human development.* Englewood Cliffs, NJ: Prentice-Hall.

Dawson, A. M., and W. R. Baller. 1972. Relationship between creative activity and the health of elderly persons. *Journal of Psychology* 82:49–58.

Douvan, E., and J. B. Adelson. 1966. *The adolescent experience.* New York: Wiley.

Elder, J. L., and D. R. Pederson. 1978. Preschool children's use of objects in symbolic play. *Child Development* 49:500–504.

Evans, N. 1993. Leisure and human development. Unpublished paper, Indiana University.

Flinchum, B. 1988. Early childhood movement programs: Preparing teachers for tomorrow. *Journal of Physical Education, Recreation, and Dance* 59, no. 7:64.

Freud, S. 1955. Beyond the pleasure principle. In *The standard edition of the complete psychological works of Sigmund Freud, vol. XVIII,* edited by J. Strachey. London: Hogarth.

Freysinger, V. J. 1994. Leisure with children and parental satisfaction: Further evidence of a sex difference in the experience of adult roles and leisure. *Journal of Leisure Research* 26, no. 3:212–26.

Ginsburg, H., and S. Opper. 1969. *Piaget's theory of intellectual development: An introduction.* Englewood Cliffs, NJ: Prentice-Hall.

Gordon, I. J. 1962. *Human development: From birth through adolescence.* New York: Harper & Row.

Harlow, H. F. 1969. Age-mate or peer affectional systems. In *Advances in the study of behavior, vol. 2,* edited by D. S. Lehrman, R. A. Hinde, and E. Shaw. New York: Academic Press.

Hartman, L., and P. J. Walker. 1989. Outdoor recreation participation by disabled people. *Outdoor Recreation Benchmark 1988: Proceedings of the National Outdoor Recreation Forum.* USDA Forest Service, Southeastern Forest Experiment Station.

Hendrick, B. N. 1985. The effect of wheelchair tennis participation and mainstreaming upon the perceptions of competence of physically disabled adolescents. *Therapeutic Recreation Journal* 19, no. 2:34–46.

Hooyman, N. R., and H. A. Kiyak. 1993. *Social gerontology: A multidisciplinary perspective.* Boston: Allyn and Bacon.

Iso-Ahola, S. E., E. Jackson, and E. Dunn. 1994. Starting, ceasing, and replacing leisure activities over the life-span. *Journal of Leisure Research* 26, no. 3:227–49.

Jersild, A. T., and F. B. Holmes. 1935. *Children's fears.* Child Development Monograph No. 20. New York: Teachers College Press.

Kelly, J. R. 1982. *Leisure.* Englewood Cliffs, NJ: Prentice-Hall.

Kleiber, D. A., and W. H. Richards. 1985. Leisure and recreation in adolescence: Limitations and potential. In *Constraints on leisure,* edited by M. G. Wade. Springfield, IL: Charles C Thomas.

Kowinski, W. S. 1989. Kids in the mall: Growing up controlled. In *Life studies: A thematic reader,* edited by D. Cavitch. New York: St. Martin's Press.

Lewis, G. H. 1989. Rats and bunnies: Core kids in an American Mall. *Adolescence* 24:881–89.

Lorenzen, L. 1989. Self-perceived creativity in the later years: Case studies of older Nebraskans. Unpublished doctoral dissertation, University of Nebraska.

Lowe, M., and A. Costello. 1976. *Manual for the symbolic play test; experimental edition.* London: NFER.

Matthews, S. H. 1986. *Friendships through the life course.* Beverly Hills, CA: Sage Publications.

McGinnis, J. M. 1987. The national children and youth fitness study II: Introduction. *Journal of Physical Education, Recreation and Dance* 58, no. 9:50.

Meyer, J. 1993. Leisure and human development. Unpublished paper, Indiana University.

Oppenheim, J. F. 1987. *Kids and play.* New York: Ballantine Books.

Ostrow, A. 1980. Physical activity as it relates to the health of the aged. In *Transitions of Aging,* edited by N. Datan and N. Lohmann. New York: Academic Press.

Paffenbarger, R. S., R. T. Hyde, and A. Dow. 1991. Health benefits of physical activity. In *Benefits of leisure,* edited by B. L. Driver, P. J. Brown, and G. L. Peterson. State College, PA: Venture.

Paffenbarger, R. S., R. T. Hyde, A. L. Wing, and C. Hsieh. 1986. Physical activity, all-cause mortality, and longevity of college alumni. *New England Journal of Medicine* 314:605–13.

Patterson, R. H. 1992. Interactive video games raise questions. *The Herald-Times,* 20 October. Bloomington, IN.

Piaget, J. 1926. *The language and thought of the child.* New York: Harcourt Brace.

Ragheb, M. G., and J. McKinney. October 1992. Campus recreation and perceived academic stress. Paper presented at the Leisure Research Symposium, National Recreation and Park Association, Cincinnati, OH.

Rapoport, R., and R. N. Rapoport. 1975. *Leisure and the family life cycle.* London: Routledge & Kegan Paul.

Rosenzweig, M. L., and E. L. Bennett. 1976. Enriched environments: Facts, factors, and fantasies. In *Knowing, thinking, and believing,* edited by L. Petrinovich and J. L. McGaugh. New York: Plenum Press.

Ross, J. G., and R. R. Pate. 1987. The national children and youth fitness study II: A summary of findings. *Journal of Physical Education, Recreation and Dance* (December):51–56.

Rothe, T., C. Kohl, and H. J. Mansfeld. 1990. Controlled study of the effect of sports training on cardiopulmonary functions in asthmatic children and adolescents. *Pneumologie* 44:1110–114.

Rothschadl, A. M. 1993. The meaning and nature of creativity in the everyday lives of older women. Unpublished doctoral dissertation, Indiana University.

Russell, R. V. 1987. The importance of recreation satisfaction and activity participation to the life satisfaction of age-segregated retirees. *Journal of Leisure Research* 19:273–83.

Sackville-West, Vita. 1984. *All passion spent.* Garden City, NY: Dial Press.

Schwarts, J. I. 1981. Children's experiments with language. *Young Children* 36:16–26.

Seals, D. R., and J. M. Hagberg. 1984. The effect of exercise training on human hypertension: A review. *Medicine and Science in Sports and Exercise* 16:207–15.

Sheehy, G. 1974. *Passages; Predictable crises of adult life.* New York: E. P Dutton.

Smith, E. L., and D. M. Raab. 1985. Osteoporosis and physical activity. *Acta Medica Scandinavica Supplement* 711:149–56.

Sutton-Smith, B., and B. G. Rosenberg. 1971. Sixty years of historical change in the game preferences of American children. In *Child's play,* edited by R. E. Herron and B. Sutton-Smith. New York: Wiley.

Sylva, K., J. S. Bruner, and P. Genova. 1976. The role of play in the problem-solving of children 3–5 years old. In *Play: Its role in development and evolution,* edited by J. S. Bruner, A. Jolly, and K. Sylva. New York: Basic Books.

Symmonds, P. 1946. *The dynamics of human adjustment.* New York: D. Appleton-Century.

Taylor, C. B., J. F. Sallis, and R. Needle. 1985. The relation of physical activity and exercise to mental health. *Public Health Reports* 100:195–202.

Tipton, C. M., A. C. Vailas, and R. D. Matthes. 1986. Experimental studies on the influences of physical activity on ligaments, tendons and joints: A brief review. *Acta Medica Scandinavica Supplement* 711:157–68.

Vandenberg, B. 1980. Play: A causal agent in problem solving? Paper presented at the meeting of the American Psychological Association. Montreal, Quebec.

Leisure is not only significant to us
personally, but it is also a vital
shaper of us culturally. How we
express ourselves through our
pastimes helps define who we are
as a community, nation, and
society. Our pastimes also are
shaped by who we are collectively.
It is this cultural interrelationship
with leisure that we explore in
chapters 5 through 8. Chapter 5
sets the tone by discussing
leisure's uniqueness according to a
culture's level of technological
development. Chapter 6 explores
popular culture—the typical
pastimes of a majority of people in
a social group. In chapter 7, the
darker side of leisure's cultural
expression is discussed, labeled
taboo recreation because of laws,
customs, or beliefs that make
some pastimes forbidden. Finally,
chapter 8 demonstrates how our
cultural lives are a mixture of
leisure, time, and work.

Leisure as a cultural mirror—societal context

leisure

"Leisure helps to shape who we are as a culture."

"Leisure is both a victim and a tool of modernization."

leisure's anthropology

Digital Stock

What is leisure's cultural significance?

Leisure is so much a part of the patterns of life that it can describe how cultures are both similar and different.

Did the earliest human cultures have leisure?

Contrary to the standard view, new data suggest that prehistoric people had abundant free time and spent it relaxing.

How is leisure unique in technologically advanced cultures?

In highly developed cultures, leisure tends to be more commercial.

How is leisure unique in developing cultures?

Leisure can be used as a tool for development. As such, leisure is also typically changed by development.

In Finland, there is a wide variation in the

amount of daylight and darkness during the year. The day is shortest during the winter and longest during the summer. In midsummer, there are twenty-four hours of daylight, whereas in the middle of winter there are days with no daylight. Tuija Sievanen wrote, "In the countryside, where I am used to go at Christmas time, I developed some kind of a tradition to make moonlight walks in the late afternoon. The full moon above the white snow landscape is enough to give light to find the way through the woods and fields" (1987, 23).

*****

Before the massive urbanization of black South Africans into white South African areas, which began in the 1930s, few parents of black children had money to buy toys. The result was all sorts of play inventions. The girls played with dolls made from rags and beads. The boys, sometimes eagerly assisted by their fathers and elder brothers, made elaborate wire cars, complete with wheels that could turn and a functioning steering system (Grobler 1985). With urbanization and increased foreign influences, cheap plastic toys became available, which brought an end to this fascinating ingenuity.

*****

In Iran, there is a game called *Borkum Topa*. Several old hats are needed for the game. To begin, a circle is drawn three feet in diameter on the ground. The player who is "it" puts a hat in the circle and stands on guard with one foot on the rim of the circle. Other players try to knock the hat out of the circle, using their hands and feet. While they try to do this, "it" tries to tag them. The one who is tagged becomes "it" next. When someone succeeds in knocking the hat out of the circle without being tagged, the person who is "it" may run away from the circle and tag anyone at all. That person then becomes "it" (Harbin 1954).

*****

A comparison of the number of paid vacation days and holidays each year specified in union contracts for industrial workers in different countries reveals some interesting distinctions. Workers in the Netherlands, for example, receive the most paid vacation days: forty-one days per year. Italian workers have forty paid holidays each year, and the French enjoy thirty-five. At the other end of the scale, Japanese workers receive twenty-five paid holidays, and American workers receive twenty-three (U.S. Bureau of Labor Statistics 1993).

*****

Cultural anthropology: the branch of anthropology that focuses on the patterns of life of a society.

In this chapter we consider topics that feature leisure from various societies—specifically, leisure from the perspective of **cultural anthropology.** The anthropology of leisure is interesting for several reasons. First, recreative elements from one culture tend to be adopted by other cultures. Particular games, songs, dances, and crafts introduced in one culture spread to others and are often changed in accord with the dominant values of the receiving culture. For example, Heider (1977) described a game of physical skill that was developed in Java (Indonesia) and later introduced in a highland New Guinea tribe. The New Guinea culture valued noncompetitiveness, so when they played the Java game, they disregarded score keeping and rules. This more casual attitude toward the rules of the game were in keeping with their cultural values.

Second, certain forms of leisure act as tools for maintaining the **culture.** For example, traditional games of Native Americans and First Nation Canadians, such as lacrosse, helped ensure the continuity of tribal groups. In rural Peru, the daily market is an important focus of social, as well as economic activity.

Finally, leisure in some cases is a fertile ground for cultural innovation. Inventions, such as the automobile, were developed in the context of being playful. In fact, the wheel itself was first important not for work, but as a toy. For example, excavations of ancient Aztec ruins in Mexico revealed wheeled pottery toys.

In this chapter, a comparison of the leisure expressions of various cultures sheds light on a more general interest of how cultures are both similar and different. We discover that cultural complexity exists in the use of such daily human experiences as free time, rest, and pastimes.

To begin our travels, we consider the earliest cultures: paleolithic peoples. The case is made that these people may have been the original affluent society. Next, we will contemplate examples of leisure in technological cultures, such as Japan, Germany, and the United States, as well as technology's antagonism to leisure. Finally, leisure within developing cultures will be explored. Examples of leisure as a tool for cultural development are presented for the cultures of Poland, Malaysia, and Costa Rica.

Hunches about Paleolithic Cultures

Humans are classified by biologists as belonging to the Primate Order, a group that also includes lemurs, tarsiers, monkeys, and apes. Present evidence suggests that humans evolved from the small, apelike ramapithecines, which lived between 15 and 8 million years ago. By 4 million years ago, this apelike creature became fully adapted for moving about on its hind legs in a distinctive human manner, and by 2.5 million years ago, the appearance of the earliest stone tools, along with the gradual enlarging of the brain, set the stage for the human of the present (Haviland 1990). The early tools (found in Ethiopia) were choppers, scrapers, gouging tools, and hammerstones for cutting meat, scraping hides, and cracking bones to extract marrow. Their invention marks the beginning of the **Paleolithic era,** or Old Stone Age, time of human existence. Scientists estimate that only a few thousand people lived in all of Africa, and a similar number in Asia during this prehistoric period.

For more than 2 million years, people lived by hunting and by gathering plants, for it was only about 10,000 years ago that people learned to farm. Instead, Paleolithic people lived in groups and moved from place to place in search of food. A group usually stayed in one place for only a few days. They ate the animals and plants in the area and then moved on. They built shelters only if they found enough food in an area to last a few weeks or months. No one knows when the first clothing was worn. Early people probably didn't begin to sew primitive clothes until about 17,000 years ago.

In addition to inventing simple tools and clothing, Paleolithic people painted the first pictures. In fact, they developed several forms of artistic expression. They painted on rock, modeled in clay, and engraved antlers, bone, and ivory. Animals were the most common subject of their paintings, but Paleolithic artists also painted people. They used four colors: black from charcoal; white from clay and lime mud; and red and yellow from animal blood, red clay, and ground up iron flakes.

Beyond these art legacies, we don't know much more about the leisure of people of the Paleolithic era. The standard anthropological view of this hunting and gathering society is that because they were constantly on the move in search of food for minimal survival, these people must have lacked the time for leisure.

Is there another plausible guess about leisure in the Paleolithic era? Marshall Sahlins, in an anthropological study, suggested that prehistoric people were the original leisure society (1988, 257). Sahlins based this hypothesis on two recent conjectures. First, Paleolithic people may not have spent as much time hunting and gathering food as formerly assumed. Second, Paleolithic people had comparatively few material goods and thus were free from the labors of protecting and maintaining them. Let's ponder each suggestion in turn.

First, Sahlins cited research about two hunter-gatherer groups living in Australia in the 1960s as examples of what life could have been like for Paleolithic people. The results are surprising. As shown in figure 5.1, the hours per day spent by one of the groups in hunting and gathering activities were not great. The most obvious conclusion Sahlins made from the data was that the people did not have

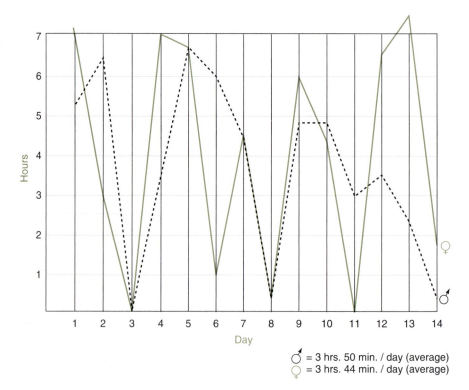

Figure 5.1 The hours per day spent in hunting and gathering activities by one of Sahlin's groups.

♂ = 3 hrs. 50 min. / day (average)
♀ = 3 hrs. 44 min. / day (average)

Part Two   Leisure as a Cultural Mirror—Societal Context

to work hard to survive. The average length of time each person spent per day collecting and preparing food was three to four hours.

Moreover, they did not work continuously. "It would stop for the time being when the people had procured enough for the time being, which left them plenty of time to spare" (Sahlins 1988, 260). What might prehistoric peoples have done with their spare time? As indicated in figure 5.2, much of the time freed from the necessities of food-connected tasks could have been spent in rest and sleep. According to Sahlins, other free time activities may have also included chatting, gossiping, and general sociability.

The idea that Paleolithic people were the original leisure society also has to do with consumerism. In contrast to the many affluent societies of today, with their focus on materialism, early people possessed very little. The customary quota of material goods for Paleolithic people (as it is for today's remaining hunter-gatherer groups, such as the Bushmen of Kalahari) was most likely a few pieces of clothing, portable housing materials, a few ornaments, spare flints, some medicinal quartz, a few tools and weapons, and a skin bag to hold it all. Contrast this with the collection of possessions you have! Further, think about all the time you spend purchasing, repairing, cleaning, putting away, transporting, sorting, finding, protecting, and storing your possessions.

In terms of leisure today, it appears that consumption is a double tragedy. We have to work in order to purchase material goods and work some more to take care of them. As Sahlins pointed out, Paleolithic people were comparatively free from material pressures. In fact, they lived in a kind of material plenty because they adapted the tools of their living to the materials that lay in abundance around them, free for anyone to take, such as wood, reeds, stones, bone, and grass. For them (unlike for us), the accumulation and hoarding of objects was not associated with status. To Sahlins, it is not that Paleolithic people learned how to curb their materialistic impulses; they simply never made an institution of them. Some might think hunter-gatherers poor because they didn't have anything. Another view is to think of them as rich in the freedom of time.

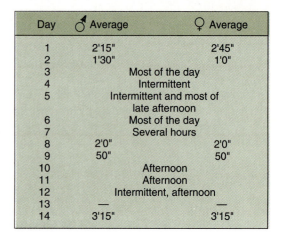

Day	♂ Average	♀ Average
1	2'15"	2'45"
2	1'30"	1'0"
3	Most of the day	
4	Intermittent	
5	Intermittent and most of late afternoon	
6	Most of the day	
7	Several hours	
8	2'0"	2'0"
9	50"	50"
10	Afternoon	
11	Afternoon	
12	Intermittent, afternoon	
13	—	—
14	3'15"	3'15"

Figure 5.2 Amount of daytime devoted to sleep. According to Sahlin's hypothesis, free time activities could have included rest, sleep, chatting, and general sociability.

Leisure in Technological Cultures

In this section, we compare the leisure of three modern societies: the United States, Japan, and Germany. These countries represent what we call the modern cultures of the world: North America, western Europe, Australia, New Zealand, and increasingly the Pacific rim countries. These cultures are modern in the sense that they are industrially, technologically, and commercially advanced.

The point of our discussion is that leisure within the context of modernization is uniquely expressed. For example, leisure behavior in these cultures

tends to be consumption oriented. Because the standard of living is high, people have large amounts of discretionary money with which to buy leisure goods and experiences. Before we consider all this, let's consider the concept of **modernization.** The process of modernization might be described as consisting of four subprocesses: technological development, agricultural development, industrialization, and urbanization (Haviland 1990). These elements of modernization are interrelated and occur simultaneously. First, with modernization, traditional knowledge and techniques are replaced by scientific knowledge and techniques. Likewise, the culture shifts from an emphasis on subsistence farming to commercial farming. Industrialization is the third subprocess; work is now done by machines rather than humans and animals. Finally the population becomes urbanized by moving from rural settlements into cities.

Modernization: involving implementation of recent techniques, methods, or ideas.

If we examine this perspective, we realize that modernization is actually an **ethnocentric** notion. Looking closely at its definition reveals that "becoming modern" really means "becoming like us." Accordingly, there is a clear implication that not being like us is to be antiquated and obsolete. Modernization can also mean undesirable losses of traditional customs.

Ethnocentric: the belief that one's own culture is superior in every way to all others.

United States

Occupying over 3.5 million square miles, the United States is one of the world's larger countries. Its population is slightly more than 251 million, making its density approximately sixty-nine persons per square mile. The predominant languages are English and Spanish. The literacy rate is 96 percent. The gross national product is over $4,862 billion with a per capita annual income average of $19,800. The economic growth rate of the United States is 3.8 percent. Major religious groups are Protestant, Roman Catholic, and Jewish.

While the context of leisure in the United States is peppered throughout this book, we consider this culture here in an anthropological way in order to draw direct comparisons. Because the American constitution guarantees every citizen the right to pursue happiness, the leisure pursuits of the people in the United States have become recognizable worldwide. Today, Americans have the reputation of enjoying a recreation-focused lifestyle. We draw our comparisons specifically from the areas of relaxation, mass media, sports, tourism, outdoor recreation, and volunteerism.

In a guidebook written for first-time visitors to the United States, Americans are described in the following way:

> Most Americans are eager to assure non-Americans that they live in a casual, relaxed manner. This may be far from true, in spite of the American tendency to accept as an article of faith that the good life is the relaxed one. To Americans relaxing symbolizes having a good time (as evident in magazine and television advertisements), but relaxing is exactly what many Americans cannot do very well.
>
> (Wanning 1991, 50)

People from other cultures have generally characterized the leisure habits of people from the United States as demanding. An Indian married to an American said, "We went to see the Grand Canyon and as soon as we got there my wife wanted to go rushing down to the bottom. These Americans never relax." (Wanning 1991, 51). People in the United States have a tendency to believe that useful activities are the most valuable and meaningful. When they do get away from work, their leisure often seems another form of labor. Americans are busy taking night classes, doing needlework, competing on a bowling league, leading scout troops, playing cards, reading newspapers, running church groups, lifting weights, redecorating a room, counting calories and jogged miles, and making holiday decorations. Weekends are full of camping, skiing, home improvement, and gardening.

Another quality highly recognizable in Americans is the importance they place on mass media. This reputation may be a bit unwarranted, because the broad pattern of television viewing time in daily life differs relatively little around the industrialized world. In most developed societies, for example, people who have jobs spend roughly one third of their time pursuing leisure activities (Szalai 1972). Of this one third of waking free time, the activity that absorbs the most time in all modern societies is watching television (Kubey and Csikszentmihalyi 1990).

Nonetheless, as confirmed not only by studies but from casual observation through the windows of home after home where the distorted bluish flickering rectangle of television prevails, it is clear that watching television is the most popular leisure pursuit among Americans. According to the figures of Mediamark Research, Inc. (1992), 92.8 percent of Americans stated they watch television for an average of two hours and fifty-one minutes a day. Listening to the radio came next with 84.7 percent stating they do so daily, followed by reading the newspaper (83.9 percent).

American's attention to television is supported also by United Nations (1985) figures that indicate the United States has the highest ratio of television sets to persons in the world with one television to every 1.68 persons. Great Britain is second with one television per 1.96 persons. To compare, there is one television for every 375.5 persons in India. The United States also has the most hours of transmission and the widest variety of programming. According to Nielsen (1982), at any given moment on any given evening, over one third of the people in the United States are watching television. On weekday evenings in the winter, half the population is sitting in front of the TV. The only activities absorbing more time than TV are sleep and work.

The most popular sport activity in the United States is exercise walking. This is followed in popularity by swimming and bicycle riding (National Sporting Goods Association 1990). As in many parts of the world, golf participation is rapidly increasing. For example, in the U.S. in 1970, 11,245,000 people reported having played at least one round. Twenty years later, this number had more than doubled (National Golf Foundation 1990).

In sports Americans are primarily known for their enthusiasm for spectating. This reputation could be partially attributed to the fact that the United States was the first country to televise sports events. In terms of gate receipts, horse racing has been the most attended spectator sport in America, attracting about 64 million people annually (Association of Racing Commissioners International 1992). This is followed by professional baseball with over 57 million spectators, college football with 36 million spectators, and men's college basketball with 34 million spectators per year. To compare sport spectating with participation, there are about 24 million golfers and 17 million tennis players (U.S. Bureau of the Census 1993). Soccer, although the number one participant and spectator sport in almost every other country in the world, has not yet enjoyed the same popularity in the United States.

Americans are also fond of traveling. They travel to national parks and state beaches, theme and amusement parks, resorts, and the homes of family and friends. Statistics indicate that the number of Americans who traveled abroad from 1980 to 1990 increased by 50 percent, which is almost ten times more than the increase in population during that same time (U.S. Census Bureau 1992). Americans travel widely, but when not visiting within the United States, they are most likely traveling to Great Britain, Germany, Canada, Mexico, Japan, and China.

Another important quality of the American leisure character is the outdoors. Nearly 50 percent of Americans describe themselves as "outdoors people," and another 16 percent consider themselves a combination of indoors and out. It is a rare American who does not engage in some form of recreation outdoors (President's Commission 1987). Collecting mushrooms in the forest, studying ocean tide pools, fishing along a stream bank, camping, cross-country skiing, and even a Sunday afternoon drive to admire the autumn colors have real and symbolic importance to Americans.

Perhaps due to Americans' rich legacy in the outdoors, literature, art, and music frequently celebrate it as well. Mark Twain's tales of Huck Finn's escapades on the Mississippi River and the adventure stories of Jack London are famous. Currier and Ives paintings of outdoor scenes, photographs of Yosemite by Ansel Adams, and Aaron Copeland's composition *Appalachian Spring* are recognizable the world over.

Finally, the American penchant for volunteerism is unique. Since its founding, the United States has been based on a strong **philanthropic** philosophy. Americans in the colonies helped each other raise a barn or make a quilt. During the early 1900s, Americans formed organizations to assist those in need. Today, close to 38 million people use their free time to help improve the quality of life of others by working without pay in charitable, religious, community, and other services (U.S. Bureau of Labor Statistics 1990). For Americans, to be of service to others is a satisfying choice of leisure activity.

In summary, the leisure patterns of Americans are wide-ranging, and sports, travel, and outdoor recreation pursuits are of major importance. Nonetheless, Americans are more recognized for their pervasive interests in

Philanthropy: a love of humankind that manifests itself in donating time, money, or services to others.

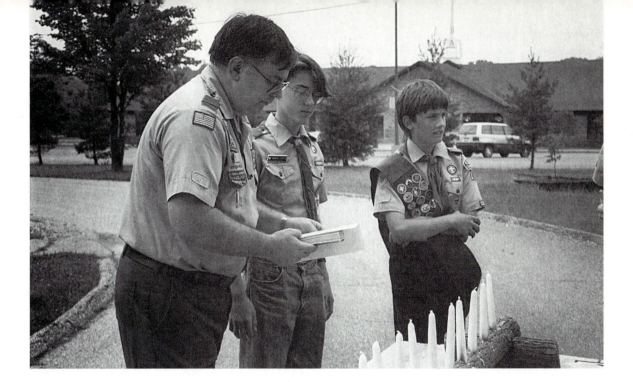

mass media and sport spectating. Americans are demanding in their pastimes; there is a strong ethic that maintains it is best to be busy—to be unleisurely about leisure—which may explain the American fondness for volunteering.

Volunteering is a popular pastime for Americans.
© Ruth V. Russell

Japan

Japan is an archipelago of about 4,000 islands extending more than 1,744 miles in the Pacific Ocean. Its total geographic size of 143,574 square miles supports a population of about 123 million, or 857 persons per square mile. Adding to a sense of density is the fact that about 67 percent of Japan is mountainous and covered with forest. Seventy percent of the people live on the strip of coastal plain between Tokyo and the northern part of Kyushu Island, Tokaido, and the Sanyo area. The language is Japanese, and the literacy rate is 99 percent. The major religious groups are Shintoist and Buddhist.

In the period immediately following World War II, Japan's economy was in a state of devastation. Recovery was accelerated to such an extent that nearly all economic indicators had reached prewar levels by the mid-1950s (Ebashi 1990). Today, Japan has an economic growth rate of about 4.5 percent; its gross national product is more than $1,843 billion, yielding a per capita annual income of $15,030. This makes Japan one of the most industrialized countries in Asia.

Since World War II, Japan has come a long way in improving the quality of life for its people. Due to its present powerful economy and high standard of living, along with recent reductions in working hours, leisure activity participation rates are beginning to catch up. For example, the Japanese used to work about forty-eight hours per week. In 1988, a law was enacted, reducing the standard workweek to forty hours, primarily by cutting out Saturday work hours. The annual average number of working hours per person of 2,150 is still greater than other modern cultures. In France, for example, the average is 1,643 work hours per year. Also, according to the United Nations, Japan leads the world with the longest life expectancy, meaning that large sectors of the population are enjoying extended retirement years. Thus, "Japan seems to be just entering a new, more leisure-oriented era" (Nishino and Takahashi 1989, 11).

Indicators of this new emphasis on leisure are numerous. One is simply involvements in leisure activities. According to a survey on leisure demand conducted in 1986, the most popular daily activities are watching television, shopping, eating out, attending movies, and socializing with friends and family. Sunday in Japan is for sleeping, spending time with the family, and playing golf. In the same survey, people indicated they would like to do more activities on a daily basis including sports (such as walking and other light athletics) and two-day or longer domestic trips (Leisure Development Center 1986).

Tourism is very popular in Japan. Dramatic increases have occurred in the past twenty years in both domestic tourism and travel abroad. For example, in 1971 the number of Japanese tourists going abroad started to exceed the number of foreign tourists coming to Japan (Ebashi 1990). Since then, the gap between the two categories of tourists has widened.

Where do Japanese tourists go when traveling abroad? The most popular destination is the United States, followed by Hong Kong, Germany, and China. In characterizing the Japanese tourist, Ebashi (1990) described them as primarily male and between the ages of twenty and thirty years. They prefer package tours because of language barriers, and they like to travel quickly, wishing to visit as many places as possible. They are enthusiastic buyers of souvenirs and take many photographs.

There are other indicators of the new leisure era as well. The Japanese have recently invested in large scale leisure-related facility development. These include national parks, craft parks, culture parks, urban ecology parks, cycling roads, walking trails, and marine recreation areas. Thanks to the passage of a "resort law" in 1987, the development of lake resorts, coastal community zones, and river recreation facilities is also expected to increase (Nishino and Takahashi 1989).

This development comes with difficulties, however. Land acquisition for new facilities in urban and suburban areas has been hampered by rising land prices. For example, in Tokyo, land costs in the past decade have increased as much as 86 percent (Nishino and Takahashi 1989). Also, the rush to build golf courses and resorts has taken its toll on the natural resources of the country. Golf courses have been constructed in steep mountain areas with escalators for the golfers, and in national parks, like Mt. Fuji, empty cans and other trash have caused pollution.

A contemporary concern for the Japanese is that the popularization of Western and modern forms of leisure is eroding participation in traditional pastimes. While the traditional combative sports of judo and sumo continue to be popular, baseball has grown to such an extent that the Japanese are now providing strong competition with major league teams in the United States. Avid lovers of beauty, the Japanese have a tremendous interest in gardening and nature, but golf in Japan, with over 500 courses, now ranks fifth in the world. This popularity is in spite of the fact that golf has the potential of changing the natural beauty of the landscape.

Perhaps this contrast can best be seen through the traditional culture expressed in Tokyo's parks. According to the Tokyo Metropolitan Government, only 2.4 percent of the city is devoted to greenery, a scant 4.5 square yards per citizen. That's not much compared to such cities as San Francisco, which is 32 percent parkland, or London, which is 30 percent greenery. Tokyo's 2.4 percent however, is developed to its fullest potential. The city's greenery has been diced into more than 7,600 separate parks (Lazarus 1993). While there are several large-scale parks—notably Ueno Park, Yoyogi Park and Shinjuku Garden—the majority are tucked into small lots between buildings or snaked narrowly through residential neighborhoods. Because the Japanese people feel a close kinship with nature, these small areas are greatly appreciated. In certain ways, Tokyo's parks are like the well-tended rock gardens found at temples throughout the country. They are pristine. They are peaceful. If you visit one, even for a brief time, you feel as though you have left the city behind you. In one park, a small bridge is designed in a zig-zag shape so that evil spirits, which according to mythology turn only with great difficulty, will hop over the wall and into the water.

Japan offers a glimpse of a culture where leisure expression is rapidly growing. With prosperity has come more free time and discretionary funds for leisure. This has produced a growth era for leisure in Japan, one which has not only meant increased participation and developments for recreational pursuits but also changes in the character of Japanese leisure in a more Western direction. Leisure can be seen, therefore, as a means for making diverse cultures more homogeneous.

Germany

Combining the formerly West and East German territories, the total area is 137,777 square miles, and the population is estimated to be 80 million. In the former East Germany, the population density is about 397.4 people per square mile, while in the former West Germany the density is considerably more—640 people per square mile. The language of Germany is German and the major religious groups are Protestant and Roman Catholic. The literacy rate is 100 percent.

The reunification of East and West Germany in 1989 has had some disappointing effects. While changing much more slowly than expected, the

Art/graffiti on the Berlin Wall before the reunification of East and West Germany.

© Beth Elliot

economic standards in Germany as of 1993 included a combined gross national product of about $1,327 billion with an estimated economic growth rate of 2.7 percent. Considerable differences still exist between eastern and western German standards of living. The per capita annual income average of $18,370 in the west and $12,500 in the east are examples. With a 40 percent jobless rate in the east, the $65 billion a year that the government is pouring into the east has been mostly for unemployment and welfare payments, as well as make-work and retraining programs.

Nonetheless, Germans have a reputation for pursuing *freizeit* (leisure) with intensity. This is even more interesting since the word *freizeit* was not coined until about one hundred years ago (Hintereder 1988). Today, approximately 20 percent of western Germans' income is used for leisure (Tokarski 1991). Such rapid growth in enthusiasm for leisure is explained by many factors, including the recent history of working hours in Germany. The first attempt to regulate working hours was undertaken (in what was then Prussia) in 1839. According to this policy, workers under the age of sixteen were limited to ten hours of work a day. In 1910, the ten-hour workday became the norm for all German workers.

After World War II, with West Germany's rapid economic development, a five-day workweek was adopted and today the typical German worker puts in thirty-five to thirty-eight hours of work per week. For many people, working time ends on Friday somewhere between 12:00 and 2:00 P.M. Most workers in western Germany are also entitled to four to five weeks paid vacation in addition to ten holidays per year. "Since the middle of the 60's people in Germany have more free time in their lives than work time" (Tokarski 1991, 27).

What becomes of these large amounts of free time? For one thing, as in other industrialized countries, television viewing occupies a considerable portion of time. It is estimated (Hintereder 1988) that 89 percent of households in western Germany own a television set, with an average of sixty-one to seventy-two minutes of viewing per day. Even though people in eastern Germany are grappling with economic problems, they averaged about fifty-six minutes of TV watching daily in the 1970s (Ibrahim 1991). Today, with large numbers of unemployed people in the east and the advent of satellite television reception, it is estimated that people in eastern Germany are spending even more time watching the TV. This interest does not seem to have decreased the German enthusiasm for reading, however. The publishing rate for books is one of the highest among all nations.

During the nineteenth century, Germany was one of the first nations to develop a strong gymnastics and physical recreation movement (Weiskopf 1975). In the early post World War II years, however, sport suffered in the western areas under a stigma left over from the Nazis use of sport as propaganda and paramilitary training. In an effort to combat an increasingly sedentary way of life, the "Sport for Everyone" movement developed in western Germany. An interest in fitness and sport has grown steadily since then, and today, sports are enjoyed by most sectors of the population. It is estimated that one in every three West Germans belong to one of the country's 60,000 gymnastics and sport clubs (Neumann 1985).

In the past, emphasis was on drill, calisthenics, and **turnverein** type movements, emphasizing precision and agility. While still very popular, German physical pastimes are now more than gymnastics. The German people are known for their avid participation in all forms of sports. In addition to football (soccer), handball, and track and field, other favorites include hiking, swimming, bowling, skiing, and tennis. Jogging is also a popular pastime. Many of the sports are managed by amateur sports organizations and clubs, as well as active for-profit organizations.

Turnverein: to perform gymnastic exercises.

Following World War II in the eastern portions of Germany, sport became an important tool for building a socialistic society. Along with child and adult education, and artistic activities, sport was named in the German *Dictionary of Marxist-Leninist Sociology* as an important and productive force in the development of socialism. This did not mean that leisure was intended as freedom for self-expression, rather its purpose was to rejuvenate one's working capacity.

Accordingly, in East Germany, government authorities promoted only certain leisure activities. In a report published in the late 1960s (Lippold 1972), sport, traveling, and walking were listed as the most desirable activities for the people. Actual participation at that time, however, appears to have been different. The study showed that the young workers ranked sport, traveling, and walking seventh instead of first, second, and third as the government desired. In fact, the average time spent on these three activities was fifteen minutes per day. Only 15 percent of the persons polled in another study at that time reported that they participated in sports on a regular basis (Ibrahim 1991). As a result, the East German government began to invest heavily in sport. Under Marxist-Leninism it was not considered a mere pastime, but vitally important to the society's ability to achieve the goals of socialism. Such government support of sport helped East Germany become internationally visible in such events as the Olympics.

In the nineteenth century, Germany established many parks and outdoor activity areas. Since then, particularly in western Germany, city governments have developed comprehensive and well-planned systems of both small and large parks. In the eastern section of Germany, large development projects have been underway to spread at least a veneer of Western affluence. New hotels, restaurants, and shopping malls have been the first to be completed. At the same time, unfortunately, youth clubs and day care centers have closed.

Germans also have a reputation for being fond of music and dancing. Traditional German music, demonstrating both a love of pleasure as well as gloom and brooding, has always symbolized the inner emotions of the people. Jazz became popular in the 1920s, was banned by Hitler, but came back strong in the west after 1945. In the 1960s, rock music became the symbol of youth protests and remains so today (Ibrahim 1991). The traditional German restaurants and open-air gardens are also famous for singing, eating and drinking, and dancing. Festivals and fairs are held throughout the year.

Theater-going is quite popular in western Germany as well—aided by government subsidies that keep admission costs low. Ballets, operas, and concerts are similarly popular. Films have also been produced in western Germany, but following their strict use for propaganda in the Nazi era, have been slow to resume their former vigor.

In all, leisure in Germany is currently transitional and uncertain. With the political changes that reunited eastern and western Germany have come harsher realities of extreme differences in life quality within the same country. This has had an impact in perhaps two ways. First, the differences in economics, employment, and abilities for consumption are starkly visible within leisure. Opportunities for commercial pastimes in eastern Germany lag behind not only what exists in western Germany, but also what used to exist in the east.

Second, and more worrisome, eastern Germans have recently claimed feelings of passivity and dependency. Because of the collapse of industry and jobs in the east, morale is low in eastern Germany. As Kurt Biedenkopf, premier of the eastern state of Saxony, commented, "We lack comparable living conditions. Western Germans see the East as a burden they need to unload as fast as possible. There's a terrible lethargy here now" (*International Herald Tribune* 1993). This state of mind is not conducive to healthful expressions of leisure.

Leisure's Contradiction with Technology

From the invention of the wheel for clay toys in ancient cultures to the perfection of robotic techniques in modern societies, technology has always had an impact on leisure. For example, vulcanization of rubber by Charles Goodyear in the 1830s led to the development of elastic and resilient rubber balls for tennis and golf. The mass production of paper and the invention of the printing press have contributed immeasurably to the pastime of reading. Technology helped cause a tripling in the last twenty years in the number of people who sport fish with fiberglass rods that enable amateurs to match the professionals (Hammel and Foster 1986). We can now ice skate year round, our bowling pins are automatically reset, and special pockets of air now cushion our feet during jogging. New pursuits have been created by technology. How would modern children survive without video games or mall walkers without Sony Walkman's?

One of the greatest dreams of technological advancement has always been the release from labor. The postindustrial economies of countries, such as the United States, Japan, and Germany, were supposed to make possible the growth of the "leisure society" (Gunter, Stanley, and St. Clair 1985). In such developed nations a combination of increases in free time and a corresponding growth in leisure facilities and activities is expected to result. The evidence to support this is indeed compelling: shortened workweeks, longer vacations, the lengthening retirement period, higher annual salaries, and increased sales of sport equipment.

In the midst of all this, however, are the beginnings of a doubt: perhaps leisure is victimized in a technological society. For example, there are increasing indications that during the last decade the amount of leisure time available has actually declined (Godbey 1989; Schor 1992). Taking the United States as an illustration, the largest percentage of the population is now in the labor force; overall employment grew 16 percent from 1979 to 1985 (Godbey 1989). This is due both to increases in women working outside the home and a higher percentage of working teenagers.

This change is partly associated with an increase in the actual average hours per week worked in the United States, from 40.6 to 47.3 (Harris 1987). Modernization with its shift toward a service economy and more salaried workers has meant generally longer work hours. The change is also associated with an increase in time spent commuting, going to school, studying, and doing yard and house work. Small business owners, such as retailers, work an average of 57.3 hours per week and professional people work an average of 52.2 hours per week.

On a more philosophical level, Goodale and Godbey (1988) also argue that technology is no friend to leisure. They claim that a large amount of the leisure afforded us today by technology is at best trivial. Modern society produces a life that is wasted in a frenetic rush for meaningless pleasures. Leisure in advanced cultures is equated with materialism and consumerism, and this is a sordid route to human happiness (Trafton 1985). Do you agree? Arguments can be made on both sides of the issue, of course, but the conclusion remains essentially identical. Leisure is affected both positively and negatively by modernization.

Leisure in Developing Countries

Development: a general level of technology, economic sophistication, and standard of living.

Development simply means the extent to which the resources of an area or country have been brought into full productivity. In common usage it refers to the amount of economic growth, modernization, and production and consumption of goods. Countries can be identified according to the extent of their development. For example, Canada, Australia, Great Britain, France, the United States, and Japan are categorized as more developed, whereas India, Paraguay, Nepal, Saudi Arabia, Senegal, and Mexico are less developed. These countries are labeled developing areas.

Developing was the term United States President Harry S Truman introduced in 1949 as a replacement for *backward,* the unflattering reference then in use. This term implies that sooner or later, all portions of the world will reach a highly industrialized stage of development. Development is a fluid condition, however, so this may not necessarily be the case. Some areas of the world are unlikely to progress much beyond their current stage. Other areas that are recognized as developed now could experience economic decay and revert to a more undeveloped state. While the standard of living in most countries of the world has improved, a serious trend is the widening of the development gap. Rich countries have grown richer, and poor countries have become relatively poorer. It is more difficult now for a less developed society to advance to full modernization by its own efforts. Thus, such organizations as the Peace Corps and the World Bank attempt to marshall some of the resources of more developed areas to help less developed areas.

Development also has implications for changes in traditional social and cultural structures. While development can enhance an area's standard of living, it may be detrimental to other aspects of a culture's uniqueness. The accumulation of wealth, whether at national or individual levels, is not necessarily a recipe for a high quality of life.

To illustrate, Norman (cited in Cole 1988) developed an interesting measure of happiness, which she labeled the "hedonometer," and used it to compare Great Britain and Botswana. Happiness was measured in terms of psychological satisfaction, rather than money. Using six principal factors for happiness, her comparison resulted in the claim that people in Botswana were happier than people in Great Britain. Upon what basis? Norman's six factors for happiness follow:

1. Understanding of your environment and how to control it

2. Social support from family and friends

3. Species drive satisfaction (such as sex and parenting)

Leisure and Nigerian Tribes

Location of Nigeria.

Christopher B. Stage

Nigeria is located along the eastern edge of the African continent. Its diverse terrain ranges from southern coastal swamps to tropical forests, open woodlands, grasslands, and semidesert in the far north. With a population of 115 million, Nigeria is the most populous country in Africa. It accounts for one quarter of Sub-Saharan Africa's people. The variety of customs, languages, and traditions among Nigeria's 250 ethnic tribal groups gives the country a rich diversity.

A study (Ekpo 1991) was conducted in Nigeria that presents an example of leisure in a developing nation and for people with a diversified social, religious, cultural, economic, and educational background. Three major tribal groups were identified: the Hausas, the Igbos, and the Yorubas. An in-depth investigation into each tribes' history, culture, religion and social patterns was conducted, followed by the distribution of a questionnaire to 500 people in each tribe. Questions relating to the tribe members' understanding of free time and leisure involvement and interests were asked.

In all three tribes, more males than females responded to the questionnaires. The sample included participants who ranged in age from twenty-five to fifty-five years, were married with children, and employed. Eighty percent of the participants had at least a secondary school education. The two main religious practices among the participants were Christianity and Islam.

According to the researcher's analysis of the findings, as expected, some differences exist between the tribes in leisure perceptions, interests, and behaviors. These distinctions are deeply rooted in the religions and cultural backgrounds of the people. As one leaves the confines of a tribe, however, one observes a nation-wide pattern in the pastimes of Nigerians. For example, until very recently many Nigerians believed leisure on a regular basis was an exclusive reserve of the rich who could afford the time and cost. While this perspective is changing, some constricted views remain, such as for women leisure rarely exists. It is felt that a conscientious woman would not have time for leisure as her work is never ending.

The findings on types of leisure activities and amount of leisure time spent also revealed differing perspectives that were less tribe-based and more socio-economic in influence. For example, among more literate groups, free time and leisure have become a necessary period of each day. What is pursued, however, depends on social class. Common leisure activities in the upper class include overseas tours, sports club memberships, casino gambling, polo, and golf. For middle-class Nigerians, leisure activity preferences include indoor and table games, sports, and spectating. Among lower-class persons, leisure is desired but infrequently pursued.

Basically, the study revealed that education, occupation, family background, family size, and residential area greatly influence the Nigerians' expression of leisure—more so than does tribal membership. As it is with the rest of the world, leisure in this developing country is greatly influenced by socio-cultural and socio-economic factors.

4. Satisfaction of physical well-being drives (such as hunger, sleep)

5. Satisfaction of aesthetic and sensory drives

6. Satisfaction of exploratory drive (such as creativity, discovery)

According to these factors, Norman judged the people of Botswana to be higher in all but one—physical well-being. While this is arguably a subjective way of measuring how well off a society is, more conventional measures of development, such as energy consumption and gross national product are subjective too. The point is that development can be described by more than the purely economic and physical indicators. Development must also be viewed as individual and collective well-being, safe environment, freedom from want, opportunity for personal growth and enrichment, education, security, and similar noneconomic criteria.

Leisure is one of these criteria. Leisure can contribute to cultural development. It can be instrumental in the personal development of each inhabitant and important to social harmony. It can widen every person's relations to the environment and can help build a social identity of a group or community. It can even be an important source of economic development as we will explore later.

Several themes can be noticed in the leisure differences between the developing countries presented in this section—Poland, Malaysia, and Costa Rica—and more developed areas. One is the notion of time (Westland 1990). In parts of Central and South America, southeast Asia, and parts of Africa a concept of "cyclical time" dominates. This concept is based on the principle that the day that passes is never lost but comes back, just like the ocean tide, in a never-ending sequence. Time is not something to be spent wisely and efficiently as in developed, industrialized cultures but is something to enjoy. While money is scarce, time seems plentiful in less developed countries. This is perhaps why Javanese Gamelan music lasts for many hours throughout the night and why taking the time to bargain for a price with a merchant in Mexico is possible.

While there are differences, leisure behaviors and interests have been greatly diffused worldwide. Leisure products from vastly different cultural environments penetrate virtually everywhere in the world.

Poland

Poland, located in north central Europe and bordering the Baltic Sea, occupies 120,727 square miles, has an estimated population of 38 million, and a density of 316 persons per square mile. The language is Polish, and the major religious group is Roman Catholic. Poland maintains a 98 percent literacy rate. In 1988, Poland's gross national product was about $280 billion, with an annual per capita income of about $8,380, and an economic growth rate of 2.1 percent. The years since 1989, following the downfall of communism in Poland, have been characterized by acute economic problems. In transition to a market economy, the gross national product fell by some 25 percent. The purchasing

biography

Rosa Luxemburg

Twentieth-century Poland has endured rebellions, wars, and foreign occupation. Earlier, as well, Poland had been controlled by Austria, Prussia (later Germany), and Russia, but with the coming of World War I in 1914, independence for Poland was begun. The Russians were driven out of most of Poland by 1915, and through the 1919 Treaty of Versailles, Poland regained large amounts of its territory from Germany. There were many heroic Polish political figures of the time, including Jozef Pilsudski and Roman Dmowski. One largely unsung political figure of Poland from this effort for independence was Rosa Luxemburg.

Rosa was born in Zamosc, Poland, in 1871. She quickly became known as a socialist revolutionary. After graduating from high school, Rosa began to read the writings of Karl Marx, which spurred her into political activism on behalf of the working class. Almost immediately, at age eighteen, she was forced to flee Poland for Switzerland to avoid arrest. There she earned a doctorate in economics from the University of Zurich in 1898 and that same year moved to Germany and joined the Social Democratic Party. This party was one of several socialist political groups that formed and grew strong in Europe and North America during the early 1900s. The movement included moderates, radicals, and revolutionaries, and Rosa earned a reputation among them as a brilliant writer and speaker.

She spent most of the period of World War I (1914–1919) in and out of prison. Prison was an integral part of life for a socialist at the time. Her notion of a life "worth living," as she put it, was not only a public life of hard, stubborn, and not always rewarding political activism but a personal life of joy and harmony. Her letters from prison reveal some of this.

"I walk in the yard hatless."

"I promise myself to live life to its fullest as soon as I'm free."

"To do without life's little ornaments, is harder than to endure big trials."

(Ettinger 1986)

Rosa's daily prison regime speaks of a fulfilled life as well. In accordance with prison rules, she rose at 5:40 A.M. and retired at 9:00 P.M. Her time was devoted to reading, writing, and tending the tiny garden in front of her cell. Gardening was a hobby she had started two years earlier when for four months "I did literally nothing else," she wrote to a friend. "I must always have something that absorbs me completely" (Ettinger 1986).

Rosa was assassinated in Berlin, Germany, in 1919. She was a socialist, and history has stereotyped her accordingly. What is largely ignored is that Polish socialism was socialism with a romantic tinge. The poets of the time promised deliverance to all oppressed people, and Rosa was inspired by this. Later elaborated into the theory of spontaneous revolution, she was proved right by the revolutionary movements of the 1980s.

---

power of consumers fell by 40 percent, and unemployment rates now hover around 13 percent.

The people of Poland have a rich cultural heritage that includes many folk traditions, but the 1900s have brought tumultuous changes. Before World War II, Poland was largely agricultural and most people were farmers. After the war and during political control by the Communist Party, Poland began to modernize. Great efforts toward industrialization were made, and more people took jobs in the cities. Today, about 60 percent of the population live in cities and towns. As a result, many old traditions have disappeared from everyday life in Poland, yet for most Poles, social life still centers around church and family gatherings. Relaxing in a sidewalk cafe and listening to music provided by strolling musicians continues to be an important pastime, as it has been for hundreds of years past. Camping and hiking also remain a part of Poland's traditionally popular pastimes.

Poland's leisure is reminiscent in some ways of typical leisure patterns in fully industrialized cultures. For example, in a **cross-cultural** time-budget study in the early 1970s that compared the town of Torun, Poland, with Jackson, Michigan, there were more similarities than differences in how people spent their free time (Skorzynski 1972). Watching television occupied the greatest portion of free time available for people in both towns. Also reading newspapers and magazines, and socializing with friends and family were popular daily activities for both.

In our discussion of leisure and Poland, we should give special attention to the arts. Poland has produced many outstanding artists, musicians, and writers as cultural life in Poland has flourished at various times in its history. For example, the composer Frederic Chopin wrote many works based on Polish dances, such as the mazurka. The novelist Henryk Sienkiewicz won a Nobel Prize in 1905 for his works, including *Quo Vadis,* and the novelist Wladyslaw Reymont won a Nobel Prize in 1924 for *The Peasants.* However, beginning in the late 1940s, Poland's communist leaders restricted cultural activity that did not promote the goals of communism. Sanctions were removed in the 1960s when the preservation of traditional folk music and folk arts was again encouraged by the government. Many Poles have recently achieved fame in the graphic arts. The cinema is also a popular art form.

Perhaps the more interesting story to tell about leisure and Poland is what has occurred with the downfall of communism. While the tale here is about Poland, the problems of development in other central and eastern European countries are similar because they have a common heritage of communist political systems and less developed economies. The solutions to these problems are also commonly crucial in determining what leisure patterns will develop or survive.

Formerly, under the communist system, government owned companies were required to generate cultural and social funds. These were set aside as a fixed percentage of sales and used to subsidize holidays and trips for employees, recreation services for employees' children, book purchases for company libraries, and tickets for the theater, cinema, and concerts.

In shifting from a communist system to market-oriented reforms, an essential feature is the privatization of public enterprises. For example, some privatization has taken place with cinemas and sports clubs (Jung 1992). As well, unfortunately, some formerly recreational establishments have shifted to other uses. Higher rates and commercialization of recreational activities, as a result of **privatization,** have made them available only to more wealthy consumers.

Privatization: to change
from government to
individual control or
ownership.

On the other hand, the economic reforms have brought an end to shortages which formerly plagued Poland. In particular, the abundance of imported Western goods has increased markedly. This also applies to goods and services for recreational needs (Jung 1992). Unfortunately, however, the liberalization of foreign trade has also meant realistic and unsubsidized prices. This put many products, including food, clothing, and rent at very steep prices, leaving practically nothing from a Pole's paycheck to spend on leisure.

In spite of the end to passport limitations, opportunities for travel have actually diminished in Poland (Jung 1990). Problems of inflation are compounded by restrictions by other countries against Polish travelers as protection from potentially massive immigration. Thus, less than half of the Polish population takes holidays away from home (Paczynska 1986).

On the other hand, the post-Communist era has opened new opportunities for leisure. These include new, more self-managed, forms of sponsorship of leisure events. A new sponsor of recreation is the Roman Catholic Church. The involvement of the Church in fine arts, as well as in various forms of youth recreation, has grown tremendously (Jung 1992). Also, newly created foundations and private firms are now sponsoring mass sports events.

With these changes has been born a new class of people. New wealth acquired partly from opportunistic luck, illegal sources, and manipulation of the ever-changing systems has mushroomed. Unprecedented private fortunes have been manifested by conspicuous consumption. "For these Polish capitalists of various social origin and background, leisure has become one of the very important fields for showing off wealth and ascertaining their social position through status symbols" (Jung 1992, 11–12). Meanwhile, at the other end of Polish society, poverty is quickly expanding.

In all, leisure has been both enhanced and damaged in the new post-Communist Poland. It seems as though the replacement of political constraints with economic ones has produced an uncertain future for some forms of leisure and thus society.

Malaysia

Until independence in 1963, Malaysia was a British colony. Today, its territory in southeastern Asia occupies 128,328 square miles split between a peninsula and the island of Borneo. Its population is estimated at 18 million, with a density of 137 persons per square mile. While Bahasa Malay is the official language, Chinese, Tamil, and English are also widely spoken. The official religion is Islam (53 percent), but other important religious groups are Buddhist (17 percent), Chinese folk religions (12 percent), Hindu (7 percent), and Christian (6 percent). The literacy rate is 65 percent. Malaysia's estimated gross domestic product is $35 billion, and the annual per capita income is $3,000. The economic growth rate is about 8 percent.

More than two-thirds of Malaysia is dense jungle. The rainforests are the oldest in the world, making those in Africa and South America seem adolescent in comparison. In addition to flour-fine sandy beaches, along the coastline there are extensive areas of mud swamps and mangroves. In the *kampong* (village), life is closely tied to the simplicity of an uncluttered outdoor life. Meanwhile in Kuala Lumpur, the capital city, the ultra-modern architecture rivals that in other major cities of the modern world, while noisy car horns and congested sidewalks compete for attention.

In Malaysia, many sports, games, and festivities are enjoyed whose traditions stretch back for centuries and are still taken as seriously today. For example, *silat*

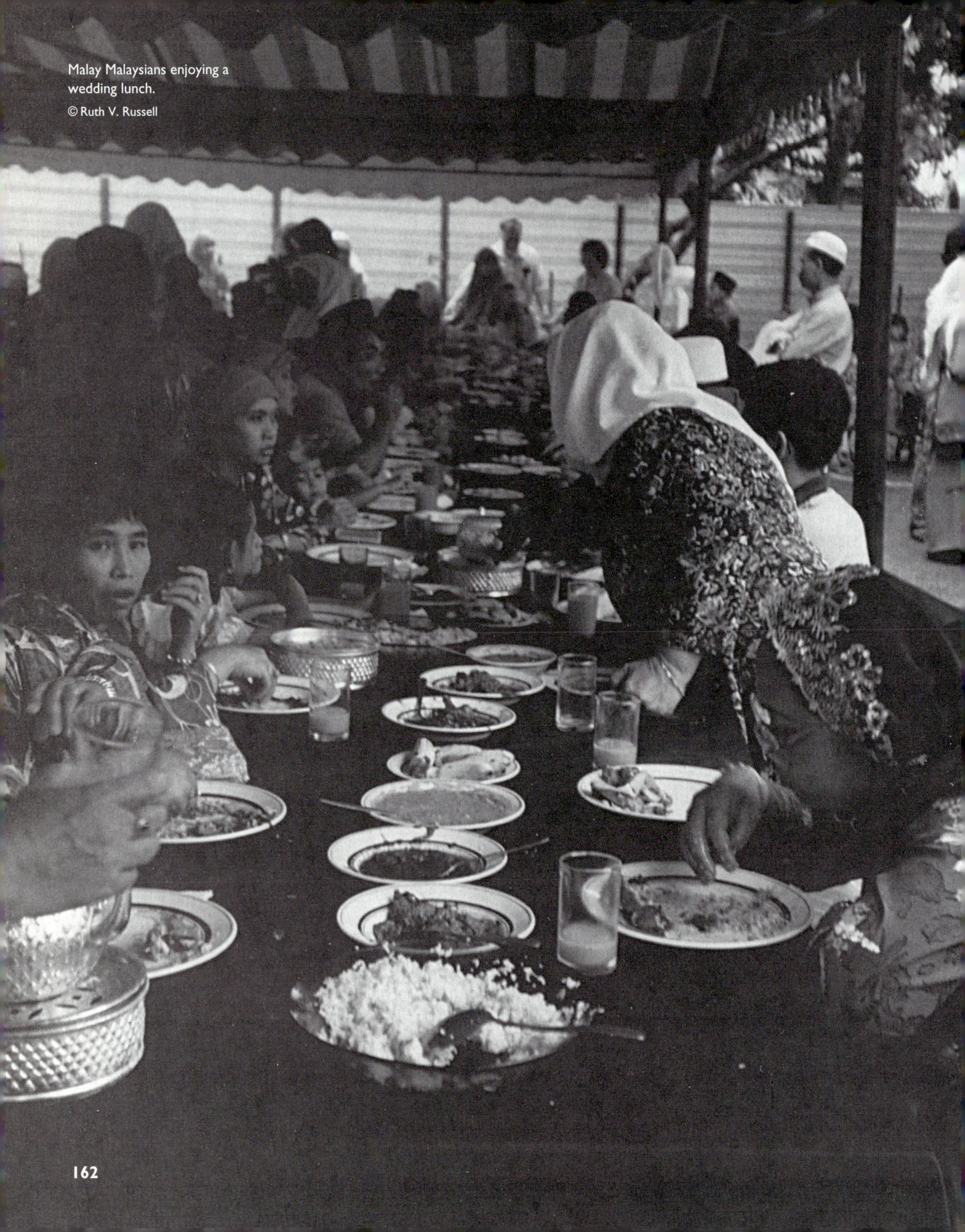

Malay Malaysians enjoying a wedding lunch.

© Ruth V. Russell

Figure 5.3 The *sepak takraw* ball made of woven rattan.

Christopher B. Stage

is the ancient Malay art of self-defense. Today, unarmed fighters mimic a dagger duel to death that was once real. Like karate and other martial arts, expertise in *silat* involves meditation and spiritual powers, believed to help ward off evil blows.

Sepak takraw is a national pastime that can be played almost anywhere as long as there is the small, woven ball made of rattan, and a wide, open space (see fig. 5.3). The aim of the game is to keep the ball off the ground using any part of the body except the hands. Other southeast Asian countries play variations, and the game was standardized in 1965 for championship purposes. Malaysia has dominated the competitions ever since.

Throughout most of the country, top-spinning is a teenage pastime, but among the communities of the northeast coast, a champion spinner is the town folk hero. With the harvest completed and all the rice stored, farmers settle down to watch and bet on the local team. There are two types of competitions. At times, contests feature the spinning time, and it is said that the record time for spinning is one hour and forty-seven minutes (*Insight Guides Malaysia* 1990). Other contests feature the fast-paced warlike top spinners who's striker tops spin down other tops faster than a speeding bullet. Skill and strength is required, since the defending team contrives tricky formations of their tops designed to eliminate an attacker's top from the tiny playing circle.

In these pastimes, we are describing only one part of Malaysia's population—the Malays. They are Muslim and despite major changes in the last decades are still to some extent rural rather than urban people. The Malays make up about 50 percent of the population, and they control the government. What other ethnic groups make up the Malaysian population?

While the Malays came originally from Polynesia, the indigenous people in Malaysia are the Orang Asli. Their name means "original people" in the Malay language, and their tribes have been there for thousands of years. They number only around 60,000, and while many have been absorbed into modern Malaysian society, several groups still live in the jungles. The majority have chosen not to take on world religions, such as Islam and Christianity, and have mostly **animistic** beliefs. Their diverse and sometimes difficult languages and their oral tradition of tales of old are little known outside their tribes.

Animism: believing that spirits inhabit nature or natural objects.

The Chinese population (most arrived during the nineteenth century) makes up about 35 percent of Malaysia's population, yet their presence makes their numbers seem far greater. The Chinese are very hard working, which has brought them relatively great financial successes. Most of the Chinese are Tao Buddhist, and splendidly colorful temples are the center of their community where both religious and secular festivals are celebrated. Orchestra practice is also held in the temple, and during festival times, stages are often set up in the grounds of the temple for an opera or puppet show.

The major Buddhist festivals are celebrated not only in the temples but in homes as well. The biggest is the Chinese New Year, which non-Chinese also celebrate. Younger and unmarried members of the family receive *ang pows,* small red and gold packets containing gifts of money. Much of the festival is spent visiting relatives and friends, and eating special food. The latest movies from Hong Kong are shown at the cinemas, and public performances of lion dances are held. For this dance, two or more energetic dancers hidden within the half-fierce, half-humorous lion costume twist and leap to the beat of a drum. The lion's eyelashes flutter and jaws flap while cymbals clash.

The Malaysian Indian population (originally from India) makes up less than 10 percent of the population, but their culture is pervasive. About 80 percent of the Indians are Tamils and Hindus, and what they lack in numbers they make up for in a rich and colorful festival life. Celebrations are held year round, with every inch of the Hindu temples' walls and ceiling brightly decorated. *Deepavali,* with its emphasis on lights, gloriously celebrates the triumph of good over evil. This is a time for indulgent eating, especially sweet cakes and candies. Traditional Hindus start the day by having an oil bath before sunrise and saying their prayers. Afterwards friends and relatives, including non-Hindu friends, attend open houses.

What is particularly fascinating about all these festivals in Malaysia is the role of Christmas. Most shops and companies use decorations and lights similar to the ones used for Christmas, regardless of the religion. They are put up to first celebrate *Deepavali*. They are left up for their Christian customers over December, and most even last until Chinese New Year, thus binding three faiths together with a kind of commercial ingenuity that spans three months.

As with most developing countries, the rift between the countryside and the city, the traditional and the modern, widens as progress is made. Those in Malaysia from the Malay group are subject to the laws of Islam (an Arabic word for submission), which immediately sets them apart from fellow Malaysians. For instance, pork, a food relished by the Chinese, is forbidden to the Muslim Malays. The resurgence of Islam in Malaysia, as elsewhere in the world, has led to some particular stresses that must also be reconciled with the modernization process of the country, as well as with leisure. Let's briefly explore a bit of this.

Islam is the official religion of Malaysia, even though only the Malay group tends to be of this faith. This means that the government plays a much larger part in controlling some things than it does in other countries—including leisure activities and products. For example, the government controls the mass media. The government gives warnings and conveys advice about the content of newspapers. Foreign produced movies are censored for sexual language and scenes. Radio and television transmit the message of Islam (Milne and Mauzy 1986). Following the student demonstrations of 1974, university and college students are now prohibited from supporting or becoming members of organizations without university approval.

To conclude, Malaysia's economic performance has been superior to that of most developing countries, and it is well on its way toward the goal of complete modernization by the year 2020. In addition, Malaysia's wealth of cultural diversity has created leisure pursuits that divide its people along ethnic lines—chiefly for the Malays, Chinese, and Indians. Here lies the problem. The government recognizes the need for a national culture, but it also insists that this culture should be founded on the Malay culture, including Islam (Milne and Mauzy 1986). This may mean strife for Malaysians in the future.

Costa Rica

The Republic of Costa Rica, located in Central America, occupies 19,652 square miles, which makes it about the size of West Virginia. With a population estimated at over 3 million, the density per square mile is 151. Spanish is the language, and the literacy rate is 93 percent. The major religious group is Roman Catholic. Costa Rica's gross domestic product is about $4.5 billion, and the per capita annual income is estimated as $2,529. Its economic growth rate is 4 percent. In 1949, Costa Rica abolished its army.

Costa Ricans call themselves *Ticos* on account of their tendency to use *tico* as opposed to *tito* as their diminutive ending on words or even to tack it onto an existing diminutive, e.g., *chiquito* which means small one becomes *chiquitico* or tiny one. Their passion for this double diminutive extends to everything, whether it be something to drink or a trip to the coast. It is this sort of light-hearted friendly spirit that makes Costa Rica a very special place. As in other societies in the developing world, they are undergoing the stresses of modernization, yet unlike much of Latin America, Costa Rica is peaceful (the only one with no army), the most democratic, and has the highest literacy rate.

In fact, democracy is perhaps the most cherished value of Costa Ricans (Biesanz, Biesanz, and Biesanz 1982). Surrounded as they have been by military dictatorships, they are most keenly aware of their individual liberty and equality. They like to tell visitors that they have the longest continuous democracy in the Western Hemisphere. One of the manifestations of this is a strong formal education system. *Ticos* boast, "We have more teachers than soldiers," and school children rather than soldiers parade in the streets on patriotic holidays. There is also a strong tendency to localism. Most Costa Ricans are oriented primarily to their families, neighborhoods, and communities.

Although less true in urban areas such as San Jose, a short school day, a two-hour noon break, a four-and-a-half-day workweek, and seventeen national holidays, make leisure time abundant for many Costa Ricans. *Ticos* are not compulsive about leisure. Their free time activities need not be constructive (in contrast with their North American neighbors), yet a concern of youth in smaller villages is boredom. They say their community is *muy tristes* (very melancholy) without the excitements of the city. Costa Ricans seem to enjoy crowds and liveliness. A radio or tape player is a typical item for a picnic.

Crowds and noise are also the feature at the street fairs that are commonly held for raising money for churches, schools, and other causes. Announced by noisy rockets before dawn, the fair normally lasts all weekend. Horse shows, mechanical rides, clowns, fireworks, a greased-pole contest, and corn liquor are typical highlights (Biesanz, Biesanz, and Biesanz 1982). A neighboring town may send a team for a soccer game, and the music will include a nonstop marimba band. Invariably a queen is chosen from among teenagers whose bikini-clad figures have graced the newspapers for days ahead. Typically, the money is raised with raffles, bingo, and lotteries.

Sunday is an important leisure day. Although some *Ticos* complain that they are bored on Sundays, many others use it for dressing in their best, attending mass, strolling, window shopping, consuming ice cream, and watching a soccer game. Others may see a movie, go to the mountains for a picnic lunch, or attend a dance.

Most Costa Ricans prefer passive, commercialized diversions to active participation (Biesanz, Biesanz, and Biesanz 1982). Popular spectator sports are soccer and bullfighting. The unique feature of the bullfights is that the bull is never injured. For decades, they have been avid movie fans. Violence, though taboo in *Ticos'* interpersonal relations, is a great attraction in films. Radio is everywhere in Costa Rica, and television antennae sprout from almost every home. Most live programs are of soccer games, popular music, giveaway shows, and newscasts. Most viewing time is occupied by old cartoons, movies, and soap operas from the United States and Mexico.

Soccer, as a popular saying goes, "is not the sport of Costa Ricans; it is their existence." Introduced early in the twentieth century, soccer is played mostly by young males, who began kicking a soccer ball around at age two, and spent much of their free time during the next two decades playing with others in any available space. Like softball in the United States, even the smallest town has at least one team. Neighborhood teams broadcast challenges over the radio and usually find a taker every Sunday.

Basketball, volleyball, and tennis are also popular, particularly for wealthier boys. Middle-aged men of means enjoy tennis and golf at private clubs. Pool is popular among men as well, and baseball teams are often

Costa Rica is gaining a reputation as an ecotourist destination.
© Ruth V. Russell

sponsored by large companies. Cockfights, once so popular, are now much less so; they are also illegal. While once considered to be unhealthy for women, in recent decades women's sport participation and fitness have increased. Nonetheless, *Ticos* consider themselves mostly "gallery sportsmen" (Biesanz, Biesanz, and Biesanz 1982).

The scenery is so beautiful in Costa Rica that it has been called the "Switzerland of Central America." Accordingly, a final feature of leisure and Costa Rica is tourism. Truly the new challenge facing the country is how best to cope with the growth of tourism. Smoking active volcanos, dense tropical jungle, beaches backdropped by lush palms, and nesting sea turtles have made Costa Ricans (and tourists too) proud. However, naturalists lament that Costa Rica is no longer the paradise it seemed a few decades ago. Some large stretches of virgin forest still exist, and some extensive areas (currently about 12 percent of the total territory) are now preserved as national parks, but many others have been destroyed. This has been the cost of development. Tourist money provides a much needed injection of currency into the flagging economy (about $266 million in 1990). Therefore, authorities are not yet fully decided about the direction tourism should take.

Capitalizing on its lush rainforests, sandy beaches, and fascinating wildlife and in an effort to stymie the ecological damage resulting from

Nepal packs more geographical diversity into fewer square miles than any other country in the world. The people who inhabit this land mirror that diversity. In Nepal, no majority population exists—all are minorities. One of the most famous of these are the Sherpas. The Sherpas live in the high valleys in the southern shadow of Mt. Everest in the region known as the Khumbu. They are Buddhists (rather than Hindu as much of the rest of Nepal), culturally Tibetan (tracing their roots to eastern Tibet some 450 years ago), and a numerically insignificant portion of the population (Fisher 1990). Their villages, which are at altitudes between 10,000 and 13,000 feet and connected to one another only by narrow mountain footpaths, have names like Namche Bazaar, Lukla, Tengboche, Thame, and Pheriche.

Most of the Khumbu region consists of rock, ice, and snow, and less than a fifth of one percent of it can be farmed. Sherpa lifestyle has, nonetheless, traditionally consisted of farming fields around sturdy permanent houses in the villages. They follow their yak herds to more make-shift shelters in higher pastures in summer and to lower ones in winter. In this climate, potatoes, turnips, and coarse greens can be grown. Milk, yogurt, and cheese from cattle supplement a largely vegetable diet.

Sherpas have traditionally operated at a very low technology level—weaving woolen cloth by hand and repairing rope-soled shoes. Religious and community celebrations follow a pattern set mostly by the passage of the seasons and often center around local monasteries. The monasteries have been the main source of education in the

Khumbu as well. Many Sherpa men have spent a few years learning to read Tibetan in a monastery, even if they eventually left it to lead secular lives. As a result, Sherpa literacy rates—estimated at one-third of the adult male population—have been uncharacteristically high for such a remote area (Fisher 1990).

Beginning in 1961, life began to change for the people of the Khumbu. First, the construction and operation of elementary schools in all villages, thanks to the efforts of New Zealand mountain climber Sir Edmund Hillary, brought literacy in Nepali and English. The establishment of a hospital in Khunde had wide-ranging effects, including the virtual elimination of thyroid deficiency diseases. Perhaps the most change inducing event for the Sherpas of the Khumbu was the construction of an airstrip at Lukla, which shortened the travel time from Kathmandu (the capital) to the Khumbu from fourteen days to forty minutes. This development has brought the Khumbu more than 6,000 tourists per year.

What has this torrent of tourists meant for the Sherpas? Those who observe and comment on the impact of tourism generally divide themselves according to two perspectives. One view is that tourism ultimately dehumanizes and destroys the cultural integrity of an area. Tourism is considered to place "the whole of the visited culture on sale, distorting its imagery and symbolism . . . transforming a way of life into an industry" (Smith 1980, 60). As one Khumbu tourist wrote in a visitor's log book "A hot shower, steaks, and 500-foot viewing tower with central

This airstrip in Lukla brings more than 6,000 tourists a year into Nepal's Khumbu region. © Ruth V. Russell

heating would definitely be in order" (Fisher 1990), which makes the culture-for-sale perspective on the impact of tourism imaginable.

The other view is that tourism is good because of the economic benefits it brings to local people. This happens by not only bringing in foreign money, but by increasing employment as well. Not surprisingly, governments are usually convinced by this second perspective and for good reason. The government of Nepal's earnings from tourism are substantial.

Which perspective is true for the Khumbu? Let's answer the question both ways.

Residents of this mountain region of Nepal now work as guides, cooks, and porters for trekking and mountain climbing trips. In fact, the word *sherpa* has come to describe a particular job—the sherpa assists the trekking party by setting up tents, managing loads, and other odd jobs during the trip. The village of Namche Bazaar in the Khumbu is geographically situated so that all tourists (and all Sherpas too) who enter the region must travel through it. Namche entrepreneurs have quickly met the challenge by opening roughly thirty shops and hotels. The Khumbu contains over one hundred lodges and teashops in all. In the village of Khunde, 85 percent of all households have at least one person working in tourism (Fisher 1990).

While most of tourist spending goes to the trekking companies outside the Khumbu that arranged the trips, Sherpa income has still increased dramatically. From 1964 to 1988, porter's wages have increased by 730 percent and guides by 369 percent (Fisher 1990), but inflation has occurred as well. The price of rice between 1964 and 1988 has gone up by 900 percent.

Is this the end of the story? Not quite. Partly because of inflation, partly because the pay is seasonal and unstable, and partly because most Sherpas have little experience in business, they have saved and invested little. Instead they have spent their increased earnings on formerly unavailable goods. For example, there is now a wider variety of fruits and vegetables in the region. Jewelry (especially watches) is another popular expense, and there has been a frenzy of activity for repairing and upgrading houses. Some traditional crafts are dying out. With so much ready cash, people now tend to buy manufactured items instead of making them themselves.

Class differences are also emerging as a new "tourist Sherpa" class develops. Formerly, land and yak herds were the sources of wealth and status. Now an almost nouveau-riche group can be distinguished by the imported hiking

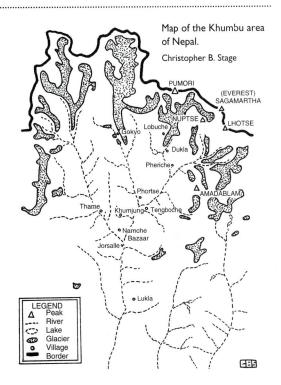

Map of the Khumbu area of Nepal.

Christopher B. Stage

boots, down parkas, baseball caps, and American university labeled sweatshirts. Another result of wide-spread employment in tourism is that people no longer live the way they used to. For instance, Sherpas who work as trekking guides or porters spend more time—roughly ten months a year—away from their villages.

Questions to Consider and Discuss

1. Which perspective do you think best portrays the effects of tourism in the Khumbu region? What are the opinions of your classmates? Why do you feel this way?

2. If you were managing tourism in the Khumbu, what policies would you establish and what would you hope these policies would accomplish?

3. As a class project, select an undeveloped area near you that has recently promoted itself as a tourist attraction. This could be a small town or a county. Interview local people to find out tourism's impact on them. Has tourism brought both good and bad outcomes?

modernization, Costa Rica has recently focused on promoting a reputation as an ecotourist destination. **Ecotourism** is a product that all Latin American countries have decided to develop to benefit from the "green" or "ecological wave" that has captured the attention of people in the developed countries. For example, nature lodges have sprung up in hitherto untouched wilderness areas, and newly trained guides are on hand to shepherd tourists along spectacular byways. Rain forest exploration, white-water rafting, deep-sea fishing, and nature study are now being aggressively marketed worldwide.

Promoting ecotourism is a potential means of making conservation profitable. The idea is that as more tourists visit the country's natural areas, the government and local inhabitants will become more interested in protecting them. For example, some tour operators help protect the tropical forest they take people to see by donating part of their profits to environmental groups. Others organize tours that focus on visitor efforts for conservation. In addition to horseback riding, snorkeling, and jungle trekking some tour groups actually work to maintain the natural areas they visit. Costa Rica has the largest number of ecotourist destinations.

With so much natural beauty, will Costa Rica be able to manage even ecotourism? To help insure the future for its 560 species of mammals, amphibians, and reptiles; 850 species of birds; 130 species of freshwater fish; and 9,000 species of plants; the government has decided that 25 percent of the territory will be part of the national park and wildlife reserves system. Let us hope; the alternative is something akin to the Acapulco or Cancun styles of development.

Leisure as a Development Tool

Leisure in developing countries like Malaysia, Poland, and Costa Rica—as well as in India, Egypt, and Mexico—is richly laced with the traditions and folkways of the culture. Music, dance, and art forms are woven into the fabric of society. In developing countries, particularly among poorer and rural residents, leisure is often mistakenly perceived as the domain of wealthy urban dwellers. When compared to people in developed countries, commercialized leisure does fare poorly for these people. One of the reasons, of course, is their low per capita income.

As countries (or any underdeveloped area, such as a rural county or an abandoned city center) seek to modernize, they embark on new income-generating efforts. Ironically, leisure has become an important means for doing this. Traditional arts and crafts are "updated" and exported. Sporting events are held to bring in outside money. Today, perhaps the single largest use of leisure as a development tool is via tourism. For Malaysia, as example, tourism is the third largest foreign exchange earner. It is also the prime motivator for the country's infrastructure enhancement. Within the past several decades tourism has been used as part of modernization strategies in most developing countries.

Summary: Leisure as Anthropology

In this chapter, we featured leisure in various societies to demonstrate that there is substantial complexity in the use of such daily human expressions as free time, rest, and recreational activity. Moreover, we concluded in our cultural comparisons that leisure is both a victim and a tool of modernization. On the one hand, the more industrially, technologically, and commercially advanced the culture, the more discretionary money people have for buying leisure. Is this a recipe for a high quality of life? In this chapter, we suggested that leisure may actually suffer from modernization. On the other hand, leisure can contribute to cultural development. It can be instrumental in enhancing social harmony, community development, and people's relations to the environment. Leisure can even be an important source of economic development.

Our exploration of leisure in this chapter was from a cultural anthropology perspective. This view of leisure is important for three reasons: (1) there is a diffusion of leisure practices from one culture to another, (2) certain forms of leisure act as tools for maintaining a culture, and (3) leisure can be a fertile ground for cultural innovation.

References

Association of Racing Commissioners International, Inc. 1992. Lexington, KY.

Biesanz, R., K. Z. Biesanz, and M. H. Biesanz. 1982. *The Costa Ricans.* Englewood Cliffs, NJ: Prentice-Hall.

Cole, J. B. 1988. Anthropology for the nineties. New York: The Free Press.

Ebashi, S. 1990. Tourism in Japan. *World Leisure and Recreation Association Magazine* (Spring):17–21.

Ekpo, K. 1991. Socio-cultural views of leisure in a multi-tribal setting. *World Leisure and Recreation Association Magazine* (Summer):13–16.

Ettinger, E. 1986. *Rosa Luxemburg: A life.* Boston: Beacon Press.

Fisher, J. F. 1990. *Sherpas: Reflections on change in Himalayan Nepal.* Berkeley: University of California Press.

Godbey, G. 1989. *The future of leisure services: Thriving on change.* State College, PA: Venture.

Goodale, T., and G. Godbey. 1988. *The evolution of leisure: Historical and philosophical perspectives.* State College, PA: Venture.

Grobler, J. E. H. 1985. The developing patterns of leisure time activities in South Africa's black cities since ca. 1930. *World Leisure and Recreation Association Magazine* (April):35–41.

Gunter, B. G., J. Stanley, and R. St. Clair. 1985. *Transitions to leisure: Conceptual and human issues.* Lanham, MD: University Press of America.

Hammel, R., and C. Foster. 1986. A sporting chance: Relationships between technological change and concept of fair play in fishing. *Journal of Leisure Research* 18:40–52.

Harbin, E. O. 1954. *Games of many nations.* New York: Abingdon Press.

Harris, L. 1987. *Inside America.* New York: Vintage Books.

Haviland, W. A. 1990. *Cultural anthropology.* Orlando, FL: Holt, Rinehart, and Winston.

Heider, K. 1977. From Javanese to Dani: The translation of a game. In *Studies in the anthropology of play,* edited by P. Stevens. West Point, NY: Leisure Press.

Hintereder, P. 1988. Leisure: Boon or bane. *Scala* (November/December):28–38.

Ibrahim, H. 1991. *Leisure and society: A comparative approach.* Dubuque, IA: Wm. C. Brown Publishers.

Insight Guides: Malaysia. 1990. Singapore: APA Publications.

International Herald Tribune, 1993. 28 June, 17.

Jung, B. 1990. More freedom, less leisure: The case of economic reforms in Poland. *World Leisure and Recreation Association Magazine* (Fall):5–11.

Jung, B. 1992. Economic, social and political conditions for enjoyment of leisure in central and eastern Europe of 1992—The Polish perspective. *World Leisure and Recreation Association Magazine* (Winter):8–12.

Kubey, R., and M. Csikszentmihalyi. 1990. *Television and the quality of life: How viewing shapes everyday experience.* Hillsdale, NJ: Lawrence Erlbaum.

Lazarus, D. 1993. Looking for a little peace and quiet in Tokyo? Try one of the city's 7,600 parks. *Northwest Airlines Magazine.* (October):69–72.

Leisure Development Center. March 1986. Survey on Leisure Demand. Tokyo, Japan.

Lippold, G. 1972. *Annotated bibliography on leisure: German Democratic Republican.* Prague: European Centre for Leisure and Education.

Mediamark Research, Inc. 1992. Multimedia audiences—Summary. In *Statistical abstracts: 1992.*

Milne, R. S., and D. K. Mauzey. 1986. *Malaysia: Tradition, modernity, and Islam.* Boulder, CO: Westview Press.

National Golf Foundation. 1990. Selected recreational activities: 1970–1990. In *Statistical abstracts: 1992.*

National Sporting Goods Association. 1990. Sports participation in 1990: Series I. In *Statistical abstracts: 1992.*

Neumann, H. 1985. The healthiest of pastimes: Sports for everyone. *Scala* (November/December):18–30.

Nielsen, A. C. 1982. *Nielsen estimates: National audience demographic reports.* Northbrook, IL: Nielsen.

Nishino, J., and K. Takahashi. 1989. Current leisure and recreation research in Japan. *World Leisure and Recreation Association Magazine* (Fall):11–14.

Paczynska, J. 1986. Women in Poland and free time activities. *World Leisure and Recreation Association Magazine* (August):30.

President's Commission on Americans Outdoors. 1987. *The Report.* U.S. Government Printing Office.

Sahlins, M. 1988. The original affluent society. In *Anthropology for the nineties,* edited by J. B. Cole. New York: The Free Press.

Schor, J. B. 1992. *The overworked American: The unexpected decline of leisure.* New York: Basic Books.

Sievanen, T. 1987. Midsummernight in the northern country—The change of light in the year's cycle. *World Leisure and Recreation Association Magazine* (April):23–24.

Skorzynski, Z. 1972. The use of free time in Torun, Maribor, and Jackson. In *The use of time: Daily activities of urban and suburban populations in twelve countries,* edited by A. Szalai. The Hague: Mouton.

Smith, A. 1980. *The geopolitics of information: How Western culture dominates the world.* New York: Oxford University Press.

Szalai, A., ed. 1972. *The use of time: Daily activities of urban and suburban populations in twelve countries.* The Hague: Mouton.

Tokarski, W. 1991. Economics of leisure and sport facilities: The German case. *World Leisure and Recreation Association Magazine* (Spring):26–28.

Trafton, D. A. 1985. In praise of three traditional ideas of leisure. In *Transitions to leisure—Conceptual and human issues,* edited by B. G. Gunter, J. Stanley, and R. St. Clair. Lanham, MD: University Press of America.

United Nations. 1985. *Statistical yearbook.* Paris: United Nations.

U.S. Bureau of Labor Statistics. March 29, 1990. *News,* USDL 90–154.

U.S. Bureau of Labor Statistics, 1993. How workers fare. U.S. Government Printing Office.

U.S. Bureau of the Census. 1992. Total population: 1980–1991. In *Statistical Abstracts: 1992.*

U.S. Bureau of the Census. 1993. *Statistical Abstracts of the United States: 1993.* Washington, DC: Government Printing Office.

Wanning, E. 1991. Culture shock! USA. Singapore: Times Books International.

Weiskopf, D. C. 1975. *A guide to recreation and leisure.* Boston: Allyn and Bacon.

Westland, C. 1990. Leisure in an emerging community. *World Leisure and Recreation Association Magazine* (Spring):5–7.

chapter

popular culture

six

PREVIEW

What is popular culture?
Popular culture is the everyday pastimes of a majority of people in a social group. It is mass leisure.

What are examples of popular culture?
In Western industrialized nations, such as the United States, examples of popular culture are television, radio, the cinema, magazines, books, newspapers, and other amusements and entertainments.

How is popular culture different from high culture and folk culture?
Whereas popular culture is the commercialized pastime expression of the masses, high culture is the typical pastime of the elite. Folk culture is transmitted orally and directly. Jokes are an example. In some cultures popular, high, and folk culture are the same.

Digital Stock

KEY TERMS

Baby boomers 176
Demography 186
Totalitarianism 188
Commercialism 189
Gramophone 189
Kinescope 189
Pluralistic 191

Do you remember what you did yesterday?

Did you listen to music on your radio or sound system? Did you watch television, read a newspaper, eat a McDonald's hamburger, jog while listening to your Sony Walkman, go to a bar or movie, or shop at the mall? You probably did at least one of these things; these are what most people in Western societies do with most of their free time. These are examples of popular culture.

Popular culture is not defined by its content or form; it could be music, literature, drama, or even sport. Popular culture is defined as the most typical pastimes of a particular group. The pastimes just listed represent the popular culture of young, single adults in Western societies. What were your typical pastimes when you were younger? Did you watch cartoons on TV? Did you read comic books, play with GI Joes or Barbie dolls? These represent the popular culture of children. In other words, popular culture is mass leisure. It denotes majority recreation. Everyday recreational activities and habits of many people are popular culture.

Eating at McDonald's is an example of popular culture in many countries. The restaurant is even located in Beijing, China.

© Ruth V. Russell

Popular culture can be tentatively distinguished from both folk culture and high culture. High culture is a label used to distinguish the typical pastimes of the elite. The elite in a society could be intellectuals, the wealthy, or upper socioeconomic classes of people. Generally, high culture is considered to be more serious than popular culture. Examples of high culture include ballet, classical music, and the fine arts. In some societies, high culture can also be very popular. For example, classical ballet is one of Russia's most popular pastimes (Kando 1980). Folk culture, on the other hand, is those pastimes that are shared through direct, oral communication, as in tribal and folk societies. Stories, jokes, and children's street games are common examples of folk culture. Sometimes folk culture can also be considered popular culture, such as when a particular joke becomes so widespread that it crosses subculture boundaries and becomes commercial.

Thus, more accurate than defining popular culture, is listing its characteristics. Perhaps you have already guessed the following four qualities. First, popular culture is those pastimes that are engaged in most often. It is the leisure activity of most of the people in a social group, most of the time. It is popular because it is a fundamental leisure expression of the culture. The most popular leisure expressions of college students may be different from those of retirees, but what these different popular cultures have in common is their popularity within that social group.

A second characteristic is that popular culture is commercial. It is leisure that is marketed and sold as a product. In the five years between 1981 and 1985, for example, annual music cassette sales climbed from $46 million to $611 million (Cieply 1986). McDonald's earned $6,142 million in 1989 (*Fortune 500* 1990). As of 1993, the top moneymaking films worldwide were *E.T. The Extra-Terrestrial, Star Wars,* and *Jurassic Park*—earning over $400 million each (United Press International 1993).

You may be wondering what are this year's top moneymaking films. This introduces a third characteristic of popular culture; it is trendy. Popular culture typically does not last long. While television, magazines, and films as popular culture categories have been more enduring, particular programs or titles have not. *A Chorus Line* had the longest run of all Broadway shows (1975–1990) but can no longer be seen there. At one time hoola hoops and trampoline parks were the rage, but they are difficult to find now.

A final characteristic of popular culture is its dependency on the tastes of youth. Often popularity in CDs, movies, foods, or sports is determined by the interests of young people. This is related, of course, to popular culture's trendy and commercial qualities. The businesses of popular culture focus on youth because of profit; that is, most youths do not save money. They tend to spend money they earn and money they receive from parents. They represent a high consumption sector of a population. According to a 1994 survey by Teenage Research Unlimited, American teens spend about $89 billion per year, an average of $61 a week each.

Combine this buying power with young people's need to be "in" by possessing the most desired products, and you understand why commercial enterprises target teens. Some radio stations, for example, program exclusively for

Mowing the lawn is a popular activity for suburbanites.

© Ruth V. Russell

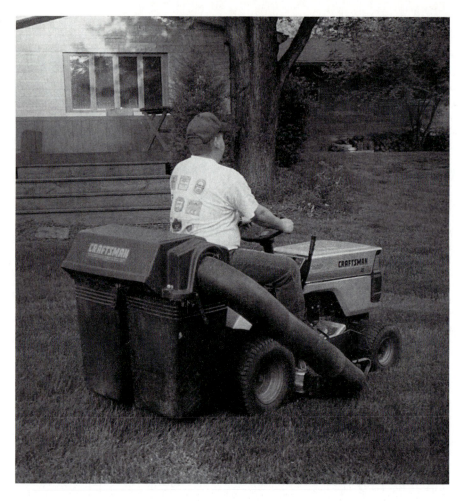

Baby boomers: the label given to the largest segment of the American population. Born between 1946 and 1964, they are the best educated generation to reach middle age, and they control nearly half the nation's income.

young listeners. Certain films are produced because of their perceived appeal to young moviegoers. For example, eight of the ten top money making American films have targeted older children and teen audiences.

While youth are important, other segments of a population control popular culture as well. For example, in the domain of popular music, some is ethnically and some is regionally popular. Rural America tends to be the largest market for religious music, and the American Midwest and the South can be typified by large interests in country music. The **baby boomers,** now in middle age, also affect popular culture. Because of their sheer numbers and higher incomes, their purchasing power also has an impact on mass recreation trends.

While entire books on popular culture have been written (Kando 1980), this chapter focuses on perhaps the most pervasive forms in modern Western societies. We begin with the most omnipresent of them all: television. Next, we briefly explore films, newspapers, magazines, and books. Finally, we discuss the thread that weaves these popular cultures together: the roles of entertainment and amusement in modern society.

Television

The hub of popular culture is television. Not only does it hold a central place in the use of free time, but it has become a primary means of communicating and validating what is popular (Kelly 1982). The A. C. Nielsen Company (1989) estimated that people in the United States view an average of seven hours of television every day. Given the possibility that this estimate is inflated, let us assume a more conservative estimate of two and a half hours of television viewing per day over the period of a lifetime (Kubey and Csikszentmihalyi 1990). This lower estimate means that a typical American would spend more than seven full years of life watching television out of the approximately forty-seven waking years each of us lives by age seventy (assuming eight hours of sleep per day). Such a realization is even more striking when we consider that Americans have only about five and a half hours a day of free time, or approximately sixteen years available for leisure in the same forty-seven year span. This means (based on conservative estimates) that Americans are spending on average almost half of their free time watching television!

Further, the number of hours spent viewing TV continues to rise by a few minutes each year, and people from almost every country in the world are becoming just as "hooked" on this form of popular culture. *Dallas,* for example, has aired in over ninety countries. Television has become not only our species' most preferred pastime but our most powerful means of mass communication as well. In spite of this, much is unknown about why people watch as much as they do and exactly how it affects them. For example, what is it about TV that would make one in four adults say they wouldn't give it up even for a million dollars? (*TV Guide* 1993).

The word *television* comes from the Greek word *tele,* meaning far, and the Latin word *videre,* meaning to see. Thus, *television* means to see far. Many scientists contributed to the development of television, so no one person can be called its inventor. Experiments leading to its invention began in the 1800s, but progress was slow. Television as we know it today was not developed until the 1920s, and it had little importance until the late 1940s. However, during one ten-year period—the 1950s—television became part of everyday American life. People became fascinated with having so wide a range of visual events available in their homes. Those who didn't have a set often visited friends who did just to watch television. Many stores placed television sets in windows, and crowds gathered on the sidewalk to watch. Today, about 98 percent of American homes have at least one television set; the typical home has two sets (Television Bureau of Advertising 1992). Television developed more slowly in other parts of the world. The television boom decade worldwide occurred in the 1960s.

While many uses exist for television—ranging from education to security and surveillance—television is watched chiefly for entertainment. Through television, it is possible to get caught up in the glamorous lives of daytime serial characters, vicariously win a cruise or a dining room set on a game show, and argue with a political commentator in a news broadcast. You can go on a shopping spree through television, and with video entertainment systems, use it as a game board.

Table 6.1
Percentage of Americans Who Participate in Specific Popular Culture Forms According to Education Levels

Form of Popular Culture	Total	High School Graduate	College Graduate
Radio	86	87	91
Newspapers	84	85	95
Television	94	94	91

Mediamark Research Inc. 1992

Television is a potent and intimate entertainment presence in people's lives (Nietzke 1978). You've already noticed some households where the television is on all day, even if no one is watching it. Other households may turn on the set for only certain programs, and still others have made an almost moral decision not to own a TV set. On the other hand, certain television "events" do have pervasive viewerships. For example, in 1978, the eight-day series of Alex Haley's *Roots* had 130 million viewers. The 1990 Super Bowl was watched by close to 40 percent of American households, and figure skating in the 1994 Winter Olympics was watched by 48 percent of households. While conclusions about television's ultimate impact remain questionable, some tentative answers are available. Do some population groups view more TV than others? When do people view the most?

From the research of Kubey and Csikszentmihalyi (1990), several conclusions can be drawn about who watches television and when. For example, African-American respondents in the study reported watching more television than did white or hispanic respondents. Single and married subjects reported watching television about the same proportion of time during the week, whereas divorced and single widowed subjects reported less TV viewing. Women tended to spend fewer minutes in front of the television than men, and viewing was slightly higher for all adults living with children. Finally, the research indicated that the more educated the respondents, the less television they watched. Data from another study (table 6.1) also led to the conclusion that persons with less education tend to watch more TV.

But these viewing comparisons actually varied a good deal less than might be suspected. Another survey of over 2,000 Americans (Bower 1985) indicated that a person's age, sex, race, education, and income made relatively little difference in how much TV was viewed. Bower concluded that everyone views TV about the same amount except when prevented from doing so by "external factors, like work" (p. 41). For those who work outside the home roughly forty hours a week, time left free to view television is limited. This at least partially explains why viewing time is greatest for children and older adults. For example, according to A. C. Nielsen (1990) men past the age of fifty-five spend an average of thirty-eight hours and twenty-two minutes per week watching television, while men between the ages of eighteen and thirty-four spend an average of twenty-four hours and fifty-one minutes per week watching TV.

Almost all television watching occurs in the home (mostly in the living or dining room) or at friends' or relatives' homes. A total of 25 percent of all time spent at home is spent watching TV (Kubey and Csikszentmihalyi 1990). Television viewing absorbs less than 15 percent of time at home between 5:00 and 7:00 P.M., whereas by 9:00 to 10:00 P.M., television has become the dominant activity. What do people do while watching television? In Kubey and Csikszentmihalyi's research (1990), the majority of respondents reported that their viewing was accompanied by other activities. Very few people consistently watched television exclusively. Typical accompanying activities are talking, eating meals or snacks, smoking, getting dressed, chores, child care, and even reading.

As a form of leisure, how is television experienced? Do we have a good time when we watch TV? A common criticism of television watching is that it replaces more active leisure. As a consequence, activity that is more physically, emotionally, or socially engaging may be postponed or eliminated from people's lives. Have you experienced this effect?

Kubey and Csikszentmihalyi (1990), found that respondents in their study generally reported "wanting to" view television over 90 percent of the time and wanted to work only 15 percent of the time. In short, television viewing is among the most freely chosen leisure activities. Also of note is the relatively high incidence of subjects (19 percent) indicating that they watched television because they said they "had nothing else to do."

Television viewing experienced by adults can be contrasted with other activities. The research results shown in table 6.2 demonstrate this contrast. In the

Rank Ordering (1–5) of Experience Qualities for Television Viewing and Other Activities

Experience Qualities	TV Watching	Working Outside the Home	Public Leisure	Idling	Meals
Concentration	3	1*	2	5*	4
Challenge	5	1*	2*	4	3
Skill	5	1*	2*	4	3*
Cheerful	3	4	1*	5*	2
Relaxed	1	5*	2	4*	3
Sociable	4	3	1*	5*	2*
Alert	4	2*	1*	5*	3*
Strong	4	2*	1*	5*	3*
Active	4	1*	2*	5*	3*

*Activities whose means are significantly different from TV watching means.

From Kubey/Csikszentmihalyi, *Television and the Quality of Life*. Table 5, p. 82. Permission by Lawrence Erlbaum Associates, Inc.

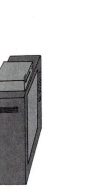

People today use electronic media extensively for leisure.

Christopher B. Stage

study, other activities included working outside the home (excluding coffee breaks, lunch, and other socializing), public leisure (dining out, parties, sports, club meetings, and cultural events), idling (waiting, daydreaming, resting), and eating meals. In the table, activities whose rankings by respondents were significantly different from those for television watching are marked with asterisks.

In summary, television viewing is a passive and relaxing, low-concentration activity. For example, the average levels of concentration, challenge, and skill perceived by the respondents in table 6.2 were lower for watching television than for all other activities. In other words, TV watching is quite easy. In fact, some information decoding processes necessary for understanding television messages happen almost automatically (Hawkins and Pingree 1986). Study respondents described TV as the most relaxing of the activities; that is, it was rarely stressful. It is said that television watching can cause anxiety and tension in younger people. It would be interesting to contrast a survey of children with the survey of adults reported in table 6.2.

What else do we know about the experience of watching television? For example, what is its impact on the family? As early as 1949, Riley, Cantwell, and Ruttiger claimed that television's presence in the home enhanced family togetherness because it provided one of the few opportunities for the family to spend time together. Later, Coffin (1955) argued that television was to be credited with increasing the family's opportunity for common experience, but also blamed it for decreasing conversation and face-to-face interaction. More recently, Kubey and Csikszentmihalyi (1990) supported the latter argument. Their findings revealed that heavier amounts of television viewing were related to slightly more positive experiences with family members by increasing the total time family members spent together. There was also evidence in their research, however, that people felt significantly less "quality" family interaction during family television viewing than in other family pastimes.

Another quality of the television experience seems to be the motivation to watch. For adults, viewing is often driven by a wish to escape or avoid negative feelings. Kubey and Csikszentmihalyi (1990) found that loneliness and negative feelings in the afternoon preceded heavy television viewing later the same evening. Heavier viewers also reported feeling significantly more negative during the week than did light viewers. It was found that television viewing was related to feelings of passivity and nonalertness after viewing. In other words, a passive spillover effect followed television viewing among adults, children, and adolescents. People reported feeling less able to concentrate after television viewing, too.

Television seems to become less rewarding the longer it is viewed. Although it is relaxing, as the amount of time spent watching increases, satisfaction and enjoyment in the experience tends to drop off (Kubey and Csikszentmihalyi 1990). Furthermore, heavier viewers feel worse than light viewers generally and particularly when alone. This relationship may be explained by the heavier viewer's tendency to use television to cope with loneliness.

What can be learned from this discussion? As a form of mass leisure, television has by far the most frequent participation of all pastimes. However, research suggests that while television viewing is freely chosen and provides relaxation and escape, it is the least enjoyable and invigorating of all pastimes. Then why is it so popular? Perhaps because it is so easy. The only constraints on watching television are free time and a TV set. No talent or skill is required. Television watching can be done anywhere with no other equipment, special uniforms, or players required, and after the initial purchase of the set, it is an extremely inexpensive activity. Is it a waste of time?

Many feel that TV is a waste of time. Television has been particularly criticized in relation to its impact on children via TV violence. For several decades, research has demonstrated that negative effects of television violence do exist. For example, Slaby (1994) has shown that some viewers of television violence, particularly those who strongly identify with the aggressor, manifest the "aggressor effect." They are more likely than nonviewers to display aggressive behavior and even serious violence toward others. The "victim effect" has also been documented. Some viewers of television violence, particularly those who identify with the victim, are more likely to show fear, mistrust, and self-protective behavior, such as carrying a gun. Finally, viewers of television violence may demonstrate the "bystander effect." They are more likely than other people to be callous toward victims of violence and to be apathetic toward others who engage in violence, because they have been desensitized to the point of accepting it. Unfortunately, particularly high levels of unrealistic television violence are presented to those most vulnerable to these distorting effects—children.

Just as worrisome are other potential negative outcomes of television watching for children. When too much time is spent watching television, is the development of social interaction and communication skills impeded? Is growth, experimentation, creativity, and the development of physical and mental skills stifled?

Similar worries exist for adults too. For example, the percentage of individuals engaging in vigorous physical activity appears to decline with increasing age. Older adults tend to be heavier television viewers, and television watching is a very passive activity. A sedentary lifestyle is a problem because it accelerates the aging process. It reduces opportunities for remaining physically flexible, strong, and coordinated. Exercise can add fifteen or more years to an inactive seventy year old's life (Bortz 1980).

For the elderly, television is an obstacle to a full life from another perspective as well. While television viewing can help give shape and distraction to the days of the retired, the time spent in TV viewing by older adults is typically spent alone and at the expense of more social pursuits. There is also the issue of role identity. Often, the elderly are portrayed negatively in television programs (Bammel and Bammel 1992).

The irony of all this is that television may benefit most those who need it least. Television does provide interesting and thought-provoking entertainment. It can influence viewers so that their feelings and thoughts are enhanced. Both drama and comedy can help deepen our understanding of ourselves and others. We can learn things from TV that help us be who we want to be. Overwhelmingly, the literature indicates that people who are already reasonably happy and in control of their lives will be more inclined to discover television's appropriate use and be less habitually dependent on it (Zillmann, Hezel, and Medoff 1980) but not always. As cited by Kubey and Csikszentmihalyi (1990), one man hospitalized for alcoholism spoke of how television "helped" him, "I have my drinking under pretty good control. I don't have my first drink of the day until noon when the *$20,000 Pyramid* comes on" (p. 185).

If television were eliminated, would people replace it with writing poetry, attending the opera, going camping with the family, volunteering at the community food pantry, or even playing cards? Many people would, but more than likely television is a form of popular culture that is impossible to replace. Perhaps the solution is in making television viewing more worthwhile. An obvious first step is the improvement of television programming (Quillian 1989). Ultimately, improving the viewing habits of the audience is needed as well.

This simply means that we need to become more mindful of our television watching. We need to view television as a method of personal growth, rather than simply as a way of killing time. Perhaps the question we should ask is "Given that I have at most five years' worth of free time left to live, do I want now to sit down and turn the set on?" (Kubey and Csikszentmihalyi 1990, 213). The answer might be either yes or no, depending on how we are feeling, the time of day, the choice of programs at the time, and our other pastime options and resources. The important thing is that watching television doesn't just happen mindlessly; it need not be an indiscriminate absence of choice. It should be chosen because of its contribution to the quality of our lives.

Films

Movies have a more limited audience than television and have experienced declines in attendance in industrialized countries since 1950. For example, an average of 80 million Americans went to the movies every week in 1946 (Chubb and Chubb 1981) compared to only 23 million in 1991 (Motion Picture Association of America, Inc. 1991). This decline may be attributed to such reasons as higher ticket prices and home video competition. While some have predicted that movie theaters will practically disappear as technology continues to affect the visual media, this is doubtful because going to the movies means more than simply seeing the entertainment on the screen. It serves as a relatively inexpensive outing in a special environment created by movie poster glitz and popcorn temptations. It provides a social occasion for family and friendship groups, and with the advent of special effects, creates a visual and sound sensation not yet copied by television.

To illustrate, let's consider the video movie impact on the film industry. In 1989, *Batman* earned $150 million as a home video rental (*Variety* 1989). Beyond the economic effects, how does video compare with traditional cinema movie viewing? A study reported by Wachter (1992) found that viewers liked video movies primarily because of the nature of the home environment. They felt more comfortable and private, could control the movie machinery to their own liking, and could do other activities while viewing the movie, particularly socializing. The disadvantages cited by respondents were that the home environment also had distractions, disruptions, and an inability to create the same emotional response as the cinema. The study found that viewing a film such as *Batman* in the cinema is valued for its unique ability to create a sense of separateness from reality and to provoke emotional response. This separateness is achieved by the specialness of the experience created by meeting friends, dining out, waiting in line, and going out for coffee afterwards. Also, the physical environment of the theater—the large screen and high-quality sound—projects images that stimulate an emotional response.

Changes in the popular culture of cinema cannot be singularly measured; thus, the conclusion is not always one of decline. For example, until the early 1970s, American film companies produced about 200 feature films per year. In 1977, only 118 films—the fewest ever—were released, yet that year U.S. box office receipts reached a record $2.4 billion (Chubb and Chubb 1981). This was the year of *Star Wars* and *Close Encounters of the Third Kind.*

Another change that makes the claim of a decline in film popularity less certain refers to where films are now produced. Prior to the 1970s, the major American film companies were the world's suppliers of motion pictures. Although the United States and Canada continue to be important markets, fewer films are being produced there. Now other countries (such as Japan, China, Sweden, and France) generate $600 million per year in film rentals compared to $700 million for American and Canadian rentals. This suggests that now the popular culture of films may simply be more widespread, and some film critics maintain that the contemporary foreign film industry has produced the majority of socially and artistically worthwhile works.

Not all movie theaters feature the same kinds of films. Out of the estimated 25,000 commercial movie screens in the United States, some feature currently released blockbuster movies, while others show foreign films or documentaries. Recent decades have witnessed the emergence of such genres as satanic possession (*The Exorcist*), ethnic history (*Malcolm X*), 1960s nostalgia (*The Big Chill*), political intrigue (*All the President's Men*), macho-violence (*The Terminator*), social commentary (*Do the Right Thing*), disasters (*Earthquake*), and science fiction (*Alien*). About 780 U.S. theaters feature pornographic films, seen by some 2 million people a week.

Today's cinema audience is as varied as the movies they watch. They are a heterogeneous collection of ethnic, social, and cultural groups. Unlike the docile television audience, moviegoers are assertive and capricious (Jarvie 1970). Who goes to the movies? From the research of Robinson (1977), we

Case Study   Reflections of the Culture from Horror Films

The Texas Chainsaw Massacre. In this film, a family of men, driven out of the slaughterhouse business by advanced technology, turns to cannibalism. The film features the slaughter of a group of young people traveling in a van and dwells at great length on the pursuit of the last survivor of the group, Sally, by the man, Leatherface, who hacks his victims to death with a chainsaw.

Friday the Thirteenth. A New Jersey camp that's been closed for twenty years after a history of "accidental" deaths reopens and the horror begins again. Six would-be counselors arrive to get the place ready. Each are progressively murdered: knifed, speared, and axed. The numerous sequels continue the gruesome murders by a maniacal Jason, who in succession escapes from the morgue and rises from the dead to slice up teenagers at a lakeside cottage and a halfway house.

Halloween. A deranged youth returns to his hometown with murderous intent after fifteen years in an asylum. *Halloween II* begins with the escape of vicious killer Shape, who continues to murder and terrorize the community of Haddonfield, Illinois.

Have you seen any of these movies? Like their predecessors (such as *King Kong* and *Rosemary's Baby*) contemporary horror films—the so-called exploitation or slasher films—provide many examples of the culture that pays money to see them. During the 1970s and 1980s, this category of film became part of the popular culture in North America. What does the popularity of these films tell us about the nature of the culture from which they emerged? There have been several content analyses of slasher horror films, so let's explore these for clues to the answers.

First, many of these films are engaged in an assault on all that bourgeois culture is supposed to cherish—youth, home, school, and even the shopping center (Modleski 1986). The individual, the family, and the institution are dismembered in the most gruesomely literal ways in these films. In *Dawn of the Dead,* the plot involves flesh-eating zombies running amok in a shopping mall, a scenario depicting perhaps the worst fears of modern culture! A few of the films, like *The Texas Chainsaw Massacre,* have actually been celebrated for their adversarial relation to contemporary society. This film has been analyzed as a critique of capitalism, since it shows the horror of people quite literally living off other people. It is also described as a critique of the institution of the family, since it implies that the monster is the family (Wood 1979).

Another illustration of this critique is in how women are considered. In contemporary horror films, an attractive young woman school teacher is beaten to death by midget clones (*The Brood*), a blond teenage girl is threatened by a maniac wielding a chainsaw (*The Texas Chainsaw Massacre*), and a beautiful female babysitter is terrorized by a grown-up version of the little boy killer revealed in the opening sequence (*Halloween*). According to Modleski (1986), in many of the films, "the female is attacked not only because, as has often been claimed, she embodies sexual pleasure, but also because she represents a great many aspects of the specious good" (p. 163).

Second, the slasher horror films often delight in fulfilling the audiences' expectations for nonclosure. In *Halloween* and *Friday the Thirteenth,* the slashers rise and kill over and over again even after they are presumed dead. Film analysts claim this reflects the impermanent nature of the culture: these films are allowed to dispense with the need for a plot and character development. People, and their personal stories, are not important. Thus, in films such as *Friday the Thirteenth,* the characters are so dispensable they are practically interchangeable, since we learn nothing of them as individuals. Likewise, there is virtually no building of a climax in the plot—only variations on the theme of slashing victims.

Worse yet, the camera location seems to place the audience in the perspective of the often unseen nameless presence which annihilates people one by one. This is a strategy that delights audiences as they cheer and applaud each outrage from their vantage point of the monster. This kind of joyful destructiveness on the part of the audience has been analyzed to mean that the masses are reveling in the demise of the very culture they appear most enthusiastically to support. For example, *Dawn of the Dead,* the film about zombies taking over a shopping center, has become a midnight favorite at shopping malls all over the United States.

Questions to Consider and Discuss

1. Have you seen any of the slasher films? What was your reaction to them when you saw them? If you haven't seen them, why not? How do your classmates feel about them?

2. What do you think these films portray about the culture? Do you agree with the analyses in this case study? Why or why not?

3. Overall, in your opinion, has American cinema improved or deteriorated in recent years? Why? How might the Supreme Court's rulings on pornography and the film companies' policies on film ratings affect future trends in the United States? Discuss the pros and cons of censorship, self-regulation, and governmental intervention in popular culture.

know that as with other forms of popular culture, film attendance is affected by employment status. Men attend movies more frequently than women, and full-time homemakers attend the least. As reported by Kando (1980), employed women attend movies nearly twice as much as unemployed women. Overall, less than 20 percent of movie attendance is done alone, and about 60 percent of moviegoers are married (Jarvie 1970).

Several studies have supported an already well-known fact; movie audiences are young. According to one older study (Opinion Research Corp. 1957), 15 percent of all individuals fifteen to nineteen years of age had seen a movie "yesterday." A second study found that 70 percent of all moviegoers are under thirty years of age and 50 percent under twenty (Nye 1970). The highest interest in cinema is by teens for whom the theater provides a place to get away from home, meet friends, and obtain a measure of privacy.

Finally, movies, which began as a form of entertainment for less affluent people, have begun to be a common pastime for the more affluent. Several studies (Kando 1980) have reported that the lowest educational, occupational, and economic levels are now underrepresented among movie audiences. Today's adult movie audiences tend to be better educated and from the professional occupational levels. They are also more likely to be from urban areas.

Newspapers, Magazines, and Books

Reading has been part of popular culture in Western societies since printing was first possible from woodcut, through the invention of movable type in the fifteenth century, to today's electronic publishing tools. In the United States and Canada today, more than 100 magazines share a total circulation of over 250 million readers. *Reader's Digest* and *TV Guide* are the most popular with combined circulations of about 32 million (Audit Bureau of Circulations 1988). There are approximately 1,626 daily newspapers in the U.S. with a combined circulation of over 62 million (*Editor and Publisher International Yearbook* 1990). Some 54,000 different book titles are published in the world annually (Bowker 1991). These are impressive numbers even though the production of printed materials continues to grow mostly in only developing countries. In this section, we focus on newspapers, magazines and books as popular culture.

People read newspapers for a variety of reasons. For some, the morning ritual of coffee and the newspaper is a means of waking up. Other people use newspapers for study as they would a textbook; some fill time with it while waiting in line or during TV commercials. Businesses follow the financial reports. Politicians pay clipping services to monitor the public's moods. Children race with their parents for the Sunday comics. Sports fans consider the paper a daily scoreboard. In any case, about 84 percent of adults in the United States read a newspaper to some extent (See table 6.1).

One of the better ways to distinguish newspaper reading behaviors of people is to compare their educational levels. For example, a study reported by Kando (1980) found that people who had not completed high school in the United States spent 80 percent of their reading time on newspapers versus only 48 percent for college graduates. College graduates spent more of their reading time reading books. College graduates also spent more time reading overall, an average of thirty-six minutes a day versus nine minutes for those who had not completed high school. Persons with less education replace reading time with television viewing.

In addition to time expenditure differences according to education level, qualitative differences appear in newspaper reading habits. An older study by Bogart (1964) showed that the readers' interest in local affairs decreases and their interest in national and international affairs increases with increased education. Also, the higher the education the more active the use of the newspaper. Such actions as clipping newspaper items, writing letters to the editor, or placing a classified ad increase for readers with higher educational levels.

A magazine is a collection of articles or stories—or both—published typically at weekly or monthly intervals. Most also include illustrations. They provide a wide variety of information and entertainment. The earliest magazines probably developed from newspapers or from bookseller catalogs, which first appeared during the 1600s in France. The first large-scale magazine boom occurred in the middle of the nineteenth century in industrialized countries. Today, subscription and newsstand sales can be quite lucrative.

In the United States and Canada, *National Geographic Magazine* has an annual circulation of over 11 million; *Better Homes and Gardens'* circulation is about 8 million; a more specialized magazine titled *Travel and Leisure* has a circulation of slightly more than 1 million (Audit Bureau of Circulations 1988). Of course, far more people read magazines than purchase them. Some magazine titles have four to five readers for every subscriber (Kando 1980) thanks to their availability in libraries and in the waiting room of doctors, dentists, and hair dressers.

Demography: the statistical study of human populations.

Magazine titles are popular to different readers. An assortment of **demographic** factors provides the distinctions. Perhaps more than any other popular culture category, magazines target specific segments of the population. For example, in no other medium are the sexes considered such separate audiences. Age levels, too, represent typical distinctions in magazine audiences. For example, *YM, Sports Illustrated, Popular Mechanics, 'Teen, Redbook,* and *Ladies Home Journal* make specific claims about the gender and age of their readership. Likewise, such magazines as *Ebony, Working Woman, The New Yorker,* and *Gourmet* target audiences distinguished by other demographic factors, such as race, occupation, education, and income.

Demographic factors also relate to the amount of magazine reading. The cross-cultural research of Szalai (1973) indicated differences according to country. For example, West Germans averaged twelve to thirteen minutes per day reading magazines, Americans four to six minutes, and Hungarians one minute. Also from this study, for the United States, blue-collar workers spent less time than others reading magazines. In this and other studies, however, educational level was the largest factor in the amount of time spent reading magazines; more educated persons read more.

Books are also part of the popular culture landscape. Most books for pleasure reading were originally published in Europe. In the United States,

Messages in Women's Magazines

Women's leisure is frequently described as "other-oriented." That is, it is likely to occur in conjunction with day-to-day responsibilities to others, such as children, spouse, and parents. Where might there be evidence of this? As a reflection of people's way of life, popular culture is often studied for answers to such questions. For example, a study by Simmons and Valerius (1992) examined whether popular women's magazines funnel women's leisure into such limited and traditionally-viewed, role-related activities. To determine this, the content of a year of issues of *Good Housekeeping* and *Cosmopolitan* were analyzed.

It was found that both magazines portrayed a limited scope of leisure for women. Approximately two-thirds of the advertisements and articles relating to leisure emphasized leisure in relation to others by depicting women in familial and traditional relationships. Women's activity interests were portrayed as woven into the leisure of children and male mates. The researchers concluded that the study raised important issues about stereotypes, gender inequality, and perceived passivity of women.

Try this yourself. At the library, sit down with a year of issues of a popular women's magazine. Study the content (articles and advertising), and every time leisure for women is depicted note the circumstances. For example, what is the social setting? Who is she with: colleagues, children, spouse and children, spouse alone, male friends, female friends, mixed friends, or is she alone? Where is she? Is the leisure taking place at a place of employment, at home, or somewhere else away from home? Is the woman in the article or ad engaged in role-determined leisure? That is, is she depicted doing something because of her responsibility as mother? Finally, how active is her leisure? Is she engaged in a passive or active pursuit? What conclusions do you draw? Are they similar or different from those of Simmons and Valerius? Why?

during the 1840s, "dime" novels began to appear in large quantities (Kando 1980). Some books sold—for as little as a nickel—100,000 copies in one year (Nye 1970). Today, book publishing continues to be a major industry that consumes millions of tons of paper a year, and according to surveys (Bammel and Bammel 1992), nearly one-third of the American adult population reads at least one book a month.

Subjects of popular books are wide ranging: history, the arts, sports, travel, games, gardening, poetry, and politics. Fiction, however, is the most popular, cutting across a wide spectrum of readers from adolescents to older adults. Most fiction readers are female, with historical, mystery, and romance fiction selling best. Biographies and autobiographies also appeal to a large segment of readers, as do cookbooks and books on popular psychology, sociology, and finances.

Science fiction is a frequently read category of books as well. Its popularity is particularly interesting in terms of its cultural and social significance. Lewis (1972) has pointed out that much of its theme centers around the struggle of humans against the encroachments of mechanization and bureaucracy.

Specifically, one strong science fiction theme is the dehumanizing impact of technology—often represented by the computer or the robot. Other pervasive science fiction topics are super-person or super-race situations and political doomsday prophecies predicting **totalitarianism.** How do you think these themes are characteristic mirrors of the culture?

People read books on city commuter trains, in backyard hammocks, at dining room tables, or in bed. Books are available everywhere as well. Popular books are sold not only in bookstores, but also in drugstores, airports, and grocery stores. Public libraries lend books for free. Books-on-tape also allow us to listen to books as we drive. Now CD-Rom and interactive video technology change how and where we read. For example, *Eurodisc* is an interactive video on the history of Europe. It is a package of eight laser disks containing 70,000 still and moving images, thousands of maps and pages of text, plus a stereo sound track of music through the ages.

In spite of all this, the inescapable fact about book reading as popular culture is its long-term decline. It is being gradually eclipsed by television. In 1935, the average amount of time spent reading a book in the United States was fourteen minutes per day. Thirty years later, it was four minutes (Robinson and Converse 1972).

Historical Reflections of Popular Culture in Modern Society

The functions of popular culture in modern society are significant. It's very definition as the most popular pastime of most of the people most of the time reflect its fundamental position in the culture. Perhaps its contemporary reflection can best be explored by comparing popular culture's impact on history. The variety and changes of popular culture were different at different times. From studying the past, we can begin to trace its important reflection in today's society.

To begin, in the late seventeenth century in the United States, we discover that ballads were sung about life and love, reflecting the more isolated character of the pioneer settlement. Although there were the popular attractions of shooting matches and horse races, contemporary pastimes are traced to the mid-eighteenth century when opportunities for mass popular pastimes began to increase.

Most characteristic at that time were rough team sports (Cross 1990). In England, sport was nearly without rules. In Derby, England, until the 1830s, Shrove Tuesday afternoon was devoted to a free-for-all between the boys and young men of two churches in the town. As many as a thousand youths on a side crowded around a ball pushing, kicking, and in general fighting to drive the ball toward their goal (such as a garden gate) a mile or so out of town. The whole town was the playing area. Some historians argued that these annual contests were socially accepted forms of war between closely-knit villages (Cross 1990).

In the eighteenth century, English cities offered more commercial pastimes. Urban living made possible entertainments for the masses in cheap forms. Public baths, coffee houses, and seaside amusement centers for music and dancing, as well as gaming, bowling, and shopping, occupied much of the people's free time. By 1790, there were fourteen morning papers in London, and by 1799, the first of a great institution, the Sunday newspaper, had arrived (Turberville 1933). In eighteenth-century American colonies, commercialized entertainments spread as well. Gambling (particularly card playing) and drinking alcohol were the popular pastimes of adult males. Of course, gambling and drinking have been common in many cultures, but the problems that emerged from them later in the nineteenth and twentieth centuries in the U.S. contributed to numerous contemporary efforts to control these pastimes.

How do we explain these passions? This was a time of a tremendous spread of **commercialism.** The commercial enterprise enjoyed a growing legitimacy and gambling, as a speculative commercial activity, complemented the times. Gambling reflected the spirit of risk taking and opportunism in establishing the new country. It channeled the excitement of competition into relatively peaceful directions. It was a means of displaying wealth and bravery. It expressed the value of individuality and the dream of gain (Cross 1990). It was also at the heart of how colonization and the western movement in America worked. For example, the Virginia Company sponsored a lottery in England in 1612 to raise funds for the financially struggling colony. Since then, Americans, who never fully endorsed such games as roulette, have felt no guilt over using lotteries to finance public projects.

Industrialization in the nineteenth century produced new forms of popular culture in the U.S. The creation of new wealth and technology gave birth to a penchant for novelty (Cross 1990). To capitalize on this, a mass entertainment industry emerged selling new pastime opportunities focused on a common denominator—the market. Great advances in transportation and communication resulted in a homogenization of pastimes. For example, although literacy was not extensive at the time, the demand for accessible pleasure reading was great throughout the century. Weekly newspapers (later to become magazines), chapbooks (paper-covered booklets), and cheap reprints of classic books were popular. The demand for indoor music was also universally insatiable. At first, this demand was met with variety shows in often disreputable saloons. Later, more respectable audiences were attracted to the opera house, followed later by the music hall.

Other public amusements of the nineteenth century, which reflect the new variety possible through technology, were penny theaters with thirty second pantomimed melodramas viewed on kinescopes, and five-cent theaters, which projected slides to tell popular stories of murder and revenge. Crowds were also drawn to the dime museums in New York City with their sideshow-like exhibitions (where Charles Stratton, or General Tom Thumb, first began his career) and wax displays depicting biblical and historical figures.

Gramophones and the **kinescope** opened the way for the projected film in 1895. The American nickelodeons (the first appearing in Pittsburgh in 1905) were the first movie houses. Often cheaper than other popular culture forms, they attracted the less affluent, often immigrant workers. Since these early films were silent and cost initially five cents, non-English speaking

Commercialism: excessive emphasis on or exploitation of people and resources for profit.

Gramophone: an early phonograph.

Kinescope: motion picture made from an image on a picture tube.

people could enjoy them on their way to or from work. By the turn of the century, the dance hall was also popular. In 1910, there were at least 500 public dance halls in New York City alone (Cross 1990).

Technology and the consumer market, which were so powerful in creating commercialized popular culture in the nineteenth century, played an even greater role in the mass recreation of the twentieth century. Foremost examples were the entertainments of film, radio, and television. What did they indicate about the culture?

Historians have stressed the complex impact of movies upon cultural values. Films, for example, contributed to changing attitudes toward women. About 1915, the childlike innocence and moralism of Mary Pickford's *Pollyanna* gave way to the aggressive sexuality of Theda Bara's *Vamp*. Still later, despite motion picture codes, films sanctioned sex by placing eroticism in an environment of affluence and sensuality. This continues as a contemporary characteristic of film. The 1920s were culturally hedonistic and glamorous, and at the core was the pursuit of excitement and success in the movies. Meanwhile, other contrasting values have been reflected in the cinema. For example, such films as *Grapes of Wrath* (1939) and *The Jazz Singer* (1927) portrayed themes of hardship and family tradition.

Radio, too, revealed a great deal about the times. Only one radio station existed in the United States in 1920. Ten years later, there were over 600 broadcast programs. By 1932, Americans devoted about four hours per week to radio listening. The radio was perfect for its time; it was very inexpensive and could be enjoyed by everyone. It especially provided entertainment for the homebound and companionship for the lonely. During the economic depression years, radio also functioned as a major form of relief from tensions. Through its policy of fifteen-minute shows, it also may have led to a reduced attention span.

American radio produced the peculiar arts of the soap opera and the situation comedy. Soap operas were originally aired in fifteen-minute segments each weekday afternoon. The situation comedy began with the racial humor of *Amos 'n' Andy,* which, oddly enough, was about two black men played by two white men. Radio also brought orchestras and vaudeville music to national audiences. On the other hand, it limited job opportunities for local musicians and killed Americans' interest in singing at home (Cross 1990).

Today, there are about 543 million radios in the United States, which means about two radios for every baby, child, adult and older person (U.S. Bureau of the Census 1993). However, radio listening behaviors have changed. While people no longer sit together to listen to an hour or two of radio in the evening, they do spend time listening to radio as a secondary activity—while eating, driving, reading and working.

Television was an extension of radio. In addition to taking over most of radio's functions, it also took over low-budget adventures from movies, plus various elements from vaudeville, variety shows, and nightclub acts (Sklar 1978). It was nearly a perfect expression of suburban lifestyles. It celebrated domesticity in its situation comedies and warned of urban dangers in its police shows, while enticing viewers through commercials to the joys of fast food and shopping. By the mid-1950s, American critics claimed that television was an excellent example of Gresham's Law in culture: "bad stuff drives out the good, since it is more easily understood and enjoyed" (Cross 1990). Other critics viewed television as an electronic version of nineteenth-century popular culture—sideshows for freaks and sensations. Supporters claimed that in situation comedies and soap operas a comfortable "family" was offered to a society suffering from the loss of extended families.

In some situation comedies of the 1970s, the "family" portrayed was not all that comfortable as television led the way in upgrading social consciousness. Watch some reruns of *All in the Family, Maude,* and *The Mary Tyler Moore Show* for examples of this. All these shows picked on the white, male head of the household and his alleged bigotry (Kando 1980).

Reflections in Popular Music

Popular music has been a tremendously important barometer of cultural character; some examples follow. Nationalism became a force in the music of Spain in the early 1900s. Russian composers, while ruled by their communist government's policy of socialist realism, nonetheless, wrote very romantic music. Latin American music reflects the festive temperaments of its people. Likewise, from the beginning of America's history, music has interpreted its various cultures. America has been characterized by its hymn, folk, jazz, blues, soul, rock, and even rap music.

For example, in the 1950s and 1960s, popular music was dominated by rock. First, it was the more primitive working-class style of Bill Haley's Comets and Elvis Presley's blend of country and African-American styles (Kando 1980). In the mid-1960s, Bob Dylan and other performers combined folk lyrics with the beat and instruments of rock. This produced folk, or progressive, rock which dealt with a variety of social issues of the time: civil rights, dissent, drugs, poverty, war, and the lifestyles of young people. The antiestablishment hard rock of Led Zeppelin and Frank Zappa also were popular. Some of the rock music of the late 1960s and 1970s was combined with other musical forms to yield a different genre, such as with opera (*Tommy*) and religion (*Jesus Christ Superstar*). For the most part, however, rock music in the 1980s and 1990s has been more traditional. Today's rock has moved back into the cultural fold, singing primarily about love and emotions among young people. American rock music has become accepted worldwide. Today, the performers may be Dutch, Chinese, or Brazilian, and the beat more syncopated, but the music is by and large an imitation of American rock.

American popular music is not just rock. It is at heart **pluralistic.** Different forms appeal to different Americans, but foremost it is an interweaving of various ethnic strands. Perhaps jazz best illustrates this characteristic of American popular music. Jazz has often been labeled the only music form to originate in the United States. While most of the best jazz today is still played in America, more and more musicians in other countries are playing good jazz as well.

Pluralistic: ethnically, religiously, racially, and socially diverse.

biography
Bessie Smith

"The Queen of the Blues," Bessie Smith (1894-1937), won stardom as America's premiere jazz singer in the 1920s, reaching millions through performances in vaudeville and on radio and records. She broke attendance records at theaters throughout the country. Among the first recordings she made—"Down Hearted Blues"—sold over 700,000 copies in six months. Ultimately, Bessie's rich, powerful contralto voice was captured on a total of 160 records (Wilson 1992).

Bessie was born in 1894 into extreme poverty in Chattanooga, Tennessee. In 1912, she and her brother Clarence, a dancer, joined a road show playing in Chattanooga. She was quickly "discovered" and the next year began singing at the "81" Theatre in Atlanta (Wilson 1992). After her performances, people threw money on the stage. For several years she traveled the African-American vaudeville circuit and by 1920 was appearing in her own show. Her opening at the Koppin Theater in Detroit caused a near riot. The streets of Birmingham were blocked by the overflow crowds trying to see her performance at the Frolic Theatre. It was the same in city after city.

By 1925, Bessie was writing her own lyrics. Perhaps her most famous was "Black Water Blues," written and recorded in 1927. One summer night that same year, Bessie, alone, chased away hooded Ku Klux Klansmen gathered outside the show tent. Based on this experience, Bessie wrote "Poor Man's Blues," a song of social protest. Some consider it her finest record. Also in 1925, Bessie began performing with top accompanists. Jazz history was made on January 14, 1925 when Bessie and Louis Armstrong made what many critics consider the definitive recording of "St. Louis Blues."

When the record market collapsed in the early 1930s, Bessie's road show struggled through the Depression years until 1937, when she was fatally injured in an automobile accident in Mississippi. During the years of her greatest fame, from 1923 to 1928, the African-American public bought millions of her records. Unfortunately, her work was almost unknown to white audiences until shortly before her death.

However, the claim remains that jazz, more than any other popular music form, more directly interprets the emotional language of Americans.

In the beginning, jazz was a simple form of folk music, developed by nonprofessional musicians. While several cities make claims, no one really knows exactly where jazz was born. The music is a mixture of rhythms from West Africa; harmony from European classical music; religious music from the gospel traditions of spirituals; and work songs from the days of slavery. Much of the earliest jazz was performed informally at African-American funerals in the South. Between 1910 and 1920, it began to spread out of the South to such places as Chicago and New York City. The first jazz band to make records was The Original Dixieland Jass Band (the spelling was soon changed to jazz). These were white musicians who paved the way for commercial jazz popularity by both black and white musicians, such as Louis Armstrong, Bix Beiderbecke, Count Basie, Charlie Parker, and Duke Ellington. During the 1920s, jazz flourished; this was the Golden Age of Jazz. Bessie Smith became the most famous of the great jazz singers.

Jazz has gone through several stylistic phases that reflected the times. For example, an early form of jazz that became popular was ragtime. This is an energetic style of piano playing that uses a more formal composition. Later, the blues became popular. This music could be identified by the mournful blue note—usually the third or seventh note of a scale played or sung a quarter or half tone flat. It reflected the sadness and misery of the slave years. By the 1930s, jazz took its next step when swing—a happy and relaxed jazz beat—became wildly popular. Swing was usually played by big bands using set musical arrangements that also included improvisation by soloists. The famous swing bands of Artie Shaw, Tommy Dorsey, Benny Goodman, and Glenn Miller helped Americans get through World War II. Benny Goodman was the first bandleader to present black and white musicians working publicly together. Bop, and later cool jazz, started in the 1940s and featured more subtle syncopation and a more even beat. In the 1940s and 1950s, jazz began to lose its reputation as a low-class music and gained acceptance among intellectuals and college students.

There was also international growth of jazz at this time; the first big jazz festival was held in Newport, Rhode Island, in 1954. Since then, annual festivals have taken place all over the world. Jazz began to be used as an instrument of international goodwill when in 1956 the U.S. Department of State sponsored tours of the Middle East and Latin America by Dizzy Gillespie. Through the 1950s, much of the development in jazz was made by small combos, such as the groups of Miles Davis and Dave Brubeck. During the 1970s, many musicians blended jazz and rock music to create fusion jazz. Fusion combined the melodic and improvisational aspects of jazz with the rhythms of rock—mastered by such musicians as George Benson and Herbie Hancock.

Today, jazz continues its subtle changes as the American culture continues to change. While remaining true to its multicultural roots, jazz still reflects the dreams and fears of people in contemporary society.

Reflections from Amusement Parks

Perhaps the most fascinating reflection from popular culture is the amusement park. As the nineteenth century gave way to the twentieth century, jugglers, tight-rope walkers and pantomimes performing in tents, theaters, and wagons were gradually displaced by carnivals. Perhaps the most dramatic demonstration of the nineteenth-century carnival occurred in 1893 with the Columbian Exposition in Chicago. Educational exhibits of "mosques and pagodas, Viennese streets and Turkish bazaars, South Sea island huts, Irish and German castles, and Indian tepees" (Cross 1990) offered the exotic four corners of the world to almost 21.5 million visitors. Meanwhile, dominating the midway was the Ferris wheel (fig. 6.1). This was the first and largest of its kind, built by G. W. Gale Ferris, a mechanical engineer from Illinois. The wheel was 250 feet in diameter. Each of the thirty-six cars could hold sixty people, and one revolution took twenty minutes.

The Ferris wheel was quickly copied in pamusement parks around the world, as was the extravagance

Figure 6.1 Drawing of the Ferris wheel at the 1893 Columbian Exposition in Chicago.

Christopher B. Stage

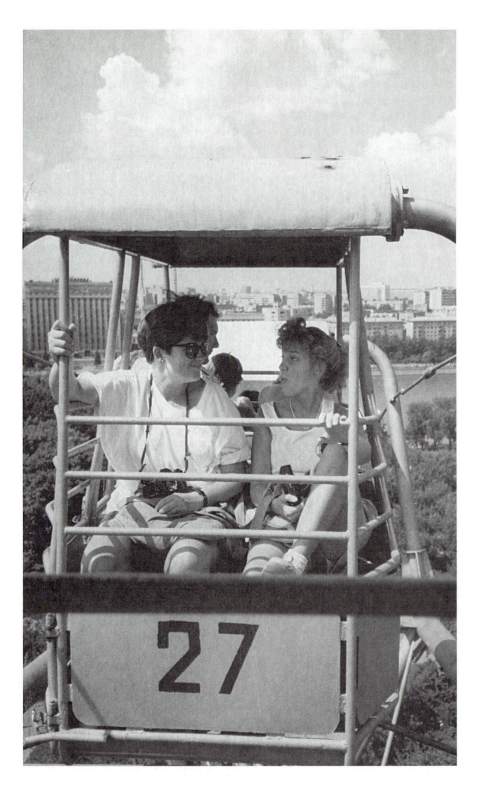

Tourists enjoying the Ferris wheel at Gorky Park in Moscow, Russia.
© Ruth V. Russell

of the pseudo-exotic themes of the Chicago exhibition. Also, electric-powered rides like the roller coaster and the loop-the-loop began to attract young people in particular to amusement parks. By the 1930s, this form of popular culture was in full swing. Typically constructed along waterfronts and on the outskirts of cities, millions of people flocked to them on weekends. One of the most famous was Coney Island in Brooklyn, New York. Here, excitement could be had for five or ten cents a ride.

> Coney Island allowed people to subtly break moral codes. The "Barrel of Fun" threw young men and women together; air jets lifted women's skirts; and post cards offered slightly risque themes.

> (Cross 1990, 135)

Historians claim that Coney Island attracted people because of its allowance for breaking accustomed social norms. It mocked the established order.

> Coney Island in effect declared a moral holiday for all who entered its gates. Against the values of thrift, sobriety, industry, and ambition, it encouraged extravagance, gaiety, abandon, revelry.

> (Kasson 1978, 50)

Today, amusement parks no longer are examples of popular culture. While there remain a few outstanding locations (such as King's Island in Ohio), many are finding it difficult to compete with other forms of entertainment. Theme parks have taken the place of amusement parks. Sesame Place, a children's water park featuring the characters from the television program, and Knott's Berry Farm, which draws on a western theme, are representative of the coordinated package of attractions around a single theme that defines theme parks. Theme parks are typically lavishly and imaginatively landscaped, with clean and friendly staff. They are good places for family entertainment.

The pioneer in this was, of course, Walt Disney. The concept that Disney demonstrated for the rest of the world since the opening of the first theme park—Disneyland in California in 1955—was the shutting out of the surrounding problems of the urban environment and an emphasis on wholesomeness. The four Disney theme parks are organized around themes of fantasy, the future, adventure, the frontier, and Americana. In Walt Disney's own words:

> Disneyland will be based upon and dedicated to the ideals, the dreams and the hard facts that have created America. And it will be uniquely equipped to dramatize these dreams and facts and send them forth as a source of courage and inspiration to all the world. Disneyland will be something of a fair, an exhibition, a playground, a community centre, a museum of living facts, and a showplace of beauty and magic.

> (Mosley 1985, 221)

Recently, a few critiques have emerged about what the Disney theme parks reveal about the culture. Let's briefly discuss these as our final look at the role of entertainment in society.

biography
Walt Disney

Walt Disney (1901–1966) was the most famous entrepreneur of popular culture in history. In the two worlds of the cinema and amusement parks, his singular reputation is unmatched as the creator of wholesome and uplifting entertainment.

He was born in Chicago, the son of a small-time businessman and a school teacher. Because his father dreamed of living away from the city, the family moved to Missouri when Walt was a child. He returned to Chicago to study art at the age of sixteen, but his fledgling artistic career was interrupted by World War I when he served on the western front in France. In 1923, Disney moved to Los Angeles with the goal of becoming an animator and for several years struggled just to pay his expenses. Finally, in 1928, he released the first Mickey Mouse cartoons (*Plane Crazy* and *Steamboat Willie*), which brought his first success. Disney himself provided Mickey's voice.

From 1929 to 1939, Disney produced a cartoon series called *Silly Symphonies,* in which Mickey Mouse and the newly introduced Donald Duck, Goofy, and Pluto made appearances. In 1937, he released the first full-length cartoon film ever made: *Snow White and the Seven Dwarfs.* It became one of the most popular movies in history. Other full-length animated films followed, including *Pinocchio* (1940), *Fantasia* (1940), *Dumbo* (1941), and *Bambi* (1942).

Disney's work in cartoons was interrupted during World War II when his studio made educational films for the United States government. After the war, instead of returning to cartoons, he concentrated on making films featuring real human and animal actors. His first full-length movie of this type was *Treasure Island* (1950). *Mary Poppins* (1964) probably ranks as the most successful of these Disney films. All in all, the Disney studio has won more than forty-five Academy Awards for its movies and for innovations in film making.

After television became popular in the 1950s, many film makers fought it as a threat to the movie industry. Disney adjusted easily to the new form of entertainment and produced a number of movies especially for television. He also hosted a weekly television show.

However, Disney achieved one of his greatest successes outside of film and television when he opened Disneyland in 1955, a theme park in Anaheim, California. A similar park, The Magic Kingdom, opened near Orlando, Florida, in 1971, after Disney's death. These parks, as well as Disney Tokyo and EuroDisney in France, feature shows, exhibits, and rides based on Disney characters and other adventure and fantasy themes. In Florida, the Magic Kingdom park is joined with Discovery Island, Disney-MGM Studios Theme park, EPCOT Center, and Typhoon Lagoon to become Walt Disney World. This is a 28,000 acre complex that also includes a night club theme park, campgrounds, five championship golf courses, resort hotels, and a shopping village.

How did it all happen?

It came about when my daughters were very young and Saturday was always Daddy's day with the two daughters. So we'd start out and try to go someplace, and I'd take them to the Merry-Go-Round and I took them different places and as I'd sit while they rode the merry-go-round and did all these things—sit on a bench, you know, eating peanuts—I felt there should be something built where the parents and children could have a little fun with them, too.

Walt Disney only lived to see Disneyland in California. He died in 1966 of emphysema (Schickel 1986).

First, Rojek (1993) has written that Disney theme parks present not just entertainment but a moralistic and idealized version of the "American Way." He described it this way. The moral order of the parks is based on a nostalgic picture of American society: the "authentic" American barbershop quartet; "real" turn-of-the-century streets of small town America; shiny faced youth dressed in red, white, and blue playing their hearts out in a brass band; ever smiling and lively characters from Disney animated films; and throughout, a narrative of the moral and economic superiority of the American way of life.

Disney World in Florida.
© Ruth V. Russell

Even the layouts of the parks, claimed Rojek, suggest an idealized space. The journey from the parking lot via monorail is set up as a crossing from the mundane world into a place filled with excitement and magic. Once past the turnstiles, we are in Main Street, USA. "Everything is freshly painted, neat, tidy and clean: a de-racialized, de-politicized space which symbolizes the original purity of the American community" (Rojek 1993, 127). Then, in Adventureland, the armchair traveler goes to far-off and mysterious destinations, such as a tropics jungle and the Caribbean. In spite of "ferocious" wild animals and "barbaric" pirates, these dangers are always defeated by the "superiority of white, middle-class power" (Rojek 1993, 128). The next stop is Frontierland, which "symbolizes the triumph of white, male culture over nature" (p. 128) and Tomorrowland where a "sense of eternal progress" is portrayed (p. 128).

Rojek's critique continues in the same vein. Essentially, the criticism is that the Disney theme parks overstep their entertainment role. They are underpinned by powerful political and social values; they present white, male-dominated, upper-class culture as perfect; and they distort history, presenting the American society as free of conflict. What do you think? If you've visited a Disney park, do you agree or disagree with Rojek?

A second perspective of the Disney theme parks as a cultural mirror, is from the anthropologist Conrad Kottak (1987). He compares a trip to The Magic Kingdom with a religious pilgrimage. Just as in many cultures where religious systems focus on sacred sites, the world flocks to the Disney "shrines." Just like pilgrims, visitors to the park share a common social status—at least for a few hours. They wait for hours in carefully controlled lines, they eat only that food served to them (no picnics allowed), and they worship the same "gods." For example, in Liberty Square's Hall of Presidents, "pilgrims silently and reverently view moving, talking, lifelike dummies" (Kottak 1987, 554). While on the Splash Mountain ride, they pay homage to a fictional rabbit (Brer Rabbit) as a build up to the big baptism (flume drop into water) at the end. Of course, the most potent religious symbol worshiped in the Magic Kingdom is Cinderella's castle, complete with a moat where pilgrims throw coins and make wishes.

Kottak concedes that most people probably visit Disney World for amusement—a vacation. In this sense, they do differ from pilgrims to religious shrines. They do not appear to believe that the visit has curative properties. Nonetheless, Kottak observed, "television news programs occasionally run stories about communities pooling their resources to send terminally ill children to Disneyland. Thus, even though a visit to a Disney park is not regarded as curative, it is an appropriate last wish" (Kottak 1987, 555). What do you think? If you have visited a Disney theme park, do you agree or disagree with Kottak's comparisons?

Summary: The Popular Culture Mirror

Popular culture, or mass recreation, is an important mirror of a society. Because of its commercial, trendy, and youth dependent characteristics, it is a pervasive expression of the culture itself. Examples include culture's reflection in television, radio, film, newspapers, books, magazines, popular music, and theme parks.

Television by far is the most frequently participated in pastime. It is a potent and intimate presence in culture, yet research suggests that while television viewing is freely chosen and provides relaxation and escape, it is the least enjoyable and invigorating of all pastimes. Research has also demonstrated that television is reflected in viewers' moods and behaviors—most of which is negative.

References

Audit Bureau of Circulations. 1988. Publishers' statements for six-month period ending December 31, 1988.

Bammel, G., and L. L. B. Bammel. 1992. *Leisure and human behavior.* Dubuque, IA: Wm. C. Brown.

Bogart, L. 1964. The mass media and the blue-collar worker. In *Studies of the American Worker,* edited by A. B. Shostak and W. Gomberg. Englewood Cliffs, NJ: Prentice-Hall.

Bortz, W. M. 1980. Effects of exercise on aging: Effect of aging on exercise. *Journal of American Geriatric Society* 28, no. 2:149–51.

Bower, R. T. 1985. *The changing television audience in America.* New York: Columbia University Press.

Bowker, R. R. 1991. *Publisher's Weekly.* New York: Reed Publishing.

Chubb, M., and H. R. Chubb. 1981. *One third of our time? An introduction to recreation behavior and resources.* New York: John Wiley & Son, Inc.

Cieply, M. 1986. Risque business. *The Wall Street Journal,* 21 April, 20D.

Coffin, T. 1955. Television's impact on society. *American Psychologist* 10:6.

Cross, G. 1990. *A social history of leisure since 1600.* State College, PA: Venture.

Editor and Publisher Yearbook. 1990. New York: Reed Publishing.

Fortune 500, 1990. The Time Inc. Magazine Company.

Hawkins, R. P., and S. Pingree. 1986. Activity and the effects of television on children. In *Perspectives on media effects,* edited by J. Bryant and D. Zillmann. Hillsdale, NJ: Lawrence Erlbaum Associates.

Jarvie, I. C. 1970. *Movies and society.* New York: Basic Books.

Kando, T. M. 1980. *Leisure and popular culture in transition.* St. Louis, MO: Mosby.

Kasson, J. 1978. *Amusing the millions: Coney Island at the turn of the century.* New York: Hill and Wang.

Kelly, J. R. 1982. *Leisure.* Englewood Cliffs, NJ: Prentice-Hall.

Kottak, C. P. 1987. *Anthropology: The exploration of human diversity.* New York: Random House.

Kubey, R., and M. Csikszentmihalyi. 1990. *Television and the quality of life: How viewing shapes everyday experience.* Hillsdale, NJ: Lawrence Erlbaum Associates.

Lewis, G. H., ed. 1972. *Side-saddle on the golden calf: Social structure and popular culture in America.* Pacific Palisades, CA: Goodyear Publishing.

Mediamark Research Inc. Fall 1992. *Multimedia audiences.* New York: Mediamark Research Inc.

Modleski, T. 1986. The terror of pleasure: The contemporary horror film and postmodern theory. In *Studies in entertainment: Critical approaches to mass culture,* edited by T. Modleski. Bloomington, IN: Indiana University Press.

Mosley, L. 1985. *The real Walt Disney.* London: Futura.

Motion Picture Association of America, Inc. 1991. New York, NY.

Motion picture revenues. 1989. *Variety, Inc.,* 31 December.

Nielsen, A. C. 1989. *Nielsen report on television.* Northbrook, IL: Nielsen.

Nielsen, A. C. 1990. *Nielsen report on television.* Northbrook, IL: Nielsen.

Nietzke, A. 1978. Getting it on with "Gunsmoke." *Human Behavior,* (June):63–67.

Nye, R. 1970. *The unembarrassed muse: The popular arts in America.* New York: The Dial Press.

Opinion Research Corporation. 1957. The public appraises movies. A Survey for the Motion Picture Association of America, Inc., Princeton, NJ.

People Pick TV over $1 million. 1993. *TV Guide,* 10 October.

Quillian, R. 1989. Better than mercenary democracy. Unpublished manuscript.

Riley, J., R. Cantwell, and K. Ruttiger. 1949. Some observations on the social effects of television. *Public Opinion Quarterly* 13:223–24.

Robinson, J. P. 1977. *How Americans use time.* New York: Holt, Rinehart, and Winston.

Robinson, J. P., and P. E. Converse. 1972. Social change reflected in the use of time. In *The human meaning of social change,* edited by A. Campbell and P. E. Converse. New York: Russell Sage Foundation.

Rojek, C. 1993. Disney culture. *Leisure Studies* 12:121–35.

Schickel, R. 1986. *The Disney version: The life, times, art and commerce of Walt Disney.* London: Pavillion Books.

Simmons, B., and L. Valerius. October 1992. Women's leisure: Messages in women's magazines. Paper presented at the Leisure Research Symposium, National Recreation and Park Association Congress, Cincinnati, OH.

Sklar, R. 1978. Popular culture, no. 5: Hollywood gave us dreams. *Centre Daily Times,* 15 February, 19.

Slabey, R. G. 1994. Combating television violence. *The Chronicle of Higher Education,* 5 January, B1–B2.

Szalai, A. 1973. *The use of time: Daily activities of urban and suburban populations in twelve countries.* The Hague: Mouton.

Teenage Research Unlimited 1994. Teen spending down. *Parade Magazine,* 13 March, 21.

Television Bureau of Advertising 1992. *Trends in television annual.*

Turberville, A. S., ed. 1933. *Johnson's England: An account of the life and manners of his age.* London: Oxford.

United Press International. 1993. 'Jurassic Park' tops $400 million. *International Herald Tribune,* 10 August.

U.S. Bureau of the Census. 1993. *Statistical abstract of the United States: 1993.* Washington, D.C.: Government Printing Office.

Wachter, C. October 1992. The movie experience: A comparison of cinema and home video. Paper presented at the N.R.P.A. Leisure Research Symposium, Cincinnati, OH.

Wilson, V. 1992. *The book of distinguished American women.* Brookville, MD: American History Research Associates.

Wood, R. 1979. *American nightmare: Essays on the horror film.* Toronto: Festival of Festivals.

Zillmann, D., R. T. Hezel, and N. J. Medoff. 1980. The effect of affective states on selective exposure to televised entertainment fare. *Journal of Applied Social Psychology* 10:323–39.

taboo recreation

chapter

seven

PREVIEW

Is there a negative side to leisure?

Yes, in spite of leisure's vital importance to the health of individuals and society, our pastimes can also produce negative outcomes.

What is taboo recreation?

Pastimes that are forbidden by law, custom, or belief are taboo recreation. Examples are gambling, substance abuse, vandalism, and harmful sex.

Why does taboo recreation occur?

There are at least two explanations. First, anomie is a concept that says that once viable social norms no longer control people's actions. Second, the idea of differential association claims that deviant behavior is learned through interaction with others.

© Ruth V. Russell

Leisure is a major contributor to people's

well-being. Leisure can help relieve tensions, maintain physical fitness, enhance mental equilibrium, and teach us how to get along with others. It is one of the best methods of health insurance, is vital to the human development process, builds strong communities, yields a productive workforce, and can serve as a catalyst to protecting and rehabilitating the environment. Specially trained professionals working in clinics, hospitals, and treatment centers use leisure activities and counsel in leisure attitudes to help patients return to the mainstream of life. Leisure is, in fact, one of the most positive and wholesome aspects of contemporary life.

However, leisure is not always positive and worthwhile. It also has a negative side. Unpleasant, as well as pleasant, results are possible through our pastimes. People can be injured while participating in recreational activities. Exhaustion, apprehension and nervousness, guilt, disappointment, and frustration can be experienced from participation in outdoor pastimes and sports in particular (Lee, Howard, and Dattilo 1992).

Beyond this, leisure has an even darker side. Under certain circumstances, individuals engage in pastimes that society considers deviant. In the American society, for instance, only certain forms of gambling are legal in only certain locations. Buying sexual pleasure is considered a problem in many countries of the world. Combining the two popular leisure pursuits of driving for pleasure and drinking alcohol regularly results in death. Vandalism can be fun for the participants, but costs other individuals and society billions of dollars.

Taboo: a social restriction based on tradition.

Pursuits such as these are considered **taboo** in many societies. The word *taboo* comes from the Polynesian word *tapu,* which means something sacred, special, dangerous, or unclean. While certain actions or objects are forbidden by law, many others are informally frowned upon on the grounds of morality or taste. For example, some societies believe that people who go to a taboo place or touch a taboo object will suffer injuries. Often sacred objects or persons are considered taboo because they are believed to have a mysterious force that enables them to harm others. All social groups of people in the world have taboos, but they are not universally the same taboos. For example, Australian Aborigines must not say the name of a dead person aloud. Muslims must not eat pork. A Western taboo, incest, is not considered taboo by all societies.

Taboo is a useful descriptor of the pastimes we consider in this chapter because they are typically forbidden by custom or belief. That is, a recreation activity wears the label deviant or socially unacceptable because of a subjective value held by society. Various societies have differing pastimes that are considered taboo. Even within the same society, taboo recreation can also change its degree of wrongness and rightness. For example, in colonial America in the 1700s, Puritan taboos were observed. There were laws forbidding participation in such activities as card games, dancing (women with men), and even theatrical performances. These laws no longer exist in the United States. In fact, local, state, and federal governments contribute financial support so that the performing arts might thrive.

Today, other taboo forms of recreation are practiced in industrialized cultures. For example, recreational marijuana use, which is illegal in the United States, was nonetheless enjoyed by nearly 34 percent of college students in 1989 (University of Michigan 1989). Alcohol is the number one substance problem among youth, however. By their senior year of high school, almost all students will have tried alcoholic beverages, even though it is not legally available to them. One in twenty high school seniors will be daily users, and 54 percent of seniors used alcohol in the last thirty days (U.S. Department of Education 1992). Each year in the United States approximately 326,000 persons are arrested for vandalism and 111,400 for prostitution (U.S. Department of Justice 1991).

As in all things, there are two sides to the story. Going for a jog may build fitness levels—so might hooking hubcaps. Joining a Scout troop may provide outlets for socialization and building self-esteem—so could joining an urban gang. The purpose of this chapter is to expand our understanding of leisure by considering the relationship between leisure and acts of deviance. We begin by developing possible explanations for taboo recreation behaviors. Two systems for describing these actions are discussed and followed by examples of pastimes that can be injurious to participants and injurious to others and society.

Leisure and Deviance

The occurrence of **deviance** in leisure is not only documented in police records and social work files but in research as well. For example, in one study (Agnew 1990) a national sample of adolescents indicated the reasons for their engagement in fourteen types of delinquent activities. Personal pleasure was most frequently cited as the motive for theft and fraud, and ranked second for hard drug use, marijuana use, alcohol use, trespassing, and illegal entry. Thrill-seeking was most often identified as the explanation for illegal entry and hard drug use. Social pressure was the reason most respondents engaged in alcohol and marijuana use, and boredom was frequently cited as an explanation for involvement in vandalism, illegal entry, and alcohol use.

Deviance: behavior that is different from an accepted norm.

Further, Aguilar (1987) provided rationale for considering delinquent behavior a game. "In theft or vandalism activities, the object of the game is to complete the task without getting caught. If done as a group activity, the youth might play various roles: leader, thief, vandal, guard, or distractor. If one youth gets caught, the unwritten rule is never to identify the others. A violation of the rule means exclusion from future delinquent games with friends and peers" (p. 5).

Purple Recreation

Two classifications have been developed to describe the connection between leisure and deviance. First, Curtis invented a concept for describing the "dark" side of pastimes. He termed it purple recreation (implying "off color") and defined it as delinquent activities that bring pleasure to participants, but to society, they are destructive and negative uses of free time. Some purple recreation ventures may result in only mild harm to the occasional participant, while others can cause major physical or mental damage, financial loss, or even death if engaged in heavily or for long periods of time (Curtis 1979, 1988).

Purple recreation, according to Curtis, is a matter of degree. Activities fall on a continuum ranging from such destructive acts as premeditated murder and torture, to such wholesome activities as church singing. Labeled The Curtis Scale, this continuum simplistically illustrates the range of "good" versus "bad" pastimes.

The Nash Pyramid

Nash also provided a way of thinking about taboo recreation. His model shows a hierarchy of leisure values (Nash 1953). As shown in figure 7.1, creative activity is the highest use of free time, while criminal activity is the lowest. Nash designated leisure pursuits that harm others or society as the sub-zero levels. The zero level is where injury may occur to the self as a result of excesses in leisure pursuits. Above this are four levels of more positive pastimes, and according to Nash's model, the higher the level the more personally and socially redeeming its value. A little of each above zero, depending on work patterns, may be good, but too many activities low on the scale are dulling, and in the end progress and development of the individual and the group are restricted. Thus, according to Nash, it is better to be actively involved in leisure than simply entertained.

Figure 7.1 An illustration of The Nash Pyramid.

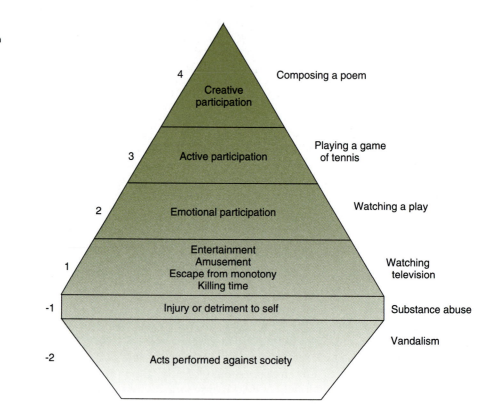

Part Two   Leisure as a Cultural Mirror—Societal Context

Why Taboo Recreation?

Why do people engage in socially unacceptable pastimes? As with most problems in society, explanations for taboo recreation have been sought in attempts to reduce its incidence. This has typically been approached by first studying deviant behavior in general and then extending the findings to understand deviant recreation behaviors. As a result, there are several theoretical explanations currently available. We'll consider two: anomie and differential association.

Leisure's Potential for Anomie

One explanation for taboo recreation is the concept of **anomie.** Anomie occurs when once viable social norms no longer control people's actions (Merton 1957). For example, at American River College in Sacramento, California, table games—including chess, checkers, cards, and dominoes—have been banned. Why? Formerly workable and informal social norms no longer controlled students' behaviors. The disruptive behaviors of people playing in the cafeteria and library had become such a problem that campus police must now uphold the new legal norms.

> Anomie: a lack of purpose and identity in a person or a society resulting in the demise of formerly useful social norms.

Typically anomie can be traced to an imbalance between a goal and the means to attain it. While it does not cause deviant forms of leisure, anomie does provide an environment in which these pastime choices are nurtured (Moore 1982). Taboo recreation activities, such as vandalism or substance abuse, occur because of a breakdown in formerly useful social regulations due to frustrations over not having the means to achieve goals. A tagalong concept is periodic anomie (Matza and Sykes 1961) from which taboo recreation pursuits temporarily arise, often in the form of thrill seeking.

Anson (1976) was one of the first researchers to study anomie in leisure. He found that a perception of a lack of recreational opportunities, economic means, and a poor self-concept led some adolescents to engage in deviant pastimes. Later, Moore (1982) investigated the leisure choices of young offenders. In comparison with young people who were not legal offenders, offenders exhibited a greater preference for taboo recreation and a higher level of anomie. In other words, the nonoffender group tended to perceive greater availability of positive recreational opportunities than offenders.

A useful example of anomie as an explanation for taboo recreation is the pastime of sport spectating. In the United States, the most popular spectator sports are thoroughbred horse racing, major league baseball, and college men's basketball (U.S. Department of Commerce 1992). As shown in table 7.1, spectator sports are big entertainment! And why not? A wonderful vicarious pleasure results from watching top athletes perform. We can have the fantasy of participation. We see ourselves dancing a pirouette to the top of the hoop for a slam dunk in basketball, or stretching across the court to make an impossible match point in tennis.

Table 7.1

Number of Spectators at Major Sports Events

Sport	Attendance in 1990 in millions	Average Player's Salary
Horseracing	64	
Major league baseball	55.5	$598,000
Men's college basketball	33.5	
Greyhound racing	28.5	
Professional basketball	18.5	$817,000
NFL football	17.5	$350,000
Professional ice hockey	12.5	$254,000

From U.S. Department of Commerce, *Statistical Abstracts*, 1992, p. 239

Yet, something has gone wrong! With greater frequency we read about rioting and violence in the crowd at sporting events. Fires have been started in the stands and property destroyed; fans have crossed barricades to attack and sometimes kill the fans of the other team or an athlete; referees have been assaulted. It seems the attitude has quickly gone from "it doesn't matter whether you win or lose, but how you play the game" to "in your face."

Eitzen (1984) examined newspaper accounts of sixty-eight episodes of collective violence or riots among spectators during or after sporting events, and concluded that in three-quarters of the cases, the precipitating event was violence in the game. Several attempts have been made through research to understand what goes wrong when violence in sport spectating occurs. Eitzen's observation reflects one reason: aggression breeds aggression. When athletes are violent on the field or court, there is a greater likelihood for violence by the fans. Confirming this, a study by Leonard (1988) found a slight tendency for spectators of violent sports to score higher on hostility after an event than spectators of nonviolent events.

Another possible answer to violence of spectators is that of self-selection. Hostile spectators may gravitate toward aggressive games (like ice hockey), whereas nonhostile spectators may gravitate toward nonaggressive events (like gymnastics). Is there a profile that describes a violent fan? Another study reported by Leonard (1988) found that more aggressive spectators tended to be male, students, season ticket holders, and have varsity athletic experience.

How do these hunches explain recent increases in spectator violence? The concept of anomie may provide a useful clue. According to anomie theory, society prescribes norms of success for people. For many roles in sport—athlete, athletic director, coach, trainer—this success means winning. However, since virtually all sport contests create both winners and losers, someone is bound to be thwarted in the quest for victory. Ways of coping with

Thoroughbred horse racing spectators at Keenland, Lexington, Ky. Spectator violence is an example of anomie.

© Ruth V. Russell

losing include conforming and rationalizing, but there are also socially deviant responses, such as cheating and rebelling. Thus, the social norms that customarily rule sports may no longer have control over players' (and spectators') behavior, and violence may result.

Leisure's Potential for Differential Association

A theory of differential association is a second attempt to explain taboo recreation. This theory is based on the idea that delinquent behavior is learned through interaction with others in intimate personal groups. Accordingly, leisure behavior is learned from association with social and friendship groups. If this group is delinquent, deviant forms of leisure may be learned. An individual's social groups can include family, peers on sport teams, housemates at college, classmates, and neighborhood or work friends. Young people are particularly affected by their associations with social groups; thus, the values and activities of the people with whom they most relate may differentiate whether or not their pastimes will be deviant.

Research also supports the differential association explanation of taboo recreation. A similar study of 3,000 adolescents in Canada (Bippy and Posterski 1985) found that the majority considered friendships to be more important than family. Agnew (1991) found that the impact of delinquent peers on establishing delinquency behaviors was conditioned by the level of attachment and the amount of time spent together. When time or attachment is minimal, deviant behavior is less likely to result. These data suggest that in order to reduce socially unacceptable behavior, emotional closeness with delinquent peers needs to be minimized.

Sanyika Shakur, also known as Monster Kody Scott, was born in 1963 into the gang world of south-central Los Angeles. He was initiated into the Eight Trays, a "set" of the Crip gang based in his neighborhood, at the age of eleven. His initiation rite included shooting several members of the rival Blood gang. At thirteen, he says, he robbed a man and stomped his face so badly that the police told bystanders the person responsible for the crime was a "monster." At fifteen, he was arrested for carjacking and assault. At sixteen, he was ambushed by rival gang members and shot six times. In the next few years, he was convicted of armed robbery, mayhem, and possession of an AK–47 assault rifle. By 1993, he was serving a seven-year sentence in Pelican Bay State Prison in northern California for beating a crack dealer.

Writing from prison, these are some of the things Monster said in his book: *The Autobiography of an L. A. Gang Member* (1993).

In a perverted sort of way I enjoyed being Monster Kody. . . . Nothing I knew of could compare with riding in a car with three other homeboys with guns, knowing they were as deadly and courageous as I was. To me at this time of my life, this was power.

An obvious example of the differential association explanation of taboo recreation is youth gangs.

Meet Roach and Shorty T. Their uniform consists of extra large pants held up with a belt. Added to this is a sweatshirt worn under a T-shirt. Often posed in a Charlie Chaplin-style stance, they are rarely seen without dark sunglasses and a hairnet. Roach is twelve years old and Shorty T is seventeen.

Motivated by love, pride, notoriety, self-worth, a sense of belonging, and the need for praise, Roach and Shorty T are members of a youth gang in a southwestern city in the United States. Originating in the 1940s, their gang is territorial—marking their space with graffiti.

The main activity in a typical day is protecting and challenging territory. This means Shorty T, Roach, and other members challenge the territory of other gangs by replacing the original graffiti with their graffiti. Encroachment of another's territory is grounds for killing each other. Their girlfriends help out.

This profile is based on a panel discussion presented by police and recreation staff of the City of Santa Monica, California (NRPA 1990). The panel's purpose was to describe a critical, increasing, and hard-to-solve problem shared by many communities. Costing millions of dollars in police services and thousands of wasted lives, youth gangs and accompanying violence are major problems for young people today.

Youth gangs can provide an example of the differential association explanation of taboo recreation. Adolescents are attracted to participation in gangs because of opportunities for power, recognition, excitement, and independence (Manson 1990). This creates associations that can potentially lead to anti-social actions, depending upon the strength of the relationships. A study of gangs in a southern California beach community (Lowney 1984) reported that gang members felt that although basic needs were fulfilled through the family, the gang provided companionship and opportunities for the pursuit of pleasure. Further, condemnation by society strengthened the bonds of individuals to the gang, alienating them further from society and limiting their access to socially acceptable forms of leisure (Vigil 1988).

Injuring Self

Perhaps you've heard the expression "victimless crime." As described by sociologist Stephen Pfohl (1985), this label applies to a wide range of social exchanges punishable by criminal law. For example, substance abuse is considered deviant because society deems it so. Its harm is mainly to those who participate. Although it may certainly be argued that substance abuse has a potential for harming others (drunk driving can kill innocent people), victimless crimes are primarily focused on the participant's pursuit of enjoyment.

A concept that attempts to explain these activities is ideational mentality (Heise 1988). Laws based on ideational mentality are primarily morally derived. That is, people have an "idea" that something is bad; even though they do not wish to participate in it themselves, they feel the need to prohibit others from being involved because they have the idea that such restriction is for the public good. They have labeled a behavior, such as drug use, as deviant and use the powers of law to make that label stick (Stiefvater 1993). Let's explore two examples of ideational mentality: substance abuse and gambling.

Substance Abuse

A group of children used a playground as headquarters for a make-believe drug ring, selling neatly packaged bags of sugar and grass clippings that looked like cocaine and marijuana, police said Wednesday.

Narcotics are essential in the practice of medicine; they are the most effective agents known for the relief of particular diseases and pains. They can literally keep people alive. Pharmaceutical production is also a lucrative enterprise: prescription and over-the-counter drugs comprise roughly a $40 billion a year business (Stiefvater 1993). Alcohol is also useful. In modern cultures, it provides a means for relaxation and temporary escape from hectic pressures, providing both physical and psychological benefit. A daily glass of wine or beer is considered by some experts on old age to increase longevity. However, when drugs and alcohol are abused—overused—problems can result.

Substance abuse is perhaps the most prevalent type of taboo recreation in the world. A ten-year study by the United States Department of Health and Human Services (McGinnis and Lashoff 1988) reported that illicit use of drugs other than marijuana is highest in the U.S. today among adults aged eighteen to twenty-five years. The report also stated that the use of cocaine by high school seniors increased 13 percent between 1984 and 1985. Americans use an estimated 40 percent of the world's illegal drugs (CNN 1988). In Great Britain, a national survey found half of all sixteen-year-olds had visited a public drinking house during the previous week, and over one-fifth of fourteen- to sixteen-year olds spent regular evenings in pubs (Roberts 1983).

The use of alcohol and drugs for recreation is not a new phenomenon; it has existed since ancient times. In fact, it can be traced to the beginnings of human history. The invention of agriculture seems to have been motivated both by a need for a constant food supply and the discovery of the use of cultivated grains for beer. Noah is reputed to have discovered grape wine (Lazare 1989).

Drugs and alcohol provide temporary escapes from everyday life. As with any pastime, this escape can be pleasant. Executives can wind down together after a day on the job with a martini. Marijuana helps warm up a group of young friends for a social conversation. Interestingly, a euphemism for using drugs is "taking a trip"—enjoying a change of pace just as we do when we leave home for a holiday or vacation. Thus, alcohol and drug use often begin in a leisure context. Alcohol and drugs are typically combined with other recreational activities because it is believed these substances enhance the fun. Cocktails are served at parties; beer is sold at baseball games; hallucinogens are popped before a concert. Unfortunately, these substances provide only "temporary detours" rather than enriching charter trips (Bammel and Bammel 1992), and their abuse can lead to sometimes insurmountable social and personal problems.

In spite of widespread use as a pastime and as an enhancement of other pastimes, drugs and alcohol are prohibited in many societies. In the United States, for example, people must be at least twenty-one years of age in order to drink alcohol, and the use of certain drugs is authorized only by medical officials. Nonetheless, each year in the United States about 910,000 people are arrested for drunkenness and 1,811,000 for driving while under the influence of

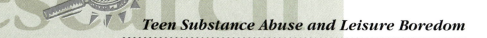

Substance abuse typically begins in adolescence (Czechowicz 1988). Today, the majority of high school seniors drink regularly and about half use illicit drugs. One question might be, why?

For drug use, research has unequivocally shown that family and peer influences play a crucial role (Halebsky 1987; Kaplan et al. 1986; Stein, Newcomb, and Bentler 1987). Personality factors also relate to drug use among adolescents (Chassin 1984; Mayer 1988). For example, substance abusers are more likely to be sensation seekers with a low tolerance for repetitious experiences.

What about the leisure connection? Substance use most frequently occurs during free time; thus, wholesome recreation activities are typically a deterrent or substitute to such antisocial activities. For example, one research team (Purdy and Richard 1983) found that the probability of a teen becoming involved in delinquent activities was directly related to the amount of unstructured and unoccupied time available. The busier they are, the less time available for getting into trouble.

Might there be another side to the story? Iso-Ahola and Crowley (1991) conducted a research study that asked a different question about leisure and drug use. Is it possible that a lack of personal leisure skills combined with restricted recreation opportunities can cause feelings of boredom in leisure, which gives rise to drug use in free time? In other words, is it more than just a lack of something to do? Are adolescent substance abusers more likely to experience their leisure as boredom than non–substance abusers?

For the research study, Iso-Ahola and Crowley selected a group of thirty-nine substance abusers (including those who had used alcohol, marijuana, cocaine, PCP, LSD, steroid injectives, hashish, and inhalants) ranging from fifteen to eighteen years of age, who were being treated in hospitals. Another group, a control group of subjects, consisted of eighty-one non–substance abusing adolescents of the same age range who were attending a private school. A questionnaire, asking about their frequency of participation in a variety of leisure activities, was given to both groups of teens. A second questionnaire asked about their perceptions of boredom while participating in these activities.

As was hypothesized, the results indicated that the substance abusers were significantly more bored with their pastimes than non–substance abusers. Interestingly, the substance abusers participated significantly more in certain pastimes: football, baseball, gymnastics, skateboarding, rollerskating, attending concerts, and going for a drive. The non–substance abusing teens participated overall in fewer leisure activities, except for reading, tennis, and going to the movies.

Thus, the researchers concluded, as expected, that substance abusing teens are more likely to experience leisure as boredom. This suggests that substance abusers with high levels of boredom in leisure seek optimal arousal through illicit substances as a way to decrease the boredom. Unlike other research, this study also concluded that teens who abuse substances have a tendency to be more active in total leisure participation. It seems paradoxical that substance abusers were more bored with leisure and yet more active in leisure.

What could help explain this paradox? What other factors do you suggest that could be studied to understand more about why teens use drugs and alcohol?

alcohol. Annually, drug abuse violations result in approximately 1,090,000 arrests (U.S. Department of Justice 1992).

In some recreation and park facilities and programs, substance use as a pastime is prohibited. For example, many city and state parks do not allow alcohol for picnics; college stadiums forbid alcohol consumption by spectators; and members of youth clubs, such as Scouts, can be kicked out for drug use. Why? If alcohol and drugs have the restorative and relaxing properties important to leisure, why have we worked so hard to prohibit their use?

Good leisure experiences enrich and improve the participant. While the use of drugs and alcohol may provide momentary sociability and relaxation, their abuse prevents any real leisure benefit from taking place. The more heavily we indulge in alcohol or drugs, the more destructive the effect. Therefore, we are less likely to have an authentic leisure experience. Leisure can be joy, freedom, intrinsic reward, and spirituality, as well as pleasure and risk. Abuse of drugs or alcohol inhibits these qualities. Therefore, the relationship between dysfunctional use of substances and dysfunctional use of leisure is a reciprocal one. While substance use often begins in a leisure setting, as the use of the substance increases, the individual's leisure becomes secondary to the substance.

Compulsive:
psychological obsession.

Compulsive overuse of substances produces many of the same problems as compulsive eating, gambling, television viewing, and even running; however, greater severity often results with substance use. Drug- and alcohol-related problems cost law enforcement agencies billions of dollars in crime management. It costs employers billions of dollars in lost working time. Families and friends lose loved ones to disease, such as the spread of AIDS through intravenous drug use, and death, such as from drunk driving. One entire generation of Chinese was essentially wiped out by extensive opium use early in the twentieth century (Godbey 1989). Even if this form of taboo recreation were decriminalized in the future, some of the problems that result from irresponsible use would remain. It is indeed a complex pastime.

Gambling

Nevada is the driest state in the United States with an average annual rainfall of only about seven inches. As a result, much of Nevada is uninhabited, sagebrush-covered desert. Nevada was first made famous by the discovery of the fabulous Comstock Lode in 1859, and its mines have produced large quantities of gold, silver, copper, and other minerals since. In 1931, the state created a new industry: gambling. Nevada is the gambling entertainment capital of the United States. In almost every public place, one can enjoy slot machines, and the casinos of Reno and Las Vegas are legendary. Gambling taxes account for about 42 percent of state revenues.

Nevada is not the only place where gambling is enjoyed. The country of Monaco, for example, has had internationally popular gaming tables since 1856. In 1981, Atlantic City drew 18.5 million gamblers, an increase of 11.5 million since the opening of its first casino four years earlier. Gambling, in both legal and illegal forms, takes place in nearly every American town and city. Dog and horse racetrack betting, poker games, bingo, sport bookmaking, state

As a leisure activity, drinking alcohol and using mood altering drugs can become addictive and a problem for the users, their family and friends, and society. Can this also be true for those leisure activities we typically consider wholesome? What about running, for example? Is it possible that running can become addictive?

Forty males who are regular runners were divided into two groups and studied for six weeks. One group continued their normal running (three times a week for a total of ten miles). The other group was stopped from running for the middle two weeks of the study. Questionnaires were completed at the end of each week by everyone. According to the findings, symptoms of depression were greater for those who stopped running for two weeks. Such complaints as anxiety, insomnia, and feelings of being under strain were also greater after both the first and second weeks of the withdrawal period in the group that stopped running. These complaints disappeared by the last two weeks of the study when both groups were running again. The researchers concluded that stopping regular physical exercise produces psychological problems and that physical exercise, therefore, may be considered addictive (Morris et al. 1990).

lotteries, riverboat casinos, church raffles, and numerous other forms of gambling thrive. In 1993 in the United States, an estimated $392 billion was spent on gambling, a 17 percent increase from 1992 (CNN 1994). One out of every three American adults gambles at least once a month (Godbey 1990).

Gambling is betting on the outcome of a future event. While people bet on almost anything with an unpredictable outcome, they bet most often on games of chance, such as dice or card games. People also gamble on games of skill, such as horse races and other sports. Gambling's basis in games is reflected in its other label—gaming.

Some gamblers believe it is a quick way to make money without the effort of working. In many gambling games, however, the chance of winning is small, and most people lose money. Psychologists believe that the real attraction of gambling lies in the thrill of uncertainty, the daring involved in taking chances and the challenge of testing one's skill. For example, according to a study conducted by Smith and Preston (1985), 91 percent of gamblers sampled said they gamble because it is a form of play and recreation. Forty-five percent said they gamble to relieve boredom and generate excitement. Only 39 percent gamble to gain monetary profit.

Some gambling is done informally with family and friends. In fact, revenues from such unauthorized gambling represent about 28 percent of the total gambling market (Leonard 1988). With the advent of televised sports, informal sport gambling increased—primarily by middle-income people. Men, it is estimated, average about 123 gambling sessions a year, and women gamble about 35 sessions a year (Downes et al. 1976).

This is not the "only game in town"! In the United States within the last decade, government sponsorship of gambling has increased. This has

Case Study   Bingo

A thick cloud of smoke, much like the one that enveloped Pompeii when Vesuvius lost its temper, hung over the bingo parlor at Saint Rose of Lima . . . Nerves were razor-sharp because Mutzi Elliott, the caller and greengrocer, was instituting new games. Mutzi had just returned from bingo school. Up until tonight we'd played bingo the way everyone plays bingo. You get a diagonal line filled up or a straight line and you yell "Bingo." We were graduating into advanced bingo . . . The Ping-Pong balls with numbers flew up in the air in a glass cage . . . "Railroad tracks. Next game is railroad tracks. You remember now, you've got to get two parallel columns. Ready." He paused for effect. "Steady. Go." A ball popped up. "Number two." Mutzi sang, "Tea for two and two for tea." (Brown 1988)

Bingo is a simple game. Numbers are selected randomly, called out, and marked off on cards by the players. The first player to cancel the appropriate pattern of numbers on their card wins. Even if the patterns get "advanced" as they did for the caller Mutzi, the only real challenge occurs if you're trying to fill a lot of cards at once.

Bingo is relatively cheap to play. Clubs tend to be local and handy. Bingo has been quite popular with lower-income women because it overcomes many of the constraints facing them. Commitment to it can be flexible; if she has no money or a child is ill, nothing is lost by not going. By contrast, if an evening crafts class has already been paid for, money is lost if she doesn't go. It is easy to see why women frequently make up more than 75 percent of bingo players.

Why might women participate in bingo? Beyond getting out of the house, is there anything else to it? Dixey (1987), a researcher in Great Britain, asked some women in her country this question. Here is what some of them said:

> They do come socially, but they all come to hope to win some money, you know . . .

> . . . say they won £ 1000 on a Wednesday night, right, so they'll go back next Wednesday and say "Maybe I'll get it again." Well that's human nature.

> . . . there are a few people that go just because of the fact that they want to win, and they get very upset and angry if they don't win.

(Dixey 1987, 207–8)

As we might expect, playing bingo for the chance to win money is important to them. In actuality, winnings tend to be small and infrequent. It is not a good investment as the cost of bingo is not usually offset by winnings. However, even players who know they are unlikely to recoup their money still hope to win. Was this all the women in the bingo hall told Dixey? Here are some more quotes.

> I like bingo. It cheers you up, keeps your mind off anything troubling you, keeps you in touch with your family when you don't live near them.

> I like the club because it is warm, comfortable and I think it is more of a social club rather than just a place to play bingo.

> Where one can go and feel content at my age and feel that one is among friends.

> Being a widow, I come to bingo to meet people, and have a good laugh and a chat.

(Dixey 1987, 213)

Lottery: a gambling event where prizes are distributed to the winners whose "lots" are drawn among persons buying a chance.

accompanied a general liberalization of attitudes toward gambling, brought on in many cases by attempts to raise funds through gambling for government treasuries. The most common form of government gambling sponsorship is state **lotteries.** States without lotteries are missing out on a potential $2.7 billion in revenues annually (Leonard 1988).

Interestingly, government sponsorship of gambling raises a question about the taboo label for this pastime. A contradiction exists if state laws continue to maintain that gambling is immoral and prosecute people for en-

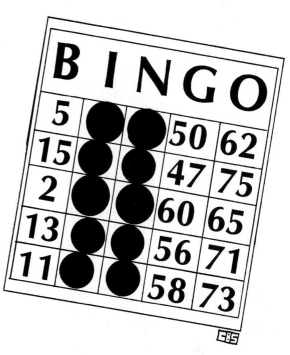

"Picture frame" and "railroad
tracks" in bingo.

Christopher B. Stage

Questions to Consider and Discuss

1. In the first set of quotes, the players spoke about winning and losing. Do you think bingo is a form of gambling? Is it a different activity than other forms, such as sport betting? Why?

2. If you did not know this case study was about bingo, looking only at the second set of quotes, where might these women be? What have been your experiences with bingo?

3. In the second set of quotes, the bingo players spoke about sociability. Does bingo provide a support network? How?

From *Bingo* by Rita Mae Brown. Copyright © 1988 by Speakeasy Publications, Inc. Used by permission of Bantam Books, a division of Bantam Doubleday Dell Publishers.

gaging in it (there were 20,600 arrests for gambling in 1989) yet increasingly sponsor state lotteries. It appears the rule is that all gambling from which the government doesn't earn money is illegal. Further, some research points to another controversy over government's support of lottery gambling. According to an Indiana University study (School of Public and Environmental Affairs 1993), lottery play is on the rise for the poor. The study claimed that lottery players in the lowest-income bracket (under $15,000) spent a whopping 8.42 percent of their money on lottery tickets. Because of the attraction of instant wealth, such active participation in gambling by lower-income people may cost governments more in the long run.

Injuring Others

Gambling and substance abuse are taboo activities because of an ideational mentality—people believe they are wrong. Activities that directly result in damage to property or other people are based on another concept termed sensate mentality. This explanation focuses on the more tangible and physical aspects of laws: antisocial acts or crimes with victims (Heise 1988). These are crimes we can detect through our senses. We can see that they are harmful.

In exploring taboo recreation behaviors that injure others, we consider harmful sex and vandalism. Human sexual behavior is an important aspect of leisure, yet it also has a potential to be inappropriately expressed and thus cause injury to others. Likewise, the destruction of property in the name of fun costs others money and, at times, causes physical injury or death.

Vandalism for Fun

Vandalism may be considered as recreation to the participants, but to society it is destructive, inappropriate, and negative. For these reasons, people perform vandalism at increasing rates, while other people continue to pay for it with

Outdoor art—or is it graffiti?
© Ruth V. Russell

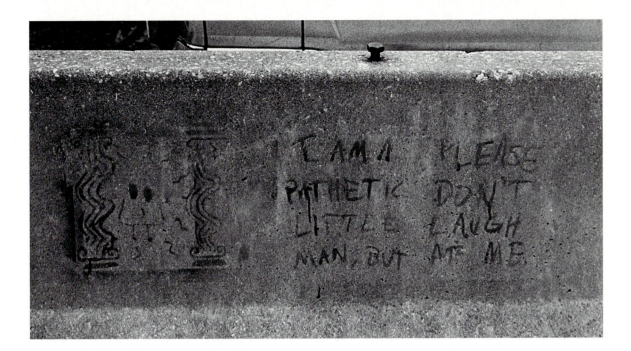

greater costs. In 1990 in the United States, 326,000 estimated arrests were made for vandalism. Of this, 89 percent were male and 32 percent were under eighteen years of age (U.S. Department of Justice 1991).

Vandalism is the destruction of property, which is done for entertainment, as well as out of ignorance of rules. Ironically, places of recreation, such as parks, suffer most from vandalism. According to a study of campgrounds in a national forest, a national park, and a state park, 60 percent of the vandalism was directed at facilities, while 30 percent was against the environment, and 10 percent was directed at property. Vandalism toward facilities was done mainly by children, and vandalism toward the environment was done mainly by adults (Campbell, Hendee, and Clark 1968).

Is all vandalism related to leisure? Are vandals simply playing too vigorously? The answer to both these questions is no. Knudson (1984) developed a typology of vandalism that distinguished it according to the following types:

1. Overuse vandalism. Often appears to be vandalism but is the unintentional result of too many people using a property or facility, such as the destruction of grass on a game playing field.

2. Conflict vandalism. Doing what is most logical and natural, regardless of the facility designer's intent, such as paths that result from people choosing the most direct route through an area and not using the designed sidewalks.

3. "No-other-way-to-do-it" vandalism. Damage resulting from sitting on a fence because there is no bench or leaning a bicycle against a tree because there is no bike rack.

Case Study   Camp Wathana

Final 1991 crime statistics released by the FBI showed that an estimated 14.9 million offenses were reported to U.S. law enforcement agencies (U.S. Department of Justice 1992). Most dramatic were the increases in arrest rates for youth aged ten to seventeen. The increases were present in all geographic regions of the country and involved all ethnic groups.

On October 26, Camp Wathana, located in Michigan and sponsored by Camp Fire, Inc., began a fourteen-day session. Thirty adolescent female campers attended. These campers were not members of the Camp Fire program; they had been adjudicated by the courts to a secure institution, which meant they were locked in their buildings at the Vista Maria treatment center. Eighty percent of them were runaways; they had been rejected by other agencies, had assaultive behaviors, short tempers, and short attention spans. What could possibly have been accomplished given these characteristics?

First, the planning committee was made up of two Vista Maria administrative staff, two Camp Fire staff, the director of the children's sector of the courts of Michigan, and two staff from a local community services organization. The committee decided that the girls would be divided into four groups with Vista Maria staff and Camp Wathana staff facilitating the groups. After several other decisions about the goals of the experience, there was a two-week planning session with the campers themselves.

The girls and their leaders decided that the everyday institution rules would be suspended during the camp, but that there would be some guiding parameters: no running, no serious assault, no smoking in the woods, and no destruction of property. If the girls couldn't accept these rules, they could not stay for the rest of the meetings or participate in the program. Then, each group of six to eight girls set up their own group goals. They brainstormed activities based on these goals, and if an activity didn't have a goal match, it was eliminated. The girls selected such goals as "learning to get along with others" and "having fun." Each girl also chose three personal goals to work on while at camp. Each camper wrote a goal statement and signed it. They then planned the activities for the first day of camp, agreeing to choose the schedule for the remainder of the program once they arrived.

Then it was time for camp. They sang silly camp songs, made crafts, rode horses, found their own secret spots to share with counselors, and tested themselves on a ropes course. They designed their own programs, and obeyed their own rules. Amazingly, for the first time in being together, they did not run away, and they did not physically assault one another. Everyone involved had much at stake. For many, it was the first time they had ever been able to be children.

The last camp fire was a combination of Camp Fire tradition and Vista Maria therapy. After everyone said how they felt about the experience, candles were lit and silent wishes made. Then came the problem the planners had not planned for—leaving camp! The experienced camp staff was not prepared for the emotional attachments that had formed. There were not only teary hugs for the staff, but the hugs between girls whom two months earlier did not know if they could resist fighting were a surprise. After camp, there was a great deal of testing. Results indicated that three out of the four groups moved significantly toward their therapy goals. Beyond the tests, the girls stated it best:

You felt like you were freer. I was tired of being in a locked setting.

I learned some things I never learned before—I found out I couldn't run away from my problems.

I tested my mental and physical endurance and I made it. Now I want to be a camp counselor.

(West 1983, 14–16)

Questions to Consider and Discuss

1. More typically outdoor recreation "treatment programs" for adjudicated youth have been high-risk adventure experiences. Camp Wathana was just a regular resident camp. What factors do you think contributed to its success?
2. If you designed your own recreation program for at-risk youth, what might be your "secrets to success"? Do some library inquiry and find other examples of this sort of treatment.
3. What does research say about the long-lasting potential of recreation programs for problem youth? Why might residential outdoor experiences have effects that last longer than other types of recreation programs?

4. Inventive vandalism. Destruction that results from solutions to needs, such as using a picnic table plank to make a springboard for diving into the river.

5. Curiosity vandalism. Damage stems from irresistible temptation or lack of personal discipline, such as pulling up a small tree to see what the roots look like or riding motorbikes to the top of a knoll to see how steeply the bike can climb.

6. Self-expression vandalism. An attempt to be noticed in the anonymity of modern society, such as graffiti on the walls of public places.

7. Spin-off vandalism. Occurs when other activities lead to the destruction of property, such as a baseball through a window or damage of property during a gang war.

8. Slovenly vandalism. An expression of bad manners and carelessness, such as littering.

9. Malicious vandalism. Usually the result of feeling mistreated and wanting to get back at society or a particular agency, such as defacing a park sign.

10. Thrill vandalism. Arises from the goading or dare of friends or an individual desire for excitement, such as the threat of private property damage from swimming in limestone quarries.

The most common form is self-expression vandalism. Slovenly vandalism is the least destructive but ultimately the most expensive. Thrill vandalism, on the other hand, can be very dangerous to the individual and to the public.

Taboo Sex

If leisure is considered a voluntarily chosen experience that is playful and provides pleasure, then many kinds of sexually related activities can be considered leisure. In fact, according to Comfort (1973), sex has three important uses in modern societies: (1) procreational (enabling children to be born), (2) relational (enabling intimacy between people), and (3) recreational (physical play). While not all institutions in society acknowledge sexual activity for pleasure, recreational sex is nothing new.

For example, in early colonial America, there was a custom called bundling. Originally justified so that the courting boy would not have to walk home at night in bad weather, it also represented a kind of courtship contest. Bundling was the custom of allowing a girl and her beau to get into bed together with their clothes on after the girl's parents had gone to bed. In some cases, parents provided obstacles such as a board dividing the bed in two.

Kissing games have also continued in many cultures through the decades. In fact, such games as "Spin the Bottle" provide a kind of transition in the sexual development of youth. They do this by allowing for sexual experimentation within the safety of the rules of the game. A study on adolescents by Avedon and Sutton-Smith (1971) found three categories of kissing games: chasing kissing games, usually played outdoors by older children; mixed kissing games typically for teenagers, in which couples do not pair off before the game but pair off momentarily once the game has started; and couple kissing games, in which pairing occurs before the game.

There are, however, particular forms of recreational sex that are considered inappropriate, immoral, or illegal by some societies. Among these could be categorized several actions, such as rape and exhibitionism. However, we will consider pornography and prostitution here because they demonstrate the taboo nature of recreational sex. That is, they are pursuits that may provide benefits of leisure to the participant but are sometimes forbidden by societies because of the harm inflicted on others.

Many forms of pornography are enjoyed by people today. It is typically available through popular culture media, such as books, magazines, music, and films. Newsstands readily provide it, and some video rental shops devote entire rooms to it. Erotic literature and art are found in most societies, but whether they are considered obscene or lewd varies from society to society and from time to time, according to custom and tradition. Today, it is hard to imagine that Clark Gable once shocked the nation in the film *Gone with the Wind* with the word "damn"! Graffiti is often considered obscene, but let's remember that graffiti provides archaeologists with valuable clues about ancient cultures! Nonetheless, what is pornography and what is not is frequently and hotly debated in some societies. Within the United States, for example, the range of opinion concerning what is considered lewd is extremely broad.

Pornography has historically been a product of the male imagination (Godbey 1990). *Playboy* is one of the most successful men's magazines, for example, because of its intellectual approach to sexuality. This dominance by male interests is changing in contemporary society, however, with the availability of more magazines, books, and films that appeal to women's erotic interests. Some pornography victimizes women and children by making them the target of degradation or violence. Public outcries have heralded what is believed by many to be an increase in this form of pornography.

The relationship between exposure to pornographic material and the committing of sex crimes is not yet clearly understood. ". . . viewing sexual material does cause an erotic response in some people, but so does daydreaming" (Godbey 1990). The impact of such an erotic response, which is more prevalent in males than in females, is not known. Some research findings show that after the initial exposure to pornographic films many viewers do not attend others. On the other hand, some rapists have reported they were carrying out fantasies first suggested through films. A few scholars have argued that pornography acts as a substitute for antisocial sexual behavior, while others maintain that it increases the incidence of such actions. Others view pornography as an indication of the extent to which sex has become shallow and meaningless in our society; some feel that it may help free us from our puritanical inhibitions and enhance our capacity to love.

Prostitution is the business of selling sexual activity. It is also nothing new. It was evident in Christian societies in the Middle Ages where it was accepted as a necessity for controlling male sexual needs and combating rape. In early Greece, prostitution was an important element of life for the male upper classes and was incorporated into religious worship as well. Some ancient Greek prostitutes had high social rank and considerable influence. In Rome, over 36,000 prostitutes were registered at one time (Evans 1979). Prostitution was also widespread in ancient Egypt and China.

Today, prostitution is a major tourist attraction in some southeast Asian and European countries where it is both legal and government controlled. Several counties in the state of Nevada also offer legal prostitution, where strict codes help provide safer and healthier practices for both male and female prostitutes.

Prostitution has been only haphazardly accepted as legal elsewhere, however. At various times brothels have been picketed and the names of famous patrons published. Following the gold rush in the 1850s in California, vigilante mobs drove out the houses of prostitution. The infamous districts of the Barbary Coast of San Francisco and Storyville in New Orleans were the objects of legal harassment in the early 1900s. During World War I, redlight districts in America were cleaned out to make way for urban renewal (Cross 1990). Recent attempts to rid society of prostitution have taken place as well, yet, it still thrives. For example, in the United States, there are four times as many sex "emporiums" (brothels, peep shows, or live sex shows) than there are McDonald's restaurants (Osanka and Johann 1989).

What is the harm in prostitution? As long as those who participate in prostitution are consenting adults, why is there such concern? Why would U.S. legal authorities bother to arrest close to 111,400 people annually for prostitution (U.S. Department of Justice 1991)? One answer, of course, is in the definition of taboo recreation; prostitution has been considered immoral by many in society as a matter of personal belief and tradition, but there is another, more frightening answer.

In Nevada, patronage at the Chicken Ranch, Desert Doll House, and Mustang Ranch has recently declined. On the other side of the Pacific the industry is likewise struggling. In Tokyo, for example, the drop in customers at some establishments is estimated at 90 percent. Why? The threat of AIDS. AIDS has made many of our sex practices—not just prostitution—life-threatening. People can carry the HIV virus for many years without developing symptoms of AIDS. Without knowing it, they may infect a large number of people, all of whom will eventually die. "While the civil rights of the victim must be respected, the fact that those who have AIDS can, by their personal 'leisure' choices, kill many other people means the rights of the public will have to be considered . . ." (Godbey 1990, 199).

The Dilemma of "Goodness"

Aristotle wrote in *Politics* that the cultivated ability to use leisure properly is the basis of a person's and a society's entire life. In other words, making moral and healthy free-time choices is leisure—not simply doing anything one pleases. To Aristotle, moral conduct dictated what leisure was, making the right choices among life's myriad alternatives and doing them well (Sylvester 1991). Today, we call this concept of positive life choices **wellness.**

Wellness: psychological, sociological, and physiological health.

Professionals who work in leisure agencies have always worked to achieve the goal of helping people achieve moral and healthy free-time choices. The YWCAs and YMCAs, for example, have always known that leisure provides an ideal opportunity to holistically develop the body, mind, and spirit. Youth-serving agencies, such as the Girl Scouts and Boys Clubs, understand that they are in the business of helping children achieve their full potential as individuals and citizens. Those in outdoor recreation and camping organizations have always focused on helping people develop self-confidence, cooperation with others, and understanding and respect for the environment. Professionals in municipal parks and recreation have a unique opportunity to teach that "children and trees should grow together" (Parks and Recreation Federation of Ontario 1992, iv). Those in therapeutic recreation advocate leisure activities that enhance life balance and develop motor and group living skills. Professionals such as these consider leisure a force of good that allows us the space and time to develop our moral and healthy selves. The goal of our institutions, then, is to encourage meaningful lifestyles and behaviors.

Is leisure only leisure when it is healthy and moral? Contrary to the teachings of Aristotle and the goals of park and recreation agencies, some contemporary philosophers answer the question differently. This alternative perspective maintains that leisure is derived from personal feelings alone—it is a subjective concept. By this definition, leisure is in the heart and mind of the individual and has nothing to do with outside factors, such as other people and the environment. Accordingly, leisure is considered a private choice based on intrinsically motivated joy and freedom and not a matter of morality. This suggests, then, that experiencing a mood uplift from walking through an inspiring natural landscape and experiencing a mood change induced by a hallucinogenic drug are equally leisure because leisure is in the mind of the beholder. It is a matter of private feelings and not social responsibility. What do you think?

This dilemma of goodness is not as simple as it may appear. If leisure is not a matter of private feelings alone, if it can be rated, so to speak, on a goodness or worth scale (such as was done in the Curtis Scale and Nash Pyramid presented earlier in the chapter), some leisure expressions are better than others. Even though it is easier to see a distinction of worth between child pornography and a family picnic, other comparisons reveal the complexity of the dilemma more sharply. For example, is attending the opera better than attending a country music concert? Is playing golf better than participating in roller derby?

Prole leisure: the recreational activities of the lowest social or economic classes of people.

Some would argue that such **prole leisure** as motorcycling, demolition derbies, and professional wrestling are just as worthy as any other leisure expression because leisure is a matter of personal definition. It would be elitist to assume otherwise. On the other side is the argument that a society in which prole and taboo leisure dominate is a mediocre and even debased civilization. This means that taboo pastimes dehumanize and ultimately demolish "good" culture.

The answer to this dilemma is grounded in leisure's purpose. Is leisure a means for personal or cultural well-being? Is leisure the freedom to do as one pleases no matter the harm to self or others, or does leisure expression include a responsibility to the public good? Of course, to Aristotle the answer was clear: moral conduct and leisure conduct are intertwined (Owens 1981).

Summary: Leisure as Taboo

Leisure holds tremendous potential for people's well-being, but at times leisure can have negative outcomes. In addition to such unpleasant results as fatigue, disappointment, and frustration, under certain circumstances, people choose to engage in pastimes that society considers inappropriate or taboo. Taboo recreation are those pastimes that are typically forbidden by law, custom, or belief. As presented by Curtis in the purple recreation model, these are delinquent activities that bring pleasure or escape to the participant, but to society, they are unconstructive and negative uses of free time. Similarly, according to Nash's hierarchy of leisure values, these are leisure pursuits that harm the participant and/or others.

Using Nash's model, this chapter explored substance abuse, vandalism, gambling, and harmful sex as examples of taboo recreation. While there are many attempts to explain such activities, the concepts of anomie and differential association were featured. Anomie occurs when once viable social norms no longer control people's actions. These result from a lack of purpose and identity in a person or a society. Violence in sport spectating is an illustration of anomie. Differential association is based on the idea that delinquent behavior is learned through interaction with others in social groups. A ready illustration of this is urban youth gangs.

Underneath all this is a dilemma of goodness. Is there such a phenomenon as "good" and "bad" leisure? If leisure is a matter of personal attitudes and feelings, distinctions of worth for specific pastimes are useless. Was Aristotle correct when he insisted, on the other hand, that leisure is making moral free-time choices—not simply doing anything one pleases?

References

Agnew, R. 1990. The origins of delinquent events: An examination of offender accounts. *Journal of Research in Crime and Delinquency* 27, no.3:267–94.

Agnew, R. 1991. The interactive effects of peer variables on delinquency. *Criminology* 29, no.1:47–72.

Aguilar, T. E. May 1987. A leisure perspective of delinquent behavior. Paper presented at the fifth Canadian Congress on Leisure Research, Halifax, Nova Scotia, Canada.

Anson, R. 1976. Recreation deviance: Some mainline hypotheses. *Journal of Leisure Research* 8:177–80.

Avedon, E., and B. Sutton-Smith. 1971. *The study of games.* New York: John Wiley & Son, Inc.

Bammel, G., and L. L. B. Bammel. 1992. *Leisure and human behavior.* Dubuque, IA: Wm. C. Brown.

Bippy, R. W., and D. C. Posterski. 1985. *The emerging generation: An inside look at Canadian teenagers.* Toronto: Irwin.

Brown, R. M. 1988. *Bingo.* New York: Bantam Books.

Campbell, F., J. Hendee, and R. Clark. 1968. Law and order in public parks. *Parks and Recreation* 3, no. 12:28–31, 51–55.

Chassin, L. 1984. Adolescent substance use and abuse. In *Advances in child behavioral analysis and therapy,* Vol. 3, edited by P. Karoly and J. Steffen. Lexington, MA: D. C. Heath.

CNN. 15 April 1988.

CNN. 10 August 1994.

Comfort, A. 1973. Future sexual mores: Sexuality in a zero growth society. *Current* (February): 29–34.

Cross, G. 1990. *A social history of leisure since 1600.* State College, PA: Venture.

Curtis, J. E. 1979. *Recreation: Theory and practice.* St. Louis: Mosby.

Curtis, J. E. 1988. Purple recreation. *SPRE Annual on Education* 3:73–77.

Czechowicz, D. 1988. Adolescent alcohol and drug abuse and its consequences—an overview. *American Journal of Drug and Alcohol Abuse* 14:189–97.

Dixey, R. 1987. It's a great feeling when you win: Women and bingo. *Leisure Studies* 6:199–214.

Downes, D. M., B. P. Davies, M. E. David, and P. E. Stone. 1976. *Gambling, work, and leisure: A study across three areas.* Boston: Routledge & Kegan.

Eitzen, D. S. 1984. *Sport in contemporary society.* New York: St. Martin's Press.

Evans, H. 1979. *The oldest profession.* London: David & Charles.

Godbey, G. 1989. *The future of leisure services: Thriving on change.* State College, PA: Venture.

Godbey, G. 1990. *Leisure in your life.* State College, PA: Venture.

Halebsky, M. 1987. Adolescent alcohol and substance abuse: Parent and peer effects. *Adolescence* 22:961–67.

Heise, D. R. 1988. Delusions and the construction of reality. *Delusional beliefs.* John Wiley & Son, Inc.

Iso-Ahola, S. E., and E. D. Crowley. 1991. Adolescent substance abuse and leisure boredom. *Journal of Leisure Research* 23, no.3:260–71.

Kaplan, J. B., S. S. Martin, R. J. Johnson, and C. A. Robbins. 1986. Escalation of marijuana use: Application of a general theory of deviant behavior. *Journal of Health and Social Behavior* 27:44–61.

Knudson, D. 1984. *Outdoor recreation.* New York: Macmillan.

Lazare, D. 1989. Drugs 'R' Us. *Drugs, society, and behavior 91/92.* Guilford, CT: The Dushkin Publishing Group, Inc.

Lee, Y., D. Howard, and J. Dattilo. October 1992. The negative side of leisure experience. Paper presented at the Leisure Research Symposium, National Recreation and Park Association Congress, Cincinnati, OH.

Leonard, W. M. 1988. *A sociological perspective of sport.* New York: Macmillan.

Lowney, J. 1984. The wall gang: A study of interpersonal process and deviance among twenty-three middle-class youths. *Adolescence XIX,* no. 75:527–38.

Manson, G. W. 1990. *Why join a gang?* Burnaby, British Columbia: Burnaby Parks and Recreation Department.

Matza, D., and G. M. Sykes. 1961. Juvenile delinquency and subterranean values. *American Sociological Review* 26:712–19.

Mayer, J. E. 1988. The personality characteristics of adolescents who use and misuse alcohol. *Adolescence* 23:383–404.

McGinnis, J. M., and J. Lashoff. 1988. *Disease prevention/health promotion: The facts.* Office of Disease Prevention and Health Promotion, U.S. Public Health Service. Palo Alto, CA: Bull Publishing.

Merton, R. K. 1957. *Social theory and social structure.* Glencoe, IL: Free Press.

Moore, T. H. 1982. A study of leisure choices of young offenders and young non-offenders and the impact of social structure and anomie on these choices. Unpublished Master's thesis, Acadia University, Nova Scotia, Canada.

Morris, M., H. Steinberg, E. A. Sykes, and P. Salmon. 1990. Effects of temporary withdrawal from regular running. *Journal of Psychosomatic Research* 34, no. 5:493–500.

Nash, J. B. 1953. *Philosophy of recreation and leisure.* Dubuque, IA: Wm. C. Brown.

National Recreation and Park Association. 1990. Educational session on urban gangs by the City of Santa Monica. Phoenix, AZ.

Osanka, M., and S. L. Johann. 1989. *Sourcebook on Pornography.* Lexington, MA: Lexington Books.

Owens, J. 1981. Aristotle on leisure. *Canadian Journal of Philosophy* 11:714.

Parks and Recreation Federation of Ontario. 1992. *The benefits of parks and recreation: A catalogue.* Ontario, Canada: Parks and Recreation Federation of Ontario.

Pfohl, S. J. 1985. *Images of deviance and social control: A sociological history.* New York: McGraw-Hill

Purdy, D. A., and S. F. Richard. 1983. Sport and juvenile delinquency: An examination and assessment of four major theories. *Journal of Sport Behavior* 6, no. 4:179–93.

Roberts, K. 1983. *Youth and leisure.* London: Allen & Urwin.

School of Public and Environmental Affairs. 1993. *Lottery sales higher from lower-income groups.* Bloomington, IN: Indiana University.

Shakur, S. 1993. *Monster: The autobiography of an L.A. gang member.* New York: The Atlantic Monthly Press.

Smith, R., and F. Preston. 1985. Expressed gambling motives: Accounts in defense of self. *Transitions to leisure: Conceptual and human issues,* edited by B. Gunter, J. Stanley, and R. St. Clair. Lanham, MD: University Press of America.

Stein, J. A., M. D. Newcomb, and P. M. Bentler. 1987. An 8-year study of multiple influences on drug use and drug use consequences. *Journal of Personality and Social Psychology* 53:1094–1105.

Stiefvater, R. E. 1993. The fun of being naughty: The concept of purple recreation. Unpublished Manuscript.

Sylvester, C. 1991. Recovering a good idea for the sake of goodness: An interpretive critique of subjective leisure. In *Recreation and leisure: Issues in an era of change,* edited by T. L. Goodale and P. A. Witt. State College, PA: Venture.

U.S. Department of Commerce. 1992. *Statistical abstract of the United States.* Lanham, MD: Bernan Press.

U.S. Department of Education. 1992. *Digest of education statistics.* Washington, D.C: U.S. Department of Education.

U.S. Department of Justice. 1991. *Sourcebook of criminal justice statistics.* Washington, D.C.: U.S. Department of Justice.

U.S. Department of Justice. 1992. Federal Bureau of Investigation Press Release. 20 August.

Vigil, J. D. 1988. Group processes and street identity: Adolescent Chicano gang members. *Ethos* 16, no. 4:421–45.

West, L. S. 1983. Youth-at-risk. *Camping Magazine* (March):14–16.

of time and work

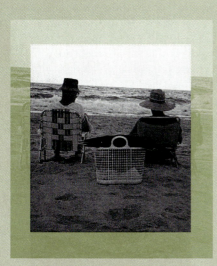

© Ruth V. Russell

PREVIEW

How do we know what time it is?

How people view time differs according to history, biology, and culture. Since ancient times, we have gone from a cyclical to a mechanical concept of time. Also, we all have an internal, biological clock that paces our daily lives. Social-cultural differences shape our notion of what time it is as well.

Why do we work?

Work (like time) is a modern phenomenon that is the result of the influences of early Christianity and the industrialization of society. It is necessary for human survival, yet it may or may not provide for living well.

How is time used for leisure?

Leisure is shaped by four time factors: personal perceptions of free time, adherence to clock time, the time needs of activities, and a culture's time sufficiency.

Is time ever a problem for leisure?

Free time for leisure is decreasing for people in modern society due to such time tyrannies as time urgency and time deepening.

What is leisure's relation to work?

There are conflicting answers to this question. Some argue that work is less desirable, and leisure is needed to overcome it. Others claim that work and leisure are both satisfying. Finally, there are those who claim that work and leisure are simply separate but equal spheres of life.

eight

They lost a weekend.

The nearly 3,000 Americans living on the remote Pacific atoll of Kwajalein, Marshall Islands, didn't remember Saturday, August 21, 1993. For good reason, the day didn't happen. It never will. Residents went to bed Friday night and woke up Sunday morning. That was because at midnight Friday Kwajalein switched its system of time from one side of the international dateline to the other. Kwajalein is west of the line, but for the past forty years had synchronized its time with the United States mainland to the east in order to match the workday there. They did this by pretending they were located east of the dateline.

In 1993, however, The Republic of the Marshall Islands requested the change so all its islets would be on the same side of the dateline. The inhabitants of Kwajalein (almost all are American military and civilian workers) still wanted to match the U.S. work schedule, so their workweek shifted to Tuesday through Saturday, which is Monday through Friday in the United States. Religious services are still held on Sunday, yet it seems like Saturday because it is the first weekend day off. Much ado about nothing? Indeed not!

Inhabitants of many societies take these notions of time and work very seriously. In part, this seriousness is what distinguishes technological cultures and "modern" human beings from others. Also, the concepts of time and work relate in important ways to leisure. Leisure is frequently restricted to a specific timetable and used as a reward for work. Although in this chapter we explore how these assumptions are incorrect and stifling, they represent a common understanding.

Our purpose is to think about the relationships among time, work, and leisure. We draw these comparisons in the same chapter because, as is suggested in the situation for the people of Kwajalein, time, work, and leisure are intertwined in contemporary society.

Types of Time

"Clock time cannot be free."

(DeGrazia 1962, 310)

Time has become one of the most complex phenomena in contemporary life. Indeed, it was Aristotle in the book *Physics* who first asked the question, "In what sense, if any, can time be said to exist?" (Barnes 1984, 369). Scholars still do not dare declare that time is well understood.

Time has become an important phenomenon in life because time is the framework on which all our behavior rests, including leisure behavior. Our understanding of time is personal; we continually adhere to time's structure in often very emotional ways. Perhaps no other noun in the English language (interestingly the word is also a verb, adverb, and adjective) is applied to so many different actions. For example, we save time, spend time, hoard time, make up time, speed up time, make good time, kill time, mark time, and while away time, and of course, time is money!

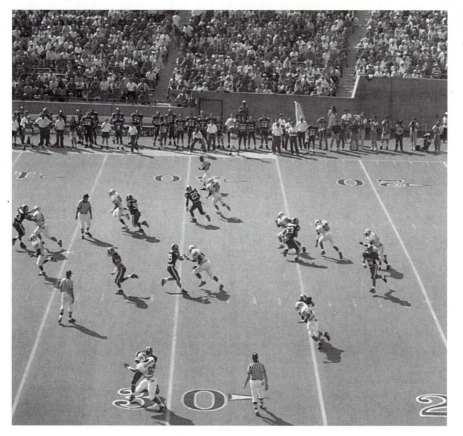

Most of us are very time conscious—even in our pastimes. We have the thirty-five-second shot rule in basketball. The playing periods in football are bound by two thirty-minute halves. The crafts class at the recreation center lasts fifty minutes, and our at-home aerobics exercise breaks are timed to the television commercial breaks. We want to be an "instant" lottery winner, and if we don't get our pizza delivered in an hour, the restaurant pays for it. We are more likely to stay out late partying on Friday or Saturday night, rather than Monday or Tuesday night. Before going to bed at night, many people allow themselves ten minutes for pleasure reading. Has it always been this way? What conditions and changing perceptions have altered the time resource of humans?

Cyclical Time

To the Navajos of North America, real time is the here and now, with the future holding much less importance. Similarly, the Balinese in Indonesia know time only as the present and not as a progression to an end. Such notions of time are assumed to be the original human experience. Early humans are said to have all thought of time as part of the regular patterns of nature. For example, nomadic hunting life was conditioned mainly by the rising and setting of the sun. Archeologists report that ancient tribal societies marked the passing of time by the levels of the tide, the passage of the seasons, and the location of the moon in the sky (Green 1968). Even with the invention of devices that produced measurement of time, such as a sun dial, the human experience of time was similar to nature: it recurred regularly.

Time originally was perceived as circular, that is, constant and returning. This is called cyclical time. This perception meant that time was never lost or wasted because time, just as life, repeated itself. Imagine what this natural perception of time might have meant to the quality of daily life! People must have not only had a strong sense of harmonious living in the natural world but also of inner peace. Humans did not control time since most measures of time came from nature, thus they felt no responsibility for it. In the words of Solomon in the book of Ecclesiastes:

> To every thing there is a season, and a time to every
> purpose under the heaven:
> . . . A time to weep, and a time to laugh; a time to mourn,
> and a time to dance;
> . . . A time to get and a time to lose; a time to keep, and a
> time to cast away;
> . . . A time to love, and a time to hate; a time of war, and
> a time of peace.
>
> (Eccl.3:1, 4, 6, 8)

Mechanical Time

The cyclical definition of time began to change, however. Isaac Newton's edict in the late 1600s that there is an "absolute, true and mathematical time, of itself and of its nature, flowing equably without relation to anything external" had an enormous impact (Ibrahim 1991). Newton's theory suggested that time is not circular but linear. This shift in thinking meant that every moment of time is new. A period of time can pass, and when it passes, cannot be recovered. Time, unlike other economic resources, cannot be accumulated; we cannot build up a stock of time. Thus, time could now be spent, saved, and wasted. Plans could be made for something to occur in the future along the absolute line that was the future. This all meant that time could also be measured mechanically, and Western societies in particular began to coordinate their lives to the clock.

The cyclical idea of time gave way to a linear idea of time as the influence of Christianity increased. Unlike the religions of Eastern societies, Christianity was an expressly temporal religion, assigning importance to the date of the birth of Jesus and looking forward to the time of his second coming (Bammel and Bammel 1992). While waiting, early Christians were to use their time in the service of God. For example, the activities of the monks in medieval monasteries were regulated by the keeping of time. Thus, early clocks were important for dividing the day accurately into times for prayer, meditation, and work.

Mechanical clocks existed around the ninth century in China, but the earliest survivors are from fourteenth-century western Europe (Priestley 1968). Since time was now viewed as linear, without beginning or end, and never pausing or veering off course, even crude clocks such as notched candles, the hour glass, water-column vessels, and sand clocks were able to mark time in a more or less absolute way. The first clock with wheels was made in Paris and presented to Charles V in 1364. The first pocket clock appeared in 1510. The second hand was invented in 1609 (Anderson 1964). These early wheeled clocks were weight driven and most ran unevenly and inaccurately. With the invention of the pendulum, the accuracy of timekeeping improved immensely.

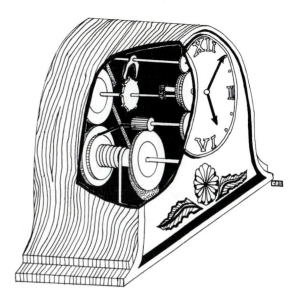

Mechanical timekeeping regulates human lives to the machine's pace.

Christopher B. Stage.

Such accuracy of time was integral, of course, to the ability to work. Mechanical time and the work ethic have always been mutually supportive. With the development of the concept of time as linear, people specialized their labors and set meeting times for conducting the business of bartering. The environment of mechanical time, which demands precision, punctuality, regularity, and reliability, was vital to creating an industrial, work-focused civilization. Clock time became a tool of industrialists to regulate the flow of production; timekeeping became an economic weapon to eliminate the gaps in the traditional day of work and assured a uniformity and continuity of output (Cross 1990).

The factory of the late 1800s, for example, forced people into the lockstep, clock-driven movements of the machine. This period in history was called the Industrial Revolution, and among other changes, it imposed a new division in the lives of ordinary people: work time (in the office or workshop) became important as it separated from the rest of life. It was now possible to feel guilty if one was not spending time productively. A favorite American statesman, Benjamin Franklin, is widely recognized for the following practical advice:

> Lose not time; be always employed in something useful.
> Sloth like Rust, consumes faster than Labour wears.
> Do not squander Time, for that's the stuff of Life.
> The sleeping fox catches no poultry.

> (*Poor Richard's Almanac* 1733 to 1758)

Franklin's proverbs were enormously popular at the time and established a legacy for the importance of using time wisely—a perspective also conducive to the rhythm of machine time.

To this day, technology and the belief in the regularity of mechanical time has continued to sever our ties with nature. Alertness to natural daily and seasonal cycles has been eliminated by lights and heating and cooling systems

biography

Benjamin Franklin

Benjamin Franklin (1706-1790) is often cited as the best example of the American Dream. He shed a boyhood of poverty for a famous and rich manhood. Born in Boston in 1706, he was the youngest son in a family of seventeen children, and he attended school for only two years. His father kept him home after the age of ten to help in the family's candle and soap shop. Thus, Franklin's schooling ended, but his education did not. He read every book he could find. He taught himself algebra, geometry, logic, navigation, grammar, and the natural and physical sciences. He studied French, German, Italian, Spanish, and Latin.

At age seventeen, Franklin ran away to Philadelphia, then the largest city in the British colonies. The story of his arrival has become a classic in American folklore. The tale describes him trudging up Market Street with a dollar in his pocket, carrying one loaf of bread under each arm and eating a third. From these beginnings, Franklin went on to distinguish himself as a printer, publisher, civic leader, statesman, and scientist.

His accomplishments were astounding. He established the nation's first circulating library and the first city hospital. He organized the first fire department and the first paid police force. He introduced fire insurance and caused the streets of Philadelphia to be paved, swept, and lighted—radical innovations for the time. He founded a school which later became the University of Pennsylvania. He held public office on municipal, state, federal, and international levels. As a scientist, his experiments with lightning began the study of electricity. Although his experiment with the kite and the key are familiar to many, how many know that he was the first to identify the presence of the Gulf Stream (Clark 1983)? He studied and composed music, played four instruments, and invented the glass harmonica for which Mozart and Beethoven wrote pieces. He invented both the "Franklin" stove and, at the age of eighty-three, bifocal glasses.

Perhaps Franklin's greatest legacy was his lifelong concern for the happiness and dignity of humanity. For example, his last public act was to sign an appeal to Congress calling for the abolition of slavery. So adamant was he in the pursuit of how best to live that in his autobiography he set forth the proper "order" of his day:

THE MORNING	5	Rise, wash, contrive the
Question. What good	6	day's business, and break-
shall I do this day?	7	fast
	8	
	9	Work
	10	

	11	
NOON	12	Read, or overlook my
	1	accounts, and dine
	2	
	3	Work
	4	
	5	
EVENING	6	Put things in their places,
Question. What good	7	supper, music or diver-
have I done to-day?	8	sion, or conversation.
	9	Examination of the day.
	10	
	11	
	12	
NIGHT	1	Sleep
	2	
	3	
	4	

(Franklin 1932, 93)

Franklin accompanied this precise idea of how daily time is best ordered with a belief that one must earn leisure. For example, in a preface to *Poor Richard's Almanac* for 1758 he wrote:

> Methinks I hear some of you say, Must a Man afford himself no Leisure? I will tell thee, my friend, what Poor Richard says, Employ thy Time well, if thou meanest to gain Leisure; and since thou art not sure of a minute, throw not away an Hour. Leisure, is Time for doing something useful; this Leisure the diligent Man will obtain, but the lazy Man never; so that, as Poor Richard says, A Life of Leisure and a Life of Laziness are two Things.

(Franklin 1932, 208)

Franklin's critics have found fault with this attitude. They have complained that he was obsessed with attaining material things. From his youth, he was obsessed in getting what he wanted (Clark 1983). From these aspects of his example, some say the national character suffers from a drive for material acquisitions at the expense of spiritual growth.

Benjamin Franklin was a jack-of-all-trades and master of many. Thomas Jefferson, himself an accomplished person, hailed him as "the greatest man of the age and country." When Franklin died on the night of April 17, 1790, he left $5,000 each to Boston and Philadelphia, part to be used for public works after 100 years and the rest after 200 years.

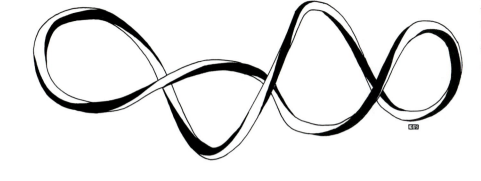

Figure 8.1 A spiral with feedback loops and simultaneous shapings may be the concept of time in the future.

Christopher B. Stage.

that come on and off automatically. Time clocks determine how much money hourly paid workers will receive. Digital alarm clocks wake us in the morning to prepare for work or school, while the sunrise is still sometimes hours away. Communication systems allow us to have conversations with multiple people at different locations at the same time. Wristwatches beep out the time it takes us to jog around the block. The post office announces the deadline for sending Christmas cards.

We live by artificial distinctions of time. This shift to a mechanical notion of time is perhaps the most important change in human life which has yet taken place. Time has become finite and standardized, and as a result, it rules our lives. While we still use the word *pastimes,* for many of us it is almost impossible to think of simply letting time pass.

Some predict that our sense of time is shifting again—to the rhythm of the computer. While the circle represented time for ancient peoples, and the straight line suggests society's experience since then, the double helix is considered the time-shape of the future (Rifkin 1987). This spiral with its feedback loops could represent an unnatural attempt to link biological rhythms with a speeded up, computerized view of time (fig. 8.1). These simultaneous shapings may take us even farther from our rhythms in nature.

Biological Time

In the 1930s, Kleber, a German scientist, discovered an interesting rhythm in certain nectar-producing plants. They secreted nectar only at specific times of the day. Bees seemed to know this and always showed up exactly at the correct feeding time (Pittendrigh 1972). Later, scientists tried to outsmart the bees by moving them via airplane across several time zones in order to throw off what appeared to be their biological clocks. Bees that collected nectar between 10:00 A.M. and noon Paris time were flown to New York. The scientists failed, the bees continued to collect nectar in New York according to Paris time (Whitrow 1980).

Thus, it was realized that another type of time we live with is biological time. This is an organism's internal awareness of time. Plants and animals have biology-based sources of knowing what time it is. The first source, photoperiodism, is a plant's sensitivity and response to light. The second, celestial orientation, is observed in birds and insects. Third, endogenous rhythms are common for many plants, as well as animals, including humans. These endogenous rhythms are cyclical physiological functions. For example, the heart beats about sixty to eighty times per minute. For women there is a twenty-eight-day menstrual cycle. Hunger occurs on about a ninety-minute cycle.

Endogenous rhythms are not regulated by a precise sixty-minute hour or twenty-four-hour day. However, they happen with precision in all of us all the time—often in conflict with mechanical time. Because we have become so dependent on external factors of timekeeping, such as the clock and television, we are not always able to experience time according to our own biological, endogenous rhythms. For example, one endogenous rhythm that has been most problematic in contemporary life is the daily rhythm of activity and rest. This is called the **circadian** rhythm. A single activity and rest cycle ranges between twenty and twenty-eight hours. As an illustration, without clocks or light cues, people in experiments who have been free to live according to their circadian rhythms, go to bed progressively later each day (Wever 1985).

When our circadian rhythms become too far out of synchronization with external time factors, such as daylight and darkness, we suffer. Common sources of this internal time desynchronization are changing to a night shift at work or taking a jet plane across several time zones. Much has been written about jet lag. From one-half to two-thirds of long-distance passengers suffer from jet lag, including infants (Blume 1993). In a study on the impact of jet travel on metabolic rate, reaction time, and decision making, differences were found mainly for longer flights. For example, when these factors were checked on a flight within a one-hour time zone, no changes occurred. In a flight with a seven-hour time zone difference, reaction time was the most impaired. Both reaction time and metabolic rate needed four days to return to normal. In a longer flight with a ten-hour time zone difference, in addition to changes in reaction time and metabolic rate, subjects suffered from mental dullness for twenty-four hours (Blatt and Quinlan 1972).

How does this relate to leisure? For one thing, rhythmic flow is associated with comfort, even pleasure. That is why we appreciate experiences that are essentially rhythmic, such as light, color, music, and poetry. Professionals who manage leisure services, must realize that people will want to participate in and will benefit most from recreation during times when their circadian rhythms are highest. For many people, this is midmorning and midafternoon. Elite athletes, for example, have used circadian rhythm charting to help predict peaks in performance.

Social and Cultural Time

In addition to mechanistic time with its linear schedule and our biological time pattern of activity and rest, cultural time aids our ability to know what time it is. Each social environment—whether it is school, home, shops, hospital, or even a nation—has its own routine. For example, in some families 6:00 P.M. is dinner time. On college campuses, most students attend classes between 10:00 A.M. and 2:00 P.M. In the workplace, many jobs begin at 8:00 A.M., and at 5:00 P.M.

Endogenous: caused by factors inside the organism.

Circadian: daily rhythm of activity and rest.

Circadian Rhythms

The heliotrope raises its leaves by day and lowers them at night. As long ago as 1792, it was noticed that even in a darkened room the heliotrope continued to worship the sun in time with its rising and setting. Since then, rats, hamsters, airline pilots, shift workers, and many others have been the subject of the inquiry of biological rhythms. Studies also have been done on cross-country skiers, distance runners, standing broad jumpers, and relay teams.

For example, one study evaluated the effect of circadian variation and the standing broad jump (Reilly and Down 1986). The subjects were twelve athletic males, aged eighteen to twenty-two years. Over the course of two weeks, the jump was performed six times a day: at 2:00, 6:00, 10:00 A.M. and at 2:00, 6:00 and 10:00 P.M. Results showed that the effort in making the jump was influenced by the time of day. Performances were about 3 percent better in the morning than later in the day.

In another study, circadian rhythm and performance in a twenty-four-hour relay race were considered (Krombholz 1990). Data were collected during the International Twenty-Four-Hour Race in Morlenback, Germany. This competition is a race for teams of ten members, and the course is a circular track of about 1,400 meters. Runners can alternate after each lap. The competition lasts twenty-four hours, from 2:00 P.M. until 2:00 P.M. The team achieving the longest distance is the winner. As expected, both teams studied showed a clear decline in performance during the twenty-four hours. At the end of the race, the average performance of both teams was about 20 percent less than that at the beginning. A circadian variation in performance was also found in one of the teams. Their performance was lowest during the night and increased during the morning hours.

What other ideas for research on leisure and circadian rhythms do you suggest would be interesting? How would you set up the study?

workers leave for home. Television programs begin and end on either the hour or half hour. In some countries, shops are closed between 1:00 and 3:00 P.M.

People get so used to certain time expectations in particular social situations that they become alarmed at deviations. If the newspaper is not delivered before a certain hour of the morning, we call the distributor to find out what happened. In the United States, if a professor is more than ten minutes late for class, students debate how long they should wait. In Brazil, university students define lateness as slightly over thirty minutes after the scheduled start of a class (Levine and Wolff 1985). Certain time periods are established as the norm for various life events, and people use these for making judgments about events that occur too soon, too late, too long, and too short. In other words, the cultural context dictates the appropriate timing of activities. The best time to eat dinner or arrive at the office will vary according to the social group.

Adherence to clock time and planned schedules for activities is more common in North America. There people plan life to correspond to fiscal years, eight-hour workdays, two-week paid vacations, academic semesters,

C ase Study   Northern Exposure

In 1993 in Barrow, Alaska, the sun set on the 18th of October and did not rise again for sixty-five days. Here, the sun always rises and sets once each year. Because of the earth's asymmetrical shape, however, there is not an equal amount of time each year in darkness and in lightness. In 1993, for example, daytime lasted 190 days.

Questions to Consider and Discuss

1. Do you think patterns of leisure in Barrow might be different than those where you live?
2. What might life be like in a culture where people's biological clocks are at such odds with the cues of light? Interview classmates from different time zones and latitudes to discover how their recreation is affected by when the sun rises and sets.

and tax day. This is less prevalent in Europe, and in developing nations, it can be completely absent. When deciding to do something, people in some cultures check their appointment books; whereas the Andamanese (from small islands in the Bay of Bengal) smell the odors in their surrounding environment before deciding.

People waiting in line at Williamsburg Historical Park, Virginia.

© Ruth V. Russell

One explanation for such cultural distinctions is that mechanical time is related to technological development. The more industrial the country, the more the reliance on a linear notion of time and a greater urgency to live by it. Let's consider a visual example of this—standing in line.

People spend time in sometimes very long lines to make a bank deposit, purchase food at the grocery store, board an airplane, see a movie, and ride a roller coaster. It has been estimated that Americans spend at least 37 billion hours a year waiting in lines (Denny 1993). Envisioning waiting as linear is not a universal phenomenon. Instead, it is an acquired social trait that began and was compulsively developed in Great Britain during the World Wars. It was then passed on to the United States, Canada, and a number of European countries. Even here there are differences. In southern Europe, it's part of the culture to jockey for position in lines, while in Britain and the U.S., first come, first served is rigidly enforced. Some observers of this custom suggest that lining up thrives only in cultures obsessed with punctuality and fearful of wasted time. For example, in a study of the notoriously nonqueuing Brazilians, it was discovered that they had far fewer clocks and watches per capita than similarly developed countries. Meanwhile in Israel, people waiting for buses stubbornly resist forming lines, yet when the bus comes, they board according to the first-come, first served principle as if they had been in line all along. The fact that forming waiting lines is unknown in some cultures was a fact missed by the Disney Corporation when it opened Euro-Disney in France and expected ticket-buyers to line up in an orderly fashion.

Time for Leisure

"I advocate mandatory increases in free time."

(Schor 1992, 150)

Leisure takes place in time. For the majority of adults in modern societies about fifty to sixty hours each week are not committed to work or maintenance obligations. Considered another way, without taking into account evening hours, a conservative schedule of weekends, holidays, and vacations gives us over four months a year of free time. Let's add it up. In the U.S. each year, most workers have nine days off for holidays, fifty-two Saturdays and fifty-two Sundays, and about ten days of annual vacation for a total of 123 days (or over four months) each year free! What has happened to all this free time? Free time usage varies from person to person and culture to culture. Also, there are dangers on the horizon for leisure as society's notions of time continue to shift.

Leisure's Expression in Time

Time usage for leisure is essentially shaped by four factors:

1. personal perceptions of free time,

2. adherence to clock time,

3. the time needs of leisure activities, and

4. a culture's time sufficiency.

Let's explore each of these factors.

Case Study   My Perception of Free Time

For the following set of statements, check the one that best expresses your view of free time:

____ 1.   I like to use my free time wisely on things that are personally beneficial and socially constructive.

____ 2.   Free time is my chance to get away from work and daily routines.

____ 3.   I am frequently afraid I'll have nothing to do in my free time.

____ 4.   I don't like to waste my free time.

____ 5.   Free time is a personal thing—it is mine to use exactly as I wish.

These are different perceptions people have of free time that affect the role of leisure in their life. Compare your choice to the description in the text.

People's perceptions of free time influence how they use it for leisure. If free time is regarded as a privilege, it is likely that it will be used wisely in pursuits that are perceived as personally beneficial and socially constructive. Others may view free time mainly as a chance for temporary escape from the physical and mental environments of work and daily routines. They regard it as an opportunity rather than a privilege, thus the goal is "getting away from it all." Others see free time as neither privilege nor opportunity but an empty space that if left unfilled becomes frightening. These are people who work so hard at leisure that it almost becomes another job. They feel compelled to be busy. Similar behaviors may arise from a perception of free time as a precious commodity. Every spare moment must be crammed with activity to be sure it is not wasted. Finally, others perceive free time as a private possession. It is theirs to use exactly as they wish—whether it be sleeping, watching television or immersed in a favorite hobby.

Adherence to clock time also affects people's leisure. Time can be a tyrant against leisure, for example. Even when no clock or other indicator of time is visible, people are still aware of time and regulate behavior accordingly. They may even stop an activity they are enjoying because they sense it is the conventional time to quit in order to eat a meal or go to bed, for example. Similarly, people will not begin a leisure pursuit if it appears there is too little or too much time available. Individuals with limited time available for leisure often try to squeeze as much fun as possible into the time allotted or are constantly worrying about how much time they have left.

Leisure as experienced in time is also based on the amount of time an activity requires. A game of Monopoly can take an entire evening. Some people hold off playing golf until they retire from employment because it takes most of a day to play. One of the sadnesses of contemporary society is that activities requiring more extensive time are being displaced in popularity with shorter time-framed activities. For example, complicated and time consuming games, such as bridge and chess are less popular. Part of the popularity of jogging is that it takes less time than walking to achieve the same fitness benefit. The

Cultural Time Sufficiency and Leisure

Distinction	Time Surplus	Time Scarcity
Time	Time rich; much free or idle time	Time poor; no or little free time
Wealth	Poor	Rich
Production	Low	High
Work	Not dependent on mechanical time; no time related work stress	Highly dependent on mechanical time; time stress causes illness
Leisure	Numerous holidays Popular recreation activities occupy large time blocks Much spontaneity Little consumption of special equipment	Few holidays Popular recreation activities occupy small time blocks Less spontaneity Much consumption of special equipment

trend in vacations is multiple three-day excursions spread throughout the year rather than the traditional two-week trip in the summer.

Finally, leisure's expression within time is a function of a culture's time sufficiency. Contrary to what might be expected, this refers to the fact that as the general welfare of people increases, life becomes more hectic and time more scarce. First noted by Linder (1970), cultures can be categorized according to the amount of time they have. Cultures have either a time surplus or a time scarcity. For example, time surplus is descriptive of the least developed and poorest countries. Production and income are so low that large portions of time remain unused. The mechanical notion of time is not necessary in time surplus cultures, because there is no pacing of activities. What happens to leisure in this situation? It tends to be spontaneous, lengthy, relaxed, and frequent. Time surplus cultures also tend to designate a larger number of days as holidays (or holy days). On "the road to riches a country gradually eliminates more and more holidays," reducing the amount of free time (Linder 1970, 18). Table 8.1 outlines this distinction.

On the other hand, for wealthier cultures the pace of life is more rapid and, therefore, more dependent on mechanical time. As a result, there is a time famine. When the drive for time efficiency is dominant, free time is transferred to active use, and becomes scarce. In rich countries, all "waste" in the use of time has been eliminated, and efficiency is supremely important (Linder 1970). The appointment calendar becomes the most important book, and when it is lost, people feel lost. Punctuality becomes a virtue, and waiting is a squandering of time. For cultures with a time scarcity, there are fewer holidays, less spontaneity in pastimes, and a convenience theme to popular activity choices. Leisure becomes just another thing that must be worked into the schedule.

Table 8.2

Average Weekly Hours of Work

1820	1900	1940	1950	1960	1970	1980	1990
70	58	44	42	40.5	39.6	35.3	34.5

U.S. Department of Commerce 1992

Time Tyrannies

Let's consider time scarcity another way. It used to be a common assumption that in more technological societies the amount of free time, and thus the potential for leisure, was increasing. Indeed, illustrations of this belief are abundant. Research findings reported by Bosserman (1975) suggested that for at least Great Britain, France, Czechoslovakia, and the United States the growth in the quantity of time freed from work during a person's life cycle has been a significant evolutionary development over the past 100 years. The growth of this free time has accelerated even more over the last twenty-five years (table 8.2).

In the 1890s, the American workday began at 6:00 A.M., before breakfast, and lasted ten hours. Spurred by changes in the type of work required and the efforts of social reformers, this soon changed. As Owen (1969) reported, the proportion of life spent in work time for U.S. males decreased from 23 percent in 1900 to 15 percent in 1960. A primary contributor to this was a reduction in the workweek from nearly sixty to almost forty hours. Likewise, the paid vacation became a right of most wage earners by the mid-1930s.

The obvious predicted result of decreases in work time was leisure time taking up the slack. In fact, some historians (Cross 1990) maintain that the first forty years of this century witnessed the most dramatic expansion of leisure in modern history. According to Hammond (1933), this was an era of "Common Enjoyment." Many felt that soon leisure, rather than work, would be the core human experience. In fact, the conviction that leisure time would continue to increase led to an intense debate in industrial societies during the 1960s and 1970s about the capacity of people to adapt to ever increasing leisure. It even became labeled as "the leisure problem": how could society cope with masses of people with an abundance of free time?

Is this trend expected to continue for the future? According to some, the answer is yes. With further industrialization and automation, the average workweek may continue to decline. After all, the United States Department of Labor estimates that one-fourth of the U.S. population is capable of producing all the goods and services needed for everyone (1970).

A number of other recent indications suggest that the amount of leisure available will actually decline for the average adult and child living in a technological society. A Louis Harris survey (1987) reported a decline in leisure time among adults in the United States from 26.2 hours per week in 1973 to

only 16.6 hours per week in 1987. Part of the explanation was an increase in the hours worked due to the shift toward a service economy with more salaried workers who generally work longer hours. Also, many people now spend more time commuting to work, and more women are working outside the home, which means they often must combine family, housework, and employment responsibilities. Men, according to the Harris survey, had an average of 20.3 hours for leisure each week, while women had only 15.6 hours each week. Other surveys, such as the 1990 Decision Research Corporation Poll and the 1992 calculations of economist Juliette Schor, also reveal a loss of leisure time. According to Schor, leisure time has fallen by forty-seven hours a year since 1969.

Beyond these indicators, which are based on changes in work hours, are there other contemporary squeezes on our leisure time? (See figure 8.2.) Time tyrannies include a sense of time urgency, the nanosecond culture, time deepening, and changing geography.

A truly contemporary condition, the sense of time urgency is prevalent in time scarce cultures. Time urgency is a quickened pace of life. For instance, participating hurriedly in an activity or choosing particular activities because they take less time suggest a malady for leisure. How much real pleasure and satisfaction can be derived from learning to play the guitar in three easy lessons, eating dinner in less than ten minutes while standing in front of the microwave oven, listening to the words of a novel piped through earphones while running faster and faster on a treadmill at the gym, or traveling through Europe in a week? As Rifkin worried in the book *Time Wars* (1987):

> We have quickened the pace of life only to become less patient. We have become more organized but less spontaneous, less joyful. We are better prepared to act on the future but less able to enjoy the present and reflect on the past (pp. 11–12).

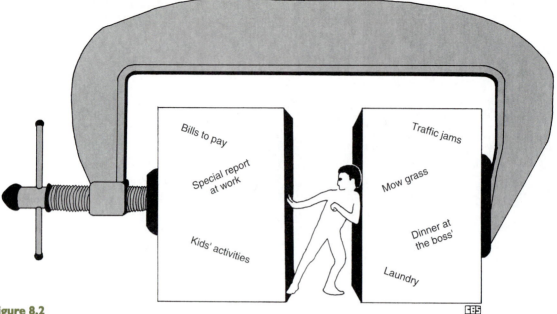

Figure 8.2
Contemporary "squeeze" on adults' leisure time.
Christopher B. Stage

Type A behavior: behavior of a personality type that is manifested in being in a hurry to do more and more in less time.

Contemporary society is lived as a restless energy that preys on speed records and shortcuts—the quick fix. The natural rhythms that characterized life for our ancestors have been shunted aside to make room for the fast track. Isn't this all rather ironic? The modern world of fast transportation, instantaneous communication, and time-saving technologies was supposed to free us from the tyranny of time. Instead, there never seems to be enough time. We rarely have a moment to spare, especially for our favorite pastimes.

Our speeded up sense of time not only affects our leisure, it also affects our health. Specific diseases can result from time urgency. An illustration is **Type A behavior** (Friedman and Rosenman 1976). Type A people are victims of "hurry sickness." Their lives are frantically driven around goals and deadlines. They are unable to approach a task in a balanced way and, in extreme cases, seem consumed by a need to accomplish more and more. Not only do they have an inward sense of urgency, their outward behavior matches. They can't sit still. They are always moving their hands, fingers, legs, or feet and are often very vocal.

Type A persons are usually ambitious and frequently highly successful in their work. In spite of these admirable qualities, they possess a characteristic that nobody envies: a high mortality rate from heart disease (Dossey 1982). The sense of time urgency displayed by Type A individuals is translated into physiologic effects: increased heart rate and blood pressure at rest, elevation of such hormones as adrenalin, increased blood cholesterol, increased respiratory rate, and increased muscle tension (Dossey 1982). Time urgency can be fatal.

Strangely enough, even as people find it more impossible to meet the time demands of contemporary society, a new and faster time is being introduced. As suggested earlier, changes in computer technology are altering our notions of time, threatening our sense of time beyond anything we have known. Welcome to the nanosecond culture. The computer works in a time frame where the **nanosecond** is the basic measurement. The nanosecond is a billionth of a second. We can perceive a second of time, but it is not humanly possible to perceive a billionth of a second. Thanks to technology, time can be experienced at a speed beyond the realm of consciousness.

This suggests that people will be using time more precisely. Already airplanes are scheduled to depart and land at very precise computer determined times, such as 12:01 P.M. and 6:14 A.M. Sport courts are also reserved for play with great time precision; it is considered bad form to fail to give up your racquetball court even a minute past your reserved time. Perhaps the best example of the nanosecond's impact on our pastimes is through computer games. These games are relentless in their demand for time-attention. Unlike pinball games or Scrabble, in which the player can dominate time, the players of computer games must surrender totally to the machine's tempo. You have to play to "the heartbeat" of the computer if you are to win (Turkle 1984).

Another contemporary condition that affects the amount of our leisure time is **time deepening** (Godbey 1980). The higher the density of a society's communication and the more educated the person, the more likely she or he is to do a number of activities simultaneously (Scheuch 1972). This is time deepening (fig. 8.3). It means that several activities are done at the same time. For example, do you simply watch television, or at the same time, are you eating a meal, reading the newspaper, writing a letter, ironing clothes, exercising, and/or talking on the phone? As you drive to work or school in the morning, are you also drinking a cup of coffee and eating a donut, glancing at your appointment calendar, listening to news on the radio, and/or brushing your teeth? The ultimate goal of time deepening is to pile multiple activities into the same time frame. This means that we can, of course, do more in our leisure—have more experiences. Time deepening can also make us feel rushed, anxious, and unfulfilled. Our leisure time becomes packed with activities, but does it provide pleasure and relaxation? "Perhaps it makes sense to say that we have become 'unleisurely' in our leisure" (Godbey 1980, 20).

Finally, the contemporary tyranny of time is also a matter of geography. The daily activities of humans—eating, sleeping, traveling between home and destination, working, or attending classes—consume space as well as time. Unlike time, an individual's spatial reach is limited because one cannot be in two places at once or engage simultaneously in activities that are in separate places. Further, since a finite amount of time exists in a day and each of us is biologically bound to a daily rhythm of activity and rest, time limits the spatial choices we can make and the activity space we can use. This is called our

Figure 8.3 Time deepening makes us feel anxious and unfulfilled.

Christopher B. Stage

time geography (Fellmann, Getis, and Getis 1990), and it is being squeezed for the average person in a technological society.

This means the farther the distance we must travel for our daily functions, the less time we have to experience them. For example, class meeting schedules, travel time from residence to campus, and dining hall location and opening and closing hours constrain a student's time. As a result, the daily function that typically gets squeezed out or reduced is leisure. This is particularly a modern problem because, in spite of the automobile, contemporary people are required to travel greater and greater distances to work, school, and other obligations.

Rescheduling Time for Leisure

As should be quite clear at this point, changes in the distribution of working hours affect leisure. One aspect of work that inhibits pastimes is the time of day when the work takes place. The office worker cannot join an afternoon aerobics class, and the factory worker must wait until Saturday to play softball. In the United States, the standard work schedule is Monday through Friday, from 8:00 A.M. to 5:00 P.M. Are there alternatives to this schedule that provide increased opportunities for leisure?

One way of giving people greater control of their free time is called **flextime.** This system allows employees to arrange their own forty-hour weekly work schedule around a core time. Core time dictates when all workers are to be present at their jobs, and is usually during the middle of the day, for example, from 9:30 to 11:30 A.M. and 2:00 to 4:00 P.M. Beyond this core time, employees are free to come and go as they please as long as they clock in the contracted amount of total work time. This means workers may take an extended lunch in order to exercise or shop, come in early and have free time later, or come in later and have free time earlier. About 48 percent of American workers now have schedules that allow them to vary their starting and finishing times (Gallup Poll 1990).

Freedom to choose work hours under flextime has given workers a greater sense of control and autonomy. Flextime employees have discovered better integration of home, family life, leisure, and work. They can choose to use recreation facilities at off-peak times, such as mornings, and often at reduced prices. The result tends to be increased job satisfaction. For example, findings in one study indicated that workers who switched to flextime were more satisfied because they had 25 percent more time with their families (Nollen 1982). Flextime works best where employees' work is fairly independent. Difficulties could occur if machines are paced according to group work, extensive communication and interaction is necessary, and continuous workplace coverage is needed.

A variation of flextime is the four-and-a-half-day workweek where employees arrange their forty hours so Friday afternoon is free. This means that on other days an employee needs to work nine or ten hours. Another variation

Linear Life Plan

Cyclical Life Plan

is the four-day workweek. Under this plan, a worker works four days during a week, at a rate of ten hours per day. The result is a three-day weekend and more opportunity for travel and other sustained leisure activities. The three-day weekend also provides a free "workday" in which people can conduct personal business and other chores while still having two days for leisure. In one study (Poor 1970), one-third of the workers reported that more money was spent for recreation once they switched to the four-day week. Participation in traveling, eating out, going to the beach, boating, dating, and shopping increased. Church activities also increased by 56 percent. Seventy-five percent reported spending more time with their families.

Earned time allows workers to go home whenever they have fulfilled their production quota for the full working day. In some cases, industrious workers can leave their jobs two, three, or even four hours before the end of their shifts and still be paid for eight hours of work. Again, larger amounts of time are freed in the week for leisure.

These alternatives for work time are based on adjustments made to the hours of the day or days of the week. What about freeing time for leisure that is an adjustment to the lifetime schedule? Most people live on a linear life plan (fig. 8.4). This consists of an extended period of nonwork at the beginning of life, a long period of education, followed by an even longer period of work, and finally retirement. Leisure is presumed to be most abundant at the beginning and end of this time line.

Could there be another way to live? As shown in figure 8.4, a cyclical life plan would redistribute some years of schooling from the childhood and youth periods and some free time from the retirement phase into the middle years of life. Work wouldn't need to be the dominant theme in middle age, nor leisure in old age (Best and Stern 1976). Advantages of a cyclical plan are a more even distribution of income over the life cycle and more people having the opportunity to realize personal goals, such as a college degree and childrearing.

Figure 8.4 A cyclical life plan redistributes schooling, work, and leisure throughout life.

Christopher B. Stage

The Intention of Work

Personally, I have nothing against work, particularly when performed, quietly and unobtrusively, by someone else.

(Ehrenreich 1988, 132)

What is work? Is it drudgery required of our existence, or is it accomplishment of something for a greater good? Is all the activity we would call work really necessary for survival? Why do people work? Why do some people work harder than is required? Is there a work "problem" in contemporary society?

Work, most simply, can be defined as the expenditure of effort. Work is the use of energy—human, animal, mechanical, electrical, solar—to produce something. The answers to questions about why people work are more complex than this. For example, some of the answers may be based on the idea that we are all, at least in part, **homo faber** (ancient Greek for "man the tool maker or worker"). That is, work is more than necessity; it is part of being human. It is in the fabric of our moral and biological character. As such, work has meaning and satisfaction in and of itself. Work is making, not just necessities, but also ideas and possibilities. Work is producing something that did not exist before for the sheer adventure of doing so.

Homo faber: human as worker.

On the other hand, does an answer lie in economics? Work's motive, at least in part, is the outcome of societal needs for goods and services? Survival takes work. People must work in order to have the money needed to buy food, clothing, shelter, entertainment, and education. The standard of living people have is directly related to their exertion of effort.

Other answers to questions about work's meaning may be found by considering its history, rewards, and satisfactions.

Pre- and Post-Industrial Work

The emergence of work as a distinct concept is a relatively modern phenomenon. Primitive peoples, some historians maintain, lived life in a more holistic sense, making no distinctions between different types of daily activities. Without the tool of mechanical time in prehistory cultures, work and leisure were fused, as were all other aspects of life. Since there was no concept of an appropriate time to work or play, such as the weekday versus the weekend, work as a distinguishable event was impossible.

The ancient Greeks did not think much of work either. Early Greek poets and philosophers found no inherent value in labor. Homer, for example, thought the Gods were displeased thus condemning people to toil. In ancient Greece, work had a very different meaning than the one we're accustomed to. In fact, the early distinction was more likely between work and labor. Roughly, labor meant providing for the necessities of life and described the activity performed by slaves or a class of laborers. This was called *ponos,* or sorrow. Work, on the other hand, was a meaningful way of life in the voluntary pursuit of intellectual and creative ideas. This was the activity of the "leisure class."

Providing for the physical needs of society (labor) was considered unworthy of the more privileged, thus they tended to approach many of their daily activities as if they were play (Parker 1971).

The ancient Romans began to change this as they faced the practical problem of overseeing a large empire. There were wars, taxes, and barbarians to manage, along with millions of citizens. Such an enormous enterprise began to take precedence over the individual's need for freedom of intellectual pursuit. This led into the medieval period in Europe which brought with it a more revered notion of work. The powerful influence of early Christianity, as maintained by Catholicism, changed and elevated work as well. It was no longer the leisure of intellectualizing nor the necessity of empire management. It was godly. Monks in the early monasteries practiced self-denial as a way of purification. Work was not for the accumulation of worldly goods but for serving God.

For example, in the Benedictine monasteries, all monks were required to engage in labor. All kinds of labor—physical, mental, and spiritual—were pursued. Monks also performed charitable work as a way of becoming more like Christ. According to the seasons and the work required to make the monastery self-sufficient, they would typically spend four to six hours a day in the fields, kitchen, or workshop (Goodale and Godbey 1988). Other hours in the day were spent on prayer and religious study. They were never to be idle. Idleness was an enemy of the soul. There were thousands of monasteries scattered through Europe at the time, and their influence was wide-ranging and long-lasting.

Over 1,000 years later, the protests against the Roman Catholic Church led by Martin Luther and John Calvin resulted in a modified interpretation of the way to salvation. The outcome was Protestantism, which had a further impact on the understanding of work. Luther stressed that work and the responsibilities of family life should be done for the glory of God. His writings were the first to suggest the idea of vocation, performing dutifully that work God wishes you to do. Calvin took up similar themes and focused on responsibilities of good citizenship and obedience.

Protestantism spread in central and southern Europe, and out of this movement, a group of dissidents emerged. Although there were several reasons for their dissent, Puritans mainly sought to purify the church along lines suggested by Luther and Calvin. By the early 1600s, they became entangled in political as well as religious struggles, a wave of migration resulted and brought the work ethic to North America. Without the Puritan's opposition to idleness and wasting time, they may not have survived the first several winters. There was no margin of abundance to allow for nonproductive members of the new settlement. Their attitudes were very practical. Work was a necessity. They believed that both their spiritual and material welfare were dependent on their own exertions.

Across several more centuries, industrialization and urbanization during the Industrial Revolution brought about another chapter in the history of work in Western cultures. The transition from a pre-industrial to an industrial society resulted in an even greater regard for work and increasing separation of work and leisure in everyday life. Work—necessary to feed the voracious machines in common use at the end of the nineteen century—was scheduled first.

Early religious groups, such as the Shakers in the United States, believed work was the supreme human activity. Here tourists observe an interpretation of Shaker singing at Shakertown, KY.

© Ruth V. Russell

Leisure became what time was leftover. Industrialism also made it possible to produce more goods that could be purchased by everyone. The acquisition, use, protection, and upkeep of greater amounts of goods made work a human priority. Leisure became associated with a materialistic style of life.

Much that we take for granted today about the purpose and nature of work is derived from this legacy. Work's history in Western cultures reveals the birth of the adage that leisure is possible only because the work has been done.

Workers' Rewards

Whether people work today because they have to or because they want to, work provides certain rewards. For example, in a research study reported by Brook (1993), the benefits of work activities were rated by a sample of men and women managers of corporations. Results indicated that work activities were more likely than nonwork activities to be creative, challenging, require mental activity, offer self-development, and involve others. Nonwork activities, on the other hand, were more likely to be enjoyable, involve emotions, provide a sense of control, be done for others, and include a freedom of choice. What other rewards might work offer?

As you are well aware, work under the auspices of employment provides money. Few people in contemporary societies grow and even prepare their own food, weave cloth and sew it into their own clothes, and build their shelter out of materials they made or gathered themselves. Most of us need money to purchase these things. Paid work provides this money. In most of the world, workers exchange their time and energy for money. The financial value of their work differs according to the work's nature, the education and training required, and even the culture where it is performed. However, anyone who has ever worked, even for the necessity of earning money, knows that work provides other rewards as well.

Another important reward to the worker is **personal identity.** In some cultures, such as those in North America, when people are asked to tell about themselves, they usually do so in terms of their occupation. Their work or career is a major source of their personhood; it gives them a place in society. Being temporarily unemployed or newly retired often brings complaints of "losing" an identity. We all have a psychological need to feel that we are important, that we have accomplished something, and for many of us this need is filled through work. No society is without its status symbols or ways of manifesting publicly an individual's worth, and in many contemporary societies, this status is provided by work. How much of your personal identity do you think is associated with your work versus your leisure interests? Might this change as you grow older?

Finally, work creates something good that didn't exist before. Artists and musicians celebrate beauty and form. Teachers rejoice when a student learns. Police officers help a neighborhood become a safer place to live. Doctors care about the health of patients, and from the testimony of a gravedigger:

Personal identity: the distinguishing character of an individual.

Not anybody can be a gravedigger. You can dig a hole any way they come. A gravedigger, you have to make a neat job. I had a fella once, he wanted to see a grave. He was a fella that digged sewers. He was impressed when he seen me diggin' this grave—how square and how perfect it was. A human body is goin' into this grave. That's why you need skill when you're gonna dig a grave.

(Terkel 1974, 507)

Work, even such monotonous chores as taking tickets, handing out towels, or digging a ditch can produce the satisfaction of a job well done. The work of people produces products and services that help others. Thus, work can provide a sense of making an important and valuable contribution to society.

Worker Dissatisfactions

Work offers the rewards of money, self-esteem, and a sense of making a positive contribution to society. Does all work provide these rewards, and is work satisfying to all workers? According to a 1991 Gallup Poll, 15 percent of Americans are at least somewhat dissatisfied with their jobs. What makes work dissatisfying?

Research has indicated that having some feelings of autonomy or control over the job situation is necessary for satisfaction with work (O'Toole 1973; Parker 1972). To work well at something important is also critical to many workers. The more knowledge or creativity used at work, the higher the potential for work satisfaction. Freedom to set one's own pace is important. Companionship with like-minded or agreeable people and having a competent boss also seem necessary for worker satisfaction. Essentially, what workers want most is to become masters of their immediate environment and to feel that they and their work are important.

There is an undocumented sense that, overall, people are less satisfied with their work than in the past. Research suggests situations that make work dissatisfying include doing a repetitive job, making only a small part of something, doing tasks that seem useless, and feeling insecure or unappreciated. For example, in an analysis (Russell 1993) of the quality of work for employees in an urban recreation department, employees perceived that having inadequate control over their work, unclear ways for increasing their position in the department, and lack of meaningful and consistent rewards for good performance were blockages to satisfaction at work.

Other reasons for dissatisfaction may be higher expectations by today's workers or an increasing mismatch between workers' educational levels and employment levels. For example, while the absolute number of jobs in the United States has increased during the last two decades, the majority of these jobs have been low-paying, high-turnover, dead end positions (Godbey 1989). Maybe managerial styles and attitudes have changed with greater focus on increasing output. Perhaps the consequences of high technology, such as the health problems associated with extensive computer use, contribute (Gamst

Table 8.3

Important Elements of Success in America

Elements of Success in America	Percent Who Say This Is Very Important
Being a good parent	95
Having a happy marriage	90
Having a happy relationship with another	86
Having friends who respect you	83
Being one of the best at your job	80
Being well educated	77
Being true to religious beliefs	68
Doing things useful to society	63
Having ample time for leisure	53
Having a job that pays above average	44
Having power and influence	16
Having a vacation home	13
Being wealthy	12
Being prominent/famous	8

Source: "The Wall Street Journal/American Dream" survey conducted by The Roper Organization, February 1987.

and Otten 1992). Perhaps a shift in human values has lessened the importance of work in people's lives. To follow this latter possibility let's look at what has happened to the "American Dream."

The *American Dream* is a term coined during the depression years of the 1930s. It described the vision of opportunity available to everyone; all could be successful, all could be rich. It was an optimistic belief in the ability of work to provide all that was needed for the good life. Is this still true? According to a poll conducted by the Roper Organization for the *Wall Street Journal* in 1987, there have been major changes in the American Dream. No longer is it a dream of being wealthy; instead, less tangible goals—things a job cannot provide—seem more important.

In table 8.3, the Roper poll results show that the most important things in life now are being a good parent, having a happy marriage and relationships with others, having friends who respect you, being good at what you do, being well-educated, doing useful things for society, etc. Fewer than 20 percent of the survey sample thought power, influence, fame, and wealth were very important. Asked to define the American Dream, respondents put

Employers concerned with maximizing worker effort might be wise to take a lesson from the games people play at work. Perhaps they should read the work of Dirkin (1985). Dirkin pointed out that for people in repetitive and boring jobs, seemingly trivial actions are regularly performed in order to reduce monotony, increase the work challenge, and enhance feelings of control and satisfaction. These are gamelike behaviors, such as rhythmically playing with the keys of the cash register, assembling a box backwards, trading jobs, or deliberately falling behind on an assembly line merely to be challenged to catch up. These games seem to be crucial to effective functioning.

Once workers have the rhythm of the job and it is not nearly as hard to do, they may begin to find other things to do with their minds (Runcie 1980). People seek comfortable amounts of stimulation, functioning most efficiently under conditions midway between extremely low or extremely high levels of arousal. For example, studies have shown that some workers in an assembly line production system adapted to the boredom and monotony by using individualized coping strategies (Dirkin 1985). They typically cope according to two patterns.

First, some individuals prefer to manipulate the task itself. They alter the required skills and challenges by covertly restructuring the task. This often takes the form of inventing a game with the machine or process (such as performing a particular task with eyes shut), experimenting with orders, creating a rhythm of loading a truck, or even sabotaging the machine itself.

Second, others compensate for boredom by dividing their attention between their task and social interactions. This could include such behaviors as "hooting" down the line to co-workers while inserting parts, listening to a radio while filling orders, chatting on the CB radio while driving a truck, cutting out recipes while answering the phone, and working crossword puzzles while watching a security television.

Csikszentmihalyi (1975) collected some interesting data that explains how these behaviors become important to basic human functioning. The study was designed to assess the effects of all noninstrumental activities on the job, including talking with co-workers, chewing gum, pacing, stretching, etc. Subjects were asked to forego these activities for a forty-eight-hour period. Results indicated that the deprivation of these behaviors affected physiological and cognitive functioning. For example, reactions ranged from increased irritability and tension to a decline in job performance.

An understanding of these trivial games on the job is informative to managers and others concerned with enhancements to productivity and worker satisfaction. Appreciating the basic desire to manipulate skill and challenge within the most routine jobs may make it possible to create a better workplace.

at the top of their lists a good education for themselves and their children, followed by the freedom to choose the way they live, a healthy and safe environment, and ample time for leisure.

These results suggest that as we finish the twentieth century, the central role of work in life is likely to change. While many social scientists and workers still believe work is central, this is becoming less true.

Leisure's Relation to Work

> But the Gods, taking pity on mankind, born to work,
> laid down the succession of recurring Feasts
> to restore them from their fatigue, and
> gave them the Muses . . . so that . . .
> they should again stand upright and erect.
>
> (Plato, quoted in Pieper 1963, 19)

According to Plato, the purpose of leisure was to refresh people from the toil of work. Is the relationship between work and leisure different today? Are these two life domains considered intertwined by contemporary people? There is wide divergence in the answer to these questions.

For example, according to Kelly (1982), the critical difference between work and leisure is that work contributes to the survival and well-being of society; thus, it is productive. Leisure, on the other hand, is nonproductive in the sense that its results are primarily personal and experiential. Do you agree with this distinction? Can you think of ways leisure may be considered productive and work nonproductive?

Meanwhile, Murphy (1981) suggested a holistic perspective. He felt meaning and satisfaction exists in both work and leisure, and both are required for realizing life to its fullest. This means that life is integrated. The freedoms and satisfactions important to life cannot be allocated to either work or leisure, but must be mutually expressed in both. For example, some people feel that if their job had more of the qualities of leisure, they would be more satisfied with it. Do you agree with Murphy? Can you imagine a good argument for keeping work and leisure separate in life?

Huizinga (1955) envisioned leisure as outside ordinary life. The differences between leisure and work were not possible to reconcile, according to Huizinga. More importantly, leisure must remain separate from the rest of life. To integrate leisure with work would destroy it. This view holds that leisure is nonrational. It is spontaneous, a celebration, and even mysterious, and it should be protected from the contamination of work's emphasis on the rational and responsible. Do you find yourself agreeing?

Parker (1971), on the other hand, tried to consider all options by proposing three kinds of relationships between leisure and work. First, the identity relationship between leisure and work suggests that the meanings, forms, and satisfactions of work and leisure are the same. At the other extreme is a contrast relationship in which leisure is needed to make up for the deficiencies of work. Finally, Parker proposed that work and leisure may be separate human experiences—neither similar nor different—simply separate. Accordingly, work and leisure have minimal influence on each other; each is a component of life with its own meaning. Which relationship do you think is more reasonable from Parker's list?

All these, as well as other attempts to describe the relationship between work and leisure, argue essentially pessimistic, optimistic, and neutral perspectives. The pessimistic perspective says that work is a less desirable human condition, and leisure is needed to control or even overcome its problematic effects. The optimistic perspective suggests that all is well with both work and leisure, and healthy people need rewards and satisfactions from both. Life is only meaningful when both are in harmony. Finally, such labels as "separate" from Parker's list suggest that none of these perspectives matter. Leisure and work are simply two separate domains in life and not necessarily related to one another. The relationship is neutral. Let us look at some special applications of each of these perspectives.

Central Life Interest

The neutral view maintains that work and leisure (and other life event categories such as education) are separate. They are parts of life that do not influence each other. One relevant illustration of this is the concept of "central life interest." The notion was developed by Dubin in 1956. Since then, sociologists have explored people's central interests in life, often using work and leisure as the two options. In his initial studies, Dubin found that 24 percent of factory workers could be defined as primarily job-oriented in their life interests. On the other hand, in a later study of managers and other upper-level employees, the orientation toward employment was much more important (Goldman 1973). This category of their lives was dominant. Those working in childcare, mental health, teaching, and public welfare showed the greatest degree of work centrality in life, while those in banking, insurance, advertising, and retail selling showed the least.

Overall, work seems to be losing out as a central life interest. For our grandparents, work was considered the way to make life better for the next generation. Today, in industrialized societies, enjoying ample and meaningful leisure, as well as having a stable and thriving family and community life, are replacing work's centrality for some people.

Workaholism

A special illustration of the pessimistic view worth further exploration is workaholism. Patterned after the word *alcoholism,* workaholism is a compulsion to work incessantly. Workaholics are people inflicted with this compulsion. The concept first appeared in a book by Oates in 1971. Since that time, the word has become widely known. Workaholism has been identified as an increasingly important factor in the work careers of many individuals, particularly those in managerial and professional occupations (Price 1980). This represents the pessimistic view because addiction to work is considered psychologically harmful; life is out of balance.

Workaholics are highly committed to work, devoting more time and energy than necessary. They feel driven to work, not because of external demands, but because inner pressures make them feel guilty when they are not working. Workaholics have been described as more perfectionistic than others and less willing to delegate responsibilities. Some research has suggested, as a result, that workaholics experience more job stress than others, and they often feel overwhelmed by their responsibilities and all they expect themselves to do. One consequence of these behaviors is poor health and illness (Spence and Robbins 1992).

The prescription for workaholism is leisure. As so enjoyably put by Ehrenreich (1988) in an essay entitled "A Farewell to Work":

> What this nation needs is not the work ethic, but a job ethic: if it needs doing—highways repaired, babies changed, fields plowed—let's get it done. Otherwise, take five. Listen to some new wave music, have a serious conversation with a three-year-old, write a poem, look at the sky (p. 135).

What is particularly interesting is that the compulsive nature of workaholism can be applied to leisure, as well. That is, we can engage in pastimes in a compulsive, worklike fashion.

Some people today overcommit themselves to the point where leisure becomes work. They find their weekends are booked full with shopping, family obligations, office work, household and garden chores, as well as scheduled social functions. No free time is left for spontaneous activities. Workaholism applied to leisure is play-aversion (Dickens 1991). Symptoms of play-aversion follow:

- Feelings of anxiety when nothing is scheduled in free time

- Staying in touch with the office while on vacation

- Scheduling numerous activities in free time

- Playing as hard as one works

- Placing a high value on always being busy, even in leisure

A play-aversionist is a workaholic in disguise. What looks like recreation is really another job to do.

Different Ways to Work

Finally, an optimistic view focuses on alternatives to work. When people see their jobs as merely a source of income, take no pride in their work, and feel no responsibility to society or employers, they are likely to come in late, leave early, take days off on the slightest pretext, and loaf as much as possible. If the best that leisure has to offer is integrated into work activities, might this change? What if the job included intrinsic rewards, freedom of choice, pleasure, spirituality, and other characteristics of leisure? Would the distinctions between leisure and work disappear?

Such efforts to do this have included the Japanese system of quality circles, on site day care centers to relieve the stress of parents, company sponsored social and sporting events, work-place opportunities for self-improvement (such as quit smoking classes and weight control counseling), and offering part-time employment. Let's look at some other possibilities.

Autonomous work groups are self-management teams of eight to twelve employees. They are given collective responsibility for whole segments of the production process. They are also given the freedom for decision making and coordination. Another idea is to integrate work support functions. For example,

Eve Smith heard herself say, "Why not? Let's give it a try." The man from the Department of Creative Technology (DOCT) had left, leaving Eve in a somewhat skeptical frame of mind. Then again, it did sound reasonable.

Eve owns a shoe factory. One thousand workers are directly involved in the production of shoes at an average pay of $10,000 per year or a yearly payroll of $10 million. She produces 1 million pairs of shoes per year, which she sells for $30 million. The difference between total sales and payroll ($20 million) takes care of other expenses and profits.

The man from DOCT had suggested that she install a computer controlled robotic system that would enable Eve to lay off 90 percent of her workforce, that is, 900 workers. Output of shoes would remain the same: 1 million pairs per year.

Eve would turn over the salary previously paid to the 900 workers (that is, $9 million) to the DOCT. They, in turn, would keep 10 percent ($900,000) of that amount to pay for the development of the robotic system and put 90 percent ($8,100,000) into a Guaranteed Income Fund (GIF).

The 900 laid off workers would be paid 90 percent of their previous salary from the GIF, either indefinitely or until they chose to seek other employment. If the latter, any negative income differential would be supplemented by the GIF. As far as Eve's profit picture is concerned, nothing would change. She would have as many shoes to sell as before and if anything, would have much fewer labor and production problems.

Nine hundred workers, human beings, would be freed from the necessity of wasting their time making a living. They would be able to develop their or their children's capabilities, skills, and talents or, if they desire, work for the betterment of society. They would be given the opportunity for leisure education, and/or training as desired and appropriate.

The man from the DOCT mentioned other alternatives for distributing the benefits. For instance, instead of freeing 900 workers totally from job obligations, the number of hours worked might be reduced or the number of free days increased, for all thousand workers. Experience will tell which of any number of methods might be best.

Just then, Eve heard a faint ringing, as of a far away bell. Then it became more insistent. She opened her eyes, realizing that she had dozed off. Had it all been a dream? (Neulinger 1989, 21–24)

Questions to Consider and Discuss

1. Is this truly a fantasy or can you see some real possibility in it? Why? What might be done to turn the dream into reality?
2. If you were given the opportunity to receive 90 percent of your salary and not work at a job, would you take it? Why? What about 75 percent of your salary or 50 percent of your salary? Would your decision change? Why?
3. Is leisure the ultimate good in life, or is the absence of leisure the ultimate problem of our time? Read J. B. Nash's classic book *Spectatoritis* (1932) to form your opinion on this.

From John Neulinger, "A Leisure Society: Idle Dream or Viable Alternative, Encroaching Menace or Golden Opportunity." (excerpts from J. B. Nash Scholar Lecture presented on April 22, 1989, for The American Association for Leisure and Recreation). Reproduced with permission from the American Alliance for Health, Physical Education, Recreation and Dance.

activities typically performed by such support units as custodial and personnel, are built into each major unit's responsibilities. How about self-government for employees? Rules could evolve from a collective experience. Everyone participates in the governance of the company.

Finally, let's consider job sharing. If many workers in a society worked four hours a day, there would probably be enough jobs for everybody and no unemployment. Job sharing is when two or more people cooperate in carrying out the hours, responsibilities, and benefits of one full-time job. Such a plan would offer numerous advantages. Workers could have more time for leisure, to help with child care, to continue their education without quitting work, and to begin a smooth transition into retirement. In one survey, one in four reported they work for employers who provide job sharing (*Employee Services Management* 1993).

Summary: Leisure Time and Work Allies

How seriously a culture takes the notions of time and work distinguishes it as modern. In contemporary life, time and work have become more important and also more tyrannical. While leisure is typically prescribed as the cure for the problems of time and work, it has also adopted many of the characteristics of time and work that make them problematic. Thus, leisure is in danger of being lost.

This chapter explored the interrelationships between work, time, and leisure in the following ways. First, types of time were compared. Cyclical time is that pace set by the rhythms of nature. In modern societies, it has been replaced by the concept of mechanical time—paced to the machine. In the future, the computer may set an even more artificial pace for life. Biological time is endogenous rhythms of rest and activity, and cultural time tells us how to pace our life according to geographical traditions.

Next, leisure's expression in time was explored as a function of personal perceptions of free time, adherence to clock time, the time requirements of particular pastimes, the amount of free time available in a society, and the unique barriers to leisure from time itself. These barriers are the time tyrannies of time urgency, the nanosecond culture, time deepening, and changing geography.

Finally, work was discussed both from the perspective of its history and what it can and cannot mean to people. While work offers the rewards of money, self-esteem, and a sense of making a contribution to society, some people are dissatisfied with work. Will leisure take work's place? There are three answers to this question. First is the pessimistic perspective that holds that work is a less desirable human condition, and leisure is needed to overcome its negative by-products. Workaholism was proposed as an example of this. Second, different ways of working were presented as an example of the optimistic view. Here both work and leisure are needed for a balanced, healthy life. Third is the neutral answer that maintains that leisure and work are not related. They are simply two separate domains in life. The concept of central life interest is an example of this view.

References

Anderson, N. 1964. *Dimensions of work.* New York: David McKay Co.

Bammel, G., and L. L. B. Bammel. 1992. *Leisure and human behavior.* Dubuque, IA: Wm. C. Brown Publishers.

Barnes, J. 1984. *The complete works of Aristotle.* Princeton, NJ: Princeton University Press.

Best, F., and B. Stern. 1976. *Lifetime distribution of education, work and leisure: Research, speculations and policy implications of changing life patterns.* Washington, D.C.: Institute for Educational Leadership, George Washington University.

Blatt, S., and D. Quinlan. 1972. The psychological effects of rapid shifts in temporal referents. In *The Study of Time,* edited by J. T. Fraser, F. C. Haber, and G. H. Muller. New York: Springer-Verlag.

Blume, M. 1993. Jet lag and the time clock repairman. *International Herald Tribune,* 2 August.

Bosserman, P. 1975. Some interpretations on the dynamics of time on industrial society. *Society and Leisure* 7:155–64.

Brook, J. A. 1993. Leisure meanings and comparisons with work. *Leisure Studies* 12:149–62.

Clark, R. W. 1983. *Benjamin Franklin: A Biography.* New York: Random House.

Cross, G. 1990. *A social history of leisure since 1600.* State College, PA: Venture.

Csikszentmihalyi, M. 1975. *Beyond Boredom and Anxiety.* San Francisco: Jossey-Bass.

Decision Research Corporation. 1990. *Decision research corporation's 1990 leisure study: Trends in America's leisure time and activities.* Lexington, MA: D. C. Heath.

DeGrazia, S. 1962. *Of time, work and leisure.* New York: The Twentieth Century Fund.

Denny, D. 1993. Waiting on down the line. *The Herald-Times,* 2 November. Bloomington, IN.

Dickens, P. 1991. Playing hard or hardly playing? *Executive Female.* (March/April):46.

Dirkin, G. R. 1985. The non-triviality of trivial acts: Implications for job satisfaction in overtly boring tasks. In *Transitions to Leisure,* edited by B. G. Gunter, J. Stanley, and R. St. Clair. In Lanham, MD: University Press of America.

Dossey, L. 1982. *Space, time and medicine.* Boston: New Science Library, Shambhala Publications.

Dubin, R. 1956. Industrial workers' world. *Social Problems* 3:134–43.

Ehrenreich, B. (May 1988). A farewell to work. *Mother Jones.*

Employee Services Management, November 1993, 36:9.

Fellman, J., A. Getis, and J. Getis. 1990. *Human geography: Landscapes of human activity.* Dubuque, IA: Wm. C. Brown Publishers.

Franklin, B. 1932. *The autobiography and selections from his other writing.* New York: The Modern Library.

Friedman, M., and R. Rosenman. 1976. *Type A behavior and your heart.* New York: Knopf.

The Gallup Poll Monthly, November 1990, p. 46.

The Gallup Poll Monthly, September 1991, p. 13.

Gamst, G., and C. M. Otten. 1992. Job satisfaction in high technology and traditional industry: Is there a difference? *The Psychological Record* 42:413–25.

Godbey, G. 1980. *Leisure in your life: An exploration.* State College, PA: Venture.

Godbey, G. 1989. *The future of leisure services: Thriving on change.* State College, PA: Venture.

Goldman, D. R. 1973. Managerial mobility motivations and central life interests. *American Sociological Review* 38:119–26.

Goodale, T. L., and G. C. Godbey. 1988 *The evolution of leisure: Historical and philosophical perspectives.* State College, PA: Venture.

Green, T. F. 1968. *Work, leisure, and the American schools.* New York: Random House.

Hammond, J. 1933. *The growth of common enjoyment.* London: Rutledge.

Harris, L. 1987. *Inside America.* New York: Vintage Books.

Huizinga, J. 1955. *Homo Ludens.* London: Paladin Books.

Ibrahim, H. 1991. *Leisure and society: A comparative approach.* Dubuque, IA: Wm. C. Brown Publishers.

Kelly, J. R. 1982. *Leisure.* Englewood Cliffs, NJ: Prentice-Hall.

Krombholz, H. 1990. Circadian rhythm and performance during a 24-hour relay race. *Perceptual and Motor Skills* 70:603–7.

Levine, R., and E. Wolff. 1985. Social time: The heartbeat of culture. *Psychology Today* 19:28–30.

Linder, S. 1970. *The harried leisure class.* New York: Columbia University Press.

Murphy, J. F. 1981. *Concepts of leisure.* Englewood Cliffs, NJ: Prentice-Hall.

Nash, J. B. 1932. *Spectatoritis.* New York: Sears Publishing.

Neulinger, J. 1989. A leisure society: Idle dream or viable alternative, encroaching menace or golden opportunity. J. B. Nash Scholar Lecture. Boston: American Association for Leisure and Recreation.

Nollen, S. D. 1982. *New work schedules in practice: Managing time in a changing society.* New York: Van Nostrand-Reinhold.

Oates, W. 1971. *Confessions of a workaholic: The facts about work addiction.* New York: World.

O'Toole, J. 1973. *Work in America.* Cambridge, MA: The MIT Press.

Owen, J. D. 1969. *The price of leisure.* Rotterdam: Rotterdam University Press.

Parker, S. 1971. *The future of work and leisure.* New York: Praeger.

Pieper, J. 1963. *Leisure: The basis of culture.* New York: New American Library.

Pittendrigh, C. 1972. On temporal organization in living systems. In *The Future of Time,* edited by H. Yaker, H. Osmond, and F. Cheek. New York: Anchor/Doubleday.

Poor, R., ed. 1970. *Four days, forty hours.* Cambridge, MA: Bursk & Poor.

Price, M. 1980. Workaholism: Fears a job can't solve. *Industry Week,* (3 March): 5, 56–59, 62.

Priestley, J. B. 1968. *Man and time.* New York: Dell Publishing Co.

Reilly, T., and A. Down. 1986. Circadian variation in the standing broad jump. *Perceptual and Motor Skills* 62:830.

Rifkin, J. 1987. *Time wars: The primary conflict in human history.* New York: Henry Holt and Company.

Runcie, J. F. 1980. By days I make cars. *Harvard Business Review,* (May/June):106–15.

Russell, R. V. 1993. Employee attitudes toward the quality of work and organizational barriers. Indianapolis Department of Parks and Recreation. Bloomington, IN: The Leisure Research Institute.

Scheuch, E. 1972. The time budget interview. In *The use of time—Daily activities of urban and suburban populations,* edited by A. Szalai. The Hague, Netherlands: Mouton.

Schor, J. B. 1992. *The overworked American: The unexpected decline of leisure.* New York: Basic Books.

Spence, J. T., and A. S. Robbins. 1992. Workaholism: Definition, measurement, and preliminary results. *Journal of Personality Assessment* 58, no. 1:160–78.

Terkel, S. 1974. *Working: People talk about what they do all day and how they feel about what they do.* New York: Pantheon Books.

Turkle, S. 1984. *The second self: Computers and the human spirit.* New York: Simon & Schuster.

U.S. Department of Commerce. 1992. Statistical abstract of the United States. Washington, D.C.: Government Printing Office.

U.S. Department of Labor, Bureau of Labor Statistics (April 1970). Employment and earnings. U.S. Printing Office.

Wever, R. A. 1985. Man in temporal isolation: Basic principles of the circadian system. In *Hours of work: Temporal factors in work-scheduling,* edited by S. Folkard and T. H. Monk. New York: Wiley.

Whitrow, G. J. 1980. *The natural philosophy of time.* Oxford: Oxford University Press.

III

In the final section of this book, we turn our attention to the more functional side of leisure: leisure's ability to be useful as a tool. We explore the use of leisure as an instrument of social good in chapter 9. In tracing leisure's history in the United States, we are able to see leisure as a positive and important force in human and community health. We also consider the use of leisure as an instrument of economics. In chapter 10, we consider how leisure mirrors a nation's level of economic development and drives its economy. Leisure as a means for achieving human equality is the focus of chapter 11, and chapter 12 presents the systems—resources and sponsors—that deliver leisure services to people.

Leisure as a Social Instrument— Systems Context

Leisure can be an instrument of social good.

leisure

Having access to leisure is imperative to the lives of individuals and societies.

using leisure for social good

Can leisure be functional?

Yes. Today leisure is seen as a positive and important force in human and community health.

How does leisure become functional?

As nations become more industrialized, they become more reliant on leisure as a tool for solving problems.

How did this view of leisure as a useful tool develop?

In the United States, what began simply as a play movement became an entire social movement. Sport, game, music, dance, and enjoying the outdoors became a means to create better personal and community lives. The movement was so sweeping that it involved cities, states, and the national government. People formed organizations, raised funds, and wrote volumes to teach people how to use their leisure productively.

University of Nebraska–Lincoln Photography

KEY TERMS

Panacea 260
Utilitarian 260
Industrial Revolution 268
Social movement 272
Settlement house 273
Accreditation 285
Certification 286

As nations of the world have become more

industrialized, they have become more reliant on leisure as a tool for social good.Unlike some earlier societies, such as the ancient Greeks for whom leisure was an end in itself, many contemporary societies see a more functional side of leisure. Today, an important focus is the useful outcomes from leisure. Leisure is considered a positive force in human and societal health. Though leisure is not a **panacea** for social and individual difficulties, it does make a vital contribution to contemporary problem solving. Our pastimes play a key role in civic celebration, release from human toil, family vitality, counteracting deprivation, and social communication and cooperation—all things that bring about a higher quality of life.

In Canada, for example, the role of leisure in creating the Canadian culture is considered to be so great that since the 1960s a number of Federal Ministries have been directly involved in providing recreation programs for citizens. Today, Canada boasts one of the largest national park systems and total expenditures on pastimes in the world (Langlois 1984). In Great Britian, post–World War I strikes by workers and the government's concern for war-weary citizens resulted in legislation granting a reduced workday. More free time for leisure was seen as a way of bringing back the country's prewar vitality. In late 1700s France, having the opportunity to read for pleasure became one of the symbols of the French Revolution. During the revolution an enormous number of books were taken from the reading rooms of the wealthy and privileged class and placed in public libraries.

In this chapter, we will use the United States to demonstrate leisure's **utilitarian** role. This example is appropriate because in the U.S. some have considered leisure completely dysfunctional to the goals of the nation, while others believed that it could solve most social problems. We tell leisure's utilitarian story through history from colonial times to the present.

Panacea: a remedy for all ills.

Utilitarian: something useful.

Colonial America

As late as the 1400s, Indian and Inuit people were the only inhabitants of the Western Hemisphere. When Columbus arrived in 1492, about 1 million members of hundreds of different native groups inhabited North America (about 20 million in Mexico and South America). Most Europeans did not know that the Western Hemisphere existed before Columbus's voyage, however, during the next 400 years, large waves of people from mostly European countries sailed across the Atlantic Ocean to North and South America. Among them were colonists—chiefly British—who settled along the eastern coast of North America between what are now the states of Maine and Georgia. They came because they thought this new world offered opportunities for wealth, power, freedom, and adventure.

Early New England

However, those Europeans who settled in the northern regions of the eastern coast did not find gold or other riches; instead, they found rugged wilderness.

Beyond the legendary hardships they experienced as they established settlements lay a vast and unbelievably rich and varied area. The resources of this land—its fertile soils, abundant water supplies, and plentiful minerals—would later help the United States grow into one of the world's largest and most prosperous nations. In the meantime, the great danger and difficulty of the wilderness of the early 1600s meant the earliest foreign colonists suffered from lack of food and from disease.

Little time and energy could be squandered on leisure. There was no abundance. Survival was meager and precarious. Leisure, with its emphasis on things nonproductive, was not only dysfunctional but dangerous. The Virginia Assembly declared in 1619 that any person found idle would be condemned to prison. In Connecticut, it was unlawful to waste time by the public smoking of tobacco.

It was not just the difficulty of taming a wilderness that sent leisure into the realm of the forbidden; the religious heritage of the new settlers also played a role. Many were motivated to come because of a belief in a "divine mission." Their rebellion against the excesses of the aristocracy in England resulted in religious abstinence from the pleasures of the privileged classes. Thus, all amusement and entertainment was forbidden on Sundays as this was the "Lord's Day." Such attitudes about the purpose of Sunday can still be found in some parts of the United States today. Also common in the New England colonies were laws forbidding participation at any time in such activities as card games, dancing by men and women together, and theatrical performances. The ban in some colonies also included bowling and shuffleboard. Penalties even existed for wearing decorative clothing.

In spite of religious dictates and the hard work to be done, the European colonists did have some fun. Each town had its own meeting house and tavern. In the taverns, the British love of game and sport was maintained. They also served as places for country dances, cockfights, and musical performances. Working groups brought together to build a barn or make a quilt took on a character of celebration and sociability as well. The wealth of deer, moose, and turkey made hunting more than just a way of getting food. In Boston, for example, close to one thousand men would gather to attend training days for practicing marksmanship. The wealthier New England colonists enjoyed private pastimes including the oft banned theatrical amusements. In the summer, they attended horse races, and dances and card parties were also fashionable.

Even though leisure was discouraged because of the notion that it got in the way of taming the wilderness, it did not completely disappear. Moreover, some of the surviving leisure expressions of the New England colonists actually had a functional purpose. Celebrations while building barns, for example, made it possible for many hands to help with the task.

The Antebellum South

Social activities were favorite pastimes of the settlers in the southern east coast areas as well but for different reasons. Unlike their northern counterparts, the lifestyle of the southern colonies more closely resembled that of the British aristocracy. Any gathering of people was a leisure event. Weddings and funerals, as well as horse races, cockfights, and bowling matches, brought people together for gala festivities. Dances, parties, barbecues, and little plays were popular forms of home entertainment. Gambling was celebrated with cards, dice, coin tossing, and lotto. Some southern gentry, such as Thomas Jefferson, enjoyed more contemplative pastimes. Jefferson was an avid reader, writer, and gourmet cook! The nature of leisure in the southern colonies, then, was similar to that of the ancient Greeks. Leisure was more an end in itself rather than a means to another goal.

What made all this devotion to pastimes possible? Slavery, which was also present in colonial New England, was more integral to the economy and social structure of the southern colonies. The enslavement of primarily black people brought from Africa began during the 1600s. It flourished in the south where great numbers of laborers were needed to work the large plantation crops. By the Civil War, about 4 million slaves supported a privileged leisure lifestyle for about one-fourth of southern white people. They cleared the wilderness; built canals, railroads, and roads; and picked the cotton that became the country's most valuable export.

While American folklore has told of cheerful slaves dancing to banjo music, in reality they experienced very little leisure. Those who worked in the fields worked daily from sunrise to sunset. If there was a full moon during the cotton picking season, the field slaves usually worked until late at night. It wasn't just the hard work that made leisure for the slaves rare; they also did not have the freedom for leisure. It is symbolic, then, that many of the music and dance forms that were prevalent in the slave culture featured the theme of freedom—a cornerstone of leisure. There was typically one break in this routine of work, however, and that was the Christmas season. Then, owners allowed a few days for feasting, dancing, music, and games.

During the late 1700s, slavery began to decline. It was abolished in the New England colonies around 1834 but continued to expand in the southern colonies until the Civil War. On April 12, 1861, the northern states and the southern states went to war over the slavery dispute. The war was a tragedy. Not only did the bloody battles take more American lives than any other war, but it left large parts of the South in ruins and created longlasting feelings of bitterness and division among the people. However, soon after the war's end in 1865, slavery was outlawed throughout the United States with the adoption of the Thirteenth Amendment to the Constitution. Today, few countries legally allow slavery with a few exceptions in some areas of Africa, Asia, and South America.

Transitions of the 1800s

During the early 1800s, European settlers by the thousands moved westward over the Appalachian Mountains into the new states and territories. These hardy people went west in search of a better life. They sought good farmland and rich mineral resources. Through hard work, they settled the western wilderness as earlier settlers had done in the east. When they arrived, they took over much of the land that native people had occupied for centuries. As these Native Americans were forced from their land, even greater hardships

In 1992, the U.S. Congress authorized a feasibility study to determine whether Nicodemus, Kansas, would be added to the national park system. The reason was that Nicodemus was important in the history of African Americans.

In the 1870s, Nicodemus, located in north-central Kansas, witnessed the great movement of African Americans from the horrors of reconstruction in the South to the Midwest. They were known as "Exodusters." Nicodemus was one of the towns that resulted from this migration. Coming primarily from Kentucky, these former slaves arrived to begin a new life. By 1881, thirty-five residential and commercial structures had been erected in the town.

At first, Nicodemus colonists had to cope with many hardships on the Kansas frontier. Their early shelters were burrows dug in the sides of dirt banks or small hills. Sod dugouts and wooden structures eventually replaced the burrows. Finding food was a far more difficult problem. Few of the settlers had any money as most spent all their funds just to get there. The Nicodemus Town Company was established to secure food and supplies from across the state. In 1879, the school district was initiated with most of the classes taught in people's homes. By the 1880s, Nicodemus had a baseball team, a literary and benefit society, a bank, lodges, and an ice cream parlor. Its citizens also became prominent in county and state political activities.

Nicodemus probably reached its peak by 1910. Its gradual decline in population mirrored that of the rest of the county, and the close of the post office in 1953 symbolized the end of its importance as a reconstruction era African-American settlement. Today, Nicodemus is the last purely African-American community in Kansas. It has forty-eight residents, yet a "strong feeling of community still permeates the town, a feeling cultivated and fueled by more than one hundred years of perseverance and unwillingness to surrender this living reminder of the contributions of their forebears" (National Park Service 1993, 12).

In conducting the feasibility study on Nicodemus, the National Park Service identified and evaluated regional land uses and trends, analyzed comparative data on the management of similar sites, and inventoried remaining structures. The study team conducted an environmental impact assessment and economic and social impact analyses. They formulated alternative management strategies and their costs. There were frequent interviews with members of the Nicodemus Historical Society and other persons interested in the town. Public meetings were also held to discuss the possibilities.

What was the decision? A report of findings was submitted to Congress in May 1993—not long before this book was written. As a special project, follow up on the story and find out what has occurred since. To begin, contact the Midwest Regional Office of the National Park Service.

were endured. For example, for the Cherokee and the Choctaw tribes, a forced march from their homelands became known as the "Trail of Tears" because of the sickness and death they endured.

Expansion into the rich interior of the continent enabled the United States to become a leading agricultural nation. Farmers were able to produce more than they needed for their own families. New farming techniques and

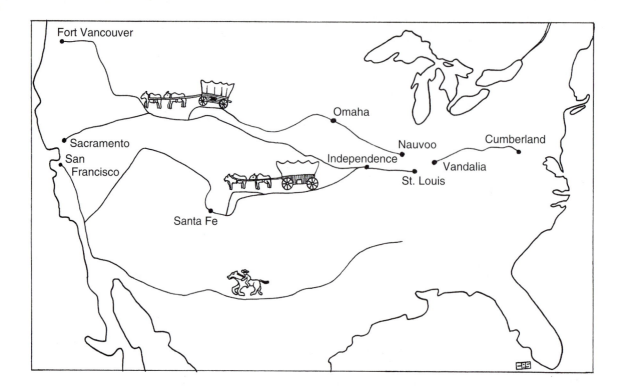

Early trails of the western movement.

Christopher B. Stage

machines boosted the output even more. The cotton gin, invented by Eli Whitney, came into widespread use. One cotton gin could separate cotton fiber from the seeds as fast as fifty people could by hand. The period also marked the beginning of large-scale manufacturing. Centered in the east, businesses erected large factories equipped with machinery to do the work. Developments in transportation also contributed immensely to the economic growth of the country. New and improved roads, such as the National Road in the east and the Oregon and Santa Fe trails in the west, eased the difficulty of traveling and shipping goods by land. In 1807, Robert Fulton demonstrated the first commercially successful steamboat, the *Clermont*. Soon the steam-powered railroad rivaled the steamboat in importance, and by 1850, about 9,000 miles of railroad lines were in operation.

These and other events meant great transitions for the new nation. Accompanying the economic and industrial upheavals were changes in how people lived, which eventually meant a more utilitarian role for leisure.

Cultural Change

After 1820, the wilderness seemed less and less hostile to the European American people. Increasingly, society glorified the frontier and nature. The public eagerly read the novels of James Fenimore Cooper, which described Native Americans and frontiersmen as pure of heart and noble in deed. American philosophers, such as Ralph Waldo Emerson, praised nature as a source of truth and beauty. In the following poem fragment, Emerson swears undying love to nature.

> For nature ever faithful is
> To them who trust her faithfulness
> Keep your gift exhaust your arts
> You shall not win our forest hearts
> When the forest shall mislead me
> When the night & morning lie
> When sea & land refuse to feed me
> Twill be time enough to die
> Then will yet my mother yield
> A pillow in her greenest field
> Nor the June flowers scorn to cover
> The clay of their departed lover . . . .

Excerpted from "Woodnotes, I," circa 1827 by Ralph Waldo Emerson, in The Poetry Notebooks of Ralph Waldo Emerson, R. H. Orth, A. I von Frank., L. Ailardt, D. W. Hill (eds.). Copyright © 1986 University of Missouri Press, Columbia, MO. Reprinted by permission of the Ralph Waldo Emerson Memorial Association.

Developments in printing made literature and art available to more people than ever before. For example, a new printing process called lithography enabled artists to produce many copies of their works more cheaply. The lithographs of Nathaniel Currier and James Merrit Ives were especially popular. They depicted everyday American scenes and customs—often in a very sentimental style. With faster printing presses, many newspaper publishers lowered the cost of their papers to a penny, a price everyone could afford. The spoken word, however, remained important. Large numbers of people attended the speeches of political candidates, scientists, clergy, and social activists.

The demand for entertainment became insatiable. City people flocked to plays performed in theaters. Groups of entertainers and magicians toured the country performing for small-town audiences. P. T. Barnum, the most famous showman of the time, fascinated the public with unusual attractions. Barnum often used exaggeration and deception to create interest in his shows. His "museums" included tight-rope walkers, pantomimes, tumblers, lectures, and plays. The variety musical show also became popular. By the 1860s, entrepreneurs like New Yorker, Tony Pastor, enticed men, women, and children to his "Opera House" on the Bowery for a program of singers, comedians, and animal and acrobatic acts. These early music auditoriums were quite different than they are today. The audience sat at tables separated into stalls, and the price of admission was not for the entertainment but for the liquor.

The traveling circus also became popular during the 1800s. The one-wagon show of colonial America, with its polar bear or elephant, gradually gave way to the three-ring circus. By about 1879, during the Golden Age of the American circus, more than ten large circuses toured the country. They traveled in colorful wagons pulled by horses (fig. 9.1) and attracted an audience before the performance by parading through the town streets. It must have been a

Figure 9.1
A circus wagon.

Christopher B. Stage

sight—the red and gold wagons, elephants, rousing band music. The parades eventually had to be discontinued because the streets were becoming more crowded with traffic. The most successful circuses were those of the P. T. Barnum and James A. Bailey partnership, and the five Ringling brothers. These two circus companies merged when the Ringlings bought the Barnum and Bailey circus in 1907, and their performances continue today.

Another change in pastime patterns in the 1800s was the increasing respectability of sport. Previously associated with gambling, drunkenness, and violence, sport gradually gained legitimacy (Cross 1990). A new attitude toward the human body helped. It no longer was thought of as merely the source of devilish temptation which had to be controlled. Instead, the body became a symbol of physical courage and disciplined will. The change in sport also resulted from the influence of other countries. For example, German immigrants introduced gymnastics when they arrived in large numbers, and Scottish immigrants imported track and field events.

As concern for the nation's health increased, public schools began to embrace the idea of fitness and sport for youth. Although colleges initially took little leadership in the growth of other sport activities, they did introduce and promote football. The first intercollegiate game was played between Princeton and Rutgers in 1869, arousing spectator enthusiasm from the start. Private athletic clubs were also founded to provide indoor exercise, primarily for businessmen. The American country club, originating in 1882 near Boston, provided first cricket and tennis, and later golf to its exclusive membership. A kind of gentleman's amateur athleticism guided many other sport developments as well, such as the founding of the YMCA and the modern Olympic Games in the 1890s. Even the founding of basketball in 1891 was based on this ideal. James Naismith invented it in Springfield, Massachusetts, to provide exercise and competition without the threat of injury common in other ball games of the time. Because of the raised goal, the player had to throw the ball softly in an arc. This was considered more "civilized" (Cross 1990).

The sport cult of the late nineteenth century, however, was militantly male, reaffirming the view that the vulnerable female was unsuited for vigorous physical activity. In the 1860s, women were allowed to play croquet, and in the 1870s, an easy form of lawn tennis was introduced. However, so powerful was the lure of sport that women gradually entered into it in spite of social constraints. One of the earliest examples is the inclusion of individual sport in the curriculum at the private women's college of Vassar in 1875.

The American Character

Along with the changes in popular culture, entertainments, and sport that gradually evolved during the nineteenth century, later decades of this period gave birth to the beginning of the modern concept of leisure as tool. Coming a long ideological distance since the colonial period, we will explain how this idea began by first describing the emerging American character.

Europeans who came to America felt intensely that they were breaking down walls and opening doors in a land of economic opportunity and freedom. The pioneering spirit of individualism, natural rights, and social mobility was vitally alive. European Americans felt confident in their ability to create their own destiny. They rejected the ideas of monarchy, caste, dynasty, and privileged birth. In fact, in the book *Democracy in America,* the nineteenth-century Frenchman, Alexis de Tocqueville, wrote of the passion with which

Ina Gittings pole vaulting in the late 1800s at the University of Nebraska-Lincoln. Still a little ahead of her time?

© University of Nebraska - Lincoln Photography

267

Americans pursued "equality of condition" (1945). This belief in equality has left a significant legacy for Americans, one that also brought some problems a century later. In the 1800s, however, it fueled a particularly American response to changing conditions of inequality.

As the nation continued to expand in commerce and industry, there were new challenges. Many of these challenges directly resulted from the development of industrialization. Historians refer to this period as the **Industrial Revolution**. Beginning in Great Britain during the 1700s, it spread to other parts of Europe and to North America in the early 1800s. By the mid-1800s, industrialization was widespread. It created an enormous increase in the production of many kinds of goods because of the introduction of power-driven machinery. The spinning mule replaced the spinning wheel; the power loom replaced the hand loom; and the steam locomotive replaced the horse. The Industrial Revolution took work out of the rural home and workshop and into the urban factory. This caused great changes in people's lives.

Some workers were displaced by machines, but others found new jobs working with machinery. Most workers lived and worked under harsh conditions. In the factories, the machines forced workers to work faster and without rest. Jobs became specialized, and the work was monotonous. Factory wages were low. Women and children worked as unskilled laborers and made only a small fraction of men's low wages. Children—many under age ten—worked from ten to fourteen hours a day. Some became deformed by the repetitious work or injured by unsafe machines. Housing in the growing industrial cities could not keep up with the migration of workers from rural areas and other countries. Severe overcrowding resulted, and many people lived in filthy conditions that frequently led to outbreaks of disease.

As a consequence, many Americans came to believe that social reforms were needed to improve their society—to correct the "inequalities of condition." Churches and social welfare groups set up charities to aid the poor. Reformers worked to reduce the working day of laborers. Prohibitionists, convinced that drunkenness was the chief cause of poverty and other problems, persuaded some states to outlaw the sale of alcohol. People like Dorothea Dix worked to improve the dismal conditions in the nation's prisons and asylums, while others like Horace Mann demanded education and better schools for all American children.

More significantly from our perspective were those reforms that used leisure. Some reformers believed wholesome and enriching leisure experiences would solve the inevitable consequences of the Industrial Revolution. The belief that all Americans had a natural right to a high quality of life was the fundamental rationale. We will use as examples the early park developments, the adult education movement, developments in therapeutic recreation, and the birth of voluntary agencies.

In the early nineteenth century, concern began for preservation of the natural heritage of the United States in the face of increasing industrialization and destruction of natural resources. One solution was parks. The need for open space for leisure was first felt in the larger cities. Following the example of William Penn who set aside five undeveloped squares in the plan for

Industrial Revolution: a rapid and major change in an economy due to the introduction of power-driven machinery.

$\boldsymbol{C}$ase $\boldsymbol{S}$tudy   Tragedy of the Commons

The city park is a relatively recent phenomenon in the United States, and its beginnings are obscure. Some historians assert that the plaza in St. Augustine, set aside in 1565, should be considered the first city park, while others refer to the Boston Common, established in 1634, as the first city park.

The common was originally a British tradition and the plaza a Spanish one. At first, the common was used as a communal pasture. People had unlimited access to this commonly held land for grazing their livestock. As the growth of cities resulted in the loss of open space, the common and plaza became a commonly held recreation resource. In recent years, the consequences of this idea have been destructive. In an essay published in 1968 by Garrett Hardin, "The Tragedy of the Commons" is explained.

Hardin asks us to imagine a pasture, fixed in size, which is accessible to all the livestock owners of a village. Each herdsman, being rational, wants to maximize his use of the pasture by grazing as many cattle as possible. Therefore, he continually expands the size of his herd, recognizing that the benefits from this will be his alone while any costs associated with the increased grazing will be shared among all the village members. Under these circumstances, reasoned Hardin, expansion seems sensible. What each herdsman fails to recognize, however, is that every other herdsman in the village is following the same logic, and the cumulative effect of their independently logical action is bound to be the destruction of the pasture. Blinded by self-interest, the herdsmen continue their exploitation of the commonly held resource.

The tragedy of the commons, then, is a situation where a group of individuals, each acting in his or her own individual best interest, finds that the collective effect of their rightful actions is actually negative. Dustin, McAvoy,

and Schultz (1982) have extended Hardin's story to apply to city parks and other public recreation places. They asked us to consider an urban resident who wishes to escape the heat, congestion, and noise of the city on a summer weekend. She looks to the mountains, or the beach, lake, or river, for a cool and refreshing two-day rest. She gathers the family, packs the car, and heads for one of America's nearby public recreation areas. After all, it is a very logical thing to do, explained Dustin, McAvoy, and Schultz. Consider also the implication of thousands of other city dwellers who are making the same logical decision. The cumulative effect of such numbers of people seeking a cool, quiet, and refreshing leisure experience at the same time means destroying the very experience for which they are searching. Instead of the peace of the outdoors, they are treated to traffic jams, noise, and crime—the very problems they attempted to escape. This too is the tragedy of the commons. It is the problem of unlimited access to commonly held resources that inevitably leads to an erosion of the quality of the leisure environment itself.

Questions to Consider and Discuss

1. What is meant by the tragedy of the commons? Is Hardin's logic applicable to public recreation settings as Dustin, McAvoy, and Schultz suggest? What other examples support this extension of the tragedy of the commons principle?
2. In a nation committed to equality of conditions, what is the symbolic significance of public recreation areas? Do some independent reading in resource user patterns and allocation policies to explore the question more fully.
3. Visit a public recreation area in your community. Can you find traces of the tragedy of the commons?

Philadelphia in 1682 and James Oglethorpe who designed public gardens and squares in Savannah, Georgia, in 1733, the grandest example of the park solution at the time was Central Park. Using a design by Frederick Law Olmsted and Calvert Vaux, New York City created the 850-acre Central Park beginning in 1853. This grand park was designed to ease the cramped conditions of the city with the joys of the countryside, to provide relief from the concrete with plants and wildlife. The model was ultimately followed by other cities. By the turn of the century, over 750 cities had set aside land for public parks.

Concern for the preservation of the natural heritage also began to be answered by the federal government during this time. In 1832, Congress passed legislation authorizing federal control of the Arkansas hot springs; the medicinal qualities of its water were reserved for everyone's use. In 1864, Congress set aside Mariposa Big Tree Park for the state of California. Later, this grove of trees became Yosemite National Park. Yellowstone National Park's establishment in 1872, however, marked the real beginnings of the national park movement in the United States. The intention was to preserve significant natural resources for the enjoyment of future generations. Several states followed this lead and claimed open spaces for the benefit of their people. The first state parks were established in California, New York, Michigan, Minnesota, and New Jersey.

Intellectual and political leaders of the time asked other searching questions about the way people lived. Considerable civic concern developed for improving the intellectual capacity of the populace. One solution was universal public education, and as education's availability increased so did its scope. A growing conviction emerged that leisure, properly used, could contribute to an elevated intellectual character of the people. Thus, the use of leisure skills, such as physical fitness, was gradually added to the curriculum to widen the horizons of people.

Another answer to the need to improve the intellectual capacity of Americans was the so-called Lyceum movement. This was a national organization with more than 900 local chapters during its peak. Its program consisted chiefly of lectures, readings, and other educational and cultural events. Its rationale was that all citizens should be educated in order to participate capably in the affairs of the country. The ideals of the Lyceum movement were also promoted by the Chautauqua organization, which took lectures and other educational programs around the country.

The prevalence of the humanistic philosophy evident in the 1800s also led to the use of leisure in health care. As the first superintendent of the Pennsylvania Hospital in Philadelphia, the first general medical hospital in the United States, Dr. Benjamin Rush is credited with recognizing the therapeutic values of recreation activities for patients (Haworth and MacDonald 1946). The use of therapeutic recreation as a treatment was most prevalent in the psychiatric hospitals of the time. Activities like chess, gardening, reading, walking, and needlecraft were used as tools in the care of the mentally ill (Carter, van Andel, and Robb 1985). Florence Nightingale, the pioneer of modern nursing, recommended in *Notes on Nursing,* published in 1873, the use of music and pets for the improvement of hospital environments.

Finally, the development of voluntary agencies provided additional leisure tools for the social reforms called for at the time. In 1851, groups of young men copied a British organization and formed the Young Men's Christian Association (YMCA) in Boston and Montreal, Canada. At first this organization provided only religious discussion groups for youth and adults. It gradually enlarged its program to include gymnastics, sports, and other recreational activities. By 1860, the first Boys' Club had been established in Hartford, Connecticut, to counteract the ills of city life. The goal was to provide a play alternative to the streets for young boys. Girls' Clubs, which grew from a concern for disadvantaged girls, weren't established until 1945. By the turn of the century, a few corn-raising clubs for boys and canning clubs for girls began a rural program that led to the founding of 4–H (MacLean, Peterson, and Martin 1985). Its purpose was to help youth gain life skills and attitudes that would enable them to become productive members of society.

Birth of Organized Leisure Systems

In spite of these nineteenth century efforts, things didn't get much better. Uncontrolled growth of urban areas continued. In 1870, only 25 percent of Americans lived in urban areas. By 1916, the figure had reached almost 50 percent. Furthermore, the long process of settling the country from coast to coast drew to a close, and Congress officially recognized that America's frontier era had ended with the census of 1890. This also signaled the end of the Native-American way of life. Through the years, the federal government pushed more and more Native Americans onto reservations. By 1900, this process was complete.

Meanwhile, the industrial boom continued to affect the lives of the European-American people. It also presented many opportunities for financial gain, and some people amassed huge fortunes. For example, there were about 3,000 millionaires in 1900, compared to only 20 in 1850. American author Mark Twain called this era the Gilded Age, describing the culture of this newly rich. Lacking tradition, the wealthy developed a showy leisure that attempted to imitate the culture of upper-class Europeans. Decorating large mansions with gaudy decorations, attending operas and horse races, holding balls and parties for over 1,000 guests, yachting, relaxing at luxurious resorts, and pursuing other "signs of refinement" created a lavish display of pleasure—the most to date in American history.

On the other hand, the industrial boom meant that the laborers who toiled in factories, mills, and mines did not share in its benefits. They usually worked at least sixty hours a week for an average of twenty cents an hour. The problem was compounded by the more than 25 million mostly European immigrants who had entered the country by 1916. They continued to crowd into cheap apartment buildings called tenements. The everyday life of the city poor was dismal at best. The crowded slum neighborhoods also bred crime, and poor sanitation and inadequate diets continued to make people vulnerable to disease. In spite of all this, the uniquely American character survived. The poor had hope. They knew that economic advancement was possible in the United States. Even if workers knew they could not advance, they believed their children would.

The strong spirit of reform that swept through the country during the late 1800s persisted into the early 1900s. Many people called for changes in the economic, political, and social systems. Workers' strikes for better wages and shorter work schedules erupted. Writers, such as Upton Sinclair, exposed the evils of corruption in government. Socialists campaigned against capitalism. Even though little progress was made during the 1800s, by 1917 the reformers had many successes.

In support of the reformers' work, organized leisure services began. The "leisure solution" was envisioned as the positive alternative to the troubles

biography **Dining at the Greenbrier Hotel**

In 1858, a large new hotel was erected in the mountains of West Virginia, and with it an exciting era of resort history began. The first floor was completely devoted to eating. A gigantic dining room (over 300 feet long) was filled with enough round tables for eight to seat a total of 1,200 people. The owners boasted it was the largest dining room in the United States. For the next sixty-four years, this hotel, called "The Old White" and known as The Greenbrier today, was the teeming center of dining and entertaining in the east.

Three times a day, the hotel guests took their assigned seats in the dining room, with dinner by far the grandest meal of the day. It was served between 2:00 and 4:00 in the afternoon and followed the busiest time, the late morning and early afternoon, when activities bustled out on the great lawn where croquet and lawn tennis tournaments were held. Three days a week, guests danced around a bandstand at noon, and on other days, they joined in champagne and fruit parties under the branches of the huge white oak trees. The dinner menu was perhaps the highlight. How about a soup of mock turtle aux quenelles to begin? This could be followed by tenderloin of beef a la duxelle or roast mutton with jelly. Then shrimps a la tartare or dressed lettuce might set the stage for a main course of fried soft shell crabs with baked sweet potatoes and green corn followed, of course, by dessert. On the dessert menu, you might find plum pudding with rum sauce, caramel pie, Charlotte Russe, and vanilla ice cream with raisins (Holmberg 1992).

If the midday meal was the grand dining experience, the evening meal, sometimes referred to as either supper or tea was more sedate and functioned as the prelude to dancing in the ballroom. It was often the staging area for the nightly display of fine dress as well. For this meal the menu might feature hot breads, cakes, perhaps eggs and some cold meats. After around 1870, the supper menu could also include such rarities as oranges, lemons, pineapples, and bananas. What made this possible? The coming of the railroad line linked the resort with the east coast, and exotic imported items, such as fresh fruits and fish, became available.

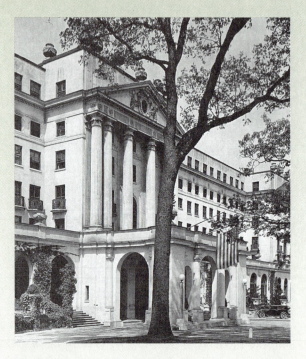

Box Figure 9.1 The Greenbrier Hotel, main entrance, 1913–1930.
Courtesy of The Greenbrier

---

of the time. It began with very little support, but it grew. Today, organized leisure services are supported by public taxes and include multimillion dollar facilities that employ thousands of university trained professionals. In tracing these roots we'll explore two early twentieth-century **social movements:** the settlement house and playgrounds.

Social movement: a significant change in the social conditions and patterns of behavior in a society.

The Settlement House Movement

The trend toward helping others improve their lives began in Great Britain as early as 1640, but it didn't become part of the American social fabric until the late

272   Part Three   Leisure as a Social Instrument—Systems Context

When American writer Upton Sinclair published *The Jungle* in 1906, it became a front-page scandal. Sinclair had written the novel to reveal the unspeakable conditions of labor in the meat-packing industry, and he hit his mark. He was vivid in describing the horrors and hazards of the workplace. There were, for example, the hands of the boners and trimmers, cut so often that they became lumps of scar tissue. There were the fingers of the wool-pluckers, eaten away by their constant immersion in acid. The backs and shoulders of the hoisters were permanently humped by incessant ducking under rafter beams, and the lungs of the men in the cooking rooms were virtually shot through with tuberculosis. Sinclair described the dangers for those who worked in the steamy tank rooms:

> . . . there were open vats near the level of the floor, their peculiar trouble was that they fell into the vats; and when they were fished out, there was

never enough of them left to be worth exhibiting—sometimes they would be overlooked for days, till all but the bones of them had gone out to the world as Durham's Pure Leaf Lard! (Sinclair 1951 edition, p. 78)

Questions to Consider and Discuss

1. Upton Sinclair was described as a muckraker. What does this label mean? Do some library investigation to learn why he was considered a muckraker.
2. Would you consider it appropriate to describe some of the early pioneers in the recreation and park movement as muckrakers? Do some additional biographical research on people, such as Jane Addams and Luther Gulick, to develop your argument for why or why not.

1800s (Bucher, Shivers, and Bucher 1984). Copying the British model of Toynbee Hall in London, **settlement houses** were established in the United States as a major tool in helping the urban poor and uneducated. The first settlement house was established by Stanton Coit in New York City in 1886. The movement then spread to Chicago three years later when Jane Addams and Ellen Gates Starr established the settlement house that became famous as the Hull House.

Settlement house: an institution providing various community services.

The objective of settlement houses was to improve living conditions in city neighborhoods, particularly for the foreign-born. To accomplish this, the houses offered educational classes, nurseries, civil rights and fair employment advocacies, and recreational services. The recreational services—typically play apparatus for young children, sports activities and social clubs for older children, and cultural arts programs for adults—not only provided a more positive balance in desperate lives but also taught skills needed for creating productive lives.

Settlement houses, now referred to as neighborhood houses, carry on this tradition. More than 300 are found mostly in midwest and east coast cities, providing social welfare and recreational services to people living in difficult conditions.

The Playground Movement

The first organized use of play as a tool is traced to Friedrich Froebel, the "father of the kindergarten movement." His kindergarten was founded in Germany in 1837. He believed children should be schooled early in a gentle manner that allowed them to develop freely. This philosophy contradicted the efforts of Robert Owen who had established "infant schools" in Scotland and New Harmony,

biography

Jane Addams and Ellen Starr

In 1889, Jane Addams and Ellen Starr went to live and work among the poor. They founded Hull House, one of the earliest settlement houses in the United States. It quickly became a model for efforts nationwide to improve the lives of people coping with urban poverty and injustice. What influenced them to leave their safe upper middle-class existence and venture into the world of urban strife when they had no experience and no guarantees that their efforts would be well-received?

Both women were products of their time. The late nineteenth century in the United States was an era of philanthropy. Perhaps their own gentle Victorian experiences as children and travels as young women provided the impetus. On trips to London following college graduation, they were impressed with the plight of the poor. At any rate, the heir of Charles Hull granted Jane and Ellen a rent-free, four-year lease on his large, dilapidated old home that had become surrounded by the sprawling, densely packed, and deteriorating immigrant slums of Chicago's 19th ward. A few days after Jane's twenty-ninth birthday, the two former college classmates moved in. They intended to share with the poor their gifts of culture.

From the beginning, Hull House was the center of every imaginable social and intellectual activity (McBride 1989). It served as a kind of halfway house, offering advice, childcare, temporary shelter, and training. Addams and Starr wanted to focus on correcting the complex social problems caused by the industrialism and urbanization of the time: juvenile delinquency, immigrant adjustment, poverty, women's suffrage, and ethnic inequalities. They were social reformers and used the diverse activities of Hull House to accomplish these reforms.

A day care center and kindergarten were held in the morning. In the afternoon, classes and clubs for teens were available, as well as adult education programs in the evening. Training was given in cooking, dressmaking, woodworking, photography, printing, and other employment skills. Financial and legal counseling was available. English and hygiene were taught. Hull House made a special reputation for itself not so much in its efforts to correct social ills, but in the methods it used. Due primarily to the influence of Ellen, the Hull House speciality was "the exaltation of art for the benefit of the masses" (Smith 1890). Jane and Ellen sought not only to change the conditions that oppressed people but also developed programs that simply made people's lives more pleasant. Concerts, dramatic readings, and lectures were weekly events; the audience was always packed. There were art history classes, literary reading groups, and art exhibits that made it possible for neighborhood ethnic groups to find continuity with their traditional heritage.

The first building to be added to the house contained an art museum, gallery, and studio. Later, they acquired another nearby building, formerly a saloon, which they converted into a coffee house and gymnasium. They then shamed a slumlord into donating a next door tenement, which they tore down to install a playground. Carefully supervised recreation in these facilities was central to their efforts to help children resist the effects of the city and prepare for a positive place in adult society. Each month, at least one child perished in a tenement fire, job accident, street gang battle, or simply from disease or neglect (McBride 1989). From the earliest age, children in the area were exposed to the influences of prostitution, alcohol, drug abuse, and family disintegration. In addition to the social services commonly available at settlement houses of the time, classes in art, pottery, rhythm and dance, music, and chorus also were offered at Hull House. Each Saturday evening, the gymnasium was set aside for athletic contests, and the neighborhood attended in large numbers.

To Addams and Starr, such organized play was training for good citizenship. Skills taught on the ball field or the playground, under proper supervision, enabled boys and girls to understand the necessity of following rules, acting decisively, and sacrificing their own interests to those of the group (Addams 1909). Their enthusiasm for leisure was so complete that Addams grievously wounded the feelings of some of her more religious neighbors. When a Methodist college inquired of Chicago's religious leaders whether it would be proper to grant Addams an honorary degree, the reply was that she "permits on the Sabbath day the playing of cards, billiards, and other amusements . . . I do not think the cause of Christ would gain advantage by giving such a degree" (Davis 1973, 118).

This was not an isolated incident in Jane's life. Because of her other well-known activities in organizing labor unions, establishing the Women's Peace Party, and leading large anti-war (World War I) demonstrations, she was for a time labeled the most dangerous woman in America (Duncan 1991). Ellen, too reached beyond Hull House to embrace radical politics. She participated in several strikes and was arrested during a restaurant workers' strike in 1914 (Stankiewicz 1989). Indeed, Starr and Addams were complex human beings trying to bring better lives to people living in complicated times. Their goal of accomplishing this through the provision of recreation set the stage for future generations.

Indiana. Owen's idea was to take children from the cradle and train them in "good habits." A little later (1860), Elizabeth Peabody started a kindergarten in Boston. In 1873, the St. Louis school system initiated kindergarten classes, leading the way for a worldwide movement of public education for the very young.

Even though Froebel's method advocated using free play as the "teaching" tool, during the 1800s many American educators felt that this did not provide enough useful training for children. As a result, American kindergartens began teaching skills that would prepare children for adult work. Meanwhile, another play movement was taking hold. Many historians trace the beginnings of the American playground to the establishment of the Boston Sand Garden in 1885. The idea was borrowed from the public parks of Berlin, Germany, where huge piles of sand were given to the city children for playing. The Boston Sand Garden was the first playground designed specifically for children. It was originally supervised by public spirited volunteer women. By 1887, when ten sand play centers were opened, women staff were employed to supervise the children.

Later, additional strides were made in Boston for promoting playgrounds. Joseph Lee helped create a model playground that included an area for small children, a boys' section, a sport field, and individual sand gardens. In 1889, the Charlesbank Outdoor Gymnasium opened; it provided apparatus for gymnastics, a running track, and space for games for older boys and men. A section was added to this playground two years later for women and girls. By 1899, Boston had twenty-one playgrounds.

The idea soon spread to other American cities, including Philadelphia, Milwaukee, Cleveland, Pittsburgh, Denver, Minneapolis, New York, Chicago, Providence, and Baltimore. The movement for publicly sponsored playgrounds was initiated in New York City by Jacob Riis, a newspaperman who recognized a great need for play space in the crowded city. The slum areas in particular had no lawns or vacant lots for play, and most schools did not have

A turn-of-the-century Boston playground.

© Joseph Lee Memorial Archives, National Recreation and Park Association

biography   Joseph Lee

Although he received a law degree from Harvard Law School in 1888, Joseph Lee never pursued that career. Instead, he chose a life dedicated to promoting leisure services. It began with his participation in a ten-year study of child delinquency in Boston. As a part of the study he researched play in Boston playgrounds, sand gardens, and streets. He made observations, drew descriptive maps, and compiled statistics. He investigated the relationship between play and population density, play and law breaking, and behavior and economic conditions (Sapora 1989). To these investigations were added trips to Europe to study playground operations. Lee was also influenced by the activities of his wife, Margaret Cabot Lee, who was a student of the teachings of Froebel, the inspiration behind kindergarten. As a result, Lee's interest went beyond the problem of delinquency. He began to develop the idea that every child needed to play—to play freely as he himself had done as a child.

To the confusion of Lee and others and in spite of the setting aside of special places for play, activities in the new Boston play areas did not differ much from those in the streets. Fights frequently broke out, often over card games. Older boys and men monopolized the game areas, and gangs prevented the smaller children from playing. Lee's solution was leadership. In 1900, he proposed that a model playground be developed. He chose for the experiment the North End playground, a barren two-acre site on the Charles River. Lee supervised the development and installation of play equipment. He had areas marked off for different age groups and designated areas for informal play. With his own money, he hired two Harvard students as play leaders and recruited several more volunteers. Before the playground opened in May, the staff completely planned the program. All this organization was a new idea at the time, and despite the lack of understanding by the local neighborhood, the program attracted over 300 children per week (Sapora 1989).

Leadership, according to Lee, was the most important factor in successful playgrounds. Although his life was devoted to many social reform projects, he continued with his model playground based on this factor. At the Columbus Avenue playground, Lee's experiment included six paid and trained recreation leaders. Fifteen boys and girls were chosen by the children to represent their interests on a kind of council. One half-time staff member spent most of her time visiting people in the neighborhood, promoting the program, and recruiting adult volunteers (Sapora 1952). Through his strong commitment and personal talents and resources, Lee was able to demonstrate the importance of organized and supervised play.

land around them that could be used for play. After considerable effort by Riis, New York City purchased two and a half acres for $1.8 million and opened Seward Park in 1899. It included play apparatus, a wading pool, and a gymnasium with changing rooms, game areas, and seats for spectators (Kelly 1982).

Other developments sprang up elsewhere. For example, Chicago established a system of small-park playgrounds. School buildings began to be used as community centers in Pittsburgh, and Philadelphia moved ahead with full playground program services in the summer. Unfortunately, most of these playgrounds were segregated. "In general, Negro playgrounds were less numerous, smaller, poorer in equipment and less adequately supervised than playgrounds for white children in the same city" (H. J. McGuinn, cited in Johnson 1930).

These early, scattered efforts of more than fourteen cities to provide space, leadership, and facilities for playgrounds finally alerted those involved to the need for communication. A small group of dedicated individuals—Jane Addams, Joseph Lee, Luther Gulick, Henry Curtis, and others—met at the White House in 1906. Their goal was to establish some means of connecting their individual efforts and concerns and communicating information gained from experiences in the different cities (MacLean, Peterson, and Martin 1985).

They felt a great sense of urgency. Their decision was the establishment of the Playground Association of America. This organization (which became the Playground and Recreation Association of America in 1911, the National Recreation Association in 1930, and the National Recreation and Park Association when it merged with other organizations in 1965) set the foundation for the organized use of leisure for social good.

In Pursuit of Happiness

In many ways, the period from about 1900 through the 1920s marked the beginning of modern American society. People continued to move from farms to cities in record numbers. The automobile, telephone, radio, and electric washing machine became common in American households. The modern aviation age was launched in 1927 when Charles Lindbergh made the first solo flight across the Atlantic Ocean. The role of women began to change as new opportunities for education and careers opened. All these changes meant broadened leisure experiences as well. The mass movement to cities meant more people could enjoy movies, plays, and sporting events. Radio brought entertainment directly into homes, and the automobile gave people a new way to travel, introducing travel for pleasure.

There was also amazing growth in the use of leisure as a problem solver. The organization of people's pastimes thrived. By 1910, for example, 336 cities had supervised recreation programs. Gradually, the example set by New York City with Seward Park, that city governments should provide recreation services, became widely accepted. In addition, colonial attitudes toward leisure had in many ways disappeared. Now, most people agreed that leisure services were necessary for all. Community centers began to offer increased opportunities in music, drama, and the arts. Schools explored ways of providing recreation programs and facilities, and therapeutic recreation services began to appear in state hospitals for persons with mental illness and mental retardation. For example, recreation activities, used at the time at the Menninger Clinic in Topeka, Kansas, took on an actual patient treatment role (Carter, van Andel, and Robb 1985). President Theodore Roosevelt encouraged the acquisition of numerous new areas for the national park system, and colleges began offering professional training for recreation leaders. Let's highlight this growth in the provision of organized leisure by listing the gains made by the youth-serving voluntary agencies.

Sir Robert Baden-Powell of Great Britain started the Boy Scout movement in 1907 when he organized a camp for twenty boys. Baden-Powell was convinced after his experiences in the Boer War that training in citizenship and outdoor skills was essential for young men. The idea was brought to the United States by William Boyce, an American businessman, in 1909 as a result of a British Boy Scout helping him find his way in a thick London fog. Boyce and others founded the Boy Scouts of America in 1910. The movement spread throughout the world, and today approximately 13 million boys, girls, and adult leaders in 110 countries are members. Total membership has numbered about 65 million since its inception.

When Baden-Powell began the Boy Scouts in Great Britain, 6,000 girls registered, too. As he "could not have girls traipsing about over the country after his

biography

African-American Roles in the Recreation Movement

In the haste to record the history of the recreation movement in the United States, the contributions of African-American men and women have largely been forgotten. The following is a collection of brief biographies of some of the African Americans who helped shape leisure's place in American society. We begin with the colonial period but spend most of our time with the twentieth century.

Phillis Wheatley. Of all the people who inhabited the thirteen rebellious American colonies, Africans were viewed as contributing little to the culture of the nation. Even then, however, with all odds against them, flashes of talent flared. In 1771, Phillis Wheatley, who had been taken from her home in Senegal as a child and raised in Boston, emerged as one of revolutionary America's best known poets (Bontemps 1975).

"Major" Taylor. One of the greatest African-American athletes in American history is practically unknown. Born in 1878 in Indianapolis, Marshall W. Taylor was destined to win world-wide honors. In 1898, 1899, and 1900 he won three national American bicycle sprint championships. Then, for three seasons he invaded Europe and Australia, defeating all of its cycling champions before huge crowds. Major was not always so well received. Early in his career, overcoming racial prejudice was very difficult. For example, when he was ten years old, Walter Sanger set a new mark of two minutes, eighteen seconds for the mile at the Capital City bicycle track in Indianapolis. Taylor could not race him because of the "color" bar, but some of Taylor's friends secured him entry to the track before the crowd had gone. After a few warm-up heats, he tore off a 2:11 mile, seven seconds under Sanger's mark. On another occasion, a seventy-five-mile road race was scheduled. Friends secreted Major in the woods, and when the race began, he rode from his hiding place behind the start. Even riding through a blinding rainstorm, Major was the first to arrive at the finish line, a full hour ahead of the nearest cyclist (Henderson 1970).

Edwin B. Henderson. Born in Washington, D.C., in 1883, Edwin Henderson was an important physical educator. After graduating first in his class from Normal School #2, he was appointed to teach in the black elementary schools. Henderson enrolled and completed a session at Harvard's Summer School during the summers of 1904 through 1907. After ranking first on the certification examination, he was appointed the first certified African-American male physical training instructor in the nation's public school system.

> I taught the rudiments of basketball to Negro boys for the first time in Washington, D.C. schools. In the next few years I taught and developed a number of teams, trained officials, and had much competition. (Henderson, cited in Coursey 1971)

Janie Porter Barrett. Janie was raised in a house with whites because her mother was the nurse to the white children. The aristocratic southern setting and white playmates were only a temporary part of Janie's world. When she reached an age at which it was considered proper for her to leave home, she was enrolled at Hampton Institute in Virginia. At Hampton, she became more aware of the difficulties confronting African Americans. As an adult, what began as a sewing class for a few girls in her home on Tuesday afternoons soon became a club. The response to the club was so overwhelming that it became necessary to form the Locust Street Social Settlement. Like the other settlement houses of the time, Locust Street activities included handicraft, poultry raising, homemaking, gardening, and reading classes. Athletics programs, child welfare services, and a playground and kindergarten were also established (box fig. 9.2). One of Janie's most appreciated programs was the summer excursion. Mothers of all ages, without their children, were treated to a day of relaxation and reflection through outings on Chesapeake Bay. During the summer of 1915, 2,200 mothers benefited from these (*Afro-American Ledger* 1912).

E.T. Attwell. As the son of an Episcopal minister growing up in New York's Greenwich Village, Ernest Ten Eyck Attwell developed a strong ethic for serving others. Perhaps his most outstanding accomplishments were made as Director of the Bureau of Colored Work with the Playground and Recreation Association of America. In this role, his first assignment was to convert the war camp community service centers built during World War I into permanent peacetime agencies. From his efforts, some twenty-seven centers were continued and others added, resulting by the mid-1960s in services to about 300 communities. Also under Attwell's direction, the Bureau made important contributions in training leaders, organizing citizen groups, and raising funds for the promotion of organized recreation services for African-American neighborhoods (Nash 1965).

George "Jake" Young. Born in 1914 in Columbus Ohio, Jake started working at the Godman Guild settlement house when he was fifteen. After high school, he was recruited to play basketball with the "Savoy 5"—predecessor to the Harlem Globetrotters—and later played football while getting a college degree from Flan-

der Smith College in Arkansas. However, his roots in recreation services were strong, and after serving with the Navy in World War II, he returned to the Godman Guild to serve as program director and summer camp director for Camp Wheeler. Here he remained until the last two years of his life. As Jake's wife commented, "he must have taught half the black children in the city how to swim" (Washington 1994).

These are some of the lives that represent the many significant contributions of African Americans to the fabric of leisure in the U.S. today. Taken together, like the pieces in a jigsaw puzzle, these African Americans help us see the historical picture of leisure more completely.

Box Figure 9.2 Janie Porter Barrett working with a Girls' Club.

Courtesy of Hampton University Archives

Boy Scouts," he got his sister, Agnes Baden-Powell, to help. They formed the Girl Guides program in 1909 (Schultz and Lawrence 1958, 299). Their first law was that they must not even speak to a Boy Scout if they saw him in uniform.

A few years later while visiting Britain, Juliette Gordon Low met the Baden-Powells and became fascinated with their organizations. When she returned to the United States, she brought the idea with her. She believed that girls, too, could benefit from the training in community service and leadership. Changing the name to Girl Scouts, Daisy, as she was known to her friends, held the first troop meeting in her home in Savannah, Georgia, on March 12, 1912. Today, Girl Guides and Girl Scouts involve more than 8 million girls, boys, and adult leaders in about 100 countries. In the United States, more than 45 million girls, women, and men from all backgrounds have belonged to Girl Scouts at some time in their lives (MacLean, Peterson, and Martin 1985).

So much more could be mentioned about other enthusiastic efforts to use organized leisure to solve social problems during this time. For example, the founding of Camp Fire Girls in 1910 (later named Camp Fire Inc.) was an effort to help youth become caring and self-directed adults who seek to improve harmful conditions of society. The camping movement began with the first private camp set up to offer a healthy outdoor experience to boys in poor health. However, it is critical that all the tremendous strides made not cloud what can be learned from this turn-of-the-century period.

The historian Rainwater made an early attempt to summarize these developments. He identified nine transitions in the expansion of using leisure for social good from about 1880 until the end of World War I.

Juliette Gordon Low with Girl Scouts.

Courtesy of Girl Scouts of the U.S.A. Archives

1. Initial limited provisions of activities to young children expanded to services for all ages.

2. Summer-only programs became year-long.

3. Indoor activities became just as important as outdoor activities.

4. Expansion of services into rural areas in addition to urban centers.

5. Support that shifted from the voluntary efforts of private citizens to government and other community agency support.

6. Play became organized instead of being freely expressed.

7. Projects became more complex and varied.

8. The philosophy shifted to include the provision of programs and not just the provision of facilities.

9. Community and group activities became more important than individual interests.

(Rainwater 1922, 192)

What began as a play movement shifted to an entire social movement. Such human expressions as sport, game, music, dance, and enjoying the outdoors became a means to create better personal and community lives. Leisure became part of a social conscience striving for humanitarian goals. The movement was so sweeping that it involved cities, states, and the national government. Hospitals, clinics, social work agencies, and voluntary welfare efforts relied more and more on leisure as a tool as well. People formed organizations, raised funds, held interminable meetings, wrote volumes of handbooks, and conducted numerous training sessions to discover better ways to teach people how to use their leisure time and experiences productively. An ethic for responsibility to ensure everyone's pursuit of happiness predominated.

The Movement's Zenith: Making a Profession

The time following World War I continued to bring monumental changes to the people of the United States. Initially, the economy entered a period of spectacular growth. Spurred on by the good times and a desire to be "modern," large numbers of Americans adopted new attitudes and lifestyles. More of the old moralism was gone, and there was greater acceptance of individual pursuit of pleasure. Women began wearing radically new clothing styles—short skirts and rolled-down stockings. Short "bobbed" hair became popular. People young and old visited supposedly secret nightclubs called speakeasies where they danced the Charleston and listened to jazz. Labeled "The Roaring Twenties," this fun decade ended with the stock market crash and a long economic depression for the United States and much of the industrial world.

The depression of the 1930s resulted in mass unemployment. Such involuntary idleness engulfed nearly one-third of the labor force. It was inevitable then that city recreation programs found themselves in difficulty. Although participation was high, tax revenues to pay for the programs declined sharply. Many employers had to lay off employees or pay them in scrip. The psychological problem of economic insecurity also tainted the pursuit of personal pleasure. In spite of all this, the depression did provide a benefit for organized leisure services. The federal government soon instituted a number of emergency work programs—many related to recreation—to reduce unemployment and stimulate the economy. President Franklin Roosevelt introduced the New Deal. Federal workers hired under New Deal programs built concert halls and community theaters, developed outdoor recreation areas and camps, and helped establish state park systems. According to Knapp (1973), such federal work projects built or improved 12,700 playgrounds, 8,500 gymnasiums, 750 swimming pools, 1,000 ice skating rinks, and 64 ski jumps.

Another unique development during the depression was the "cellar club" (Kraus 1990). These were youth-organized recreation groups that emerged in low-income neighborhoods of large cities. They were often based on ethnic and racial differences and included mostly boys and young men. They met in vacant stores, cellars, and building lofts where the youth were free of adult interference. By 1940 in New York City alone, there were 6,000 cellar clubs, each with memberships between 20 and 100. The federal government became concerned about the clubs and organized federations of them and established rules for behavior. In some cases, settlement houses also worked with club members to help end the delinquency that often erupted.

The New Deal relieved some of the hardship of many Americans, but hard times dragged on until World War II military spending simulated the economy out of its depression. The day after the December 7, 1941 Japanese attack on Pearl Harbor in Hawaii, the United States declared war on Japan and on Germany and Italy three days after that. About 15 million American men and women served in the armed forces during the war. Other women who stayed at home worked in the defense plants. Even children took part in the war effort. They collected used tin cans, old tires, and other things that could be recycled and used for war supplies.

This brought a renewed emphasis by the federal government on leisure's utility in war. The goal was to relieve the tensions, increase morale, and decrease the psychological impact of being away from home. For example, with the help of approximately 40,000 officers and enlisted men and women, the Special Services Division of the U.S. Army provided recreation facilities and programs on military bases around the world. About 1,500 officers provided recreation programs for the Navy, and even the Marine Corp offered expanded programs. Nongovernmental agencies redirected their efforts to the war as well. In 1941, the United Service Organization (USO) was formed by the joint efforts of six agencies: the Jewish Welfare Board, YMCA, YWCA, the Salvation Army, Catholic Community Services, and the National Travelers Aid. The USO provided recreation services at airports, hospitals, hotels, lounges, and special clubs near combat areas and rest centers. Their camp shows provided professional entertainment for the troops, often amidst great danger to the performers. The American Red Cross was also instrumental in aiding recreation's war effort. Some 17 million members produced supplies for army recreation rooms (MacLean, Peterson, and Martin 1985).

Meanwhile, back in American communities, the nature of organized leisure services was changing. Many programs had to be curtailed during the war because the leadership was overseas. However, city recreation and park departments started special new programs to assist the war effort. One was the establishment of facilities and programs for local war plants. Recreation services were available around the clock to help with the stress and adjustments required of the defense industry workers, primarily women. Programs included social events, sports, and child care, and set the stage for a new profession in industrial recreation services that continues today.

When World War II ended in 1945, the United States entered the greatest period of economic growth in its history. Because the war had taken place elsewhere, no widespread destruction demanded attention. Periods of inflation and recession occurred, but overall, businesses and people prospered. A new lifestyle resulted from prosperity. Vast numbers of Americans moved out of cities to suburbs where new housing was available, and by 1970, the U.S. Census showed that for the first time more Americans lived in suburbs than in cities. A rise in automobile ownership accompanied suburban growth. By 1960, over three-fourths of all American families owned a car. Increased automobile traffic led to the building of a nationwide network of superhighways. These enabled more people than ever to take vacation trips, and motels and fast-service restaurants sprang up to serve them. Television, an experiment before the war, became a feature of most American homes during the 1950s.

Changes in Organized Leisure Services

Outdoor recreation interests boomed in the 1950s as well. This boosted the services of such federal agencies as the National Park Service and the U.S. Forest Service, leading to opportunities for new initiatives. The Land and Water Conservation Fund, for example, was created in 1965 to provide federal aid in outdoor recreation development to states and local communities. The 1950s also witnessed new concerns for physical fitness. Results from a national test on muscular strength and flexibility determined that American youth were physically inferior to European youth, thus national interest centered on correcting the problem. Out of this grew such organizations as the National Collegiate Athletic Association, the Amateur Athletic Union, and the President's Council on Physical Fitness and Sports. This was also a growth period for the performing arts. The 1958 act of Congress that established the National Cultural Center for the Performing Arts (later named the John F. Kennedy Center for the Performing Arts) signaled the importance of the arts.

Stimulated by experiences of the depression and World War II, Congress held hearings in 1946 on the creation of a federal recreation service. Should the federal government become permanently involved in providing organized leisure services? The idea did not receive enough political support, so the proposal was abandoned and city park and recreation departments took up the slack and continued to develop facilities and programs.

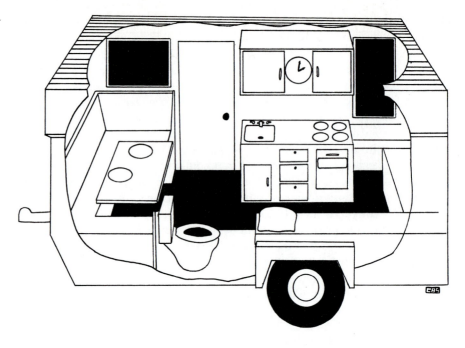

The mechanization of out-door recreation.

Christopher B. Stage

In spite of the prosperity of the 1950s, millions of Americans still lived in poverty. The poor included members of all races, but the plight of the nation's poor African Americans seemed especially bleak. African Americans faced discrimination in jobs, housing, education, and other areas in spite of the emancipation of the Civil War. During the early 1900s, African Americans and many European Americans began a movement to extend civil rights, but the movement didn't gain momentum until after World War II. In 1955, Martin Luther King, Jr., a Baptist minister, began organizing demonstrations protesting discrimination. Before long, this form of public protest became a major tool for Americans seeking change, including change in organized leisure services.

The first crack in segregation in sports occurred when the Brooklyn Dodgers brought Jackie Robinson up from their farm team in 1947. A series of legal test cases were also initiated including one against the state of Maryland for racial segregation in its state parks. African-American citizens of many cities bravely asserted their right to use recreation facilities by attempting to use segregated beaches, swimming pools, and amusement parks. In the city of Chicago, for example, black residents were excluded from public parks, playgrounds, pools, and beaches in white neighborhoods. Efforts to keep them out were supported by police and recreation workers (Drake and Cayton 1945). Not until 1964 did the Civil Rights Act outlaw discrimination in employment, voter registration, and public facilities. In 1968, the act was extended to include housing.

Other problems demanded solutions, too. Crime and violence soared after 1960, and the war in Vietnam during the 1960s and 1970s brought civil strife at home. Pollution followed industrial and population growth, and thousands of refugees fled to the United States because of hardships in their homelands. However, there were also opportunities for positive growth. For example, space exploration of American astronauts provided a high note during the troubled times. During the 1950s, 1960s, and 1970s the most significant progress of organized leisure was growth in the areas of professional education and career specialization. Let's complete our story by looking at each.

Professional Education

During the turn-of-the-century period, as agencies focused on providing organized leisure services, most of the hired leadership came from the fields of education, physical education, and social work. Park personnel were trained in such fields as landscape architecture and forestry. One of the earliest leadership training programs specifically for recreation professionals was conducted in 1887 by Luther Gulick, then a professor of Physical Education for the School of Christian Workers (now Springfield College) in Massachusetts. It was a summer school program (Butler 1965).

In 1905, Gulick joined the faculty of New York University and offered the first university course on play—Principles of Physical Education—which included units on sports and games, the theory of toys, and play and the exceptional child (Sessoms 1993). Later, the awareness of the need for special training for recreation leaders increased, resulting in the start of a one-year graduate curriculum. Known as the National Recreation School, its founding in 1926 confirmed the desirability of educating recreation professionals. Located in New York City and relying heavily on the faculty of New York University, its curriculum included the construction and planning of play facilities and administering city and county recreation departments. It graduated over 295 students in its nine years of operation.

From this beginning, professional preparation programs in recreation appeared in the curricula of forestry, education, social work, and physical education at colleges and universities across the country. Among the first were those at the University of Minnesota (1937) and the University of North Carolina (1939). By the mid-1960s, several dozen programs existed, supporting a burgeoning number of job opportunities. By the end of the 1970s, there were approximately 500 academic programs in recreation in the United States and Canada (Kraus 1993). While many of these programs were still linked to physical education, most were now administered autonomously. They had their own faculty and separate courses. Through the 1980s, professional preparation programs in recreation at colleges and universities were consolidated, and a number of weak and marginal programs were discontinued.

The road to full professional status was also aided by two other processes. These are accreditation and certification. **Accreditation** is an approval rating for college and university educational programs. If the program is accredited, it has met certain standards in preparing students for a particular profession. Its purpose is to protect the consumer or public and indicate to employers that graduates have a certain level of knowledge and ability. The effort to establish an accreditation system for recreation curricula began in the mid-1950s. It wasn't until the mid-1980s, however, that standards for

Accreditation: a process attesting to high standards for professional curricula in colleges and universities.

professional preparation in recreation became fully authorized and operational. Today, approximately 100 colleges and universities offer accredited degree programs in parks, recreation, and leisure studies.

Certification, on the other hand, is more recent. Efforts to install a certification requirement for those who deliver organized leisure services began with a professional registration program in therapeutic recreation in the 1950s. By 1990, such credentialing programs as that of the National Certification Board, the National Council of Therapeutic Recreation Certification, and the National Employee Services and Recreation Association were active. Certification is a professional credentialing process based on educational and field experience. It also includes an examination. Whereas accreditation sets the standards for college and university curricula, certification sets the standards for professionals who work in a particular field. Certification identifies individuals as qualified.

Certification: a professional credentialing process based on a specified course of study, including appropriate work experience.

Accreditation and certification have significantly enhanced the professionalism of those whose job is to use leisure as a tool to solve human and societal needs. In the past, recreation jobs were more simply based on demonstrating a general level of competence and a degree of common sense (Bammel and Bammel 1992). Employees in leisure service agencies received some on-the-job training but mostly figured out their jobs by trial and error. The competencies expected of leisure professionals today—as stipulated by the standards in accreditation and certification programs—are greater. This makes it more important that those entering the leisure service fields have specific academic preparation and work experiences.

Leisure Occupations

At the beginning of the twentieth century, a handful of volunteers worked in playgrounds and settlement houses. Today, near the beginning of the twenty-first century, it is estimated that several hundred thousand professionally trained and salaried individuals are providing organized leisure services. The list of the different job titles would fill a separate book so wide is the variety of leisure occupations.

In spite of their diversity, leisure services occupations can be divided into several programmatic areas. For example, those employed in outdoor recreation specialties use natural resources as a source of leisure service. They work in national or state parks, nature centers, trip outfitter companies, outdoor education programs, camps, forest reserves, the Boy and Girl Scouts, and so on. Their work may range from groundskeeping and turf management to wilderness preservation to adventure education. In addition to leisure studies coursework, college preparation usually includes classes in ecology, horticulture, natural resource management, nature interpretation, as well as communication, psychology, and sociology. An internship in a private or public natural resource based agency is also usually required.

Therapeutic recreation specialists use leisure as a treatment for disability or illness. Working with other medical specialists in hospitals, rehabilitation centers, corrections facilities, and mental health programs, they focus on the healing potential of leisure. Job opportunities range from working with substance abusers to children with disabilities to patients in convalescence to adjudicated youth. In addition to college preparation in leisure studies, professionals in therapeutic recreation also have mastered information and skills in allied health areas. For some, this may include special course work in anatomy and physiology, rehabilitation science, or gerontology. Usually an internship in a community or clinical therapeutic recreation setting is also required.

Tourism management occupations are centered around the pleasures of travel. These professionals organize conferences and meetings, market the attractions of a particular locale, and manage vacation destinations. Knowledge of advertising and marketing, transportation, hospitality, entertainment, business systems, and attractions management are often useful for these jobs. In addition to university programs in leisure studies, there are also special training programs in hotel and restaurant management that help prepare professionals for tourism positions.

Sport management experts organize fitness and athletic experiences. They work for such agencies as the YMCA, a city recreation department, corporations, colleges and universities, professional sport teams, and sports federations. Appropriate college courses include leisure studies, physical education, and business, as skills in leadership, sport programming, marketing, and risk management are often needed.

Community recreation workers provide services of sociability in such settings as senior centers, Boys' and Girls' Clubs, and recreation facilities of the Armed Forces. Professionals are needed to operate programs in arts and crafts, dance, sports, fitness, drama, and music. In addition to preparation in leisure studies and an internship, skills in leadership, supervision, and program planning are usually desirable.

The future for these and other leisure occupations seems quite good. According to labor statisticians, leisure will continue to be a major employment area. Estimates indicate that by 2005 the jobs in human services occupations will increase by 82 percent, for food service and lodging managers by 38 percent, and for travel agents by 70 percent (U.S. Bureau of Labor Statistics 1991). Another optimistic estimate reported by Godbey (1989) is that jobs dealing with health care (such as therapeutic recreation), and training and consulting will become abundant in the future.

Summary: Leisure as a Change Agent

As nations of the world have become more industrialized, they have also become more reliant on leisure as a tool for solving problems. Unlike some earlier societies, such as the ancient Greeks for whom leisure was an end in itself, many contemporary societies see a more functional side of leisure. Though leisure is not a panacea for social and individual problems, it is certainly one of the solutions.

This chapter traced the development of the utilitarian notion of leisure through its history in the United States. Beginning with colonial America when leisure activities were tolerated according to the difficulties of survival in the new land, the story is traced through the transition century of the 1800s to the birth of organized leisure services in the 1900s. During this time, leisure became part of a social conscience striving for humanitarian goals. Initial services to young children were expanded to services for all ages. Support shifted from the voluntary efforts of private citizens to government and community agency support. Community and group activities became more important than individual interests. Leisure, in essence, became organized.

References

Addams, J. 1909. *The spirit of youth and the city streets.* New York: Macmillan.

Afro-American Ledger. 1912. Work of uplift shown results. *Afro-American Ledger,* 31 August.

Bammel, G., and L. L. B. Bammel. 1992. *Leisure and human behavior.* Dubuque, IA: Wm. C. Brown Publishers.

Bontemps, A. 1975. Culture: Despite the odds, blacks mastered white arts, added new twists of their own. *Ebony* (August): 105.

Bucher, C. A., J. S. Shivers, and R. D. Bucher. 1984. *Recreation for today's society.* Englewood Cliffs, NJ: Prentice-Hall.

Butler, G. D. 1965. *Pioneers in public recreation.* Minneapolis, MN: Burgess Publishing.

Carter, M. J., G. E. van Andel, and G. M. Robb. 1985. *Therapeutic recreation: A practical approach.* St. Louis: Times Mirror/Mosby College Publishing.

Coursey, L. N. 1971. The life of Edwin Bancroft Henderson and his professional contributions to physical education. Unpublished doctoral dissertation, Ohio State University.

Cross, G. 1990. *A social history of leisure since 1600.* State College, PA: Venture.

Davis, A. F. 1973. *American heroine: The life and legend of Jane Addams.* London: Oxford University Press.

de Tocqueville, A. 1945. *Democracy in America.* Volume II. New York: Vintage Books.

Drake, St. C., and J. Cayton. 1945. *Black metropolis.* New York: Harper and Row.

Duncan, M. 1991. Back to our radical roots. In *Recreation and leisure: Issues in an era of change.* 3d ed., edited by T. L. Goodale and P. A. Witt. State College, PA: Venture.

Dustin, D. L., L. H. McAvoy, and J. H. Schultz. 1982. *Stewards of access, custodians of choice: A philosophical foundation for the park and recreation profession.* Minneapolis, MN: Burgess Publishing.

Godbey, G. C. 1989. *The future of leisure services: Thriving on change.* State College, PA: Venture.

Hardin, G. 1968. The tragedy of the commons. *Science,* (13 December): 1243–48.

Haworth, N. A., and E. M. MacDonald. 1946. *Theory of occupational therapy.* Baltimore: The Williams & Wilkins Co.

Henderson, E. B. 1970. *The black athlete: Emergence and arrival.* New York: International Library of Negro Life and History, Publishers Company.

Holmberg, M. 1992. *The Greenbrier cookbook: Favorite recipes from America's resort.* White Sulphur Springs, WV: The Greenbrier.

Johnson, C. S. 1930. *The negro in American civilization.* New York: Henry Holt.

Kelly, J. R. 1982. *Leisure.* Englewood Cliffs, NJ: Prentice-Hall.

Knapp, R. F. 1973. Play for America: The New Deal and the NRA. *Parks and Recreation* (July): 23.

Kraus, R. 1990. *Recreation and leisure in modern society.* Glenview, IL: Scott, Foresman/Little, Brown Higher Education.

Kraus, R. 1993. *Leisure in a changing America: Multicultural perspectives.* New York: Macmillan College Publishing.

Langlois, S. 1984. Consommation et activities de loisirs au Quebec. *Society and Leisure* 7, no. 2:327–49.

MacLean, J. R., J. A. Peterson, and W. D. Martin, 1985. *Recreation and leisure: The changing scene.* New York: John Wiley & Son, Inc.

McBride, P. 1989. *Pioneers in leisure and recreation.* Reston, VA: American Alliance for Health, Physical Education, and Dance.

Nash, J. B. 1965. *Recreation: Pertinent readings.* Dubuque, IA: Wm. C. Brown Publishers.

National Park Service, U.S. Department of the Interior. (May 1993). *Nicodemus, Kansas: Special resource study.* U.S. Government Printing Office.

Orth, R. H., A. J. von Frank, L. Allardt, and D. W. Hill 1986. *The poetry notebooks of Ralph Waldo Emerson.* Columbia, MO: University of Missouri Press.

Rainwater, C. E. 1922. *The play movement in the United States.* Chicago: University of Chicago Press.

Sapora, A. 1952. The contributions of Joseph Lee to the modern recreation movement and related social movements in the United States. Unpublished Dissertation, University of Michigan.

Sapora, A. 1989. Joseph Lee. In *Pioneers in leisure and recreation,* edited by H. Ibrahim. Reston, VA: American Alliance for Health, Physical Education, Recreation, and Dance.

Schultz, G. D., and D. G. Lawrence. 1958. *Lady of Savannah: The life of Juliette Low.* Philadelphia, PA: J. B. Lippincott.

Sessoms, H. D. (October 1993). Quo vadis physical education and recreation. Paper presented at the Leisure Research Symposium, National Recreation and Park Association, San Jose, CA.

Sinclair, U. 1951. *The jungle.* New York: Harper.

Smith, S. 1890. Sophia Smith Collection [SSC], Starr Family Papers, box 1, folder 3. Clipping dated August 7.

Stankiewicz, M. A. 1989. Art at Hull House, 1889–1901: Jane Addams and Ellen Gates Starr. *Woman's Art Journal* 10:1, 35–39.

U.S. Bureau of Labor Statistics. (November 1991). *Monthly Labor Review.*

Washington, S. 1994. Personal interviews with Marie J. B. Young, Columbus, Ohio.

paying for it all

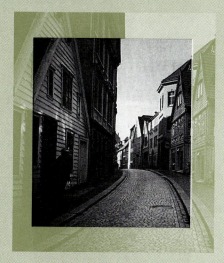

© Ruth V. Russell

What is leisure's relationship to economics?

Leisure is an economic balancing tool. For example, leisure mirrors a nation's level of economic development and its economic system. Leisure also drives an economy by fostering consumerism.

What is leisure's positive economic impact?

Leisure makes good economic sense. It benefits employment, taxes, property values, and expenditures.

What is leisure's negative impact?

Sometimes leisure results in undesirable costs. Examples are the negative economic impacts of leisure accidents and a country's balance of payments.

ten

Every nation has a system for organizing the

production and distribution of goods needed by its citizens. This organizational system is called the economic system, and it differs from country to country. Individuals also have a system for organizing the acquisition of the goods and services they need or want. This too requires an economic system. For both the nation and the individual, the resources used to produce and acquire the goods and services are usually scarce. If a person or a nation buys one thing, they may not be able to afford something else. For example, a teenager may have to choose between seeing a movie or buying a video game with this week's allowance. A nation may have to choose between weapons for its national defense and an enhanced educational system. Few persons or nations have enough wealth to buy everything they want when they want it. Thus, economic systems are based on economizing—using resources wisely to produce the things wanted most. This is the most essential task of **economics.**

Economics: the study of how people use their scarce resources in an attempt to satisfy unlimited wants.

Leisure is at the heart of economizing. Opportunities for leisure depend on how much money people have to spend, how much time away from the production of goods and services they have, and what leisure goods and services are available for purchase. The desire and ability to purchase leisure goods and services are expanding. Personal income, despite the ups and downs of the economies in many nations, seems to be climbing over the long run, making more discretionary income available to spend on pastimes. Such expenditures make the leisure industries among the fastest growing segments of the economy. Leisure is an economic tool.

Leisure and economics are bound in an intricate and delicate balance. Changes in one often create drastic shifts in the other. A healthy economy depends on relative stability between them. For example, if we reduce the amount of leisure time—perhaps if people worked longer hours—there would be less time in which to use the extra money earned. People would buy fewer boats, read fewer books and magazines, take fewer vacations, attend fewer sporting events. These industries would, in turn, earn fewer profits, and their employees would be without work. Likewise, if we increase the amount of leisure time and reduce the number of hours worked, we can assume a comparable decline in income earned. Even with time to spare, people may not have the money to buy leisure goods. Again, the balance is out of kilter.

In this chapter, we begin with the intricacies of the balance between leisure and economics. In so doing, we consider leisure in terms of free time and recreational activity. Our exploration is the relationships between leisure and economic development, capitalism, and consumerism. Then we will contrast the positive and negative affects of leisure economics. The power of leisure to positively affect economic health through employment, taxes, and property values is compared with leisure's negative economic impact from the cost of accidents and a negative balance of payments.

The Web of Leisure and Economics

Leisure is an economic balancing tool; it helps shape the economy and is affected by changes in the economy. An examination of leisure's relationships with economic development, capitalism, and consumerism illustrates this function of leisure.

Leisure and Economic Development

An economy must grow if its people want a higher **standard of living.** As an economy grows, it satisfies more and more of its people's needs and wants. The faster the economy grows, the faster the people's standard of living rises. Economists measure an economy's rate of growth by studying its **gross national product** (GNP) over a period of years. The U.S. gross national product has increased at an average rate of between 1 and 3 percent each year for the past 100 years. Another way of measuring a nation's economic growth is to study the standard of living of its people. To judge this, economists sometimes divide a nation's total gross national product by its entire population. The resulting figure is called the per capita gross national product. In 1992, the per capita gross national product of the United States was about $22,000. This means that if all the goods and services produced in the U.S. in a year were divided evenly among all the people, each person would receive about $22,000 (Schor 1992). Americans have one of the highest standards of living in the world.

> **Standard of living:** the economic level at which an individual, family, or nation lives.

> **Gross national product:** the value of all goods and services produced in a country during a given period.

The growth of the economy of a society depends on its natural resources, its technical skills in producing goods and services, and its value system (Ibrahim 1991). An economy cannot grow if it uses all its resources to produce food and clothing. These are used up almost as quickly as they are produced and cannot help produce more goods in the future. More mature economies are based on manufacturing and the production of services as well. For example, underdeveloped societies have economies based on food gathering. Intermediate economies are based on manufacturing, and modern economies focus on services and communications (table 10.1). How does this simple three-stage system of economic development relate to leisure? Using the work of Rostow (1960) as our basis, let's explore this relationship.

Such underdeveloped societies as Nepal, because of limitations on productivity, must devote very high proportions of their resources to agriculture. Family and clan connections are economically important as people perform simple economic tasks by virtue of their social position, gender, and age. In these economies, leisure is possible to only those who, because of their status, do not need to be directly involved in producing food. Often, they are supported by a slave system. In ancient Greece, for example, where leisure was considered a way of contemplative and cultured life, leisure was an ideal of the elite males and supported by slavery. Also in southern colonial America, the luxurious plantation life of certain families was possible because of slaves who took care of the production of food.

Table 10.1

Selected National Economic Statistics

Economy	Per Capita GNP: 1987 in Dollars	Percent Average Annual Growth: 1967–1987	Life Expectancy (Years)
Underdeveloped			
Chad	150	−2.0	46
Nepal	160	.5	51
India	300	1.8	58
Bolivia	580	−0.5	53
Intermediate			
Mexico	1,830	2.5	69
Hungary	2,240	3.8	70
Greece	4,020	3.1	76
Israel	6,800	2.5	75
Mature			
Canada	15,160	2.7	77
Norway	17,190	3.5	77
U.S.A.	18,530	1.5	75
Switzerland	21,330	1.4	77

Source: The World Bank 1989, Tables 1, 3, and 9.

Veblen's idea of a leisure class corresponds here. In his writings (1912), leisure was defined as nonproductive consumption of time. Thorstein Veblen was a late-nineteenth-century scholar who concluded that leisure is an aristocratic possession. He claimed that throughout history only the rich and powerful social classes possessed leisure. Their pastimes demonstrated their superior status; these people were the leisure class. To Veblen, leisure was a decadent economic exploitation because it was characterized by idleness and conspicuous consumption. Only the wealthy could be called leisurely; only the wealthy could afford to have nothing to do with work. Veblen's writing reflected a critique of his own time, for in the late nineteenth century the pastimes of the few wealthy in Europe and North America contrasted starkly with the poverty of the masses. Today, do such television shows as *Lifestyles of the Rich and Famous* continue to mirror Veblen's critique?

In intermediate economies, such as contemporary Greece, some role differentiation exists in people's labor, and the focus is on manufacturing. New industries and new agricultural techniques develop, and a class of entrepreneurs is created. A steady rate of economic growth begins. Such industrialization offers time and opportunity for more people to have leisure. Leisure, however, is not available to all people. As happened at the turn of the twentieth century in the U.S., the process of industrialization can make life more harsh. Let's look at the economy and leisure of Mexico as an example.

In 1987, Mexico had a per capita gross national product of $1,830 and an average annual economic growth of 2.5 percent (The World Bank 1989). Mexico's economy is growing faster than those of most other Latin American countries, based on government policies and programs developed after the Mexican Revolution of 1910. At that time, Mexico was mainly a land of huge estates owned by wealthy landlords. The government broke up most of these holdings and distributed them among millions of landless Mexicans. Since the 1940s, the government also has promoted industrialization. Today, manufacturing is Mexico's fastest growing industry.

In terms of pastimes, Mexico is well-known for such sports as bullfighting, soccer, and *jai alai*. Let's consider some of our images of Mexico: strolling orchestras and mariachis who perform at every possible leisure occasion; breaking piñatas at holidays and family gatherings. These pastimes, easily identified as Mexican, provide the impression of easy-going festivities. In spite of Mexico's economic progress, large numbers of its people remain poor. Wages continue to be low. Each year, more and more people move to cities in search of employment.

Nepal has an underdeveloped economy in spite of its tourism income.
© Ruth V. Russell

Greece has an intermediate economy.
© Ruth V. Russell

Oslo, Norway, has old world charm with a modern economy.

© Ruth V. Russell

This has caused overcrowding and a shortage of jobs. In addition, recession and inflation have left many people desperate for work.

When industrialization reaches a successful level of output for many people to have command over consumption, a modern economic system, such as in Norway, is achieved. People's basic needs for food, shelter, and clothing are satisfied, and they can focus on services. High amounts of discretionary income and time abound. In mature economic societies, leisure itself is an industry. Tourism is an excellent example of this.

Tourism is an aggregate of many different businesses. Tourist attractions, transportation systems, lodging, restaurants, entertainment, and advertising, focus on generating a profit from people's desires to travel for pleasure. Tourist industries create immense business activity. Estimates indicate that domestic and international tourists annually spend about $583 billion touring the United States, creating about 5.2 million jobs (Waters 1992; U.S. Travel Data Center 1991). In forty-six of the fifty U.S. states, tourism is one of the top three sources of income. Such states as Hawaii and Florida are almost pure tourist economies. Florida alone receives more than 40 million leisure-oriented visits by out-of-state residents annually. These visitors generate some 600,000 jobs and add three-quarters of a billion dollars to state tax revenues while spending a total of about $26 billion (Florida Department of Revenue 1992).

Another illustration of the economic value of this leisure industry is Baltimore, Maryland. A few years ago, the city launched a major renovation of a portion of its harbor area. New hotels, restaurants, retail stores, and entertainment facilities were constructed. These Inner Harbor developments created a concentration of attractions for the city that resulted in an increase in annual tourist spending of about $400 million. The development also led to an improvement in the psychological attitudes of residents toward their own city. Once disdainful of their city, Baltimoreans now are "frank and unashamed 'boosters' " (Millspaugh 1990, 13).

In fact, one thing we are not short on is verification of the economic benefit of tourism. In Ontario, Canada, a snowmobiling trail system is projected to boost the local economy from $9.25 million in 1992 to $34.75 million by 1996 (NordicGroup International 1991). Also in Ontario, the economy of the city of Peterborough netted $165,165 from one hockey tournament; the largest proportion came from distant teams who needed hotel accommodations (Marsh 1982). There are many other examples confirming that leisure facilities and events are attractive to tourists and enrich local economies.

Leisure and Capitalism

The web between leisure and a mature economic system is not always so positive. From some viewpoints, economic systems can be harmful to leisure. We'll use **capitalism** to illustrate this point. Capitalism is an economic system in which individuals or private business enterprises develop, own, and control much of the capital and means of production. Capitalism is also known as the free enterprise system. The central ideas for capitalism date back to as early as 1656 when the philosopher Lee suggested that, "the advancement of private persons will be the advantage of the public" (Goodale and Godbey 1988, 74). Adam Smith expanded on this idea in his book, *An Inquiry into the Nature and Causes of the Wealth of Nations* (published originally in 1776), in which he promoted the thesis that an individual's work contributes automatically to the welfare of others.

According to Adam Smith, the basic premises of economic order were that (1) self-interest is the prime motivation, (2) individual striving leads to a common good, and (c) no regulation of the economy is best (Smith 1937). Smith argued that individualism led to economic progress. He asserted that in order to make money, people produce things that other people will buy. Buyers spend money on things they need or want most, and a pattern of production develops that results in mutually supportive economic harmony. Smith said that all this would happen without any conscious control, "as if by an invisible hand." This became the basis of capitalism.

"In capitalist society . . . leisure time for a privileged class is produced by converting the whole lifetime of the masses into labor time." (Cunningham 1980, 515). This statement made in the 1800s by Karl Marx, the father of communism, criticized capitalism's suppression of leisure. Since Smith's ideas of free enterprise were based on a human progress only possible by individual labors, leisure was considered an obstruction—even by Smith himself. The more leisure, the less progress—the more progress, the less leisure (Smith 1937). The "invisible hand" of the common good from capitalism works only when people are working.

Capitalism: an economic system characterized by private ownership of goods.

biography   Adam Smith

Adam Smith (1723-1790) is generally considered the founder of modern economics. His major work, *An Inquiry into the Nature and Causes of the Wealth of Nations* established the premises of the capitalist economic system because it endorsed a free trade and self-regulating economy. Up to this time, no concept of economics existed. Throughout the previous 4,000 years, work and wealth had been distributed by force, necessity, and tradition according to the beliefs of various religious systems (Goodale and Godbey 1988). With Smith's writings came an understanding of the production and distribution of wealth (economics) that has influenced us since. How amazing that one person's thinking could have such a major effect on how life was to be lived for the next 200 years! How was this possible? What sort of person was Adam Smith, and how was he affected by the time in which he lived?

Smith was born in Scotland in 1723. He studied at the University of Glasgow and Oxford University, and became a professor of moral philosophy at Glasgow in 1751. He was the quintessential *Mad Magazine* scholar—an eighteenth-century nerd. He moved awkwardly, was pale and skinny, and had poor vision. He was chronically absent-minded and was frequently seen wandering the beaches around his home muttering to himself (Fox and Pope 1989). Despite his peculiarities, such publications as the philosophical work *The Theory of Moral Sentiment,* which argued that sympathy is the motivating force of morality, gained Smith instant success and an appointment as tutor to the young Duke of Buccleuch. With a regular income from the duke's stepfather, Smith was able to retire from teaching and devote the next ten years to writing. During these years, he wrote *The Wealth of Nations.*

The ideas presented in this book are still argued today, and the opinions of many economists of the 1990s descend from him. Where did these ideas come from? They arose from Smith's deep concern for the welfare of others. He lived during the time of the American and French revolutions. His emphasis on economic freedom fit in well with the belief in political freedom that was growing during that period. It has been said (Becker 1968) that had Smith lived at a later time, he may have been a socialist because of his belief that economically valued work was the right of everyone. In Smith's time, most people had never had more than the most meager subsistence. Smith wanted to assure subsistence plus a little bit more. He was on the side of the laborers, farmers, and others oppressed by the aristocracy. He believed that labor was the human activity that produces money, and money becomes the means to purchase the "necessaries, conveniences, and amusements of human life" (Smith 1937, 30). A free enterprise system was seen by Smith as a way to achieve a fairer distribution of wealth because of its equal access to work. He believed that by pursuing our own interests we ultimately promote that of our entire society more effectively than when we really intend to.

How ironic that an economic system that was originally motivated by a desire to distribute excess money to everyone today is associated with greed. However, it is quite unfair to attribute to Adam Smith much of what was to follow in the name of capitalism. To Smith, capitalism provided a progressive direction for society.

Since Smith's time, however, many people believe that capitalism has created more leisure for people. Economic progress through capitalism was projected to yield steady reductions in working time. Because of this economic system we are blessed with a forty-hour workweek, two weeks a year for vacation, and extended years of schooling and retirement. However, like Marx and Smith, contemporary economist Schor argues that capitalism's tendency instead is to expand work to the detriment of leisure (1992).

Schor's rationale follows:

> Key incentive structures of capitalist economies contain biases toward long working hours. As a result of these incentives, the development of capitalism led to the growth of what I call 'long hour jobs.'. . . U.S. workers experienced a new decline that now, at the century's end, has created a crisis of leisure time (Schor 1992, 7).

Table 10.2

Annual Hours of Paid Employment in the U.S.

	1969	1987	Change 1969–1987
All participants	1786	1949	+163
Men	2054	2152	+98
Women	1406	1711	+305

Source: Schor 1992, 29.

This perspective is supported by statistics indicating people in even modified capitalist societies are working harder than ever. Schor maintains that in the last twenty years the amount of time Americans spent at their jobs has risen steadily, particularly in professional occupations. Each year the increase is small, amounting to about nine hours, or slightly more than one additional day of work. Nonetheless, if this trend continues, by the end of the century, Americans will be spending as much time at work as they did in the 1920s. Unlike the assumption of a forty-hour workweek, Schor's statistics maintain Americans work an average of forty-one hours per week. Even more drastic, however, are her estimates for annual hours of labor. The average employed person is now on the job an additional 163 hours, or the equivalent of an extra month each year (table 10.2).

Other economic systems, such as communism in the former Soviet Union and socialism in Great Britain, have also had up and down relationships with leisure. For example, communism has been successful in creating free time for people but unsuccessful in producing the goods and services wanted for leisure. People in these economies cannot "buy leisure" because the products are simply not available on the retail market. A few years ago when communism was the dominant economic system in what was then the Soviet Union, the consumption of "luxuries" was discouraged. A twenty-one-inch color television cost about $1000. On the black market, Japanese-made VCRs were reportedly selling for up to $2500 and blank videotapes for $67 each. Even more problematic was that there were only a few tape rental stores, and the selection of titles was slim, mostly reruns from Soviet TV. In spite of all this, there was a ten-year waiting list to purchase a VCR. When leisure is defined as buying experiences, a communist economic system is prohibitive, whereas capitalism may perhaps be responsible for a decline in leisure as free time.

Leisure and Consumerism

The Purr-fect Garden

You'll enjoy growing nutritious, organic snacks that your cat will love. Easy-to-use kit includes reusable cat-shaped planter with enough seed for several plantings. Instructions included. $12.95.

T-shirt

Inscribed with "Older than Dirt." $14.95.

Harley Phone

Now the greatest name in American motorcycling decorates your home or office with this amazing phone. This righteous replica of Harley's #1 "hog" features cleverly disguised touch-tone dial with mute and auto redialing. Horn sounds and headlights flash for incoming calls. $79.95.

Chocolate Tool Kit

Real men won't need instructions to eat these solid milk chocolate tools: hammer, chisel, wrench, and monkeywrench. 9 delicious oz. of chocolate. Gift boxed. $12.95.

Aerobie Football

The scientific engineering of this space-age football makes it easy for anyone to throw perfect spirals at over 1,000 RPM, yet easier to catch than a regular football! Holds the Guinness World Record for the farthest thrown object. Ages 5 and up. $11.95.

(*What on Earth Gift Catalog* 1993)

Are these things we simply must have? These types of products are part of a 1990s consumer phenomenon: the mail-order catalog. According to the Direct Marketing Association, more than 10,000 American mail-order companies sent out 13.5 billion catalogs all over the world in 1993. The goal was to tap into a $51.5 billion annual market (Asher 1994).

| Consumption: all household purchases of goods and services. |

A fundamental part of any economic system is the function of **consumption.** In most economies, it is the largest spending category. Along with services, it includes purchases of nondurable goods, such as soap and steak, and durable goods, such as stereos and suitcases. Durable goods are those expected to last for more than a year. You can usually tell a lot about an individual's or family's economic status by observing their consumption patterns. Do they drive a new Mercedes or an old VW bus? What do they eat? What do they wear? Although you sometimes come across people who live well beyond their means or people who still have the first dollar they ever earned, consumption and income tend to be closely related.

As shown in figure 10.1, real disposable income and real consumer spending in the United States since 1929 have tended to move together. (The term *real* indicates that the data have been corrected for the effects of inflation.) Thus, the higher the incomes of people, the more they are likely to spend. Consumption, therefore, is an expected characteristic of mature economies.

Spending money for leisure is a common focus of consumption. As we'll highlight in the next section, expenditures for leisure are at the center of some economies. People buy tennis rackets, photo film, fishing licenses, Barbie dolls, admissions to amusement parks, golf clubs, pets, video tapes, flower

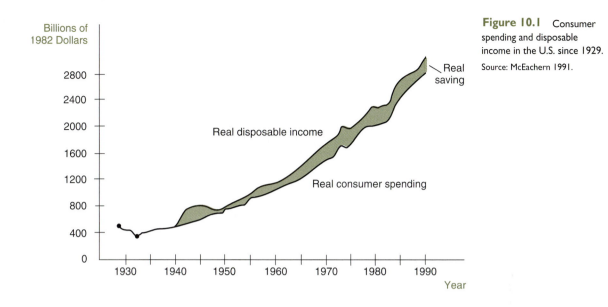

Figure 10.1 Consumer spending and disposable income in the U.S. since 1929.
Source: McEachern 1991.

seeds, jogging shoes, health club memberships, violins, CDs, magazine sub-scriptions, and even Harley telephones and chocolate tools. Buying these goods are good for the economy, but the web that entangles leisure and con-sumption is more dynamic than this. In some societies, consumption is actually a form of leisure. Let's consider shopping as an illustration.

Although we have no clear estimates of how many of us spend time wandering around the stores, a number of research studies have pointed to the prevalence of shopping as a favorite pastime for North Americans. Many individuals surveyed indicated that they preferred going shopping to most other activities, including TV watching and playing sports. Visiting shopping malls is for many a preferred evening or weekend recreation. Judging from the crowds that throng shopping malls and stores "just looking," shopping is a customary way of spending free time. In fact, when people are given more free time, shopping participation often increases. In one study of the effects of converting to a four-day workweek and thus a three-day weekend, one-third of the blue-collar workers surveyed filled the extra time by spending more money on shopping (Maklan 1977).

Is this really leisure? As one philosopher observed, what we want are things, things cost money, and money costs time (deGrazia 1962). Similarly, if we own more and more material possessions and work long hours so we can purchase them, will this lead to more happiness? These concerns lead us to the concept of the harried leisure class, which is also the title of a book by Staffan Linder (1970). Its theme is that consumption greatly limits leisure; in fact, Linder considers it the antithesis of leisure. The increased work required to have the money to buy things, the increased time needed for upkeep and maintenance on the things we buy, and of course, the time devoted to the process of buying it all result in a hectic, never-satisfied, materialistic frenzy. Is it leisure? Some say no.

*C*ase *Study*   Mall of America

When the Metropolitan Stadium in Bloomington, Minnesota, closed, the city was left with what amounted to a huge white elephant. What could be done with seventy-eight acres of land near the Minneapolis-St. Paul airport?

At 10:00 A.M. on August 11, 1992, the most discussed retail project in the United States opened and answered this question. Everything about it is big. Mall of America is 4.2 million square feet of leisure under one roof, with 2.5 million square feet of it retail. This is twenty-two times the retail footage of the average American shopping center (Guterson 1993). It includes a seven-acre Knott's Camp Snoopy theme park, the largest enclosed amusement park in the nation; a miniature golf course; and an entertainment complex of theaters and restaurants. There are also more than 330 specialty shops, 400 trees, nearly 13,000 parking spaces, 109 surveillance cameras, and 700 tons of monthly garbage (Guterson 1993). On opening day, more than 150,000 people visited it (*Chain Store Age Executive* 1992). By 1996, developers expect 40 million visitors a year, spending about $2 billion and annually generating $40 million in state taxes. Hotel rooms in the area—6,500 of them—are also filling (*Chain Store Age Executive* 1993).

Mall of America is not just a shopping trip; it's a shopping event. Never was it envisioned as simply a marketplace. No clocks or windows remind people of realties outside. The mall is square with four themed "streets" connecting four department stores. North Garden features a heavily landscaped summer decor. East Broadway is a contemporary, chrome-filled street. South Avenue features a 1920s grand hotel look, and West Market resembles a European train station. Third-floor panoramic vistas, glass-enclosed elevators, bridges, balconies, and vaulted skylights greet shoppers. At night, the outside is spotlit in the manner of a Las Vegas casino. On one recent Valentine's Day, ninety-two couples were married en masse, after which they rode the roller coaster and the Screaming Yellow Eagle. "I believe we can make Mall of America stand for all America," asserted the mall's general manager in a promotional video entitled *There's a Place for Fun in Your Life* (Guterson 1993). The idea was to position America's largest mall as an institution on the scale of Disneyland and the Grand Canyon—as a giant pleasure dome.

Interestingly, America's first fully enclosed shopping center—Southdale Center, in Edina, Minnesota—is a ten-minute drive from Mall of America. Opened in 1956, Southdale ushered in a vast new industry. Since then, shopping centers developed so rapidly that today nearly 39,000 of them operate across the country, annually grossing $747 billion (Communication Channels 1993). In the mid-1980s, malls became less profitable as shoppers turned their allegiance to factory outlet centers, catalogue purchasing, and large discount membership-based stores. Anticipating the future with the advent of cable television's Home Shopping Network, the mall industry is expecting to suffer even more. This provided the rationale for Mall of America. "Anxiety-ridden and sapped of vitality, mall builders fell back on an ancient truth, one capable of sustaining them through troubled seasons; they discovered what humanity had always understood, that shopping and frivolity go hand in hand and are inherently symbiotic. If you build it fun, they will come" (Guterson 1993, 53). If predictions come true, Mall of America will count four times the number of annual visits to Disneyland and twelve times the visits to the Grand Canyon.

It doesn't stop here. Not far away in Canada is the larger West Edmonton Mall (water slide, artificial lake, hockey rink, and forty-seven-ride amusement park). On the drawing board is Mall of Japan (ice rink, water park, fantasy-theme hotel, three breweries, waterfalls, and sport center). Is all this simply marketing gimmicks, or is it a safe, surreal, outside of time and space, potent dream—a carefully controlled fantasy life?

Questions to Consider and Discuss

1. There is, of course, nothing new in the human impulse to dwell in marketplaces. Do some library reading about the contemporary shopping mall's predecessors: the stately arcades of Victorian England, the covered bazaars of the historic Middle East, and Asia's monsoon-protected village markets. Is the use of shopping malls today different from these?

2. Is the Mall of America a marketplace or a tourist attraction? What is the role of shopping in tourism?

3. In the future, will people prefer shopping in the security of their living rooms, conveniently accessing through their televisions on-line retail companies as a form of quiet evening entertainment? Is there something about shopping in a mall that transcends simply the purchase of products? Is shopping entertainment?

Shopping for leisure goods or shopping as leisure?
© Ruth V. Russell

In fact, there may be no relationship between money spent and personal satisfaction obtained from purchases. You buy a mountain bike and then discover there's nowhere around your community to use it, so it collects dust in the garage. Then you feel frustrated because you're not exercising, so you buy a stationary exercise bike instead. Going diving in top-of-the-line scuba gear sounded like fun from the advertisements, but one time out was enough! Now the gear is somewhere in the back of the closet. You feel guilty. Since buying the latest and most expensive video and audio entertainment center, you come home every evening after work and plug in for hours. You've been feeling more isolated and alone lately.

Godbey (1989) criticizes consumerism for more than its damage to the spirit of leisure. He claims that North Americans have developed "a style of life and an attitude toward the consumption of material goods which serves as a negative model for the rest of the world, rapes the world's resources and does untold environmental harm" (p. 17). He cites as an example that United States citizens use twice as much paper per capita as the British or Japanese and have the highest rate of automobile ownership in the world. The desire for cheap hamburger has led, claims Godbey, to the removal of tropical forests in Central America to produce rangeland for cattle. These problems created by consumption directly affect leisure as well. The natural resources used for leisure are endangered. Because of ozone layer depletion, water contamination, acid rain, use of pesticides, and other outcomes of consumption, the water and land

Case Study   Noise over the Grand Canyon

Backpackers on the Bright Angel or Kaibab trails in the Grand Canyon National Park experience an eerie quiet that few people ever experience. Not even the rustle of leaves or the thunder of the mighty Colorado River disturbs the serenity of the canyon. "Generations of people have come to the canyon to experience the incredible silence of the place," says Dennis Dorwin, a Phoenix geography teacher who has hiked much of the canyon. "The quiet is more impressive than the colors of the sunsets." That is, when the almost constant roar of aircraft taking sightseers on expensive tours, doesn't crash the tranquility (Kahler 1986, 16).

With rotors beating like machine guns, helicopters swoop off canyon rims—the noise of their engines reverberating continuously throughout the canyon. The roar of the helicopters is magnified inside the canyon, and the vibrations one feels are intense. Even commercial jets at altitudes of 30,000 feet disturb the tranquility. The park, known for its cathedral quiet, now has the most disturbing noise of all.

Recently, the National Park Service has attempted to address the problem. The controversy has pitted leisure purists against commercialism. Those for whom the Grand Canyon represents a treasured national jewel want a complete ban on all tourist flights over the park. Air-tour operators, on the other hand, argue that their services make the canyon experience available to tourists on short visits, as well as to those with physical disabilities. There is also the economic advantage. Today, about half a million tourists pay about $200 each for air tours of the canyon. Flight operators estimate the tour business at the Grand Canyon is at least a $100 million per year industry.

What should the National Park Service do?

Questions to Consider and Discuss

1. This case study is not fictional. It is a problem affecting not only the Grand Canyon National Park. Other parks, such as Sequoia-Kings Canyon, Cumberland Island, and Yosemite deal with similar problems of pollution and economics. Do some library research for a more thorough briefing of the dilemma. What has happened about this problem since 1986? How is it being solved?
2. What are the main issues in this case? Is it a matter of whose rights should prevail? Which side do you favor?
3. How powerful do you consider the economic value of the flights to be in determining a solution? Is a compromise possible?

---

needed for some leisure pursuits are diminishing. The rate of extinction of animal species, for example, is about 10,000 species per year.

Many decry the problems Godbey worries about but throw up their hands in hopelessness because they claim leisure would be impossible in contemporary societies without consumption. What if we were more conserving in our leisure patterns, could we still have fun? What would happen if we didn't want faster snowmobiles, fast travel to unusual places, and hundreds of CDs? What would life be like if we did only those activities that made minimal demand on material goods, such as walking, yoga, organic gardening, reading, singing, and dancing? How would our health be affected if we chose cross-country skiing over downhill skiing, hiking over all-terrain motorcycles, playing basketball rather than watching it on TV? How would our environment be affected if each year we recycled the medals won in sports competitions, repaired and passed on to others toys our children have outgrown, and took our own cup to the refreshment stand at the ballgame? Conserving in our leisure is a matter of being and doing rather than having (Spry 1991). Would we still have a good time?

How Leisure Benefits an Economy

Our pastimes have tremendous economic significance, especially in the capitalist economies of developed countries where so many activities involve travel and the purchase of leisure-related goods and services. It is common for people to spend more money on leisure than on any other single category, including housing, food, clothing, health care, or education (Chubb and Chubb 1981). Every indication also suggests that leisure has become the primary economic base for many cities (Godbey 1989). The competition for conventions, tourism, shopping, sports, entertainment, festivals and celebrations, and fine arts have become major tools for urban renewal projects. Promoting leisure makes good economic sense; the return is always greater than the outlay.

For example, the presence of leisure facilities and programs attracts businesses and industries to particular locales. These cultural and sport events have public relation value for corporations that support them. They enhance the company's image and ultimately increase profits. Well-planned leisure services can also help reduce the costs of vandalism and crime, particularly in urban areas. Four positive economic benefits from leisure that we explore more thoroughly in this section are expenditures, employment, taxes, and property values.

Expenditures for Goods and Services

In the United States, total annual expenditures for leisure pastimes are said to be higher than $259 billion or an average of about $1,000 per year for every man, woman, and child (U.S. Bureau of Economic Analysis 1991). According to many, however, this estimate is very conservative. This is because money spent on tourism is typically not included in these leisure expenditure estimates. While money spent on such items as televisions, sports equipment, camping gear, children's toys, movie and concert admissions, and other direct purchases are fairly easy to measure, it is much more difficult to determine what proportion of the money spent on automobiles and gasoline, in shopping centers, and at restaurants should be considered leisure expenditures. Items such as these are usually excluded from estimates of leisure goods and service purchases in spite of their economic significance.

How would you make the estimate? Try this experiment. Get a copy of a mail-order catalog for a large retail store, such as J.C. Penney and Service Merchandise. Count the number of pages devoted to leisure supplies and equipment and estimate what proportion of spending is related to leisure. Do you count the pages devoted to automobile supplies, such as car stereos, tape players, and CB radios? How about the do-it-yourself home enhancement tools, such as a home woodworking center? Of course, you've counted the pages of televisions, stereos, bicycles, tents, musical instruments, photographic supplies, sleds, electronic games, bowling balls, boat and motorcycle supplies, roller skates, pool tables, and toys. What about the gardening supplies and guns?

On an Average Day Americans Spend . . .

$149,360 buying Spider-Man comics.

$212,325 on basketballs.

$973,150 on golf balls.

$1,247,280 on fishing licenses.

$1,780,825 for admission to Disney World and EPCOT.

$2,021,918 on home exercise equipment.

$13,698,630 on health-club membership fees.

$17,561,644 supporting arts charities.

$18,904,110 on video rentals.

$33,561,644 buying lottery tickets.

$272,876,712 buying products by mail order.

$434,246,575 on toys.

$1,600,000,000 in shopping malls.

Based on data by Heymann 1989.

The largest single item of leisure expenditures is tourism. According to the U.S. Travel Data Center (1991), Americans spend money on transportation (about $48 billion), food (about $182 billion), lodging (about $60 billion), and entertainment (about $44 billion). The Automobile Association of America (1994) estimates that a car trip costs $215.30 a day for a family of four, with lodging, meals, and car expenses. Tourists also buy sightseeing admissions, guides, travel clothes, travel documents, film, and souvenirs. Thanks to the spoils of development in mature economic societies, things such as super highways, car ownership, and modern airplanes, the fabric of the vacation has been forever changed. Now we can easily travel to see the wildlife of Africa and the cartoon characters in Florida. As well, the timeshare purchase of vacation lodging is replacing the full ownership of second homes. Condominium timeshare purchases are expected to double in the next ten years (*American Demographics* 1993).

After travel and vacations, sport and outdoor recreation purchases are the next largest type of leisure expenditure. The fitness boom that began in the 1970s not only meant healthier people but new ways to spend money. For example, the popularity of jogging has meant much more than simply getting motivated to get up off the couch. It has created the need to buy special shoes, clothes, watches, energy foods and drinks, portable radios, how-to books and magazines, off-season training equipment, airplane tickets to races, and more. In Canada, the total value of expenditures on goods and services related to physical activity is estimated to be $6.3 billion (Conference Board of Canada 1991). Table 10.4 summarizes selected expenditures for sports in the United States.

Case Study   This Is What You Must Have to Jog

Dateline: January 1994.

This just in! Reebok's highly secretive Advanced Concepts Group, an offshoot of its research and development department, has developed the Pump Fury. It's a running shoe that's 25 percent lighter than conventional running shoes. What's striking about the Fury is not what's been put into it but what's been left out. Let's start with the middle third of the midsole. When you run, you push off with the toe and land on the heel; thus, the middle part of the sole doesn't do much. So take it out! The Fury is also missing laces, and for that matter, most of the upper. A skeletonlike bladder, inflated with the pump button or with a disposable CO_2 cartridge, holds your foot in place, so there isn't a need for much more material there. All this subtraction of shoe pieces is good. Apparently, for every ounce laced to your feet, you lug an extra 550 pounds over the course of a five mile jaunt. Bummer. This is terrific! Less running shoe for only $125. Reebok's

Pump Fury is just the tip of the iceberg in "minimalist" athletic footwear. Plans for basketball shoes are on the drawing board. (Silverman 1994)

Questions to Consider and Discuss

1. What is the role of expensive equipment in enjoying a leisure activity? Think of the latest in running shoes advertised here. Do such shoes always enhance the experience of running? Can you think of examples of how expensive equipment might be a detriment?
2. Many leisure products, such as specialized running shoes, home computers, and videocassette recorders have not been part of the U.S. economy for very long. Some of these newer goods, such as computers, have been decreasing in price and improving in quality. Is this generally true for other new leisure products?

Table 10.4

Sport and Outdoor Recreation Expenditures

Activities	1980	1990
Fishing licenses	$35.2 mil.	$37 mil.
Hunting licenses	$27 mil.	$30 mil.
Camping equipment	$646 mil.	$1.1 bil.
Recreational boats	$7.4 bil.	$13.7 bil.
Bicycles	$1.2 bil.	$2.4 bil.
Jogging shoes	$397 mil.	$519 mil.
Golf clubs and balls	$386 mil.	$1.2 bil.
Tennis equipment	$237 mil.	$287 mil.
Baseball and softball equipment	$158 mil.	$217 mil.

Source: National Sporting Goods Association 1992.

Traditionally, outdoor pastimes had little economic effect beyond the indirect benefit of mental and physical well-being. However, today's expenditures for outdoor equipment are economically important as well. Beginning in the 1960s in the U.S., outdoor recreation became mechanized. To enjoy the

Cultural Art Expenditures

Table 10.5

Activities	1980	1990
Broadway shows	$143 mil.	$283 mil.
Symphony orchestras	$246 mil.	$680 mil.
National Endowment for the Arts	$188 mil.	$171 mil.
Music cassettes	$776 mil.	$3.5 bil.
Books	$9.9 bil. (1982)	$19 bil.

Sources: Book Industry Study Group 1992; Recording Industry Association of America 1992; *Variety* 1992; American Symphony Orchestra League 1992; National Endowment for the Arts 1992.

outdoors now, more people require dune buggies, campers, motor homes, off-road vehicles, motor boats, snowmobiles, and motorized surfers. One of the most expensive pieces of equipment for outdoor pastimes, airplanes, are also being sold at faster rates. Private and publicly sponsored flying clubs are increasing. Table 10.4 summarizes expenditures for some outdoor pursuits.

Cultural arts is the third leading category of leisure expenditure. The cost of music lessons, musical instruments, symphony orchestra concert tickets, craft supplies, museum admissions, stereos, sheet music, dancing shoes, and much more represent almost as many purchases as those in sports (table 10.5). Estimating is difficult because of the numerous aspects of the cost of a cultural arts experience. For example, crafts cover a very broad area. Decorative crafts (stitchery, weaving), survival crafts (shelter building), fine arts (sculpting, painting), school crafts (coloring), culinary crafts (cooking, baking), and even automotive crafts (painting a car body) require expenditures. The costs of craft activities include not only the materials, some of which are quite expensive, but instruction, special clothing, equipment, and sometimes fees charged for the place of performance or display. Some crafts are free, such as making a mosaic out of items found in nature, but most require at least some expenditure.

There are other categories of leisure expenditures. For example, the cost of popular culture outlets (newspapers, books, magazines, records, CDs, movies, televisions), admissions to spectator sports, driving for pleasure, children's toys, hot tubs, outdoor cooking grills, home swimming pools, pets, and eating out represent significant economic impact.

Employment

It is difficult to estimate the number of people whose income is leisure-related, yet available statistics suggest many occupations have something to do with leisure. Those in the entertainment fields, supervisors in city recreation agencies, managers in parks and forests, employees of health and fitness facilities, workers in restaurants and hotels, managers of bowling centers, travel agents, assembly line workers in factories manufacturing recreation goods, recreation therapists in hospitals, and many more leisure-related employments provide benefits to an economy. For example, the U.S. state park systems employ over 45,000 people. More than 12,000 permanent employees and more than 6,000 seasonal employees are hired to operate the recreation facilities and programs of federal agencies. In total, about 3 million jobs are directly related to leisure. This represents approximately $46 billion in income which is fed back into the economy (U.S. Bureau of the Census 1993). Other occupations, such as transportation system workers and child care specialists, are indirectly or partially related to leisure and provide economic benefit as well.

There is another angle to the positive impact leisure has on employment. Substantial research data indicate participation in some leisure activities leads to more healthy, productive workers. Since labor is a factor of production, when that factor becomes more productive, the costs of production decrease. This results in financial gain to employers (Johnson and Brown 1991). Activities that are strenuous and increase the participant's strength and endurance allow them to be more productive at jobs that require physical labor. Improved fitness also increases the productivity of workers whose jobs do not require physical labor. It reduces health care costs, lowers absenteeism, reduces on-the-job accidents, and provides other benefits that mean better profits for employers (Ellis and Richardson 1991). Otherwise, according to the Center for Disease Control, about $5.7 billion is spent each year in the United States on medical bills and lost productivity of people who could have fought off heart disease with even a little physical exercise.

Taxes

The generation of local, state, and federal government revenues through taxes typically paid in connection with leisure also contribute to the economic health of society. These include sales taxes from the purchase of leisure goods and services, income taxes on wages earned in leisure-related jobs, property taxes from private and commercial properties that are partly or totally leisure oriented, gasoline taxes, and taxes on entertainment, restaurant meals, and hotel accommodations.

Taxes and license fees are levied on bars, nightclubs, bowling centers, and game arcades. The fees for hunting, trapping, and fishing licenses and the taxes on hunting and fishing equipment usually benefit the upkeep of the fish and game habitats. Excise taxes are levied on certain imported leisure goods. Liquor taxes in some areas are quite high, and the taxes garnered from legal gambling, such as lotteries and pari-mutuel betting, have been very useful to local and state governments. In many cases, these tax revenues are used to enhance the leisure services available to people. For example, the National Endowment for the Arts allocates millions of tax dollars in federal money to be used as matching funds by local arts organizations.

research

State and local governments across the U.S. are heavily involved in the provision of outdoor pastime opportunities for the public. While it is important to measure the social and psychological impacts of these services on the people who use them, until recently methods for determining their economic impact were less common. A research study conducted in 1992 by Cordell, Bergstrom, and Watson demonstrated how this could be done.

Pomona State Park was the representative park examined in the study. It is located in Osage County in eastern Kansas. It is a moderate-sized park of about 500 acres providing both tent and trailer camping. It was selected for the study because it offers day and overnight opportunities as well as water- and land-based activities. It is open from mid-April through mid-September. The park's economic impact on the state and seven surrounding counties was measured using a microcomputer software system developed by researchers from the U.S. Forest Service. It is called IMPLAN.

In terms of economic growth, the results from the IMPLAN analysis indicated that nonresident recreational spending associated with Pomona State Park contributed about $.77 million to the local

economies and about $1 million to the state economy. Nonresident recreational spending also contributed about nineteen jobs to the local economy and twenty-three jobs to the state economy, resulting in $.51 million in employee pay. The significance of this is that if the park were to shut down or reduce services, there would likely be a "shock" to the local and state economies.

Another kind of analysis conducted by the researchers in this study was the calculation of an economic growth multiplier. For example, the multiplier for local income was 2.44. Suppose that the effect of 1,000 additional visits to Pomona State Park is the addition of $100,000 of new sales within the local region. The multiplier of 2.44 suggests that the final total impact on the local economy will be the addition of $244,000 in total income ($100,000 times 2.44). The implication of this is that increased visitation to state parks in Kansas from nonresidents could have substantial positive economic growth effects. Thus, actions taken to attract more nonresident visitors to Kansas state parks could be especially important in current times as some rural economies face dramatic shifts away from traditional forestry and agriculture as major sources of income.

Property Values

The value of land is often affected by the presence of leisure-related development. Large, attractive parks usually increase the value of adjacent property, such as the land near Central Park in New York City and Golden Gate Park in San Francisco. In some situations, the highest-priced residential property in a city adjoins parks (Maclean, Peterson, and Martin 1985). Likewise, the value of lands near golf courses, developed lakes and reservoirs, resorts, wildlife refuges, and other leisure sites tend to increase property values. Sometimes this has meant increases of fifteen to twenty times within only a few years of the development.

On the other hand, the value of property can also be reduced by certain leisure related developments. Property near X-rated movie theaters, topless bars, bowling centers, and other more commercial enterprises can fall victim to reduced financial value. Similarly, property that is adjacent to athletic fields that are used at night and noisy playgrounds may be devalued. However, these play areas can be carefully planned with plantings to muffle noise, protect privacy, and provide aesthetic views, which help the adjacent property rise in price.

The most evident examples of the positive impact of leisure on property values are found in such places as Palm Springs, California. Sometimes the best economic use of an area is for leisure. Once barren desert land, today Palm Springs has a population of approximately 40,000 residents. Why? Its whole reason for being is as a winter playground. The Palm Springs industries are tennis, golf, cultural events, bicycling, pool lounging, pleasure walking, and fine foods eating. These industries bring in not only permanent residents but conventioneers and tourists. Two million visitors a year flock to this land of 350 days of sunshine. It is estimated that there are some 109 golf courses, 600 tennis courts, and 8,000 swimming pools (*Industry Week* 1990). Based on almost a pure leisure-focused industry, where there was once nothing, Palm Springs has a median family income of about $34,000, city revenues of over $52,000,000, and a single-family home value that averages $142,000 (*Information Publications* 1993).

How Leisure Harms an Economy

Sometimes leisure results in costs rather than benefits to individual and national economies. These include the costs of property damages incurred as a result of our pastimes. Also, decreased productivity of workers through absenteeism, inattentiveness, or lethargy generally happens at times of the year closely associated with leisure. For example, the opening of baseball and hunting seasons, and the two week holiday period around Christmas and New Year's typically experience the highest rates of absenteeism and inattentiveness at work and school. In addition, leisure businesses are among the most susceptible to the whims of public taste. Fads come and go, and expensive leisure industries come and go with them. For example, what has happened to trampoline parks? Financial headaches can also be caused by the seasonal nature of some forms of leisure. Ski resorts are good illustrations.

The economic repercussions of people relocating to be close to recreation amenities can be significant as well. For example, migrations to beach or mountain areas can reduce the tax base in communities that lose population. It also causes equally serious financial harm to small communities receiving the migration if the newcomers demand substantial improvements in public facilities and services.

Frequently, society must pay high costs to solve some of the problems that result from leisure. These problems include public money spent on pet related problems. There are about 53 million dogs, 59 million cats, 12 million

Table 10.6

On an Average Day . . .

35 Americans are injured by fireworks.

68 people are injured playing golf.

7 children are injured using playpens.

15 people die from drowning.

222 people are injured using skateboards.

1,546 persons are injured using bicycles.

523 children are treated at hospitals for playground injuries.

17 forest fires are started by campfires.

341,644,383 pounds of paper products end up in the trash.

495 species are threatened and endangered.

Source: Heymann 1989

birds, and 5 million horses in the United States (American Veterinary Medical Association 1993). The cost to taxpayers for managing dogs, such as dealing with strays and removing fecal waste from public places, is about $500 million per year. Another example is the $1 billion spent annually by the U.S. Coast Guard to rescue small pleasure boats. It is estimated that dealing with the problems of pleasure drinking, such as sick pay, accidents, and lost production costs about $15 billion a year.

The problems multiply. To feature two problems, we explore the economic harm of leisure caused by accidents and balance of payments.

Accidents

Every day, on average, 24,384 Americans suffer disabling injuries (Heymann 1989). These accidents cost the U.S. economy about $323,287,671 per day in lost wages, medical expenses, insurance, rescue and emergency care, and indirect work loss. What proportion of this cost is leisure related? Estimates are not available, but perhaps you can conduct your own survey to investigate the role of leisure in accidents. Every time someone you know is injured, ask them whether their injury was the result of something they were doing for fun. You will probably find that a large proportion of the injuries have some connection to leisure (table 10.6).

How do accidents in leisure occur? There are several ways. Lack of sufficient or appropriate information can give people a false sense of security when engaged in leisure activities. A poorly informed person is much more likely to take unnecessary risks. For example, diving into murky water of unknown depth represents an uninformed action. Limited performance skills can also lead to accidents. Accidents often happen because individuals participate in activities before they have mastered the needed skills. For example, drowning victims are likely to be poor swimmers, and novice skiers are more likely to be injured than experts.

Accidents can also be attributed to carelessness, laziness, foolishness, and other inappropriate behaviors. Going down the ski slope just one more time even though one is very fatigued, bouncing on a trampoline without spotters present, not using protective eye wear in racquetball, and not using mats

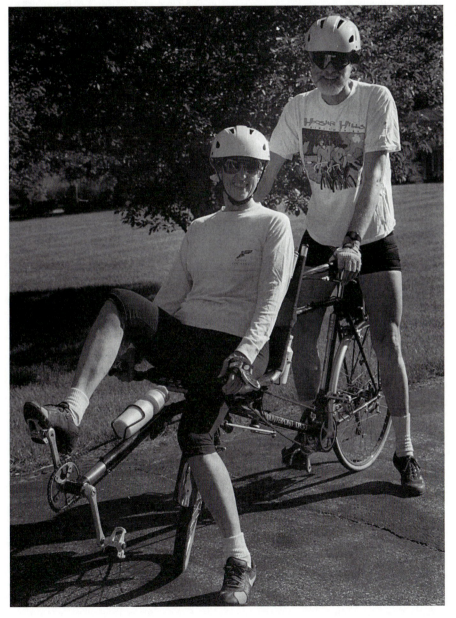

Risks to bicyclists have increased.
© Ruth V. Russell

in gymnastics are likely to lead to accidents. We can think of many others: starting down a slide before the one in front is off, ice skating fast in a crowded space, playing ultimate frisbee during an electrical storm, running around a wet pool deck, using drugs or alcohol while playing volleyball.

Careless behavior is different than dangerous behavior. Careless behaviors produce at least 90 percent of all accidents that occur at recreational places (Bucher, Shivers, and Bucher 1984). Increases in participation in high-risk activities, such as scuba diving, hang gliding, caving, rock climbing, and extreme skiing compound the problem. Even riding a bicycle around town is a more dangerous activity than it used to be because of crowded conditions.

Another category of sources of leisure related accidents is lack of proper management by sponsors of recreation. Poor maintenance of facilities can lead to accidents, as when someone is cut falling on broken glass on a ball field. Also, if recreation facilities and activities provided by agencies are not adequately supervised, such as lifeguards failing to control rowdy behavior at the city pool, accidents are more likely to occur.

Injuries sustained through leisure-related accidents have costs, of course. In addition to the human costs to health and sometimes life, they also result in financial costs. There is the expense of lost wages, lost productivity, medical treatment, and sometimes lawsuits. Lawsuits for injuries sustained while pursuing recreational activities have become economically significant. About half of all sports related lawsuits result in financial recovery for the injured; more frequently, the amount awarded is $1 million.

Balance of Payments

Balance of payments: a statement of all goods and services, as well as investments, that flow in and out of a country.

A nation's **balance of payments** is the record of transactions between its residents and residents of the rest of the world. Part of these transactions are the buying and selling of merchandise. The balance is the difference between the value of commodities exported minus the value of commodities imported. In recent years, the United States has experienced a deficit in its trade balance. The value of U.S. imports has exceeded the value of U.S. exports. In 1989, this deficit amounted to $113 billion. During most of the 1980s, Americans were consuming more than they were producing. Americans now owe more to the rest of the world than does any other nation.

How does this relate to leisure? Inventory your own leisure-related equipment. Do you own athletic shoes, golf clubs, snow skis, a bicycle, a television set, CD player, or musical instrument? What proportion of your leisure possessions were made in the U.S.? If more of them were made outside the U.S., you have just demonstrated a negative balance of payments.

Tourism provides another example. In 1985, American tourists to other countries spent about $24.6 million; that year international tourists to the U.S. spent about $17.9 million (U.S. Bureau of Economic Analysis 1992). This again is an illustration of a negative balance of payments. Since then, there has been a change in the tourism economic balance. In 1992, American tourists to other countries spent $32 million while international tourists to the U.S. spent about

$55.3 million. This is now an example of a positive balance of payments. What is clear in this see-saw is that tourism is a large commodity of international trade with the possibility of both aiding and harming the economies of the world.

Summary: Economic Significance

You come home from work too tired for anything but watching television. You see things on TV you want, so you end up buying them. Then you go to work to pay for them, and again you come home tired and watch television.

In this chapter, we explored leisure's relationship to economics. In the first place, leisure is a mirror of a nation's level of economic development and its economic system. In capitalistic and economically mature countries, leisure drives an economy by fostering consumerism. Sometimes consumption itself is viewed as a leisure experience. Does a high level of spending for leisure mean a high quality of life? As illustrated in the opening paragraph of this summary, this is not necessarily true.

We also explored the positive and negative economic impacts of our pastimes. On the one hand, leisure makes good economic sense; it benefits employment, taxes, property values, and expenditures. On the other hand, leisure has human and societal costs. Two examples are the costs of leisure-related injuries and negative balance of payments.

References

American Symphony Orchestra League. 1992. *Major U.S. symphony orchestras and their music directors.* Washington, D.C.

American Veterinary Medical Association. 1993. *U.S. pet ownership and demographics sourcebook.* American Veterinary Medical Association.

Asher, G. 1994. How catalogs lure with images, reel 'em in with words. *The Herald-Times,* 6 January.

Automobile Association of America. 1994. Family car trip expenses. *Travel and Leisure* (August): 120.

Becker, E. 1968. *The structure of evil.* New York: George Braziller Inc.

Book Industry Study Group. (September 1992). *Book industry trends.* New York: Book Industry Study Group.

Bucher, C. A., J. S. Shivers, and R. D. Bucher. 1984. *Recreation for today's society.* Englewood Cliffs, NJ: Prentice-Hall.

Chubb, M., and H. R. Chubb. 1981. *One third of our time? An introduction to recreation behavior and resources.* New York: John Wiley & Son, Inc.

Communication Channels. March 1993. *Shopping center world.* Atlanta, GA: Communications Channels.

Conference Board of Canada. (1991). *The fitness industry in Canada: Research findings and issues associated with economic measurement. Summary report.* Ottawa, ON: The Conference Board of Canada.

Cordell, H. K., J. C. Bergstrom, and A. E. Watson. 1992. Economic growth and interdependence effects of state park visitation in local and state economies. *Journal of Leisure Research* 24:3, 253–68.

Cunningham, H. 1980. *Leisure in the Industrial Revolution.* London: Croom Helm.

deGrazia, S. 1962. *Of time, work and leisure.* New York: The Twentieth Century Fund.

Ellis, T., and G. Richardson. 1991. Organizational wellness. In *Benefits of leisure,* edited by B. L. Driver, P. J. Brown, and G. L. Peterson. State College, PA: Venture.

Florida Department of Revenue. 1992. *Florida statistical abstract.* Tallahassee, FL, State of Florida.

Fox, F. W., and C. L. Pope. 1989. *American heritage: An interdisciplinary approach.* Dubuque, IA: Kendall/Hunt.

Godbey, G. 1989. *The future of leisure services: Thriving on change.* State College, PA: Venture.

Goodale, T. L., and G. C. Godbey. 1988. *The evolution of leisure: Historical and philosophical perspectives.* State College, PA: Venture.

Guterson, D. 1993. Enclosed. Encyclopedic. Endured.: One week at the Mall of America. *Harper's Magazine* 281, no. 1719:49–56.

Hagel, D. 1992. At long last, the megamall. *Chain Store Age Executive* 68:9, 53–55.

Heymann, T. 1989. *On an average day.* New York: Fawcett.

Ibrahim, H. 1991. *Leisure and society: A comparative approach.* Dubuque, IA: Wm. C. Brown Publishers.

Industry Week. March 19, 1990. 239:6, p. A6.

Information Publications. 1993. Palo Alto, CA.

Johnson, R. L, and T. C. Brown. 1991. Beneficial economic consequences of leisure and recreation. In *Benefits of leisure,* edited by B. L. Driver, P. J. Brown, and G. L. Peterson. State College, PA: Venture.

Kahler, K. 1986. Airborne views: The pure silence of Grand Canyon is shattered by constant overflights. *National Parks.* (March/April): 16–19.

Linder, S. 1970. *The harried leisure class.* New York: Columbia University Press.

Maclean, J. R., J. A. Peterson, and W. D. Martin. 1985. *Recreation and leisure: The changing scene.* New York: John Wiley & Son, Inc.

Maklan, M. 1977. How blue-collar workers on a 4-day workweek use their time. *Monthly Labor Review* 100:8, 26.

Marsh, J. S. 1982. An initial study of the economic impact of the 24th annual Peterborough church league atom hockey tournament, Peterborough, January 21–24, 1982. Unpublished Paper, Peterborough, ON: Department of Geography, Trent University.

McEachern, W.A. 1991. Macroeconomics: A contemporary introduction. Cincinnati, OH: South-Western.

Millspaugh, M. L. 1990. Leisure and tourism: Economic strategy policy issues regarding economic development and the revitalization of urban areas. *World Leisure and Recreation* 32:2, 10–15.

National Endowment for the Arts. 1992. *Annual report.* Washington, D.C.: U.S. Government Printing Office.

National Sporting Goods Association. 1992. *The sporting goods market in 1992.* Mt. Prospect, IL: National Sporting Goods Association.

NordicGroup International. 1991. *Northern Ontario snowmobiling development strategy.* Edmonton, Alberta: NordicGroup International.

Recording Industry Association of America. 1992. *Inside the recording industry: A statistical overview.* Washington, D.C.: Recording Industry Association of America.

Rostow, W. W. 1960. *The stages of economic growth.* Cambridge: Harvard University Press.

Schor, J. B. 1992. *The overworked American: The unexpected decline of leisure.* New York: Basic Books.

Season box office totals. 1992. *Variety,* 1 June.

Seldon, W. L. 1993. Timesharing sheds a shady image. *American Demographics* (May): 14–15.

Silverman, J. 1994. The next thing in running. *Outside* 19:1, 49.

Smith, A. 1937. *An inquiry into the nature and causes of the wealth of nations.* New York: The Modern Library.

Spry, I. M. 1991. The prospects for leisure in a conserver society. In *Recreation and leisure: Issues in an era of change,* 3d ed., edited by T. L. Goodale and P. A. Witt. State College, PA: Venture.

Time for a Mall of America update. 1993. *Chain Store Age Executive* 69:3, 43–44.

U.S. Bureau of the Census. 1993. *Statistical Abstract of the United States: 1993.* Washington, D.C.: Government Printing Office.

U.S. Bureau of Economic Analysis. 1991. *Survey of current business.* Washington, D.C.: U.S. Government Printing Office.

U.S. Bureau of Economic Analysis. 1992. *Survey of current business.* Washington, D.C.: U.S. Government Printing Office.

U.S. Travel Data Center. 1991. *National travel survey.* Washington, D.C.: U.S. Government Printing Office.

Veblen, T. 1912. *The theory of leisure class.* New York: Macmillan.

Waters, S. R. 1992. *The travel industry yearbook—The big picture.* Rye, NY: Child & Waters.

World Bank. 1989. *World Development Report 1989.* New York: Oxford University Press.

leisure and equity

PREVIEW

Is there equity in leisure?

No. Barriers exist in society to equal opportunities for leisure. This can be demonstrated by considering the leisure discrimination of women, persons with disabilities, ethnic groups, and people who are societally invisible.

Does leisure have the potential to enable equality in society?

Yes. Leisure is an important context for creating equal opportunities for a high quality of life.

chapter

eleven

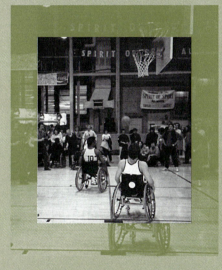

© Ruth V. Russell

Is leisure a right or a privilege?

This is a simple question to ask but much tougher to answer. Leisure has been viewed by some as a privilege—something to be earned after a hard day's work or the gift of a lucky birth into privileged circumstances. Since leisure, especially when defined as free time, is often viewed as a reward for work, it can be considered a privilege for those who work. On the other hand, much that has been written about leisure qualities comes from the perspective that it is a right—something that is as essentially human as eating and sleeping.

Is it a right or a privilege for these young adults to participate in this drum and bugle corps?

© Ruth V. Russell

As privilege, of course, leisure is something that is distributed un-equally. That is the whole point of it. As a privilege, leisure is a reward only available to qualifying people. Sometimes the qualifier is having enough money to pay for certain forms of leisure. Other times, it is the guilt-free sensation that by the time the weekend is here, you have worked hard enough to qualify for taking some hard won time off.

As a right, leisure is supposed to be distributed equally. In many cultures, there is a belief in natural or inalienable rights—rights that are impossible to surrender. These inalienable rights are often described as life, liberty, and the pursuit of happiness. With these rights comes the belief in equality—everyone has a right to the good life. Thus, leisure is felt to be the right of everyone.

In many cultures, including the United States and Canada, notions of in-alienable rights and equality form the basis of political philosophies and government policies. Governments sponsor services considered vital to a happy life. These frequently include leisure services. Leisure can be a way of achieving equity in the pursuit of happiness. However, even when leisure is considered a right of all people, it is not completely accessible or available to all people. For example, women's roles and responsibilities often constrain them from full participation in leisure; people with disabilities must continue to overcome barriers to total access to leisure expressions; ethnic minorities are sometimes discriminated against in certain leisure activities; and an opportunity for leisure is often nonexistent for people who are homeless, migrant workers, and persons who have AIDS.

The domestic political life of the United States and some other industrialized nations during the post–World War II portion of the century could be described as the drive for **equity.** In the 1950s and 1960s, African Americans challenged the political system to live up to its ideals and grant them full equality. In the 1970s, unequal treatment of women was pushed to center stage. Following leads from these groups, civil rights movements have also been launched in recent decades by Native Americans; Hispanic Americans; and gays, lesbians, and bisexuals.

Equity: freedom from bias or favoritism.

At first glance, the issue seems to focus on economics—the right to escape poverty. The government has chosen to define **poverty** according to the income needed to consume certain basic goods. For example, a household with four persons was considered in 1991 to be below the poverty level if its income was less than $13,920 (U.S. Bureau of the Census 1992). Certain groups have a much higher probability of becoming impoverished. For example, as figure 11.1 indicates, African Americans and women have twice the probability in comparison with whites and men. Since the 1960s, the U.S. has passed numerous laws to eliminate economic inequality. The Civil Rights Act of 1964 prohibits employment discrimination on the basis of sex, religion, race, and national origin. The Employment Act of 1968 prohibits discrimination on the basis of age. The Americans with Disabilities Act of 1990 requires full accessibility to educational, employment, recreation, and other resources to persons with disabilities. In spite of these and other legislation, efforts to correct

Poverty: the condition of lacking the usual or socially acceptable amount of money or material possessions.

Figure 11.1 The probability of being poor.

Christopher B. Stage

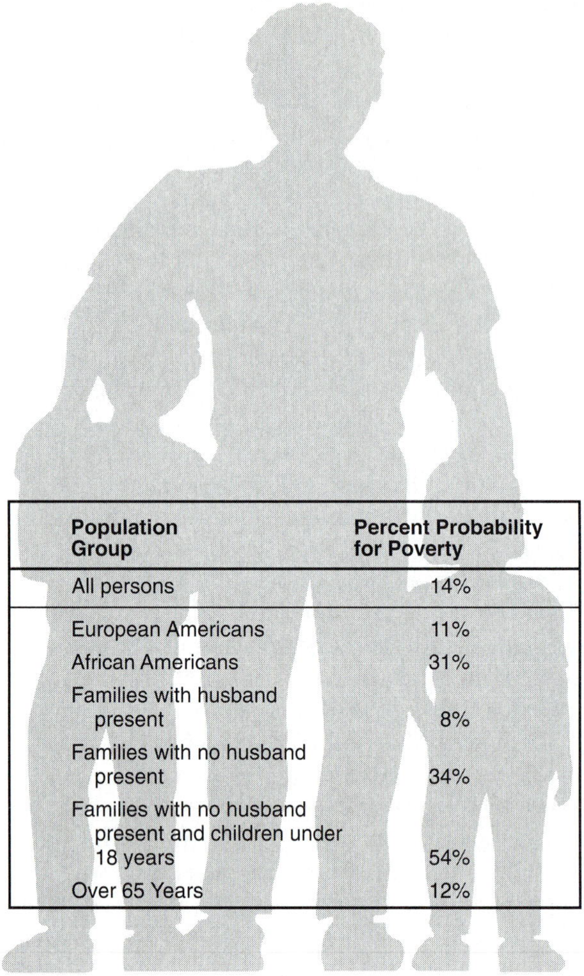

Population Group	Percent Probability for Poverty
All persons	14%
European Americans	11%
African Americans	31%
Families with husband present	8%
Families with no husband present	34%
Families with no husband present and children under 18 years	54%
Over 65 Years	12%

discrimination have been more than struggles for economic equality. They are more concerned with equality of opportunity.

Today, efforts to provide more equality of opportunity have a strong political appeal in the United States. For example, over $223 billion is spent each year by federal, state, and local governments on education with about 70 percent of these expenditures for elementary and secondary education (Fox and Pope 1989). Certainly, the provision of more opportunity through education is a major motivation for these expenditures. The federal Headstart program represents a successful effort to give very young children better early opportunities for educational achievement.

In this chapter, we make two major points about leisure and equity. First, there is not yet equity in leisure. Second, leisure has the potential of being a great equalizer. Our pastimes have been both a hurdle to equality and an enabler of equality in society.

Women's Leisure

Woman has played many roles throughout history. She has been a friend, mother, daughter, lover, and mate. She has also been prime minister of her country, a farmer, a homemaker, a political activist, a business executive, a teacher, and a scientist. Today, most women, including those who are single and without children, combine two or more of these roles, yet through the centuries, almost every society has developed definite ideas about what activities are appropriate for women. Some of these ideas have disappeared or changed greatly over time, but others have changed little or not at all.

To trace an example, in ancient India, women had quite a bit of political and social freedom, owning property and taking part in public debates for thousands of years. Around 200 B.C., Hinduism developed laws that gave women an inferior status. Parents began to arrange for their daughters to be married before reaching puberty and taught them always to obey their husbands. Today, Indian women again have the right to vote and own property, and over 10 million women hold professional jobs. However, only about 19 percent of all Indian women can read and write compared with 40 percent of the men.

In this section, we explore leisure in women's lives. What have been the implications in the changes in the roles of women for leisure? What is the meaning of leisure for women? Is leisure equitably available to women? In shaping our exploration we consider two themes: feminist philosophy applied to women's leisure, and research conclusions about the nature of women's leisure.

Teachings from Feminist Philosophy

Feminism has come to be known as the belief that women should have economic, political, and social equality with men. While feminist beliefs have existed in various cultures throughout history, they did not become widespread until recently. Prior to this time, people in many cultures regarded women as inferior to men. In the interest of family stability and unity, women were confined to the home. Laws reflected these opinions. In the United States, Canada, and most European countries women were barred by law from voting in elections, and most professional careers were closed to women. They were also barred from equal opportunity in education.

In the early 1800s, a struggle was begun that took almost a century to be taken seriously. Efforts focused mostly on achieving political equality. Leaders of the women's rights movement believed that if women had the vote, they could use it to gain other rights. Strong opposition, which maintained that women were less intelligent than men and unable to make good political decisions, heated the struggle. Finally, the right to vote (suffrage) was earned in the early 1900s for American, Canadian, and many European women. New Zealand was the first nation to grant women full voting rights in 1893. Today, all but a few countries have laws allowing women to vote.

After suffrage was won, the efforts for equality nearly disappeared. However, during the mid-1900s, when increasing numbers of women entered the

Feminism: the theory of the political, economic, and social equality of the sexes.

labor force and found that many higher paying jobs were closed to them, the struggle was renewed. This time the focus was on economic equality. The National Organization for Women (NOW) and other feminist groups fought to end job discrimination against women. As a result, by the end of this century more women are entering law, medicine, politics, and other traditionally male fields, yet full economic equality has not been achieved. In the United States, women earn about 70 cents for every dollar men earn in comparable employment.

Feminism, however, is more than the efforts to achieve equality. It has a broader philosophical framework that includes ideas of empowerment and social change, as well as equality. As such there are three major goals of feminism (Henderson et al. 1989). The first goal is the correction of the invisibility of women's experiences. As women's historical contributions, achievements in art and music, and roles in science are uncovered, it is believed that action for social change will be possible. A second goal of feminism is the right of every woman to freedom of choice. This means that women should have not only equity but also the power to control their own lives. A third goal is the removal of all forms of oppression against all people in society. According to feminism, both men and women have basic human rights. With equality in pursuing these rights, feminists believe both men and women will have freedom from restrictive gender roles.

Because of these three goals, feminism and leisure are linked. Both are based on the qualities of choice and freedom (Henderson et al. 1989). The essence of both feminism and leisure is the encouragement of freedom of choice. Women have not had the same opportunities for leisure as men, because they have not had the same level of freedom to choose leisure. Through leisure, however, women have the opportunity to take responsibility for themselves. It is a unique relationship: leisure provides both an avenue for achieving women's equality, empowerment, and social action, and leisure itself has been constrained for women because of a lack of equality, empowerment, and social action.

Opportunities and Constraints: Research Findings

Feminism provides a useful means for addressing the opportunities and constraints for women in experiencing leisure. In contrast to traditional opinion, women's and men's leisure experience is different. In achieving the goals of feminism—greater visibility, empowerment, and removal of oppression—a better understanding of these differences is possible. A good place to begin our research-based discussion takes us back again to the early 1900s.

In a study by Henderson (1993), the professional recreation literature was analyzed to answer questions about how girls' and women's leisure was viewed historically. Henderson began with books and articles published in 1907 and discovered that the time period of 1907 to 1916 could be described as the "females become visible era" (p. 169). In this early literature, it is "discovered" that girls need recreation, too. Some writers of the time thought girls had been forgotten and that the playground movement had focused only on boys. In their writing, they sought to include girls by advocating that the "spirit of play needed to be awakened in girls" (p. 169).

For example, when the early playground leaders interacted with boys and girls, they found girls to be listless. A study reported in 1910 suggested that girls were less interested in recreation. The study concluded that many girls were so tired from their household tasks that when they came to the playground, they had little energy to play (Weller 1913). Henderson suggests that there may be other conclusions. For example, recreation facilities and programs were often not made available to girls. Also the limitations of girls' clothing at the time constrained their physical movements (Rockwell 1917).

Henderson's literature analysis also revealed an interesting debate in the early part of the nineteenth century about whether girls' sport activities should be more like boys' or the other way around. This was particularly debatable because of the "corruption" in boys' activities (McKinstry 1909). One early writer suggested that boys would be better off if they adopted some of the "gentler and more conventional amusements" of girls. It was also advised that girls should have "more liberty in their recreations" (Weller 1913, 209).

Today, research on contemporary women reveals similar themes of constraint and opportunity in leisure. In a review of the research on women's leisure, Henderson (1990) outlined five broad conclusions about women's inequality in leisure and the different nature of women's leisure experiences.

1. Women experience inequality in leisure when compared to men. Much of the current literature about women's leisure from a feminist perspective suggests that regardless of social class, age, and educational level, the leisure of men and women varies considerably. Many women have less time for leisure and less of a priority for leisure. Women also, according to studies, tend to have narrower options for choosing particular leisure activities. Some pastimes, such as football and ice hockey, are still considered inappropriate for girls and women.

2. Combining role obligations with leisure is a common focus for many women. The research indicates that many women perceive themselves as family members first and individuals second; thus, they perceive their leisure as the family's leisure. For example, when a woman marries, her social life often becomes linked with that of her husband's. When she has children, her life is further sublimated to the interests and needs of the family. The meaning of leisure for women outside the family also tends to center around interactions with others. Some studies claim that the reason many women participate in organized sport is not competition but the opportunity to socialize with other women.

3. Women's leisure is more likely to occur in the home and be unstructured. The home is the most common place for women's leisure, because leisure can be easily infused with household chores and women are socialized to value home-based activities, such as crafts, gardening, reading, socializing, and cooking. Fewer leisure opportunities are available for adult women outside the home, and efforts are not provided to assist them in participating in those that are available, such as child care services and flexible program scheduling.

A women's bicycle racing team at Indiana University's "Little 500."

© Ruth V. Russell

Unfortunately, the home as a typical location for women's leisure has its problems. Studies have shown that because activity in the home does not always provide an opportunity for a change of pace, it is frequently not refreshing. Also, home-based leisure has been shown to increase feelings of social isolation for women.

4. Much of women's leisure is fragmented. A number of researchers suggest that women seldom find large blocks of time for leisure in their lives. Instead, they have to "steal" free time. They take "minute vacations." Women have difficulty planning ahead for leisure; instead, leisure occurs as the opportunity presents itself. Women are also more likely to combine leisure activities with other obligations, such as watching television while ironing.

5. Finally, many women do not feel entitled to leisure. Research findings conclude that many women do not believe they deserve leisure. If leisure is viewed as an earned reward, some women who are homemakers may never feel they earned the reward. This may be the case because leisure is so often considered the opposite of work. Even for women who work outside the home, studies have found

that they too often felt they had no right to take time off. This may be because of trying to "do it all." Overall, however, samples of employed women typically had more leisure interests than women not employed outside the home. Researchers have concluded that this was because they had more money, household help, and more ability to plan the day.

As Henderson (1990) has summarized, while leisure is considered an important part of the quality of life for people, women are often unable to take full advantage of the potential for leisure in their lives. This must be corrected because leisure experiences provide the opportunity for maintaining personal autonomy, self-definition, and choice often absent from other aspects of women's lives.

People with Disabilities

It has been estimated that 43 million Americans live with significant **disabilities.** There are a variety of disabling conditions, including visual and hearing impairments, motor impairments, and psychological and behavioral disorders. Disabilities cut across age, race, social class, gender, and educational backgrounds, but people with disabilities commonly find it more difficult to attend school, pursue a career, live independently, and enjoy leisure.

Disability: a form of physical or mental impairment that may limit ability to participate in some life activities.

During the 1960s in the United States, a movement developed that emphasized the rights of people with disabilities. Philosophically originating in turn of the twentieth-century efforts to overcome the human consequences of industrialization, the crux of the movement was advocacy (Kennedy, Smith, and Austin 1991). Health and human service organizations, as well as governments, were called upon to serve the needs of persons with disabilities.

Originally, the advocacy took the form of "separate but equal." Recreation programs in communities were instrumental in addressing the needs of persons with disabilities by establishing segregated programs (Bedini 1990). Their needs were met through services provided only for them. These included residential, educational, and recreation services separate from those services available to people without disabilities. In fact, these were often labeled as programs for "special populations."

Later, it was realized that segregation encouraged dependence by those with disabilities and fueled the community's condescension and pity (Bedini 1990). Now the focus is not simply to provide access to community facilities or leisure resources through segregated and "special" programs, but to enable persons with disabilities to become full participants in normal community life (Decker 1987). **Mainstreaming** is the term often used to describe this goal.

Mainstreaming: facilitating the goal that people with disabilities will be full participants in the traditions of their society.

Mainstreaming means providing mechanisms for individuals who have disabling conditions to participate in life according to typical circumstances, helping them become as independent as possible by joining the mainstream of society (Stein 1985). For example, once roller skating rink managers in southern Minnesota were made aware of how easy it was to push wheelchairs around the rink while skating, they began to promote family skating activities that included family members with disabilities. They encouraged these families to come regularly, supplying them with discount coupons. No separate times were set for skating by special populations. They were integrated into the community's schedule (Decker 1987).

Research on the pastimes of people with disabilities has characterized the pastimes as solitary and sedentary passive entertainments. A study of several hundred adults with physical disabilities by Kinney and Coyle (1989) found that among the top five favorite leisure activities, only one required exertion or interaction with other humans. Further, almost half of those surveyed could not identify more than three accessible recreation, sport, or cultural facilities in their community. This suggests another important concept for creating equality of opportunity for persons with disabilities. This is called **normalization.**

Normalization refers to the provision of as normal as possible life experiences, so individuals with disabilities can develop and maintain the interests and behaviors of their society (Wolfensberger 1972). When disabilities are severe, however, customized programs may be needed (Carter, Van Andel, and Robb 1985). Normalization does suggest that when there is need for customized, segregated programs, that they be as close to the cultural norm as possible, and that relatively normal behaviors be expected from participation. For example, participation in wheelchair basketball should be as close as possible to how basketball is played. Modifications to the rules should be minimal.

Maryland's Montgomery County Department of Recreation is an example of normalized and mainstreamed recreation services for all individuals (Bedini 1990). This system is based on the belief that people with disabilities

Normalization: providing normal experiences for people with disabilities.

Wheelchair basketball.
© Ruth V. Russell

are entitled to normal and integrated leisure experiences. The solution was simple. No special staff or services are provided for persons with disabilities; instead, programs and services are individualized. All people are helped to find those county facilities and activities that meet their needs. All staff are prepared to serve all kinds of people. There is also a leisure "buddy" system. Another example of the buddy system is Project Recreation, Fitness, and Development in Georgia (Cobb and Miko 1987). Each week college students who are enrolled in therapeutic recreation and adapted physical education classes at Georgia Southern College get together with nursing home residents, middle-aged adults from community mental health and mental retardation centers, and elementary school children from special education classes. They buddy up for two hours of one-on-one activities. There are fitness activities, games, social dances, crafts, team sports, tennis lessons, and swimming. Regular school, community, and home facilities are used.

To conclude, while leisure is assumed to be an important aspect in the quality of life for people, often people with disabilities are unable to take full advantage of the potential for leisure in their lives. This must be corrected, because leisure experiences provide the opportunity for maintaining personal autonomy, self-definition, and choice often absent from other aspects of their lives.

Ethnicity

Diversity of religion, thought, values, lifestyle, culture, language, and race have come to characterize contemporary life. Acceptance of such ethnic diversity is not yet complete, however. Human nature is only able to assimilate diversity slowly. Marked departures from the norm are usually viewed as inferior, threatening, and even contemptible. This is most true in democratic societies (Fox and Pope 1989) and no better example exists of people grappling with **ethnic** differences than in the United States. Americans in the year 1900 accepted far more ethnic diversity than did their ancestors a century earlier. It seems equally likely that their descendents in the year 2000 will accept far more still. Let's trace a bit of this history so we might imagine this future.

Ethnicity: a characteristic distinguished by common racial, national, tribal, religious, linguistic, or cultural background.

Changing Demographics

In the days of Thomas Jefferson, the American idea of religious tolerance generally stopped short of Catholicism. At the time, there were few Catholics in America, but with the onset of the great Irish potato famine in 1841, a flood of Irish immigrants suddenly came into the United States bringing their Catholic religion with them. Sometimes entire villages came, and because many of them were illiterate and poor, they lived in ghettos. Persecution followed. They could not find employment. Their children were denied entrance into schools. Their presence was unwelcome outside their own neighborhoods. For example, because they were perceived as being alcoholic, signs went up in saloons that read: "No Dogs or Irishmen Allowed."

Fairly easy acceptance of the Irish and their religion was ultimately possible, however, because they were never denied legal equality. No actions were formally taken against them, so they began to find work. Some even "struck it rich" in the gold fields in California—and became active in politics. As second and third generations adopted more American lifestyles and language, there were fewer ways to distinguish the Irish from everyone else. Other immigrant groups, such as European Jews, had similar assimilation experiences.

Other immigrant groups had tougher times. The horizons of toleration have not expanded fast enough for some Americans. For example, the Chinese first came to the United States as laborers. They were rounded up in groups in China and shipped to work the gold rush in California. They were model workers, which should have enabled them to easily follow the path of the Irish, but because the Chinese were a distinctive cultural and racial type, they were not accepted. Their culture was perceived as strange and evil. Rumors of fan-tan parlors, opium dens, and slave bordellos in "Chinatown" were rampant. As a result, their right to freely enjoy American society was denied. The daily persecution was worse. On the streets of San Francisco, "young hoodlums" spat in their faces and threw pepper in their eyes (Fox and Pope 1989). In 1882, Congress passed the Chinese Exclusion Act, which suspended immigration from China.

African immigrants received even worse treatment. They had the misfortune of being brought to the United States as slaves. Every horror that could befall human beings was a part of their early experience in America. They were not only enslaved but exploited, brutalized, degraded, ridiculed, murdered, and denied education. Their lives did not improve very rapidly after slavery ended. They were restricted to living in separate neighborhoods and learning in separate schools. They were forbidden to eat in what were viewed as white restaurants, see movies in white theaters, and use white recreational facilities. They endured laws and administrative actions that restricted their freedoms and denied them opportunities. In World War II, African Americans even went to war in segregated units.

By the war's end, however, the situation was ripe for change. In the Supreme Court's decision in *Brown v. Board of Education,* all United States schools were ordered to desegregate. There was no turning back. The following year, in Montgomery, Alabama, Rosa Parks, a foot-weary black woman on her way home from work, decided on the spur of the moment not to give up her bus seat to a white passenger as required by law. In a dozen other cities, African Americans sat down at lunch counters and asked for service. While some communities immediately made recreation facilities available to all citizens regardless of color, a few cities took action to dispose of their public recreation areas rather than integrate their use (Murphy 1972).

Because justice was on their side, however, under the leadership of the Reverend Martin Luther King, Jr., African Americans were slowly able to turn the power of government to their side. At Little Rock, Arkansas, in 1957, President Eisenhower called in the U.S. Army to supervise school desegregation.

biography　Sidney Poitier

Sidney Poitier is an American movie and stage actor. Born in Miami, Florida, in 1927, he spent his childhood years in the Bahamas. In 1945, he began taking acting lessons at the American Negro Theater in New York City and started appearing on the Broadway stage in 1948. His real fame, however, came from his movies. Beginning with the film *No Way Out* (1950), Poitier became a symbol of the initial breakthrough into realism for African-American performers in American films. Through such films as *The Blackboard Jungle* (1955), *Edge of the City* (1957), *Raisin in the Sun* (1961), and *Lilies of the Field* (1963), a realistic treatment of racial problems could be found for the first time.

Prior to this, popular culture helped to strengthen racism in the United States. Popular songs, jokes, magazine stories, television, and films all reinforced stereotypes of African Americans as "Sambo" and "Amos 'n Andy." With the films of Sidney Poitier, the stereotypes began to be shattered. Poitier is handsome, well-spoken, and a gentleman; this image, along with excellent scripts, helped demonstrate to the American public at the height of the Civil Rights Movement, that racism was wrong. Let's consider two films as examples.

In *To Sir With Love,* Poitier played a skilled engineer in search of employment, who winds up teaching high school on London's East Side. The tough and ill-behaved students reject his civilized ways, but he goes to work on them. Treating them as adults, speaking to them with respect, gently guiding them into an appreciation of the cultural arts, he begins to win them over. By the end of the film, "Sir," a title given to him by the students to show their respect, has completely captured their hearts. At the year's end dance, they make an emotional speech of appreciation, hand him a beautifully wrapped gift, and present a card with their signatures: "To Sir, With Love." The value of *To Sir With Love* was that race made no difference. It was his intelligence and compassion that civilized the students.

However, in *Guess Who's Coming to Dinner,* race made all the difference in the world. Joey Drayton, the daughter of a liberal San Francisco journalist, meets and falls in love with dashing John Wade Prentice, played by Poitier. Her father, of course, doubles back on the values of tolerance he so carefully instilled in his daughter as he struggles with what at the time was the bottom line of racial bigotry—interracial marriage. Eventually, Joey's father accepts the situation with open arms after he examines his principles.

Later, President Lyndon Johnson also championed racial justice. The turning point was finally reached in the mid-1960s when a series of laws gave African Americans economic and political rights.

These are the stories of immigrants to the United States. Irish, Chinese, and African, along with other major immigrant groups since the 1800s, such as those from Italy, Japan, Ukraine, Poland, and Vietnam in their turn experienced persecution for their ethnic differences. While their lives are still not discrimination-free, they have come closer to winning full economic, social, and political equality. The story of the Native Americans and many Hispanic Americans is complicated by the fact that they were not immigrants; they were here first. Lands occupied by European Americans had once been theirs.

For Native Americans, the reservation system, which gave them some protection and preserved some of their traditional cultures, also kept them separate and unequal. They were left impoverished and ill-educated. They were wards of the government, and outside the reservation were despised and persecuted. A particular animosity going all the way back to the Mexican War existed for Hispanic people. European Americans judged their culture as lazy.

While some Hispanic Americans were in the United States long before the westward movement, many came later from Cuba and Mexico as a result of political and economic turmoil. To avoid cultural conflict, most tried to be invisible by drifting from farm to farm during the growing season.

Eventually, encouraged by the progress of African Americans, Native Americans began demanding their rights. To dramatize their cause, they occupied the town of Wounded Knee, South Dakota, the site of a tragic massacre of their people in 1890. Hispanic Americans also came into a revolutionary self-awareness. In the early 1960s, they proudly renamed themselves Chicanos(as) and began speaking proudly about their race. Cesar Chavez led a successful grape boycott in California that demonstrated their political and economic power.

Gays and lesbians, whose difference crosses lines of religion, race, language, and national origin, have also made some progress in achieving societal tolerance and equality. Homosexuality is an emotional and physical attachment to members of one's own gender. It has been a part of human behavior in societies throughout history, but contemporary cultures have differed in their attitudes toward it. For example, in ancient Greece homosexuality was considered an ideal relationship; many men believed that only men could fulfill the role of true friend and lover. While some contemporary Western countries, such as The Netherlands, Sweden, Great Britain, and France have no laws against gays and lesbians, the struggle for their civil rights in the United States has moved more slowly.

Change began for homosexual Americans in June 1969 when crowds demonstrated following a police raid on the Stonewall Inn, a popular gay bar in Greenwich Village, New York City. For gay men and lesbians nationwide, the riots were considered a moral victory and a call to arms for the birth of the modern gay political movement (Pela 1994). The Gay Liberation Front was formed, and it and other groups throughout the country began lobbying for pro-gay political candidates and legislation. In 1961, Illinois became the first state to abolish its laws against homosexual acts. Since the 1970s, several U.S. cities and states have passed laws banning discrimination against gays and lesbians in employment, housing, and other areas. However, voters in some regions later repealed these laws. Today, the struggle for equality continues, but some progress has been made in overcoming legal and economic persecution.

These and other civil rights movements changed American society. Americans began to accept that they were not one people, one lifestyle, or one "melting pot" of values. They were many peoples, styles, and values. This acceptance and encouragement of diversity is called **pluralism** and is a departure from the historic human need for homogeneity. Americans have not yet achieved absolute pluralism. Such pluralism maintains that everyone should be equally accepted and free to do as he or she wishes, and Americans have so far been unwilling to carry it to its logical extreme. Many groups of people do not enjoy full societal toleration.

Pluralism: a state of society in which members of diverse ethnic groups maintain separate participation in their traditional cultures.

What has been the impact of ethnic pluralism on leisure in the United States? In a pluralistic society, everyone has opportunity and access to the good life. Have leisure values and behaviors helped or hindered the drive to acceptance of diversity?

Defining and Empowering Ethnicity Through Leisure

Leisure can be a tool for distinguishing ethnic groups. It is also a tool for empowering people of all ethnicities. Several decades ago, it was believed that leisure did just the opposite. For example, writers such as Meyer and Brightbill (1964) claimed that leisure's value was in helping assimilate people of different backgrounds—a kind of blending into the American lifestyle could be achieved by playing baseball or basketball. Now it is believed that the leisure interests and participation patterns of a particular racial, religious, or other group help to ethnically explain them. Because of unique constraints and opportunities, there is a tendency toward participation in certain activities among certain ethnic groups. Leisure provides the means for expression of ethnic individuality and identity. One example is leisure's role in the lives of black Americans.

Black Americans are diverse in their roots and their needs. Some can trace their ancestors back to different African countries, while others came to the United States more recently from other places such as the Carribean Islands. Black Americans are diverse in their pastime pursuits as well. In what ways is their ethnic identity defined by leisure? One answer is from the research literature that compares leisure interests and behaviors. A review of several studies (Stamps and Stamps 1985) concluded that southern African Americans usually participate in inexpensive, close-to-home forms of leisure. Middle-class blacks typically participate in activities comparable to whites, such as travel, and participant and spectator sports; and there is a heavy involvement in church activities regardless of economic class. The review also summarized that the leisure patterns of African Americans persist over time, even after they migrate from rural to urban areas.

Another review of research studies (Dwyer and Gobster 1992) indicated a generally lower participation among African Americans in outdoor pastimes, such as camping and hiking, and higher participation in active, social, and urban-oriented activities, such as picnicking. Other studies have also indicated a lower rate of participation in winter sports. To cite one particular study, the research by Hutchison (1987) confirmed that meaningful cultural differences between ethnic groups did produce distinctive patterns of pastimes. By doing field observations of thirteen neighborhood parks in Chicago, Hutchison found that peer groups are an important leisure context for African Americans. This was particularly true for young males.

For black Americans and other ethnic groups, the goal of pluralistic society is to provide leisure opportunities that enhance their diversity. There still are barriers to them taking full advantage of the potential for

leisure in their lives. This must be corrected, because leisure experiences provide the opportunity for maintaining personal autonomy, self-definition, and choice often absent from other aspects of their lives.

Invisible People

In addition to women, people with disabilities, and ethnic groups, leisure and equality will be considered for one final group of individuals. These are labeled *invisible* people. The term *invisible* is used to denote people living with particular situations that have left them out of customary leisure services. The discussion includes people who are homeless, people who are unemployed, migrant workers, latchkey children, and AIDS/HIV victims.

People Who Are Homeless

You know where they got this little private club, down the end of the block. . . . There's garbage cans back there, but they're paper cans, not garbage. They're clean. And many a night, you know, in the summer time, I'd go in there, turn the barrels over, and put a pasteboard box there, and turn that barrel and stick my feet in it, and maybe I'd stick my head and shoulders in this damn pasteboard box, well I was out of sight. I'd lay there with half my body in a garbage can and the upper half in a pasteboard box. Until someone kicks that can or tries to load it and you better get out!

From J. P. Spradley, *You Owe Yourself a Drunk: An Ethnography of Urban Nomads.*
Copyright © 1970 Little, Brown and Company.

Having a home. The idea conjures up images of warmth, love, safety, comfort, food, and companionship. Millions of Americans are without this basic condition most of us take for granted. Homelessness is a condition of being without regular shelter (Kunstler 1991). People who are homeless try to find a public or private sponsored shelter at night or sleep in makeshift dwellings, such as a car or building doorways. Although the homeless condition is not new to the world, its rapid rate of increase in particularly the United States is new. Although homeless people have become visible to residents of cities, they are invisible in terms of receiving leisure services. This is ironic, as the park is a common "home" for those who are homeless. Let's investigate these seeming contradictions.

Early in the twentieth century, the homeless person was depicted as the "skid row bum" or the "hobo." Usually a middle-aged, alcoholic, white male, he received little sympathy and was viewed with contempt as lazy, dangerous, and worthless. Most American cities had a **skid row,** a section of town where these men found shelter and were out of sight from the rest of the citizenry (Kunstler 1991). The economic depression of the 1930s caused an increase in the numbers and breadth of the homeless to include younger people and women. World War II quickly absorbed many homeless men and women through employment in the war industries. Post-war prosperity and more generous social security benefits enabled many more people to afford their own housing during the 1950s and 1960s.

Skid row: the label originally from a street in Seattle where logs were skidded to the sawmill. It was lined with flop houses, taverns, and gambling halls. The name for such parts of towns often became skid row as it was adopted throughout the country.

C ase *Study*   **In Search of Intelligent Life**

Trudy:

Here we are, standing on the corner of
"Walk, Don't Walk."
You look away from me, tryin' not to catch my eye,
but you didn't turn fast enough, did you?

You don't like my raspy voice, do you?
I got this raspy voice
'cause I have to yell all the time
'cause nobody around here ever
LISTENS to me.

You don't like that I scratch so much; yes, and excuse me,
I scratch so much
'cause my neurons are
on fire.

And I admit my smile is not at its Pepsodent best
'cause I think my
caps must've somehow got
osteoporosis.

And if my eyes seem to be twirling around like fruit flies—
the better to see you with, my dears!

Look at me,
you mammalian-brained LUNKHEADS!
I'm not just talking to myself. I'm talking to you, too.
And to you
and you
and you
and you and you and you!

I know what you're thinkin'; you're thinkin' I'm crazy.
You think I give a hoot? You people
look at my shopping bags,
call me crazy 'cause I save this junk. What should we call
the ones who
buy it?

Selected excerpts from pp. 13–15 from *The
Search for Signs of Intelligent Life in the
Universe* by Jane Wagner. Copyright © 1986
by Jane Wagner Inc. Reprinted by permission
of HarperCollins Publishers, Inc.

In the fall of 1985, a play premiered at the Plymouth Theater in New York City. It was strangely titled "The Search for Signs of Intelligent Life in the Universe"; it was a one actor show starring Lily Tomlin. The play was a huge success in spite of its warning that it told the "truth" about American society. In the play, Tomlin plays several different characters. The major narrator is Trudy, a bag lady who has been "certified" mad, but whose madness is really a perception of society from the underside (French 1986). The script of the play does not place blame for the social problems it addresses; it focuses on our anxiety and on our dangerous tendency to harden ourselves against these problems.

Trudy:

I made some studies, and
reality is the leading cause of stress amongst those in
touch with it. I can take it in small doses, but as a lifestyle
I found it too confining.
It was just too needful;
it expected me to be there for it all the time, and with all
I have to do—
I had to let something go.

Perhaps the reality of people who are homeless is too strong to ignore any longer. Reality has become just too needful. Today, to most Americans homelessness seems neither invisible nor insurmountable. According to a 1993 survey (Clements 1994) of 2,503 women and men, nearly nine out of ten (89 percent) viewed homelessness as a major problem throughout the U.S., and 76 percent said "something could be done." Most surprising, in contrast to earlier attitudes toward people on skid rows, 56 percent of those surveyed think that most of the homeless are not responsible for the situation they are in.

Questions to Consider and Discuss

1. Do you ever worry that you could become homeless?
2. Do you personally donate money, time, or effort for the homeless?
3. Do you think most homeless people are responsible for the situation they are in?

Beginning in the 1980s, there was again a sharp increase in the number and breadth of homeless people. Although accurate statistics are difficult to calculate, today's estimates are that every night in the United States between 2 and 4 million men, women, and children are without shelter. In addition to the typical homeless person as unemployed, middle-aged, single, white, and male, most of the new homeless are families, unaccompanied youth, deinstitutionalized mental patients, and ethnic minorities. They are young; many are children. Some have severe physical problems, such as drug and alcohol addiction, tuberculosis, and AIDS. Some are victims of domestic violence or runaways. Some do hold jobs or are employable, but they earn so little that they can't afford rent. One classic research study labeled them as "urban nomads" (Spradley 1970) and characterized their existence as mobile, alienated, and poor. Their culture possesses a unique set of survival strategies.

As with any social problem, the solutions are not simple because the causes are complex. A shrinking number of rental properties and a precipitous rise in rents have been partly to blame for homelessness. This has been caused to some degree by **gentrification.** In the 1980s, cities replaced many worn out buildings in downtown areas with high-rent property and condominiums. These areas became fashionable addresses. Other causes of contemporary homelessness are the withdrawal of the federal government from the provision of low-income housing and a reduction of federal subsidies for rent assistance. Also, real wages have fallen in the last twenty years for blue-collar and unskilled jobs. The inability of community health centers to provide needed support services to the deinstitutionalized mentally ill has also been cited as a factor in the increase of homelessness.

Gentrification: the immigration of middle-class people into recently renewed urban areas.

Providing help to people who are homeless is complicated. Negative stereotypes abound, and public policy is at a loss for remedies. For example, during the summer months and in warm climates, the homeless frequently live in parks. Should leisure service agencies be more active in providing parks as homes? Often local residents feel threatened by the presence of the homeless in their neighborhood parks and demand that the park agency bar the homeless from the park. Situations such as this have resulted in a tendency to want to punish rather than help. In trying to serve the homeless, agencies often reinforce a cycle that saps self-esteem and sense of control over life (Kunstler 1991). This happens when agencies try to distance people who are homeless from the rest of society. This is inappropriate for a group that is already desperately isolated from things that make people feel human. Services are needed to help homeless people overcome social isolation from family, friends, and the community.

The current approach to solving the problems of homelessness primarily has been providing an overnight shelter and a meal (Kunstler 1992). Most cities have responded by converting such city-owned facilities as gymnasiums into temporary shelters. While food and shelter are certainly logical places to start, some of these solutions shortsightedly see homeless people as worthless rather than victims of a societal condition of inequity. However, as attitudes have begun to awaken, so have new solutions.

Case Study KYTES

The graffiti on the bridge columns over the rail yards and abandoned warehouses reads "Eat the Rich." Until they were chased out by fire hoses, hundreds of street youths and other people without homes lived in this industrial underbelly of the city of Toronto. Now they perform Shakespeare.

"There are thousands and thousands of desperate youth who have no prospects for a better future," said Ned Dickens, the producer. "We're trying to show that you really can do something for them that means something" (Farnsworth 1993, 16). Dickens is director of the Kensington Youth Theater and Employment Skills, a local organization known as KYTES, that helps street youths change their way of life through the staging of theatrical works for the public. One of their most ambitious productions was *Romeo and Juliet.*

Each year, more than 200 youths apply for 44 places (about 15,000 of Toronto's homeless population is under age eighteen). The entire troupe includes about 100 people. They've made both a stage and sleeping quarters of an old illegal dump site a hundred feet beneath the bridge. Canadian National Railways owns the land and gave KYTES permission to use it. Each cast member also gets high school credit during the five-month program. However, the main benefit seems to be that the kids actually achieve something that they set out to do.

Katrin calls herself a "positive statistic" (Farnsworth 1993). When Katrin was fifteen years old and after her mother remarried, she left home, dropped out of high school, and was out on bail after being charged with car theft. She had been living as a vagrant when she was accepted into KYTES. She gave a stunning performance as Juliet. Eventually, she entered the University of Toronto. Another "positive statistic" is Irwin. On the streets since he was fourteen years old, he became the lightboard operator for KYTES. Since learning the necessary electrician's skills, he has plans to parlay them into permanent work.

Every night, hundreds of people walk down a weedy dirt path into this theater under the railway bridge. Sometimes the sound system has to make special adjustments because of wind or humidity. The audience sits on plastic milk cartons listening to a production that competes with sirens, trains, helicopters, and streetcars rumbling overhead.

Questions to Consider and Discuss

1. Does this sound like a bizarre solution to homelessness? Why do you think it has been so successful?
2. Conduct a community survey where you live. What is the size of your homeless population? How would you describe them demographically? What services and solutions are being tried in your community?
3. If you were a social service agency in your community (such as a parks and recreation department or a community mental health center), what solution would you want to try?

From New York City, which has the nation's largest homeless population, come these ideas (Kunstler 1992). A city hospital has established a residential treatment program for homeless mentally ill men in which a therapeutic recreation specialist helps them develop a hierarchy of daily living skills, function as group members, communicate, and express their feelings. To help them accomplish this, the men run a coffee shop and participate in discussion, music, and drama groups. Also in New York City, a network of community-based youth centers serves homeless children living in welfare hotels by providing transportation to an after-school recreation program. Elsewhere, at a city-sponsored shelter, children are provided structured and unstructured recreational activities, such as games, sports, crafts, and day trips. These services help create the capacity for independent living by raising self-esteem, learning social interaction skills, and developing a sense of community.

In conclusion, while leisure is assumed to be an important part of a quality life, people who are homeless are unable to take full advantage of the potential for leisure in their lives. This must be corrected, because leisure experiences provide the opportunity for maintaining personal autonomy, self-definition, and choice often absent from other aspects of their lives.

People Who Are Unemployed

People have jobs because they want to work. They want to feel productive and do something that has value to themselves and others. People also have jobs because they have to work. They need the income being employed provides. For both these reasons, unemployment is usually undesirable. While a small amount of unemployment (4 to 6 percent) is good for an economy because it signals adjustments to job growth, and a small amount of unemployment (such as weekends, holidays, and vacations) is good for human beings because it provides rest and recovery, unemployment in general is usually considered a sign of inefficiency in an economy and worthlessness in a person. For example, an increase of 1 percent in the unemployment rate in the U.S. causes a loss to the economy of about $75 billion, enough money to provide scholarships of $10,000 for every full-time college student in the U.S. (Fox and Pope 1989).

Unemployment is increasing all over the world. While the absolute number of jobs has gone up in the United States during the last two decades, more people need jobs (table 11.1). In addition, many of these new jobs are low-paying, dead-end positions. A recent estimate of the growth of middle- and upper-management positions over the next several years is about 20 percent, while the pool of employees hoping to secure such positions will grow by about 42 percent (Dannefer 1983).

How does unemployment affect people? Individuals who become unemployed seem to have different experiences, but for most, a decrease in financial ability results. There is also the emotional side. Based on research studies, Smith and Simpkins (1980) described the stages of people's psychological reactions to unemployment as

- Euphoria—feeling liberated from work

- Shock—realizing the economic implication of being unemployed

- Optimism—trying to get a new job

- Pessimism—feeling depressed and defeated

- Fatalism—accepting the stigma of being unemployed

The condition also usually produces feelings of humiliation, uselessness, and inadequacy, which often result in health and social problems. One theorist (Jahoda 1981) developed the latent deprivation model of unemployment. It emphasizes that most people in society require employment to obtain time structure, social experience, purpose, status, and identity. Loss of these has negative psychological consequences.

Unemployed: all individuals over sixteen years of age who are not in school and who are actively seeking work. Unemployment statistics do not include anyone over sixteen years of age who is not in school and not employed but is not actively seeking employment.

Table 11.1

Percent Unemployed, 1980 to 1992

Characteristic	1980	1985	1990	1992
Total	7.1	7.2	5.5	7.4
Male	6.9	7.0	5.6	7.8
Female	7.4	7.4	5.4	6.9
White	6.3	6.2	4.7	6.5
African American	14.3	15.1	11.3	14.1
Hispanic American	10.1	10.5	8.0	11.4
20–24 years old	11.5	11.1	8.8	11.3
45–64 years old	3.7	4.5	3.5	5.1

Source: U.S. Bureau of Labor Statistics 1993.

One outcome of these losses is a change in leisure interests and participation. In a study by Burman (1988), the unemployed people in the sample regarded free time created from unemployment not as leisure but as unwanted idleness. Some studies have found that unemployed people spend a longer time in bed than before and lose interest in previously enjoyed hobbies (Smith and Simpkins 1980). Another study (Bunker, Dewbarry, and Kelvin 1983) found an increasing interest in sedentary activities such as reading, listening to the radio, and watching television with unemployment. On the whole, unemployed people are relatively inactive (Kay 1989).

In many ways, unemployment and leisure are fundamentally incompatible. While leisure is regarded as a pleasurable and freely chosen experience, the experience of unemployment is rarely pleasant and the unemployed seldom feel free to use their time as they please. Also, the depression and lethargy that afflicts them discourages participation in pastime activities. When they are out-of-work, few adults are motivated to construct a lifestyle based on leisure.

Nonetheless, there is extensive evidence that participation in pastimes during unemployment benefits individuals: those who are active seem to find the psychological effects of unemployment less severe. In the face of research that indicates a typical decrease in leisure during unemployment, what kind of meaningful role can leisure have? Currently, providers of leisure services are trying to determine how best to help.

From the attempts so far, **intervention** seems to be a useful role for leisure. For example, unemployed workers in Norway who participated in a recreational sport program (calisthenics, volleyball, badminton, swimming) during their unemployed time said they "felt better" and had more energy (Fasting 1986). In Sault Ste. Marie, Ontario, Canada, the intervention was community-based. Services for the unemployed were carried out by many community agencies. They also found that what they thought the unemployed

Intervention: something (such as leisure) that modifies the normal course of events.

Does Jobless Mean Lifeless?

Leisure has the potential to benefit the jobless person greatly, yet does it actually do this? Can leisure activity be a substitute for work in maintaining emotional health? How does one's leisure life change as a result of the absence of work?

Let's consider these questions in more depth. A study conducted by Reid (1990) examined the changes in leisure behavior of workers who were subjected to layoffs. Respondents were both men and women, mostly between the ages of twenty-four and forty-four. The setting was the industrial community of Sault Ste. Marie, Ontario, Canada. Data about leisure participation patterns both before and after the layoff were collected using a questionnaire that asked the unemployed respondents to think back to their lives before the layoff. This is a research technique called a retrospective—remembering past behaviors.

Many of the respondents reported that their leisure activity patterns did not change drastically between the employed and unemployed condition. As shown in the following table, however, overall leisure participation for the sample decreased after the layoff. Travel, the highest cost activity, experienced the largest percent decrease. Recreational sport participation (less intense than competitive sport participation) and entertainment (attending the theater and cinema) experienced drops in participation by at least 20 percent of the sample. In fact, all categories of activities considered in the study experienced net decreases in level of activity.

The most pronounced change in leisure activity patterns happened during the first three months of unemployment with little change observed after that. In fact, a slight increase in leisure participation seemed to occur for those unemployed for five years or more. As expected, the data also demonstrated that as income decreased, activities requiring larger expenditures of money (such as travel and entertainment) decreased more than those that required little or no financial expenditures (such as home hobbies and family activities).

The results of this study seem to show that unemployment not only affects needed was opposite of what the unemployed themselves thought they needed. In response, the leisure agencies in Sault Ste. Marie found it better to set up a communication link with the unemployed (Reid 1987). In some British communities, leisure service agencies have been successful in maximizing facility use at off-peak times by the unemployed. This has also included teaching new skills and creating opportunities for people who are unemployed to enjoy social contact with others who are also unemployed (Kay 1989).

While leisure is assumed to be an important aspect in the quality of life for people, unemployed people are unable to take full advantage of the potential for leisure in their lives. This must be corrected, because leisure experiences provide the opportunity for maintaining personal autonomy, self-definition, and choice often absent from other aspects of their lives.

one's work life but has the potential to disrupt other areas of life as well. While the study found that the majority of the unemployed attempted to maintain their established pattern of leisure activities, many reduced or eliminated some activity completely during a phase in their life when free time increased. The study also found that the lack of financial resources is a major constraint in pursuing leisure activity during unemployment.

These findings might lead to the conclusion that if providers of leisure services, such as city recreation departments and sport clubs, provided activities free of charge the problem of reduced leisure in unemployment would be solved. Does the reason for decreased leisure activity during unemployment run deeper than this? What other factors, besides money, may have an impact on the quality of life during unemployment? Some researchers have suggested that the main problem of unemployment is the change of social position. They believe that decreased leisure involvement is a result of loss of social position. How would you design a study to investigate this?

Activity	Percent Decrease	Percent Increase	Percent Discontinued
Travel	30	12	27
Competitive sport	19	8	14
Recreational sport	22	10	14
Entertainment	21	14	9
Home hobbies	17	12	5
Community service	14	7	12
Family activities	17	12	11
Educational activity	18	12	17
Social activity	16	13	10

Migrant Workers

As a result of economic, political, and natural difficulties in particular parts of the world, there are again large numbers of immigrants. They move from eastern parts of Germany to western parts of Germany, from Cambodia to Thailand, and from Sudan to Kenya. The United States is also experiencing a major influx of immigrants. Currently, people of Hispanic and Asian origins make up the majority, and it is estimated that by the first quarter of the twenty-first century, Hispanic Americans will comprise the largest minority group. Already these new immigrants are changing the politics, economies, and social life of the country.

One special category of immigrants is the migrant worker. Whereas immigrants arrive with the intention of settling permanently, migrants are people who are temporarily in the country for economic reasons. They move repeatedly in search of work. They often perform "stooped labor," such as cultivating crops, cleaning public restrooms, and assembly line work. They are paid low wages and, therefore, are a pivotal part of the economy. Because many are contracted in their own countries and brought into the United States illegally, they are easily abused. They are sometimes denied basic legal rights and are often ill-housed and malnourished. In the early 1990s, the United States deported more than 1 million undocumented workers a year.

Until the twentieth century, most of the U.S. migrant workers were citizens. Now most are workers from other countries. In the U.S., migrant workers tend to be Hispanic. Unlike typical immigrants, they usually do not come as family units. Most are young males, employed primarily by large farm associations. Although much of their salary goes home, some is spent in the U.S. Unfortunately, however, much of it is spent for taboo pleasures: alcohol, drugs, prostitution, and gambling (Sessoms and Orthner 1992).

These typical activity choices of migrant workers may be the result of their invisibility. For example, migrant workers are typically unaware of the opportunities and systems for more wholesome leisure that are available to them. Also, because migrant workers are in particular areas for short periods of time—usually the planting and harvesting seasons—community systems for providing wholesome leisure are slow to respond. Differences in language and culture are major deterrents as well.

Some communities have been able to reach out to their temporary residents. They have created special programs and festivals, using religious holidays as the theme. Such a simple action as a dual-language sign to inform migrants of the policies for using a park or lake has also helped. In Florida, an after-school and Saturday program was developed for migrant children of the Everglades Labor Camp. This is supervised by bilingual (English/Spanish) recreation specialists.

To conclude, while leisure is assumed to be an important aspect in the quality of life for people, people who are migrant workers are unable to take full advantage of the potential for leisure in their lives. This must be corrected, because leisure experiences provide the opportunity for maintaining personal autonomy, self-definition, and choice often absent from other aspects of life.

Latchkey Children

As a society, we have been loathe to recognize the chronic problems that plague the American household. We prefer to romanticize the family. We want to see rosy cheeked children coming home after school to a steaming bowl of Campbell's chicken noodle soup, and mothers and fathers tumbling joyously in the autumn leaves with their kids in a game of touch football. Unfortunately this is a fantasy. One reason it is not true is that the married couple, living together in traditional ways, continues to decline in the 1990s. In 1940, 90 percent of American households were headed by married couples. Government information shows that by 1992, 55 percent of America's households were headed by married couples (U.S. Bureau of Census 1993). Today, the typical household is just as likely to be single-parent families, nonmarried adults, or people living alone. One outcome is that a growing number of school-age children are regularly without adult supervision for a part of the day. Of children aged five to thirteen years enrolled in school, about 2.1 million are considered **latchkey children.**

In spite of statistics such as these, the fantasy about the family persists. One reason is the glorification of parenting; being a mother or a father is highly respected. It is an article of faith that infants and small children need constant attention and love. As they grow older, they also require education and moral training; thus, parenting is an important job. One might expect that parenting was always esteemed. Afterall, newborn babies in the fifteenth century were just as helpless as those in the twentieth century. However, as Schor (1992) pointed out, 300 years ago, parents acted very differently—children were not "raised" in today's sense of the term.

Historians of the family have discovered that standards of parenting, particularly for mothers, have been dramatically upgraded over the years. Before the sixteenth century in England and other parts of Europe, parent-child relationships were much less emotional. For the most part, children were not cared for by their parents. The rich had little to do with their children until they were grown. Infants were given to wet nurses and older children were sent off to school. Children in poorer families fared no better. They became servants or apprentices at early ages. Economic stress made proper care of children virtually impossible; time for mothering was an unaffordable luxury because women had to work. In all families, infants and children were routinely left unattended for long periods of time. To make them less of a nuisance, babies were wrapped in swaddling clothes, their limbs completely immobilized. Children were given opium to keep them in a stupor until parents returned home (Razzell and Wainwright 1973).

Eventually, some of these child-rearing practices faded away. More caring attitudes began to emerge in the eighteenth century in both Europe and the United States. Parental affection became more common. Spurred on by religious reformers, the biggest changes came in the nineteenth century. The idealization of mother love, with vigilant attention to the needs of children, came to dominate. By the end of the nineteenth century, a bona-fide mothers' movement emerged. As the "century of the child" opened, mothers and fathers were providing their children with all manner of new services (Schor 1992, 93). The legacy of child neglect gave way to the most intensive parenting process in human history. We now teach children to read and count before they go to school. We convert whole rooms of the house to playrooms. We toilet train them, give them daily baths, chauffeur them to school and activities, worry about their nutrition and exposure to germs, and take them to psychiatrists.

No wonder that as current economic conditions require both adults in two-parent families to work and as the typical family is increasingly likely to be headed by a single adult, we feel great concern about the slipping standards of caring for children. We blame poor parenting for many problems ranging from

Latchkey child: a young child who must spend part of the day at home without adult supervision. Latchkey refers to the key to a front door and is used to describe that the children let themselves in after school.

poor academic performance to rudeness, from delinquency to being overweight, from bullying behaviors to boredom. Children appear to be less physically fit because they watch too much television. Parents are blamed for this. As parents have become busier, television has assumed a major role in raising children. However, some statistics are surprising. According to one study (Institute for Social Research 1986), the total time children spent each week watching TV was fourteen hours and forty-nine minutes for children of employed mothers and sixteen hours and thirteen minutes for children whose mothers were homemakers.

What are the effects of reduced attention by parents? Are latchkey children disadvantaged? One assumption is that children who spend a large portion of their lives without parents or other caregivers suffer from severe problems. Is this accurate? What is the role of leisure?

Historically, the school day ended at 3:00 P.M. to allow children time to reach their rural homes and help their parents with farm chores before dark. For most children in American society, this schedule is no longer relevant. Now, unless children are involved in after-school study or recreation programs, they have at least two hours of unobligated time every weekday afternoon. While the impact of this on children's school performance, safety, stability, social adjustment, and other qualities is not well understood, there is the perception in American society that this time should be meaningfully filled.

The most frequent solution has been an after-school recreation program. School systems, city recreation and park departments, churches, voluntary youth agencies, commercial day care agencies, and others offer a wide array of programs that include sports, crafts, hobbies, cultural arts, and homework tutoring. Frequently, "late" bus service is also provided. Other solutions tried in some areas are telephone check-in services where an adult calls the child at home everyday after school, and flexible work hours for parents. In one city, a community program called "police partners" turned the children into extra eyes and ears for the police.

To conclude, while leisure is an important aspect in the quality of life for people, latchkey children are unable to take full advantage of the potential for leisure in their lives. This must be corrected, because leisure experiences provide the opportunity for maintaining personal autonomy, self-definition, and choice often absent from other aspects of their lives.

People with AIDS

As of June 1993, 626,076 cases of AIDS had been reported in the United States for children and adults (*HIV/AIDS Surveillance Report* 1993). About two-thirds of these people have died from the disease. This represents the tip of the iceberg. The Center for Disease Control insists that cases are underreported by 15 to 20 percent, and other estimates maintain that 1 million Americans have been infected (Grossman 1993). This makes AIDS a public health crisis. It is also a new crises; the first AIDS cases were reported in 1981 and are believed to have been introduced and spread via tourism. While most of the cases since then have been reported in the United States, 162 countries also have reported cases, particularly in the Sub-Saharan African countries.

AIDS (Acquired Immune Deficiency Syndrome) is a virus that attacks the immune system. HIV (Human Immunodeficiency Virus) is the virus that causes AIDS. HIV infects several different cells of the immune system, and as more cells become infected, there are fewer available to fight off disease. Thus, diseases a healthy immune system can overcome, such as pneumonia, become very powerful and ultimately can kill. HIV is found in many different body fluids. Blood, semen, and vaginal secretions have the greatest concentration of HIV and are most capable of transmission of the virus between people. While most (60 percent) of the reported cases of AIDS have been spread by the sexual actions of homosexual men and improper use of needles by intravenous drug abusers (21 percent), the fastest growing rates of transmission are for women (particularly African American and Hispanic American) between the ages of twenty and forty engaged in heterosexual activities and children who acquire the virus at birth from infected mothers. AIDS is also spreading fastest in rural America. By the year 2000, it is estimated that at least 40 million people worldwide will be carrying HIV, costing about $100 billion for treatment (Grossman 1993).

No cure or vaccine for AIDS exists; thus, the human cost is the most devastating. Victims typically endure a loss of physical strength, mental alertness, ability to work and be self-sufficient, social roles, housing, and sometimes the emotional support of loved ones. The diagnosis of AIDS is traumatic because the disease takes a progressive course and ultimately ends in death. Many people with HIV and AIDS experience stigmatization and discrimination.

In the absence of effective medical therapy, education and risk reduction have become the most useful tools in fighting AIDS. These preventative measures represent an opportunity for leisure service agencies to help. Park and recreation organizations can establish HIV/AIDS hotlines, speakers bureaus, condom availability sites, needle exchange sites, and other services. Because of the stigma and discrimination associated with the disease, there is a barrier to effective prevention education. Therefore, these services could be located in places that are a part of a community's mainstream, such as the YMCA, Scout programs, and city recreation facilities.

Once people have contracted HIV/AIDS, a role for leisure service agencies continues. Therapeutic recreation professionals can be a part of health service teams that specialize in treating people. Community recreation organizations can provide support groups for HIV positive individuals, those with AIDS, and their families and friends. Government agencies can provide financial, housing, legal, and food assistance programs for people with HIV/AIDS. Most importantly is the provision of leisure experiences for people with the disease. Leisure activities can enhance feelings of self-worth, self-esteem, and integrity. They can help people achieve a sense of empowerment, hope, and friendship. Special leisure programs can help patients with AIDS learn to cope with free time due to joblessness and loneliness due to separation from families and friends. Leisure programs offer them an opportunity to express their feelings, both verbally and nonverbally, as they are dying.

While leisure is assumed to be an important aspect in the quality of life for people, persons with AIDS are unable to take full advantage of the potential for leisure in their lives. This must be corrected, because leisure experiences provide the opportunity for maintaining personal autonomy, self-definition, and choice often absent from other aspects of their lives.

Summary: Achieving Equity in Leisure

Often, through leisure, equality of opportunity can be achieved. In this chapter, leisure as part of the problem and part of the solution has been advocated. For women, people with disabilities, ethnic groups, and individuals whose circumstances make them invisible from service providers, leisure is both the context for inequality and the tool for correcting inequality. The goal is to tip the balance between these two outcomes, using leisure as an equalizer.

How can we make this happen? Leisure's ability to create wholesome and healthy lifestyles requires the removal of barriers that obstruct opportunities. A useful classification of these barriers to leisure participation (and to all of life's opportunities for that matter) are situational, dispositional, and institutional (Cross 1981). Situational barriers might include lack of time or monetary resources that prevents participation in certain kinds of activities. Another situational barrier for some, such as youth, could be lack of support from peers. Dispositional barriers are attitudinal and might include lack of confidence in one's self and abilities, lack of knowledge about available programs and services, and feelings of being unwelcome or an outsider. Finally, institutional barriers could occur when leisure services cater to the needs and interests of one group of people to the exclusion of others.

Leisure service managers must assume responsibility for eliminating these barriers. Situational barriers, especially activities that require money and separate the "haves" from the "have not's" should be prime targets. Let's consider a college or university recreation program as an example. An annual spring weekend celebration that includes a concert, a spectator sport activity, a golf tournament, and a banquet for $125 per couple is a situational barrier to many students. Students attending college with the help of financial aid will probably not be able to attend. However, by selling low-cost "work-celebrate" tickets (reduced price tickets in exchange for a certain number of hours of helping run the event), a broader array of students can be included in the event (Stage and Manning 1992).

To continue the college illustration, a common dispositional barrier to student participation in campus recreation activities is a lack of knowledge about them. For example, on some campuses, activities are publicized through the school paper, which is often available by subscription. An advertisement publicizing an upcoming deadline for intramural soccer team signups might be missed by international students who have not been provided money for the student paper in their budgets. By posting an announcement in residence halls where international students live or at an office for international students, this dispositional barrier might be overcome (Stage and Manning 1992).

Institutional barriers to leisure opportunities on a college campus could occur when needs and interests of only one kind of student are considered. While much has been gained recently to remove these barriers, many programs are deeply ingrained in the institutions and not easily altered. Homecoming, for example, traditionally reflects the tastes and values of the dominant culture of students. When campus leaders provide **multicultural** programs and events, with cooperation, recommendations, and participation of diverse students, greater equity of leisure opportunities is achieved.

Multicultural: a recognition and valuing of a broad array of cultures.

Helping to create a multicultural society is an important contemporary goal for professionals who provide leisure services. It requires that all leisure interests, values, and patterns be respected. Racial and ethnic minorities, persons with disabilities, gays and lesbians, people of different religious beliefs, and many others make up the rich mosaic of contemporary society. Since leisure represents a major societal phenomenon, with strong links to economics and politics, equality of opportunity through pastimes can be enhanced.

References

Bedini, L. 1990. Separate but equal? Segregated programming for people with disabilities. *Journal of Physical Education, Recreation and Dance* 40 (October): 40–44.

Bunker, N., C. Dewberry, and P. Kelvin. 1983. Unemployment and use of time: Methods and preliminary results of a research enquiry. In *Newsletter supplement,* no. 1, edited by S. Glyptis. Leisure Studies Association.

Burman, P. W. 1988. *Killing time, losing ground: Experiences of unemployment.* Toronto: Wall and Thompson.

Carter, M. J., G. E. Van Andel, and G. M. Robb. 1985. *Therapeutic recreation: A practical approach.* St. Louis, MO: Times Mirror/Mosby.

Clements, M. 1994. What Americans say about the homeless. *Parade Magazine.* 9 January, 4–6.

Cobb, P. R., and P. S. Miko. 1987. Project Recreation, Fitness and Development. *Journal of Physical Education, Recreation and Dance* (April): 54–56.

Cross, K. P. 1981. *Adults as learners: Increasing participation and facilitating learning.* San Francisco: Jossey-Bass.

Dannefer, D. 1983. Age structure, values and the organization of work: Some implications for research and policy. *Futures* 7: 8–13.

Decker, J. 1987. A social process: Integrating people with disabilities into community recreation. *Journal of Physical Education, Recreation and Dance* (April): 50–53.

Dwyer, J., and P. Gobster. 1992. Recreation opportunity and cultural diversity. *Parks and Recreation* 16: 19–21.

Farnsworth, C. H. 1993. Toronto's homeless turn to the Bard. *International Herald Tribune,* 19 August, 16.

Fasting, K. 1986. The effect of recreational sports on the quality of life of the unemployed. *Sport and aging. The 1984 Olympic scientific congress proceedings, Vol. 5,* edited by B. D. McPherson. Champaign, IL: Human Kinetics.

Fox, F. W., and C. L. Pope. 1989. *American heritage: An interdisciplinary approach.* Dubuque, IA: Kendall/Hunt.

French, M. 1986. Afterword to *The search for signs of intelligent life in the universe,* by J. Wagner. New York: Perennial Library.

Grossman, A. H. (March 1993). The faces of HIV/AIDS. *Parks and Recreation* (March): 44–46.

Henderson, K. A. 1990. The meaning of leisure for women: An integrative review of the research. *Journal of Leisure Research* 22, no. 3: 228–43.

Henderson, K. A. 1993. A feminist analysis of selected professional recreation literature about girls/women from 1907–1990. *Journal of Leisure Research* 25, no. 2: 165–81.

Henderson, K. A., M. D. Bialeschki, S. M. Shaw, and V. J. Freysinger. 1989. *A leisure of one's own: A feminist perspective on women's leisure.* State College, PA: Venture.

HIV/AIDS Surveillance Report. July 1993. Atlanta; GA: U.S. Department of Health and Human Services.

Hutchison, R. 1987. Ethnicity and urban recreation: Whites, blacks, and Hispanics in Chicago's public parks. *Journal of Leisure Research* 19, no. 3: 205–22.

Institute for Social Research. 1986. How families use time. *ISR Newsletter* (Winter 1985–1986): 4–5.

Jahoda, J. 1981. Work, employment and unemployment: Values theories and approaches in social research. *American Psychologist* 36: 184–91.

Kay, T. 1989. Active unemployment—A leisure pattern for the future? *Society and Leisure* 12, no. 2: 413–30.

Kennedy, D. W., R. W. Smith, and D. R. Austin. 1991. *Special recreation: Opportunities for persons with disabilities.* Dubuque, IA: Wm. C. Brown Publishers.

Kinney, W. B., and C. P. Coyle. 1989. *Predictors of quality of life among physically disabled adults.* Philadelphia: Temple University and U.S. Department of Education.

Kunstler, R. 1991. There but for fortune: A therapeutic recreation perspective on the homeless in America. *Therapeutic Recreation Journal* (Second Quarter): 31–40.

Kunstler, R. 1992. Forging the human connection: Leisure services for the homeless. *Parks and Recreation* (March): 42–45.

McKinstry, H. M. 1909. Athletics for girls. *The Playground* 3, no. 3: 3–7.

Meyer, H. D., and C. K. Brightbill. 1964. *Community recreation: A guide to its organization.* New York: Prentice-Hall.

Murphy, J. F. 1972. Egalitarianism and separatism: A history of approaches in the provision of public recreation and leisure service for blacks, 1906–1972. Doctoral dissertation, Oregon State University.

Pela, R. L. 1994. Stonewall's eyewitnesses. *The Advocate,* 3 May, 654, 50–55.

Razzell, P. E., and R. W. Wainwright. 1973. *The Victorian working class: Selections from letters to the Morning Chronicle.* London: Frank Cass.

Reid, D. G. 1990. Leisure and recreation as an instrument for maintaining life quality during unemployment. *Leisurability* 17, no. 1: 3–11.

Reid, D. G. July 1987. Overlooking the unemployed as a potential new leisure class. *Recreation Canada.* Canadian Parks/Recreation Association.

Rockwell, E. 1917. Athletics for elementary school girls. *The Playground* 11, no. 2: 94–102.

Schor, J. B. 1992. *The overworked American: The unexpected decline of leisure.* New York: Basic Books.

Sessoms, H. D., and D. K. Orthner. (August 1992). Parks and recreation and our growing invisible populations. *Parks and Recreation* (August): 62–65.

Smith, M. A., and B. S. Simpkins. 1980. *Unemployment and leisure: A review and some proposals for research.* U.K.: The Centre for Leisure Studies, University of Salford.

Spradley, J. P. 1970. *You owe yourself a drunk: An ethnography of urban nomads.* Boston: Little, Brown and Company.

Stage, F. K., and K. Manning. 1992. *Enhancing the multicultural campus environment: A cultural brokering approach.* San Francisco: Jossey-Bass.

Stamps, S. M., and M. B. Stamps. 1985. Race, class and leisure activities of urban residents. *Journal of Leisure Research* 17, no. 1: 40–55.

Stein, J. U. 1985. Mainstreaming in recreational settings: It can be done. *Leisure Today. Journal of Physical Education, Recreation and Dance* 56: 5, 3, 52.

U.S. Bureau of Labor Statistics. 1993. *Employment and earnings.* Unpublished data.

U.S. Bureau of the Census. 1992. *Current population reports.* P60–181.

U.S. Bureau of the Census. 1993. *Statistical abstracts of the United States: 1993.* Washington D.C.: U.S. Government Printing Office.

Wagner, J. 1986. *The search for signs of intelligent life in the universe.* New York: Perennial Library.

Weller, C. F. 1913. Life for girls. *The Playground* 7, no. 5: 199–207.

Wolfensberger, W. 1972. *Normalization.* Toronto: National Institute on Mental Retardation.

leisure resources for people

Digital Stock

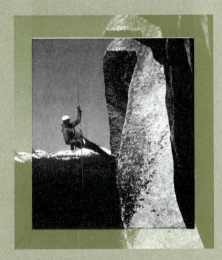

PREVIEW

Why are leisure resources important?

Having access to pastimes is imperative to the health and vitality of individuals, as well as societies. One verification of this is the concept of cultural capital.

What is cultural capital?

It is competence in a society's dominant culture. Leisure experiences help people gain this competence.

What are the types of organized leisure resources?

These resources are usually grouped into the categories of sports, cultural arts, outdoor recreation, travel, hobbies, and social recreation.

Who sponsors these leisure resources?

They are sponsored by public, private, and commercial agencies.

maggie and milly and molly and may

e.e. cummings

maggie and milly and molly and may
went down to the beach (to play one day)

and maggie discovered a shell that sang
so sweetly she couldn't remember her troubles, and

milly befriended a stranded star
whose rays five languid fingers were;

and molly was chased by a horrible thing
which raced sideways while blowing bubbles: and

may came home with a smooth round stone
as small as a world and as large as alone.

For whatever we lose (like a you or a me)
it's always ourselves we find in the sea

Where do our places for play come from?

This poem was written in 1956 by Edward Cummings (or e.e. cummings, as he preferred to sign his name). Cummings made poetic history by experimenting with different typographical arrangements (lower-case letters and unusual punctuation). In this poem, going to the beach—an everyday kind of experience—is glorified by Cummings. Like all his poems, it can be understood on several levels of meaning. We can think about a simple trip to the beach from various perspectives. For example, how do the discoveries made by the four girls explain the final line in the poem? How does the rhythm and word choice create a picture of the poet's view?

Another meaning in the poem is the beach as a place for play. Where do our places for play come from? How are they cared for so we may use them? Who manages our gymnasiums, ice rinks, playgrounds, athletic fields, art centers, concert halls, libraries, amusement parks, health clubs, and resorts? How are our forests, gardens, parks, camps, trails, reservoirs, campgrounds, and beaches cared for? These and many other leisure resources are managed by a varied collection of agencies, organizations, and companies. Funds are generated, personnel hired, services offered, and people served by thousands of organizations, big and small, all focused on leisure.

Of course, many pastimes are experienced in an informal way. People spend much of their free time in casual or independent activities, such as reading, walking, watching television, and socializing with friends. However, other pastimes require or are made better by a formal organization that provides facilities, equipment, leadership, instruction, schedules, and other support. Even such independently experienced activities as bicycling, picnicking, and swimming require safe, attractive, and accessible areas if they are to be truly enjoyed. These things do not happen automatically—they require some form of sponsorship.

In this chapter, we explore some of the typical ways leisure resources are managed. We begin by exploring reasons why leisure resources are so important. First, we introduce the concept of cultural capital. Next, ways of structuring leisure services according to type of leisure experience are presented. These include tourism, cultural arts, sports, and outdoor recreation. Finally, ways of organizing leisure services according to type of sponsorship are explored. These sponsorships are commercial, private, and public.

Leisure Resources as Cultural Capital

Having leisure resources is important. From the previous chapters in this book, we know that having access to outdoor recreation, cultural arts, sports, and other leisure forms is imperative to individuals, as well as societies. Without reservation, both philosophical writings and research reports illustrate leisure's significance in shaping people and communities. Leisure is good for our physical and emotional health. It shapes the culture, affects our economy, reflects our values, and can be a tool for solving social problems. Leisure has worth in and of itself. As we conclude our exploration of the role of pastimes in contemporary life, we consider one more claim for leisure's importance. That is, leisure has the power to enhance life's successes.

One of the concepts that supports this claim is **cultural capital.** Cultural capital is defined as an individual's store of behaviors and knowledge (Bourdieu 1977) that pays off in terms of succeeding in the culture. The importance of this for people in contemporary societies is that the more a person's own cultural capital matches that which is most highly regarded by his or her culture, the more successful—in work and school—he or she will be. How does this relate to pastimes? Bluntly, it says that the way to success is via a shared experience in the pastimes of those at the top. Before we reject this notion as elitist, let's examine it a bit more closely.

Cultural capital is acquired through life experiences and interactions. The "capital" acquired in childhood is believed to affect not only success in school but success later in occupations. According to Bourdieu (1977), the reason some children fail at school is that the schools often require cultural capital that is foreign to their lives. School's cultural capital often conflicts with the world they know and understand. This explanation maintains, for example, that young urban youth learn early that if someone is "in your face" you have to fight or you will "lose face" and respect in the neighborhood. The accepted cultural capital of school, on the other hand, dictates that by fighting you lose face. Thus, what is natural and necessary to succeed in the home community, often leads to failure and rejection in school, and later, work environments.

What's to be done about this problem? Part of the answer is in people's leisure experiences. Much of the research on cultural capital has been done on the role of pastimes for children and school success. In a study by Lareau

Cultural capital: personal resources that are useful for achieving competence in a society's high-status culture.

One of the more important studies done on cultural capital was by DiMaggio (1982). DiMaggio was trying to discover why some American high school students had more difficulty succeeding in school than others. DiMaggio had noticed that other studies on school achievement only weakly supported the role of family income, parents' education and occupation, and race in explaining the differences. Students from upper-class family backgrounds were just as likely to fail as those from lower-class origins.

DiMaggio then decided to test a different hypothesis. His notion was that certain aspects of "cultural style" make the important difference. To DiMaggio, cultural style included one's specific leisure tastes and interests. If your cultural style is shared by others, he reasoned, membership, respect, and affection will be the reward, and this translates into success in that network.

To see how cultural style, labeled cultural capital, helped American students succeed in school, DiMaggio set up a study that measured the interests and activities of almost 3000 eleventh graders in public,

parochial, and private high schools. He measured their cultural capital as involvement in art, music, and literature, including their patterns of art museum and gallery visitation, classical music concert attendance, and poetry and literature reading. He considered these to be a common cultural currency among American elites.

DiMaggio also measured the students' grades. His findings revealed a striking confirmation of the hypothesis that cultural capital is positively related to high school grades. Higher grades were associated with students who had higher amounts of cultural capital. Interestingly, this relationship differed strikingly by gender. The young women in the study sample expressed substantially more interest and reported greater participation in the high culture activities than did the young men. Therefore, the returns to cultural capital were greatest for women. By contrast, among the men in the sample, the positive impact of cultural capital on grades was restricted to students from lower- and middle-class households.

(1989), children whose parents regularly read to them performed better in school. In another study, Katsillis and Rubinson (1990) found that high school students' participation in "high culture" activities (attending lectures and the theater, and visiting museums and galleries) were important sources of cultural capital that related positively to success in school.

In the research of Downey and Powell (1993), those eighth graders who were more successful in school participated in scouting, hobby clubs, neighborhood clubs, boys' or girls' clubs, nonschool team sports, 4–H, Y activities, and summer and other recreation programs. For these and other research studies, the answer to helping people be more successful in life is a rich leisure life. Finally, researchers at the University of California at Irvine (Rauscher 1994) found that listening to music helps the brain manage complex mental functions, such as understanding mathematics and chess. For example, one of their experiments showed that preschool children who received eight months of music lessons demonstrated spatial reasoning skills that far outstripped those of preschoolers who didn't take lessons.

Packages for Organized Leisure Services

What are the sources of cultural capital? There are many. The great variety of pastimes that people enjoy is limited only by imagination—that of the participants and the agencies that serve them. Leisure interests are as broad as humanity itself. Leisure activities may require differing skill levels, take place at certain seasons of the year, have a complex or simple organizational structure, take place indoors or outdoors, involve formal or informal participation, require expensive equipment or no equipment at all, be highly competitive or passive and reflective, and require or not require a leader.

Despite this variety, we can catalog pastimes according to type of experience. While classifying experiences that offer leisure meaning and value is a difficult task and the means of classification are arbitrary, a traditional system has been useful. People's pastimes and the program services of leisure organizations can be organized according to the grouping of activity types listed in table 12.1. Although this classification cannot be all-inclusive, it is useful for describing the common types of leisure services. They provide people of all ages with the means to live fuller lives in contemporary society.

A Renaissance fair—the variety of pastimes is limited only by imagination.

© Ruth V. Russell

Types of Leisure Activities

Table 12.1

1. Sports and games
   a. Individual sports and games (archery, diving, gymnastics, ice skating, video games, weight training)
   b. Dual sports and games (badminton, billiards, chess, croquet, foursquare, racquetball, tennis, wrestling)
   c. Team sports and games (volleyball, basketball, dodge ball, ice hockey, lacrosse, soccer, softball, water ballet)

2. Cultural arts
   a. Music (barbershop quartets, opera, musical charades, orchestras, jazz clubs, guitar lessons, talent shows)
   b. Fine arts (calligraphy, sand casting, batiking, filmmaking, woodworking, ceramics, quilting, weaving)
   c. Dance (social dances, modern dance, square dance, ballroom dance, belly dancing, rhythm games)
   d. Drama (stage productions, mime, skits and stunts, pageants, puppetry, clowning, storytelling, choral speaking)

3. Outdoor recreation
   a. Camping (backpacking, car camping, hosteling)
   b. Nature-oriented (animal husbandry, stargazing, nature walks, terrarium making, bird watching)
   c. Conservation (gardening, planting for wildlife, bird census taking)
   d. Adventure (white-water kayaking, mountain climbing, spelunking, rock climbing, extreme skiing)
   e. Outdoor sports (hunting, fishing, boating, orienteering, water skiing, snow skiing, horseback riding)

4. Travel and tourism
   a. Group tours (bus tours, shopping tours, theater tours, charter flights)
   b. Cruises (barefoot cruises, ocean liner cruises)
   c. Ecotourism (conservation projects, wildlife exploration)
   d. Destination focused (independent travel to theme parks, cities, resorts)

5. Hobbies
   a. Education (reading, study, poetry writing, board games, puzzles, debating)
   b. Collecting (antiques, autographs, dolls, coins, matchbooks, recipes, rocks, stamps)

6. Social recreation
   a. Parties (birthday parties, card parties, holiday parties, hayrides, scavenger hunts, social dances)
   b. Clubs (meetings, coffee houses, drop-in centers)
   c. Eating events (picnics, banquets, cookouts, potluck suppers, ice cream socials, restaurant eating)
   d. Visiting (open houses, visiting shut-ins, receptions, telephone conversations, coffee breaks)

From this list, we now explore tourism, cultural arts, outdoor recreation, and sports more thoroughly. The question we ask is what are the resources for these pursuits?

Tourism

From earliest times, people have traveled. Trips of ancient peoples were mainly driven by religion, hunger, or to escape danger. The invention of money by the Sumerians (Babylonia) and the development of trade, beginning about 4000 B.C., probably mark the start of the modern era of travel, because people could then pay for transportation and accommodations. The first trip for purposes of tourism was made by Queen Hatshepsut to the lands of Punt (now Somalia) in 1490 B.C. Descriptions of her tour have been recorded on the walls of the Temple of Deit El Bahari at Luxor and are still admired by tourists today (McIntosh and Goeldner 1986).

Other significant early trips include those by Oceanians, who in small dugout canoes (not over forty feet long), traveled from Southeast Asia across the Pacific to the Marquesas and Society Islands. Polynesians, also in small canoes, traveled distances of over 2,000 miles from the Society Islands to Hawaii. Early Mediterranean peoples were also avid travelers. In ancient Greece, people traveled to the Olympic Games, and ancient Romans built a magnificent network of roads, on which they could travel as much as 100 miles a day using relays of horses furnished by rest stops about six miles apart. At the time of Alexander the Great, some 700,000 tourists would crowd into Ephesus (now Turkey) in a single season to be entertained by the acrobats, jugglers, and magicians who filled the streets.

Today, thanks to important inventions in transportation and communications, millions of people travel for pleasure—millions who, about a century ago,

The tin lizzie —an early automobile —marked the beginning of the modern tourism boom.

Christopher B. Stage

would have considered a few hundred miles a very long journey. Tourism has become one of the fastest growing social and economic phenomena in the twentieth century. All predictions maintain that the number of tourists, both those who travel internationally and domestically, will continue to grow. Also, the geographic spread of tourism continues to widen. Nearly all parts of the world are accessible to visitors; the whole world has become one neighborhood.

Tourism is hiking in a national park, standing at the rail of a cruise ship, attending a conference, and going to grandma and grandpa's house. It is a weekend trip with friends to the ski slope, a one-week family vacation to the beach, a honeymoon to a resort, a Sunday drive on country roads to see the autumn colors, and a business trip that is extended by a day for relaxation at a spa. It is also sitting through a showing of your neighbors' slides from their trip to Europe and helping with a tropical cloud forest conservation project in Honduras.

Regardless of the length, purpose, or destination of the trip, a complex network of agencies are relied upon. Travel experiences are not sponsored by a single type of organization but through an aggregate of entities, some appearing to have no connection to any others. In fact, tourism may be defined by this feature: it is the sum of the interactions of tourists, business suppliers, host governments, and host communities.

Tourism is a composite of activities, services, and industries that deliver travel experiences, including eating and drinking establishments, transportation, accommodations, special events, attractions, shops, entertainment, visitor services, and advertising. While these tourism segments are not organized into a cohesive and coordinated enterprise, each makes an interrelated contribution to tourism. The success of any one of these segments depends on the success of the others. For example, the success of the resort business on the island of Antigua depends not only on the marketing efforts of travel agents worldwide, the availability of transportation, housing, and restaurants but it also relies on retail shops, charter boats, diving and snorkeling guides, musicians, gardeners, and even weather forecasters. Some of this is depicted in figure 12.1. Taken together it is referred to as **the tourism system.** All components are essential for modern tourism.

First, without volumes of people, or markets, who have the desire and ability to travel, tourism cannot thrive. Travel tastes differ according to age, income level, educational level, personal health, stage in the family life cycle, occupation, and other factors. For example, families with young children take vacations closer to home and less often because of the difficulties of traveling with children. Travel patterns of people are diverse, yet tourist markets are usually systematically analyzed and segmented on the basis of such demographics. For example, some hotels cater specifically to the family market.

Figure 12.1

The tourism system.

Source: Clare A. Gunn, Tourism Planning. Copyright © 1988. Taylor and Francis.

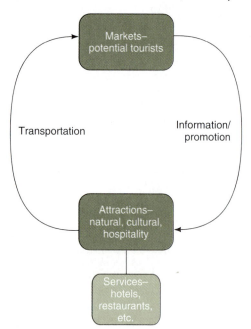

The tourism system: the interrelated services for and activities of tourists.

However, travel interests are not fully explained by demographics. Other factors determine how and where people travel. For example, fears about wars or political unrest affect travel intentions. Even differences in people's personality types shape travel interests. To elaborate, in explaining why destination areas rise and fall in popularity, Plog (1974) classified tourists according to their personality. He proposed a continuum ranging from the **psychocentric** at one end and the **allocentric** at the other. The pure psychocentric personality is self-centered, whereas the pure allocentric personality is interested in things beyond the self. Psychocentrics tend to focus on the events around their own lives. Allocentrics are outgoing and self-confident. They are willing to reach out and experiment with life. Plog found that the U.S. population was normally distributed along the continuum between these two extreme types with most people falling in the mid-centric type—a balance of both. His research was also able to identify the travel preferences of psychocentrics and allocentrics (fig. 12.2). According to figure 12.2, allocentrics tend to travel to far away and unfamiliar places, and psychocentrics are happiest vacationing close to home.

Next in the tourism system is attractions. Although all components of the system are important, attractions provide the energizing power. A wide variety of physical settings and establishments provide a pull for travelers to visit. While almost anything at one time or another may become an attraction (even

Psychocentric: a personality type characterized as focused on self and the familiar.

Allocentric: a personality type characterized as outgoing.

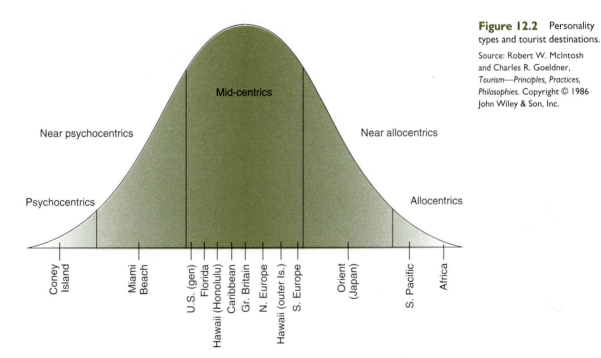

Figure 12.2 Personality types and tourist destinations.

Source: Robert W. McIntosh and Charles R. Goeldner, *Tourism—Principles, Practices, Philosophies.* Copyright © 1986 John Wiley & Son, Inc.

natural disasters, such as floods and earthquakes), tourist attractions are more typically natural, cultural, and hospitality resources. Landforms, bodies of water, climate, fine arts, history, music, shopping, sports, and even locals' welcoming spirit can attract tourists.

People travel to parks, beaches, ski slopes, golf courses, arts and crafts fairs, cities, museums, wineries, zoos, sports competitions, theme parks, convention centers, and shopping malls. They want to see religious rituals, old houses, dance performances, and the cherry tree blossoms. Tourists to Germany visit the castles. In India, they visit the Taj Mahal. Tourists to Las Vegas visit the casinos. One way of classifying attractions is according to the type of trip: touring circuit and longer-stay (Gunn 1988). As illustrated in table 12.2, touring circuit attractions seek to satisfy traveling markets—those on the move and on tours that include several locations. On the other hand, longer-stay attractions are destinations. They are used by visitors over the course of the entire trip.

Service facilities, such as hotels, restaurants, retail shops, laundries, and local transportation, support attractions, as well as provide an economic link to the local community. Tourism services are primarily commercially sponsored and are the first-contact businesses used by tourists. For example, tourist lodgings are usually private or corporate owned and hire local staff. Lodging choices for tourists range from deluxe to budget: hotels, motels, inns, timeshare condominiums, bed and breakfasts, pensions, lodges, boats, hostels, campgrounds, and hiking shelters. The deluxe to budget distinction is restricted to type of sleeping accommodation, but it also includes the presence or absence of such amenities as living rooms, fireplaces, wet bars, whirlpool bathtubs, computer-linking jacks, VCRs, and other necessities for a "good

Tourism Attraction Examples

Touring Circuit Attractions	Longer-Stay Attractions
Roadside scenic areas	Resorts
Unique natural areas	Campgrounds
Cultural sites	Homes: friends and relatives
Historic sites	Vacation homes/condos
Shopping areas	Casinos
Water touring areas	Convention and trade centers
Seasonal attractions	Festivals/events
Unusual sites	Theme parks
Ethnic areas	Sports complexes

Tourist attractions require support services, such as restaurants.

© Ruth V. Russell

night's sleep." Deluxe versus budget also refers to the availability of swimming pools, glass elevators, health clubs, game rooms, child care services, airport and attraction shuttles, and business centers. In other words, today lodging services can offer much more than just a place to sleep; they can also be the focus of the trip.

Food and beverage services are another important component in the tourism system. In fact, to some tourists eating and drinking is one of the purposes of the trip. A visit to Great Britain would be incomplete without going to a pub, or a bistro in France, or a delicatessen in New York. Shopping services are similarly critical to tourism, and for some, they are the main purpose of the trip. For example, shopping is considered the main event for tourists to Hong Kong. However, retail services are more pervasive than this. The tourist wants souvenirs from the places they visit. Attraction operators have learned that it is not enough to develop and operate the attraction. They must also offer T-shirts, postcards, and camera film.

Finally, let's consider the connectors of the market and attractions components in the tourism system. Links between the market and the attractions are of two types: information-promotion and transportation.

Although automobile and air travel tend to dominate most tourist transportation today, other modes, such as boats and bicycles, serve frequently both as transportation to an attraction and as the attraction itself. Today, tourist transportation options are quite broad and include modes previously made obsolete by new technology. For example, if tourists wish to travel by water they may choose a car ferry, passenger ferry, hydrofoil, or canoe. Floating resorts, such as ocean liners in the Caribbean and riverboats on the Mississippi River,

biography

"New" Resorts

The Loews Ventana Canyon Resort in Tucson, Arizona, has an eighty-foot waterfall cascading from the top of a mountain. The Marriott Desert Springs Resort in Palm Desert, California, takes guests to their room by gondolas through a series of artificial lakes and canals. The Hyatt Regency Waikoloa on the big island of Hawaii has a saltwater lagoon where guests swim with porpoises. Call them fantasy-resorts or just resorts, this is an industry that is getting more unique all the time.

Perhaps the most unique of the new resorts is the hotel developed by the Swedish entrepreneur, Nils Yngve Bergqvist. This hotel is called ARTic Hall. It is located in the Lapland town of Jukkasjarvi. The hotel is made entirely of ice. It features a large ice bar, a theater, a jazz club, and a chapel with reindeer-fur covered pews. Bed and breakfast in one of the ten rooms cost $40 to $45 a night, reasonable enough unless one is bothered by the absence of doors, closets, and of course heat. In 1993, the first year of operation, about 800 tourists stayed at ARTic Hall. Each were given a survival certificate. With the coming of summer, the hotel vanishes, but with so many advance guest reservations, it is sure to be rebuilt the next winter.

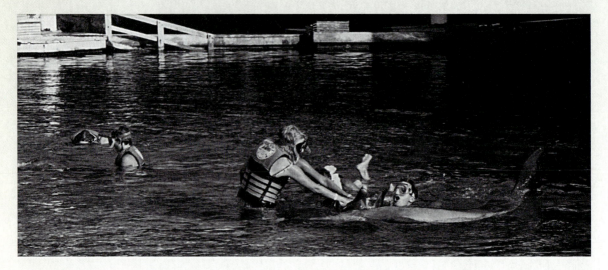

Box Figure 12.1 Porpoise lagoon at a Hawaiian resort.
© Ruth V. Russell

provide self-contained lodging, restaurants, and entertainment. By land, tourists most commonly use the automobile. Also, truck campers, motor homes, motorcycles, taxis, buses, street cars, trains, horses, and mules (and in some locations elephants and camels) can add to the trip's adventure. By air, tourists use a wide variety of aircraft, including hot air balloons. On the other hand, some tourists get there by walking.

One of the most vital aspects of tourism is the combination of modes of transportation. A commuter flight links a traveler to a major airline. The "fly-drive" mix where air travel is used to reach a destination area and a rental car provides local transportation is increasingly common. Vacationers can also get themselves and their car to a destination by train or ferry, or drive their motor home onto a barge that is pushed up and down a river by tugboats. Travelers to large cities use airline services to reach the airport, a railway connection to downtown, and a taxi to the hotel. Ownership of each mode of transportation tends to be separate, yet as you can see, decisions about schedules, pricing, convenience, and location cannot be made independently. The pieces must fit together.

People are also connected to attractions through information about and promotions for attractions. These come from many sources: travel agents, tour operators, magazines, television ads, meeting planners, visitor and convention bureaus, and friends and relatives. The goal of all of them is to create a motivation for travel. Basic travel motivators fit into four categories (McIntosh and Goeldner 1986):

1. Physical motivators are those related to physical rest, recuperation, and other health goals. This is often what is promoted for such attractions as spas and cruises.

2. Cultural motivators come from the desire to know about the music, dances, art, customs, folklore, and religion of other cultures. This is often a feature of information and promotions for foreign and historical destinations.

3. Interpersonal motivators include an interest in meeting new people, visiting friends or relatives, and escaping from a routine at work or home.

4. Status and prestige motivators concern ego needs. Trips related to business, conventions, education, research, and hobbies cater to people's desire for recognition, appreciation, and attention.

Cultural Arts

Americans have benefitted from a growth in the number of offerings in the arts in recent decades. Summer day-camp programs for children are now just as likely to include graphic art and jazz dance as swimming and games. Members of the older adults center can now sign up to learn to play the oboe or write Haiku poetry. Football players take classes in ballet, and executives join potter's cooperatives. Puppets help hospitalized children adjust to their treatment regime, and teens make videotapes to express their concerns about guns and violence. Young children and their parents go to a bookstore on Saturdays to listen to a storyteller, and youth in a correctional institution are invited to paint murals on blank walls of downtown buildings.

Communities typically have orchestras, dance companies, theater groups, and art fairs. Schools provide classes and workshops in sculpture, and voluntary organizations sponsor photography clubs, Shakespeare interest groups, and crafts guilds. The university's string quartet performs weekly at noon on the campus lawn, and the Army base provides rock band practice rooms. Governments are rapidly establishing community-wide multiple arts centers and shopping malls feature art exhibits. In one town, an old river-boat is converted into a theater, and in another town, every weekend a street becomes a stage for a talent show. A barn becomes an art gallery. An African-American youth chorus performs in the park. A retiree teaches children to play the piano in his home after school. This is all as it should be, because a smorgasbord of cultural arts appeals to people of all ages, backgrounds, abilities, and interests. In highlighting resources for cultural arts, special mention needs to be made about nonprofit theaters, commercial theaters, symphony orchestras, dance companies, and cultural centers.

First, theater is the most popular resource for the arts in the United States. For example, each year there are 184 nonprofit professional theaters giving about 48,695 performances, around 35 new Broadway shows released, and 1,152 weeks of road shows played (Theatre Communications Group 1992). The foundation for all this is the nonprofit theater. These range from large, specially built theaters in multiple arts complexes subsidized with government grants to small privately operated "attic" theaters that receive meager help from local arts councils. The network of nonprofit theaters also includes regional theaters, such as those in Houston, Louisville, Minneapolis, and Seattle. Many of these have set a national pace by developing superior acting companies and producing experimental works. Often, the productions of regional nonprofit theaters are exported to audiences outside the home region and later are adopted by the commercial theaters on Broadway. Indeed, regional theaters now function as if they were all America's theater by supplying the nation with a steady source of new plays, performers, directors, and set and lighting designers.

Although a large proportion of the finest theater productions in the United States originate in nonprofit theaters, another outstanding resource for drama are commercial theaters. Many are in the Broadway area of New York City. Broadway theaters still represent the biggest, most lavish productions performed by the most experienced performers and staged by leading directors and producers. Other major cities also support commercial theaters, and commercial summer theater is thriving. Many summer theaters are located in popular tourist destinations. Worldwide, another important resource of commercial theater is London's West End. International visitors occupy an increasing proportion of theater seats in both London and New York. For example, in London, Americans fill about one-fourth of the seats.

Growth in orchestral music has also grown in the United States. The size of audiences and the number of performers have both increased. There are now over 1,666 symphony orchestras, and annual attendance now exceeds 22.3 million people (American Symphony Orchestra League 1992). Orchestras are no longer found exclusively in the largest cities. For example, the Colorado Symphony Orchestra, founded in 1922, has a budget of up to

$10 million and an annual attendance of 225,000 for a fifty-two-week season (*Handel's National Directory for the Performing Arts* 1994).

Opera, the most expensive of the performing arts to produce, also has a history of growth. Once considered the domain of wealthy intellectuals, opera has become more widely appreciated. In 1970, attendance was calculated at 4.6 million people, and by 1989, attendance had climbed to 21.4 million (Central Opera Service 1992). Now, first rate opera performances can be seen not only at New York City's Metropolitan Opera but in thriving opera houses in smaller cities, such as Seattle, Houston, and Boston. A world renowned university sponsored opera season is even mounted in small-town Bloomington, Indiana. An important concern for the continued growth of opera, however, is cost. Even with 95 percent of capacity audiences, opera's expensive production often leaves the company risking financial loss.

What about dance companies? When the New York City Ballet first performed in Washington, D.C. forty years ago, just five people were in the audience (Chubb and Chubb 1981). Now, the company attracts a capacity crowd every night of its run there. Other American dance companies are enjoying similar success. Several explanations are possible for this increased popularity. The emergence of superstars, a growing admiration for the athletic ability of dancers, more effective promotion of dance as an art form, and the increased availability of better facilities for staging dance performances have all contributed to its success. Like opera, however, dance companies are able to earn only a portion of their operating expenses; thus, the future of dance companies as a cultural arts resource is also worrisome.

Finally, multiple purpose cultural arts centers represent a special kind of cultural arts resource. The majority of American dramatic, dance, and musical performances take place in this type of facility. **Cultural arts centers** usually are a cluster of one or more stages, an art gallery, and rehearsal and workshop areas under one roof. The idea is to provide a cost efficient resource for community expression in all the arts. One of the first multiple cultural arts centers to be constructed was New York City's $160 million Lincoln Center for the Performing Arts, which opened in 1962. The six buildings and thirteen auditoriums support The Metropolitan Opera, The New York Philharmonic Orchestra, The Juilliard School of Music, The New York Public Library for the Performing Arts, the New York City Ballet, the New York City Opera, the Film Society of Lincoln Center, the Chamber Music Society of Lincoln Center, and the Vivian Beaumont Theater. Of course, most cultural arts centers are much more modest but provide similar resources to their communities.

Cultural arts center: a facility supporting more than one art form.

Sports

A casual drive (or better yet, a bicycle ride) through the average American community demonstrates the priority of sport resources. Basketball hoops above garage doors, tennis courts behind apartment buildings, city swimming pools, private golf courses, jogging and fitness trails, health clubs, and softball

Figure 12.3 The object of curling is to glide eight 42-pound "rocks" (discs of granite with handles) as close as possible to the center of a circular target on the ice 138 feet away. Players furiously sweep with brooms to help direct the rocks.

Christopher B. Stage

diamonds can be found everywhere. In fact, it is a challenge to find a community that does not have at least one softball field or a household that does not have at least one golf club, running shoe, or tennis racket!

Likewise, each year new sports soar to popularity, new highs are reached in attendance at sporting events, and new teams and leagues in amateur and professional sports are established. For example, curling has an immensely popular following in Canada (fig. 12.3). According to a Canadian Curling Association survey, there are more than 750,000 active curlers in the country and 1,298 curling clubs. At the competitive level, curling has become a major television draw, with upwards of 3 million viewers tuning in for recent telecasts of the Canadian men's championships. A study conducted in 1990 for the Ontario Ministry of Tourism and Recreation predicted that the number of active curlers would grow by 8.9 percent annually over the next twenty-five years—a growth rate that would put curling ahead of golf, hockey, tennis, skiing, or squash (Bergman 1992).

Many agencies and organizations provide resources for sport participation and spectating. Athletic clubs, community centers, Boys' and Girls' clubs, religious groups, commercial stadiums and tracks, hotels, camps, cities, schools, and many others are examples. Even the home is an important sport resource. In fact, the residence is the "most common locale for leisure" for adults (Kelly 1987, 141). Pastimes in and around the home are common and practiced on a daily basis. They often include other important persons in our

Case Study   Leisure in Your Yard

The yard can be used as a softball, football, and soccer field. People can practice their golf swing; play volleyball, badminton, and croquet; and in winter weather, the yard can even be flooded and used as an ice rink. More and more people have swimming pools, putting greens, tennis courts, and volleyball courts in their yards. Here are some other ideas for getting more leisure out of your yard.

Questions to Consider and Discuss

1. Think about your own yard. Is it a potential resource for sports? If you live in an apartment, what spaces are available for physical pastimes? How can you make it more useful for this? What sorts of sports?

2. Is there a danger that the home as a resource for leisure will become so dominant in people's lives that community-based resources will find it difficult to attract users? Why or why not? Can you cite an example where a commercial- or government-sponsored facility or program is no longer viable because of increases in participation at home?

Features	Leisure Potential
Low-maintenance design (no hedges, fences, cultivated areas)	Less free time and money spent on maintenance; allows several adjoining unfenced yards to form a large semipublic play area for space demanding activities (i.e., frisbee, touch football).
Fences, hedges, or walls	Provides privacy for personal leisure, such as sunbathing, reading, entertaining guests, and eating outdoors.
Large trees and shrubs	Provides a more aesthetic and relaxing place for observing wildlife, enjoying a swing, tree house, or hammock.
Flowers, vegetables, and fruits	Encourages gardening as a hobby.
Installation of leisure facilities	Swimming pools, barbecue grills, sand boxes, children's play equipment, basketball hoops, and tennis courts.
Screened porches	Provides privacy and shelter along with a sense of the outdoors for all indoor leisure pursuits, such as TV watching, table games, eating, and hobbies.

Source: Chubb and Chubb 1981, 330.

lives. Typically, we think of the home as a place for solitary or social activities, such as resting, conversation, playing card games, watching television, and reading. However, as contemporary society embraces new technologies and the cost of many away-from-home events increases, home has become more

Case Study The NCAA

At 5:13 P.M. on Sunday, March 4, 1990, Loyola Marymount's Hank Gathers timed his jump perfectly, caught the pass high above the rim and slammed the ball through the net like Zeus hurling a thunderbolt (Dealy 1990, 1). The basket put Loyola ahead of Portland, 23–12, in the opening minutes of a tournament game that would decide which school would represent the West Coast Athletic Conference in the NCAA's 1990 Men's Basketball Championship. At 5:14 P.M., after slapping a high five, Gathers's expression went from triumph to bewilderment as he staggered sideways and crumpled to the floor. At 6:55 P.M. he was pronounced dead. An autopsy later revealed that he had died from cardiomyopathy—a condition he'd been diagnosed with three months earlier.

Cardiomyopathy is a thickening of the heart muscles that causes the heart to beat quickly and irregularly when stressed. In a stress test, Gathers's heart beat at over 200 beats per minute, a dangerous level. The average twenty-three-year-old athlete going all out never exceeds 120 beats per minute. Gathers had been instructed to take Inderal, a medication that slows the entire body down, and allowed to play. However, Gathers noticed he didn't perform as well under the medication, and he began to secretly reduce his dosage. On March 4, 1990, he didn't take it at all.

Hank Gathers died because he played in a basketball game. He died because he didn't take a drug that could have saved his life. When asked why the National Collegiate Athletic Association (NCAA) did not play a role in the Hank Gathers case, Frank Uryasz, the association's Director of Sports Medicine, said, "There was no call for it, really. We never get involved in something like that" (Dealy 1990, 24).

Another question involving athletes received an equally evasive answer from an NCAA official. Athletes account for less than 1 percent of the nation's undergraduate college population, yet studies show they represent 33 percent of those accused of campus rape and sexual assault. When asked to comment on the problem, David Cawood, NCAA Assistant Executive Director, said, "It's a major problem for higher education. But it's a concern the NCAA has no jurisdiction over" (Dealy 1990, 28).

In 1979, Southern Methodist University football coach, Ron Meyer, was trying to recruit running back Eric Dickerson. On the evening of National Letter of Intent Signing Day, Texas A&M University gave Dickerson a brand new Pontiac Trans Am. That same day, another school's recruiter arrived at Eric's home carrying a suitcase containing $50,000 in cash. Dickerson kept the Trans Am but rejected the cash in favor of SMU's offer, which had suddenly gotten richer. Several months later, responding to rumors that SMU was hiring its football team, the NCAA began a full-scale investigation but could not substantiate the charges.

While most colleges and universities conduct their varsity sports programs in strict compliance with the policies of the institution and while most coaches are honest and resist temptations to cheat in spite of the ever-present pressures to win, there are abuses in intercollegiate athletics. Who is responsible? What is the role of the NCAA?

The NCAA is a national organization for governance of intercollegiate athletics. Membership includes nearly 800 universities and colleges that compete in over 27 different sports for men and women. It seems the problems of college sports are restricted to the top sixty-five schools with the best football and basketball programs, the big-time schools where big-time revenues provide temptations. With television money and its resulting clout came athletic departments incorporating themselves to enhance their power. These separate legal entities are completely independent from the university. In the next eight to ten years, the top sixty-five big-time college football and basketball programs will earn over $1.5 billion from television rights fees—$160 million per year, split among sixty-five NCAA institutions.

Questions to Consider and Discuss

1. Did Hank Gathers have little choice but to cheat on his medication dosage? Are the stakes of major college sports so tempting, the pressure so intense, that he had to try to beat the odds on his health?
2. In addition to the problems discussed here, what other problems are facing college sports? Do some library research, and find out to what extent the rules of the NCAA attempt to solve these problems. Assess how well you think they are working.
3. Interview several college athletes. What do they consider to be the best role for the NCAA in solving these problems?

important for such active pastimes as sports. For example, exercise apparatus and portable swimming pools are more common.

Community agencies also provide sport services. These agencies attempt through the provision of programs and facilities to serve a variety of sport interests and needs. Schools, playgrounds, and camps often feature less-organized sport activities, such as relays, dodge ball, and tag games. Health and fitness clubs typically offer individual sports, such as swimming, jogging, walking, and weight lifting. Private clubs also usually provide opportunities for individual sports, such as boating, fishing, hunting, and horseback riding. On the other hand, some sport participation resources provide opportunities to participate in dual sports. Commercial establishments cater to bowling interests, cities offer tennis, schools provide for wrestling, and private clubs feature badminton. Also common are facilities and services for team sports, such as basketball, football, volleyball, and soccer. Team sports are typically sponsored by schools, universities, and municipal recreation agencies.

Leisure service organizations not only provide many types of sports, but they also serve a broad range of participants. Communities offer sport programs for the novice and the highly skilled, for the young and the old, for all ability levels, and for women and girls, as well as men and boys. For example, in St. Petersburg, Florida, a softball league has a minimum age requirement of seventy-five years. They call themselves Kids and Kubs, and they've been playing regular seasons since 1931. Then there's the Golden Girls—a senior women's softball league in northern Virginia. Founded in 1989, this five-team league has nearly 100 members. The minimum age to become a Golden Girl is 40, but players that young "are merely our farm team" (Tousignant 1993, 25).

Sports for people with disabilities have also become more available. As a result of a blend of more positive societal attitudes and progressive government legislation, services of all kinds are now made accessible to people at all ability levels. One prime example is in the provision of sport services. Now programs, equipment, and facilities for bowling, golf, skiing, mountain climbing, tennis, and other activities are participated in by individuals with even severe disabilities. Numerous organizations actively promote these opportunities. Among them are the Joseph P. Kennedy, Jr. Foundation, which sponsors the Special Olympics with nearly 1 million participants worldwide, the National Wheelchair Athletic Association, the International Sports Organization for the Disabled, and the American Athletic Association for the Deaf.

Outdoor Recreation

We are still children of nature. For periods of time, humans may wall themselves up in a cubbyhole, breathe noxious air, walk on a straight cement path in a canyon of steel and concrete, and work and play by artificial light. But sooner or later we break loose and seek the land—to bask in the sun, to plunge our hands into rich black soil, to cast a line after an elusive trout, or to test our skill against a mountain's height.

(Maclean, Peterson, and Martin 1985, 255)

biography   Snow Talent

The sun was bright on the snow. Florescent ski clothes decorated slopes marked by the dark hue of the evergreen trees. It was a very festive occasion. From February 23 to March 6, 1990, in Winter Park, Colorado, the First Interstate Bank World Disabled Ski Championships were held for the first time in North America. Sponsored by Winter Park's National Sports Center for the Disabled, skiers from eighteen countries, including a small team from Russia, participated. They competed in four events: the slalom, giant slalom, downhill, and super G (Crase 1990).

Ten of the teams included mono-skiers. The mono-ski is a single ski that the skier sits on. Short ski poles with a small ski at each tip are added for highly agile and fast runs. The mono-ski enabled high-leg amputees and spinal cord injured skiers to compete.

The downhill was 1,737 meters long with over a 500 meter drop for the men. The course was only 300 meters shorter for the women, eliminating only 60 meters of drop. Speeds of over 70 mph were clocked by some of the racers. For the higher-level-injury skiers, Matthew Stockford of Great Britain won the gold medal with a time of 1:41.43. In the lower-level-injury downhill events Alain Marguerettax of France and Paul Bluschke of Austria dominated.

Marit Ruth of Sweden swept the downhill gold for the women with a time of 1:20.70—almost 12 seconds ahead of second place finisher Shannon Bloedel of the United States. Marit reigned in the other events, too. She won the women's super G, slalom, and giant slalom races.

A snowstorm moved in on the last day of competition. The women were just able to complete their super G contest. A deep, silent layer of snow seemed an elegant closing ceremony to a majestic display of snow talent.

People have formed themselves into saddle clubs, hiking clubs, flying clubs, yacht clubs, bird watching clubs, and hunting clubs. They make reservations months ahead at ski resorts and oceanfront hotels. Normally sedentary and prosaic adults spend their weekends climbing rocks in a state forest, exploring caves located on private property, or following soaring bald eagles in a national park. The childhood goal is going to summer camp. Caring for plants provides therapy to patients in a convalescent center. Tourists flock to natural wonders. These and a wide list of other activities rely on the outdoors for their expression.

The outdoor resources for leisure—forests and soil, sunshine and rain, rivers and sky, the hills, the prairies, the oceans—are more than just pleasant places in which to play. Rock climbing on an indoor artificial climbing wall can be fun, but it is not the experience it is on a rock face in Yosemite National Park. Body surfing on the machine generated waves at a neighborhood swimming pool is not as thrilling as it is at Hawaii's north shore. Outdoors, people participate more intimately in their own ecology. They go outdoors for the repair of what happens to them indoors. They leave the human-made environment to seek the natural environment, because in the outdoors, they experience something greater than can be found indoors. Even the children put on their shoes and get out of the car at Niagara Falls (Rolston 1986).

Sometimes people return to nature in their pastimes to show what they can do. The notion is that we can best prove ourselves against the ruggedness and surprise of the outdoors. For example, nothing exhilarates quite

The urge to swim is so strong that residents of Moscow, Russia, turn drainage areas into swimming pools.

© Ruth V. Russell

like racing a storm across the lake in a small sailboat. On the other hand, sometimes people go to nature for leisure because of nature's beauty. They find strength in watching the flight of the hawk, hearing the silence of the falling snow, and smelling the sweetness of the pine forest. Leisure in the outdoors can seem an artistic experience.

Although the vast land and water holdings of the federal and state governments constitute the major outdoor recreation resources, local resources add considerably to the opportunities for outdoor recreation. These resources include zoos, botanical gardens, camps, nature centers, gardens, parks, forest preserves, resort ranches, marinas, ski slopes, horse trails, golf courses, campgrounds, lakes, rivers, and beaches. Even within the categories on this list, subcategories of outdoor resources for leisure are numerous. For example, let's consider parks.

Parks are a fundamental component of outdoor recreation resources. While essentially all parks can be defined as a tract of land that serves the aesthetic and recreational needs of people, they accomplish this goal in different ways. The minipark, for example, is a small area (up to about one acre) that typically provides shade trees and benches for sitting and some children's play equipment. Most miniparks are located in residential areas or downtown business areas, as they are designed to be within a ten-minute walk of users.

Neighborhood parks, as the label suggests, are intended to serve a particular residential locale. Communities are divided either officially or attitudinally into neighborhoods by such physical or social boundaries as main streets, highways, and ethnic backgrounds. A typical neighborhood has 2,000 to 5,000 people and is up to one mile wide. City planners usually try to locate a neighborhood park and an elementary school near the center of each neighborhood. Neighborhood parks range in size from one to fifty acres and provide a wide variety of facilities: swimming pools, sport fields and courts, playgrounds, picnic tables and shelters, and undeveloped natural areas.

Community parks are tracts of land that serve several neighborhoods. Some also call these areas district parks. Ideally, each community of ten to twenty neighborhoods (50,000 to 100,000 people) should have at least one large central park. Community parks range in size from 50 to 300 acres or more. Because they are larger, they are able to provide for larger crowds of users. Facilities often include golf courses, sports fields, picnic areas, playgrounds, swimming pools, bicycling and hiking trails, and a special natural feature, such as a small lake or stretch of river. Some have beaches, boat rentals, fishing, hiking, nature centers, small zoos, and gardens.

Major parks, typically located on the outskirts of large cities, are regional parks. Regional parks are larger (up to about 2,000 acres) and provide a wide range of outdoor recreation offerings. They are called regional parks because they attract users from a wide area and include features not usually found in community parks. These may include extensive trail systems, ski slopes, marinas, camp sites, and nature preserves. Regional parks generally have fewer constructed resources than community parks and many also serve as nature preserves.

State and provincial parks have an even broader jurisdiction. They differ from community and regional parks in that they usually are more remote from population centers, are of greater historical or natural significance, attract visitors from greater distances, may be larger, and focus more on providing services that relate to the natural environment. By these measures, they can be compared with national parks: state and provincial parks are usually closer to population centers, are of less historical or natural significance, attract visitors from nearer distances, are smaller, and focus more on providing recreational services for people.

State parks also differ somewhat from each other in their purposes. Several state parks in Florida offer underwater exploration, those in Indiana feature nature programs and environmental education, and parks specifically for the use of all-terrain vehicles have been created in Delaware. Some parks, like those in Kentucky and West Virginia, emphasize their appeal as tourist attractions and provide hotel, restaurant, and resort services. Others concentrate on the needs of local residents who use the parks on a daily basis.

The first state parks established in the late 1800s were Yosemite in California (later redesignated as a national park), Niagara Falls in New York, and Mackinac Island in Michigan. Since this beginning, state park systems now exist in all fifty states, managing a total of 11 million acres and over 750 million annual visitors (National Association of State Park Directors 1992). Although the total acreage of state parks in the United States does not exceed one-fifth that of the national parks, they are used three times as much.

When we think of the "great outdoors" many of us immediately picture the Grand Canyon or Old Faithful. This is because national parks are the finest

biography John Muir

In the mid-1800s, the western region of America was a land of miles of open space, acres of forests, and vast expanses of natural beauty. The concerns of the people living in this abundance of uninhabited land were riveted on survival. They believed their mandate was to conquer the land. Their daily existence was a never ending labor to claim the land for agriculture. To them, there seemed to be more than enough trees, forests, animals, soil, water, and fresh air for the taking. Into this time and place came an eleven-year-old boy who was destined to change America's thinking about its land (Ford 1989).

John Muir was born in Scotland in 1838, but his family immigrated to Wisconsin, where John, his parents, and six siblings eked out a farm living. Because John's father was stern, John's early days were spent toiling on the land and receiving his daily whipping. Because of good schooling in Scotland, Muir could read and write well, so he saved his money and bought books by Shakespeare, Milton, and others. Farm life also fostered a great love of nature. By the time he entered the University of Wisconsin, his reading focused on botany, geology, and physics. John was too busy taking courses to graduate, and after four years, he left the University of Wisconsin for the "university of the wilderness." He embarked on "a glorious botanical and geological excursion, which . . . lasted nearly fifty years . . ." (Teale 1954, 72).

In 1866, Muir arrived in San Francisco and took the quickest way out of town (Ford 1989). He headed east over the Pacheco Pass toward the land that would shape the rest of his life, yet the life of the Yosemite region was also shaped by Muir. Muir noticed how overgrazed and overlogged this beautiful area was and began his campaign to save it for posterity. It took him seventeen years of writing, speaking, and lobbying to get the area designated a national park and saved from destruction.

Muir is remembered as an explorer, naturalist, and writer. He is considered the first champion of forest preservation in the United States. In addition to his work on behalf of the Yosemite region, Muir tramped through many wilderness areas of the United States, Europe, Asia, Africa, and the Arctic. His efforts not only influenced Congress to establish Yosemite National Park but also Sequoia National Park. He is credited with saving the Grand Canyon and the Petrified Forest and playing a significant role in the establishment of Crater Lake, Glacier, and Mesa Verde National Parks. He persuaded President Theodore Roosevelt to set aside 148 million acres of forest reserves. Believing so intensely in the need to work for America's beautiful places, Muir founded the Sierra Club in 1892, and it became a leading conservation organization. Its purpose was to explore, preserve, and enjoy the mountains of the coast. Muir served as its president for twenty-two years.

For Muir, there were also some disappointments. Twenty miles north of Yosemite Valley, within the boundaries of the national park, was the Hetch Hetchy Valley. It was reputed to be as beautiful as the Yosemite Valley, but it was also considered by San Francisco authorities to be the best and cheapest location for a source of water power for the city. Muir fought a long and lonely battle to save the valley but lost when, in 1913, a bill was passed permitting the building of a dam across the Tuolumne River, flooding the valley and destroying it forever.

With so much of his life spent outdoors, it is puzzling that Muir possessed few camping skills. He wore just a coat and sometimes carried a blanket (and his never-shaved red beard) to ward off cold and snow while he slept. He built fires only to heat his coffee and carried little food other than bread. He never carried a gun, for he believed the wilderness was not something to fear; it was his laboratory and his house of worship (Ford 1989). It is amazing he didn't die from exposure. In 1914, he did contract pneumonia and died in a hospital at the age of seventy-six.

examples of a country's heritage. They feature superlative scenery and natural phenomenon, and they preserve historic, prehistoric, and scientific areas of great value. There are outstanding national parks worldwide. In addition to Yosemite and Yellowstone in the United States, other fine examples include Banff National Park in Canada, which features magnificent snowcapped peaks and large glaciers; Tsavo National Park in Kenya, which contains more than

20,000 elephants; and New Zealand's Fjordland National Park with its extensive coastline and numerous fjords.

The system of U.S. national parks is the most extensive in the world, however. It manages over 79 million acres, of which 54 million acres are in Alaska. Included are not only the famous Grand Canyon, Yosemite, and Yellowstone parks, but also 334 other units of national parks, seashores, lakeshores, and historic and cultural sites and monuments. These include such highly recognized places as the Lincoln Memorial in Washington, D.C., Independence Hall National Historical Park in Philadelphia, the USS *Arizona* Memorial in Hawaii, Mount Rushmore National Memorial in South Dakota, Statue of Liberty National Monument in New York City, Death Valley National Monument in California, and Carlsbad Caverns National Park in New Mexico.

National park is a title reserved for the most superb treasures of a country—those with outstanding and unique historical, scenic, or scientific features. National parks have dual roles. They protect the natural resources and provide enjoyment for the people who use them. This means that lodges, restaurants, campgrounds, trail systems, and visitor centers are common services for people, as are endangered wildlife reintroduction projects, reenactments of historical events, archeological digs, and coalitions of conservation organizations.

Linear parks, another park type, provide leisure experiences for people as they travel through them. For example, a lengthy walkway (or promenade) enables people to stroll along a beach, river, or lake shoreline or through a section of the city. Parkways, another form of linear park, is a landscaped road along which people can take slow, relaxing drives. Some parkways are developed as elongated community parks with occasional parking lots, picnic areas, scenic overlooks, and even playing fields. Hiking, bicycling, and horse trails can also be planned as parks. These trail parks are narrow strips of land designated for specific forms of recreational travel and are becoming increasingly important outdoor recreation resources. These parks are being built on abandoned railroad beds, on the banks of old canals, along powerline right-of-ways, and on easements between properties. Usually, motorized vehicles are not allowed on these trails.

> National park: an area of special scenic, historical, or scientific importance set aside and maintained by a national government; in the U.S. by an act of Congress.

Sponsorships for Leisure

Leisure resources may also be classified according to the type of sponsor. For example, federal, state, and local governments provide leisure services and so do nongovernmental, nonprofit agencies. Private clubs and commercial for-profit businesses also provide for the pastime needs of people. Employers often offer facilities and programs for leisure as an employment benefit. Colleges and universities accommodate the sport, social, and arts interests of students. Recreation programs are part of the treatment for the residents in correctional settings and patients in hospitals. These and many other examples form the diverse "industry" of frequently competing, sometimes cooperating, leisure service organizations.

Leisure Agency Sponsor Types

Table 12.3

Type of Agency	Purpose	Services	Funding Source
Commercial	To sell leisure experiences in order to make a profit.	Wide variety, with focus on entertainment, sports, travel, and cultural arts.	Paying customers.
Private	To meet the leisure needs of members.	Wide variety, with focus on social recreation, sports, and volunteer service.	Member dues, donations, and grants.
Public	To see that all citizens are equitably able to experience a high quality of life.	Wide variety, with focus on outdoor recreation and sports.	Government taxes, fees, charges, and grants.

To organize the discussion of leisure service sponsors, we consider them according to three broad categories. Commercial agencies provide leisure services as a business. Private agencies, in contrast, offer facilities and programs for their members, and public agencies are government sponsored and equitably available to all people. Table 12.3 compares these types of service sponsors in terms of funding sources, clientele served, and purpose.

Commercial Agencies

In contemporary societies, people are willing (and often eager) to pay for leisure services. Commercial recreation agencies sell leisure experiences to make a profit. Commercial sponsorship of leisure experiences is one of the largest and fastest growing. Expenditures for commercial pastimes far exceed those for services offered by public and private agencies. In fact, some people rely on commercial resources for most of their pastimes outside the home. Other people consider certain commercial recreation experiences, such as eating out or a trip to a theme park, as special occasions.

Leisure resources operated for commercial purposes include a variety of resources from shopping malls to ski resorts. There are commercial campgrounds, golf courses, tennis courts, bowling centers, riding stables, health spas, museums, restaurants, game rooms, playgrounds, theaters, dance studios, parks, sport stadiums, racetracks, music halls, and gymnasiums. Commercial leisure agencies are the principal industry in some cities, regions, states, and even nations.

In spite of this variety, certain types of pastimes are regarded the domain of mainly commercial sponsorship. For example, commercial agencies are more

likely to be associated with entertainment, popular culture, spectator sport, theme park, tourism, food and drink, and shopping facilities and programs. On the other hand, it is much less common that a commercial enterprise will sponsor a playground or community center. Notable exceptions to this tradition are Holiday Inn's Holidomes and McDonald's restaurant playgrounds.

Many people enjoy visiting shops for leisure, and the options are plentiful. Choices include specialty shops, department stores, discount stores, flea markets, sidewalk sales, craft fairs, antique shows, mailorder catalogs, trade shows, and Saturday markets. For example, the town of Nashville, Indiana, has a population of only 800 people, yet annually hosts about 3.5 million visitors who spend approximately $57 million in small gift shops (Brown County Convention and Visitors Bureau 1994). The thrill is in finding bargains, splendid merchandise, an interesting or aesthetic environment, or in the social interaction. In some societies, it is customary for merchants and buyers to approach each sale as a friendly contest with rituals and rules much like a game.

Another large portion of commercial recreation enterprises.are food and drink services. Since the beginning of human history, meals have been just as much social occasions as means of satisfying hunger. Perhaps the best examples of this are cafes and nightclubs. Cafes are not only resources for reasonably priced snacks, but they also serve as social centers. They are places to relax with friends, play checkers, listen to music, and watch people. In many small towns and rural areas, the single cafe often is the hub of the area's social life. Bars and nightclubs are also social centers. Depending on local attitudes and the nature of the establishment, drinking places can serve as community centers where people meet to not only drink and eat but also to play games, sing, watch television, and enjoy friends. The classic example of this is the traditional British pub.

The list of commercial leisure enterprises goes on, and so a discussion of each is impossible here. Before going on to the pros and cons of commercial leisure, let's consider some unique examples of commercial leisure sponsors: museums, towers, and sport facilities. Although most of the world's museums, gardens, and zoos are publicly owned, a few of these leisure resources are noteworthy as commercial businesses. Because entrepreneurs are adept at presenting an attraction in such a way that potential customers are lured to attend, these represent some of the more heavily visited leisure resources. For example, Madame Tussaud's wax museums, Ripley's Believe-It-or-Not Museums, Sea World parks, Florida Cypress Gardens, and Lion Country Safari are world famous.

Similarly, although the majority of stadiums, arenas, and athletic playing fields are publicly owned, an outstanding number of these are commercial developments. One such complex—Madison Square Garden in New York City— contains a 20,000-seat arena, an amphitheater, several restaurants, a bowling center, an art gallery, and convention facilities. Year round it hosts boxing and wrestling matches, tennis tournaments, basketball and ice hockey games, horse shows, rodeos, motocross competitions, circuses, concerts, and other entertainment spectaculars. Frontons (for watching and playing the sport of *jai alai*), velodromes (for bicycle racing), tracks (such as Churchill Downs for horse racing and Indianapolis Motor Speedway for car racing), and stadiums (such as Dodger Stadium) are also noteworthy commercial sports facilities.

Another unique commercial leisure facility makes scenic places more enjoyable by providing views of them. These include overlooks, towers, and the top floors of tall buildings. For example, in spite of its name, the National Gettysburg Battlefield Tower is a commercial business. Other examples are the overlooks at the top of the Empire State Building in New York City and the Sears Tower in Chicago. The Eiffel Tower in Paris, visited by more than 80 million people since its opening in 1889, was the first major commercial structure built primarily for viewing the landscape.

Taken together, commercial leisure agencies provide a magnitude of opportunities. As a frequently glamorous resource for leisure, they tend to round out the services offered by public and private sponsors. Commercial agencies are able to offer activities that are too expensive for public and private sponsors and that cater to a more limited clientele. Commercial enterprises offer opportunities for people to experience unique forms of leisure. For example, amusement park rides, gambling casinos, dog racing, ice shows, and nightclubs are exciting and not usually a part of people's everyday leisure experiences. They are special occasions.

Commercial leisure agencies can also create a demand for new resources, because they respond quickly to current trends and are sometimes more willing to provide opportunities on a speculative basis. By taking financial risks, they give new pastimes a chance. A good illustration of this is the wave pool (Chubb and Chubb 1981). Commercial developers introduced it into the United States and demonstrated its ability to entice patrons to stay longer, return more often, and pay higher admission charges than conventional swimming pools. As a result, public agencies such as city, county, and state parks now offer wave pools.

In spite of the many benefits of commercial recreation, there are criticisms. A prime complaint is the profit motive. For example, commercial leisure establishments have been blamed for being too tempted by making money and thus disregarding the welfare of people. Not always caring about the effect of their services on people, some commercial enterprises justify their programs because they sell. By glamorously advertising, they can create demands where none previously existed or where demand is not desired. One example is the selling of violence through such commercial leisure forms as television, films, and video games. Such facilities as bars, casinos, and adult bookstores have also been blamed for the demise of a positive moral order in society, as have some newer pastimes, such as war games with paint guns.

Those criticisms that ring true for a culture are, however, controlled by that culture. Such regulations as legal and trade controls, competition, and public opinion indicate what is appreciated from what is not tolerated in commercial recreation. For instance, competition is a positive approach for determining socially acceptable pastimes. A dishonest operation is likely to have to close up when a responsible competitor opens for business; thus, commercial sponsorship of leisure resources plays an important role in expanding and enriching our leisure potential.

Private Agencies

Commercial leisure agencies are just one slice of the resource pie. Another type of sponsorship for leisure services is private agencies. These are the social, civic, religious, political, fraternal, labor, conservation, special interest, and youth-serving organizations that provide for our pastimes. These services are not formed by government or for profit. Almost all of us have been touched at some point in life by these services. Have you ever been a Boy or Girl Scout, a Big Brother or Big Sister? Have you been a member of the YMCA or a 4–H program, a participant in Little League, or in a fraternity or sorority? Do you belong to a sports or health club or a video club? Does anyone you know belong to the League of Women Voters, Kiwanis, the Nature Conservancy, or the Youth Hostel Federation? So plentiful are the private agencies that provide for leisure interests, the list could consume the rest of this chapter.

Private leisure organizations are defined for the most part as organizations that provide recreation experiences for their members. These range from small groups of people gathered to express a particular leisure interest, such as the association for the owners of a group of summer cabins around a small lake to

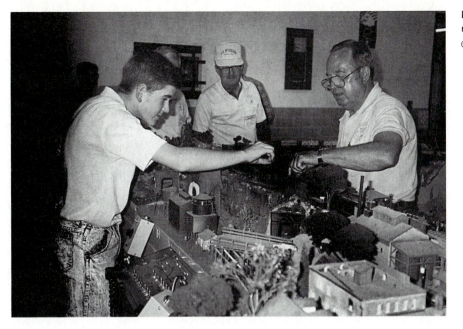

complex organizations with thousands of members, such as the Boy Scouts. A tidy system of categorizing this diversity does not exist, yet it may be useful to consider them according to those that are private leisure dominant organizations, private secondary leisure organizations, and quasi-private organizations.

Private leisure dominant organizations exist primarily to serve the leisure interests of their members. For example, social clubs provide for members' social needs. They include small, informal groups that meet to play games, such as bridge clubs, clubs for particular ethnic groups, country clubs, and college alumni clubs. Some social clubs own extensive facilities, such as retreat centers, club houses, dining rooms, libraries, game rooms, gymnasiums, and golf courses.

Other examples of private leisure dominant organizations are sports and athletic clubs. Thousands of private sports clubs were formed in the late 1800s and since then have developed extensive services for the sport enjoyment of members. Most tend to focus on one or a cluster of related sports. Golf, tennis, bowling, swimming, skiing, and track and field clubs thrive in the United States. Soccer clubs are widespread in Europe. Cricket clubs are popular in Great Britain and many former British colonies. While some sports clubs have no facilities of their own and use public facilities, others control extensive properties. Hundreds of indoor tennis centers, racquet courts, marinas, and playing fields exist for the exclusive use of club members.

Other private leisure dominant organizations focus on outdoor leisure activities. For example, hiking, bicycling, mountaineering, and camping clubs abound. The Appalachian Trail Conference is a collection of over ninety-three local clubs located along the 2,000-mile Appalachian Trail stretching from

Maine to Georgia. These local clubs help maintain the trail and the sleeping huts that are about a day's hike apart. Clubs that promote participation in drama, music, the fine arts, and hobbies are also popular. For example, model railroad clubs provide large rooms for members to build elaborate layouts of train scenes and workshop space.

Another category of privately sponsored agencies are the secondary leisure organizations. These are agencies that contribute to the supply of leisure opportunities even though their primary purpose is otherwise. For example, residential management associations, composed of owners of houses or condominiums, exist primarily to maintain and manage the shared residential facilities of roads, parking, trees, and shrubs. They also frequently manage shared recreation resources. These vary widely but typically include playgrounds, picnic areas, swimming pools, tennis courts, and party facilities.

Another example of private secondary leisure sponsors is religious organizations. Christian, Jewish, and other religious groups provide many leisure experiences for their members. The amount and extent of the opportunities depends on the attitude of the religious organization, but common provisions are suppers, games (such as bingo), sports, and youth social clubs. Some religious organizations own land and buildings in resort locations and offer campgrounds, cabins, and resort-style complexes for the enjoyment of members. While much of the resource may be used for religious meetings and retreats, many also have facilities for swimming, boating, fishing, and other outdoor activities.

To the list of examples of private secondary leisure organizations, we should add benevolent organizations (such as Veterans of Foreign Wars and the American Association of Retired Persons) whose primary objective is to promote the general welfare of their members. This includes facilities and programs for dances, parties, golf outings, card games, and banquets. Service organizations, such as the Association of Junior Leagues, Women's Clubs, Rotary, Lions, and Jaycees are also private secondary leisure organizations. While these groups are committed to raising funds for public service projects, many also have recreation facilities and sponsor events that add directly to a community's leisure resources. For example, some service clubs provide funds for libraries, museums, arenas, community centers, and swimming pools. Others pay for the uniforms of sport teams, Scout troops, and bands; large print books for people with visual impairments; and trees for parks.

Finally, a large collection of private agencies can be grouped under the heading of quasi-private organizations. These represent a special kind of private leisure resource, because while they exist to serve the needs and interests of their members, they also receive support from the public at-large or a government agency. For example, they may receive government grants or public donations, and much of the organization's work is performed by volunteers. Also, these organizations have open membership policies; participation cannot be denied on the basis of race, religion, ethnic origin, or income level.

Youth-oriented organizations fall within this category. Girl Scouts of the U.S.A., Boy Scouts of America, Boys' Clubs of America, Girls Inc., Camp Fire, Inc., 4-H clubs, the Police Athletic League, Young Men's Christian Association

(YMCA), Young Women's Christian Association (YWCA), and others strive to help children and youth develop character through wholesome pastimes. While they all were originally founded to serve the needs of youth according to gender, income levels, or religious orientation, today differences in their programs and membership policies are diminishing. For example, girls belong to the Boy Scouts, there are 4-H clubs for urban youth; and people of any or no religious affiliation are welcome to join the YMCA.

In addition to their more traditional programs of outdoor recreation, cultural arts, and sports, these youth-serving organizations have tried hard in recent years to help solve social problems. Through their leisure services, they have focused on problems of interracial and intercultural relationships, poverty, youth delinquency, and urban violence. Their programs have broadened to include vocational guidance, school tutoring, and family counseling. To illustrate, a special division of the Boy Scouts of America—Exploring—specializes in career development. Young men and women aged fourteen through twenty belong to Explorer posts co-sponsored by businesses, industries, and community organizations, and have in-depth, hands-on opportunities in occupations from accounting to zoology.

The list of quasi-private leisure organizations could continue. For example, the Fresh Air Fund, a social welfare organization, provides disadvantaged New York City children with summer vacations away from their problem-ridden neighborhoods. Other social welfare organizations are the United Service Organization (USO), the Red Cross, and the Joseph P. Kennedy, Jr. Foundation. This latter group annually sponsors the Special Olympics. The Nature Conservancy is a private preservation organization whose goal is to protect ecologically significant land. Often, efforts result in new park properties.

A final example is the many leisure services provided by corporations and industries for their employees. Typical of this type of service is the program at Phillips Petroleum where morning and midnight softball and bowling leagues are organized for off-shift workers and at the du Pont Company where employee fitness programs have yielded big savings in health care costs. Other common company sponsored recreation services for employees and their families include golf courses, picnics, parties, travel programs, adult education, basketball and volleyball leagues, youth camps, and discount tickets for entertainment performances.

Public Agencies

Of all the types of sponsors of leisure services, government agencies have the unique distinction of being the following:

- The first type of agency to be formally recognized as responsible for serving the public with recreation

- The only type of agency that can provide services on an equal basis to the entire population

- The only type of agency that has the power to secure, hold, protect, and open for use the natural resources upon which much of our leisure depends.

The primary function of government is to serve human needs. Government is the means by which people's leisure needs are met without regard to ability to pay, occupational status, or any other distinction that restricts leisure to special groups. This is best illustrated by the park and recreation services provided by local governments. These agencies serve the broadest needs and the largest clientele. Because they are at the level of government closest to the people, they are better able to respond to the needs of the people. The state serves an intermediate role. It assists local provisions through advisory services, special funding, and the management of leisure resources of wider appeal. The federal government, in turn, manages leisure resources of even greater significance, as well as aids the efforts of state and local agencies. To elaborate on government's role, we begin at the federal level.

In the United States, the federal government provides a broad assortment of leisure services. While difficult to count from election to election, there are more than ninety departments, bureaus, commissions, councils, divisions, and authorities that have at least some responsibility for leisure provisions. As you might imagine, coordination and cooperation among these many agencies has been difficult. Essentially, each agency determines its own policies and responsibilities. One of the best summaries of the federal government's role in leisure service provision was that of Maclean, Peterson, and Martin (1985). Overall, they summarized the complexity of federal activities in promoting leisure into six functions.

1. Ownership and management of land, water, and wildlife for leisure. Approximately one-third of the land in the fifty states (nearly 760 million acres) is managed by federal agencies. Of this land, about 270 million acres are used primarily for public parks, forests, and recreation areas. Examples of agencies that administer these lands are the National Park Service, the U.S. Forest Service, the Bureau of Land Management, the U.S. Army Corps of Engineers, the Tennessee Valley Authority, and the Fish and Wildlife Service.

2. Grants to state and local governments. Several federal agencies make financial grants to state and local governments for land and facility purchases for leisure; special services to certain groups (such as the elderly, those with disabilities, etc.); and wildlife protection, research, and leadership training. The Department of Education, for example, provides financial support for training therapeutic recreation personnel; the Soil Conservation Service helps local agencies fund projects of fish and wildlife protection; and the Administration on Aging provides grants for community counseling and outreach services for the aged. The National Endowment for the Arts provides grants of over $100 million a year to help local organizations operate fine arts programs.

3. Direct program operation. While this function is more likely the responsibility of local governments, some federal agencies operate

leisure services directly for participants. For example, Veterans Administration hospitals provide therapeutic recreation programs for patients, and the Department of Defense operates community recreation programs for military members and their families living on military bases.

4. Research. The federal government has supported a broad spectrum of research on leisure ranging from outdoor recreation trends, to the status of urban recreation, studies of forest recreation, and the needs of people with disabilities. For example, in 1985 President Ronald Reagan created a Commission on Americans Outdoors. Their charge was to review public and private outdoor recreation opportunities, policies, and programs, and make recommendations to ensure the future availability of outdoor recreation for the American people.

5. Regulation. Federal regulations affecting leisure include standards for air and water quality, the impact of leisure activities on the environment, regulation of hunting and fishing, boating safety, and architectural accessibility standards for persons with disabilities. For example, the U.S. Congress in recognizing the needs of approximately 43 million citizens with disabilities, passed the Americans with Disabilities Act. This act provides a national mandate for the elimination of discrimination in access to such areas as employment, housing, public accommodations, education, transportation, communication, public services, and recreation.

6. Advisory services. More than thirty federal programs offer technical assistance to local government agencies, as well as private citizens. Typically, this advisory assistance is in such areas as land use, facility development, and preservation. For example, many community programs serving economically disadvantaged populations have been assisted by the Department of Health and Human Services.

Even though the Tenth Amendment to the U.S. Constitution gives states powers in such areas as public education, welfare, and health services, the notion that leisure services are a state responsibility is relatively new. It emerged in the 1960s and 1970s as the federal government gave states more authority to dispense federal funds to their own agencies and to local communities. Because state governments are closer than the federal government to the people, they are better able to gauge local needs. Even with recent cutbacks in expenditures, states remain an important sponsor of leisure services.

States are diverse in the manner in which they sponsor leisure services. Again, we rely on the organizing scheme of Maclean, Peterson, and Martin (1985) for discussing the functions of the state government in supporting leisure.

1. Enactment of enabling legislation. States give local governments the legal authority to operate recreation and park programs. This kind of state law is called enabling legislation. It gives city, county, and/or school authorities the power to acquire properties, employ personnel, and impose taxes to support leisure services.

2. Provision of leisure resources. Each state government operates a network of parks, forests, and recreation areas. For example, about 41 million acres of state-owned land are available for pursuing pastimes. These lands include wilderness areas, natural preserves, historical monuments, cultural preserves, and such recreation areas as beaches, lakes, wayside rests, campgrounds, vehicular trails, and even underwater playgrounds. Leisure services are also offered in such state managed institutions as hospitals and prisons.

3. Education. States also provide educational services related to leisure. These may include the production of slides and films, publications, radio and television programs, traveling exhibits, workshops, conventions, lectures, and outreach programs in the schools. State affiliated colleges and universities also offer professional curriculums that prepare students for careers in leisure services and training institutes that help leisure service personnel continue their education.

4. Promotion of tourism. State departments of commerce, planning, highways, natural resources, and tourism typically make special efforts to attract visitors to the state. State agencies conduct marketing research, and advertising campaigns focused on getting their share of the tourist dollar.

5. Regulations. State standards affecting leisure are of two types: those protecting participants and those protecting leisure resources. Those protecting participants include regulations for safety, cleanliness, and health in camps, resorts, swimming pools, and restaurants. States have also prohibited certain forms of commercial amusements, such as gambling and pornography. Regulations protecting leisure resources pertain to water pollution, fire dangers, and soil conservation.

Finally, we turn to local government's role in sponsoring leisure services. The population of the United States increased from 3.9 million at the first census in 1790 to about 250 million in 1990 (U.S. Bureau of the Census 1990). Two hundred years ago about 95 percent of the population lived in rural settings. Today, about 77 percent live in metropolitan areas. In the U.S., about 186 cities have populations of over 100,000 (U.S. Bureau of the Census 1989). Most Americans now live in cities or towns.

This means that most Americans depend on municipal government to provide many important leisure services. In some areas, public school districts provide recreation and park facilities and programs, and in others, the county government operates these services. For most, however, municipal recreation and park departments have the responsibility. What are some of the primary functions of local governments in the provision of leisure opportunities?

Municipal departments acquire, develop, and maintain facilities needed for the leisure participation of local citizens. They also provide the skilled leadership and the program structure for the use of these facilities. This makes them the prime government source of leisure opportunities. Local government reaches more people in providing services than state and federal governments because it is closest to their daily lives. For example, most cities provide softball and baseball diamonds, tennis courts, swimming facilities, basketball courts, playing fields, picnic areas, playgrounds, and a community center. Frequently, the city's responsibility is not only acquiring and maintaining these facilities but conducting programs by professional staff for people's greater enjoyment. For example, playgrounds not only include the facilities of play apparatus and playing fields, but they also offer programs of games, crafts, sports, and cultural arts. These services are part of people's daily leisure expressions.

Medium to large communities also may have gymnasiums, golf courses, auditoriums, outdoor theaters, bike trails, fitness trails, handball and racquetball courts, horseshoe courts, campgrounds, nature centers, skateboard parks, soccer fields, and cultural centers. Some provide special-interest leisure opportunities. For example, there are city libraries, museums, zoos, aquariums, arboretums, and botanical gardens.

In carrying out these functions municipal agencies also lead community efforts for in-service training of volunteer and paid personnel and advisory services for other private or voluntary leisure service agencies in the community. To avoid duplication, sometimes the local government recreation and park department is the coordinator of the various community leisure services. The local government leisure services agency also works closely with other branches of local government, such as the police department, to develop effective programs. They also may cooperate with federal, state, and county authorities to develop comprehensive long-range service plans.

Summary: Putting It Together

Leisure is a significant institution in modern society. It involves a wide variety of behaviors and social structures. Once chiefly the responsibility of the family or religious group, leisure services have now become the responsibility of a number of agencies. These include cities, hospitals, schools, correctional institutions, the Armed Forces, universities, retail businesses, clubs, and thousands of other organizations. All these sponsors of pastimes can be grouped according to whether they are public, private, or commercial in purpose.

What do they provide? Leisure experiences that are planned, marketed, and presented by the staff of leisure service agencies for the enjoyment of others include outdoor recreation, cultural arts, travel, and sports. Through the provision of these opportunities, agencies try to satisfy the emotional, social, and physical needs and desires of people.

References

American Symphony Orchestra League. 1992. Washington, D.C.

Bergman, B. 1992. Canada's hot rocks. *Maclean's* 105, no. 5: 46–48.

Bourdieu, P. 1977. Cultural reproduction and social reproduction. In *The handbook of sociology,* edited by N. Smelser. Beverly Hills, CA: Sage Publications.

Brown County Convention and Visitors Bureau. 1994. Telephone conversation by author, 6 August.

Central Opera Service. 1992. Central opera service bulletin. New York: Central Opera Service.

Chubb, M., and H. R. Chubb. 1981. *One third of our time? An introduction to recreation behavior and resources.* New York; John Wiley & Sons, Inc.

Crase, N. 1990. Snow talent. *S'NS* (May/June): 265–71.

cummings, e. e. 1956. "maggie and milly and molly and may." *Complete Poems 1913–1962.* New York: Harcourt Brace Jovanovich.

Dealy, F. X. 1990. *Win at any cost.* New York: Carol Publishing Group.

DiMaggio, P. 1982. Cultural capital and school success: The impact of status culture participation on the grades of U.S. high school students. *American Sociological Review* 47:189–201.

Downey, D., and B. Powell. 1993. Do children in single-parent households fare better living with same-sex parents? *Journal of Marriage and the Family* 55: 55–71.

Ford, P. 1989. John Muir (1838–1914). In *Pioneers in leisure and recreation,* edited by H. Ibrahim. Reston, VA: The American Association for Leisure & Recreation/ American Alliance for Health, Physical Education, Recreation, & Dance.

Gunn, C. A. 1988. *Tourism planning.* New York: Taylor & Francis. *Handel's national directory for the performing arts,* vol. 1. 1994. New York: R. R. Bowker's Data Base Publishing Group.

Katsillis, J., and R. Rubinson. 1990. Cultural capital, student achievement, and educational reproduction: The case of Greece. *American Sociological Review* 55, no. 2: 270–79.

Kelly, J. R. 1987. *Recreation trends: Toward the year 2000.* Champaign, IL: Management Learning Laboratories.

Lareau, A. 1989. *Home advantage: Social class and parental intervention in elementary education.* Philadelphia: Taylor & Francis.

Maclean, J. R., J. A. Peterson, and W. D. Martin. 1985. *Recreation and leisure: The changing scene.* New York: John Wiley & Son, Inc.

McIntosh, R. W., and C. R. Goeldner. 1986. *Tourism: Principles, practices, philosophies.* New York: John Wiley & Son, Inc.

National Association of State Park Directors. 1992. *1992 Annual Information Exchange.* Tallahassee, FL: National Association of State Park Directors.

Plog, S. C. 1974. Why destination areas rise and fall in popularity. *The Cornell Hotel and Restaurant Administration Quarterly* 14, no. 4: 55–58.

Rauscher, F. 1994. Music and spatial task performance: A causal relationship. Irvine, CA: Center for the Neurobiology of Learning and Memory.

Rolston, H. 1986. Beyond recreational value: The greater outdoors preservation-related and environmental benefits. *A Literature Review: The President's Commission on Americans Outdoors.* U.S. Government Printing Office.

Teale, E. W. 1954. *The wilderness way of John Muir.* Boston: Houghton Mifflin Co.

Theatre Communications Group. 1992. New York.

Tousignant, M. 1993. A diamond life for gold girls. *Washington Post,* 1 May, A1.

U.S. Bureau of Census. 1989. *Statistical abstract of the United States: 1989.* Washington, D.C.: U.S. Government Printing Office.

U.S. Bureau of Census. 1990. *Statistical abstract of the United States: 1990.* Washington, D.C.: U.S. Government Printing Office.

index

Page numbers in italics indicate figures and illustrations. Page numbers followed by t indicate tables.